Broken to Beautiful

Broken to Beautiful

A Journey
From words that crush
to the Word of Life

A Novel
By

Sheila Summers

New York

Broken To Beautiful

A Lifelong Journey From Words That Crush To The Word Of Life

Cover Design by: Rachel Lopez
Rachel@r2cdesign

ISBN 978-1-60037-688-7

Library of Congress Control Number: 2009933337

MORGAN · JAMES
THE ENTREPRENEURIAL PUBLISHER

Morgan James Publishing, LLC
1225 Franklin Ave., STE 325
Garden City, NY 11530-1693
Toll Free 800-485-4943
www.MorganJamesPublishing.com

Table of Contents

A Dedication

For my Children-Nathan, Erin, Apryl and Joy who is in Heaven with Papa

I dedicate this book to you, my blessings, the loves of my life and the very reasons for my speaking the simple truth of a lifetime.

The journey has been arduous dear ones, but every word written has come from my heart: A heart that now bears the evidence of an incredible process of healing, a heart that loves you more now than I ever thought possible.

Why? Because I dared to ask God; why did I fall victim to the predators of the world? His answer came in the form of a journey back through time to my childhood, where most of our tragic hurts derive from… where most of yours have come from.

This book is a legacy of love, from Our Papa to me and from me to you. A hand-me-down of precious treasures unveiled and revealed from a mother to her children. If I leave you nothing else from my life on this earth, at least I will have shared the simple truth I have found in learning of God's love for His children, each and every one. A redeeming love that surpasses the understanding of most mere mortals, but when we take the time to discover how simple His love is, it is amazing how rarified the air around us becomes. It is amazing how crystal clear everything in our daily life becomes. It is amazing how much more we can love when the cobwebs are swept away.

Trust in Him and He will make the way clear

Sticks and stones may break my bones
but words will never hurt me…is a Great Big Lie!

Prologue

Fall came to the northeast corner of Pennsylvania with a vengeance this year as unusually wet weather caught the small town of Yardley by surprise and in the wee, small hours of a mid-November night a violent storm raged throughout the area. Thunder rumbled and silver shafts of lightening pierced the pitch black night sky. Threatening shadows danced across the illuminated bedroom walls of an ivy covered cottage on the outskirts of town.

Obviously troubled, an old woman named Shy tossed and turned feverishly under the warmth of a blanket. She'd had this nightmare before but the background setting of nature's fierce elements only added to its terror this night. As the storm raged outside deep furrows of anguish appeared across Shy's brow.

She murmured softly under her breath as a tiny whisper could be heard just barely audible from her lips:

"Please don't I beg you, no, no............"

Cold beads of sweat tracked down her face as the drama of the terrible dream played out in her troubled mind.

"A-a-g-h! Oh No God p-l-e-a-s-e stop him!" an unknown, yet familiar woman screamed as her pleas for help filled the darkened apartment.

Thrown down onto the hardwood floor the woman gasped for breath nearly suffocating under the tremendous weight of the man who straddled her. Her swollen belly pressed down hard against the cold wood.

"The b-a-b-y, you're hurting the baby!" she cried with exhaustion, but the pounding of his clenched fists on her head was relentless. All she could do was give in to the protective instinct of a mother shielding her young and curl up into a tight ball to wait for his anger to subside......

Shy tossed to and fro trying to escape the tragic scene muttering through a broken voice

"No, please stop!" A sudden crash of thunder pierced her subconscious and she awoke with a start. Sitting bolt upright, her heart pounded; her eyes went wide with fear.

She breathed heavily and gripped her stomach to ease the churning inside as a deep sob broke the storm-chased silence of her room.

With face in hands Shy began to rock back and forth like a child trying to erase the graphic images from her mind.

Gradually, the gentle rhythm settled her and her breathing softened as she slowly opened her eyes. It took only a few moments for Shy to realize where she was, and then the safety of her sanctuary gradually merged from a blur of ominous shadows to the gentle peace of her room.

"O.K. now!" she uttered between ever-softening breaths, wiping her brow with the back of her hand. "That was just a bad dream; it was just a dream. I'm fine now. Thank you, Lord".

Shy sighed deeply as she slipped back down between the flannel sheets and snuggled under the cozy warmth of duck down.

Her faithful little Maltese, Kylie, had jumped up onto the bed during the storm. As Shy caressed the soft curls of her coat a gentle smile broke out across her life-lined face.

"Erin and Lyric will be here tomorrow sweetie pie," she whispered softly to the little dog. Kylie cuddled into her side listening eagerly to her mistress's gentle voice.

"Thanksgiving is one of my favorite holidays, don't you think so too Kylie?"

Shy imagined the delicious aromas that would soon be permeating the beautiful old house. She let her mind drift to thoughts of great conversations with her girls and long walks down the country lanes. And of course the stories she promised to share with her precious Lyric.

"Ah! The stories..." she thought, as a sudden sparkle returned to her bright green eyes.

"Oh, I do so love being a grandma," she whispered as Kylie's ears pricked up. Trying hard to be attentive to her mistress, but having no great desire to move from her comfy spot, Kylie curled up and gave a sigh as though agreeing with the sentiment.

Shy's eyelids became heavy as she listened to the remnants of the storm dissipating into the distant night. She sighed, wishing with all her heart that the rest of her children could make it home for the holidays.

"Well." Shy looked down at her little companion as though to reassure her too that; "anything is possible if we just believe." "Isn't that right, honey, but...maybe next year?"

Part One

The mountain she saw before her that measured
the distance she had to climb to gain her daddy's favor
back from being; 'nothing but an idiot',
was too high for such a little girl
who only wanted to hear the words;
"Kieran, I love you and I'm proud of you."

Chapter 1
The Week of Thanksgiving

"Mum, aren't you ready yet?" Lyric shouted to her Mum as she fidgeted impatiently in their cozy Brooklyn apartment.

She was brimming with excitement as the time drew near for them to leave for her grandmother Shy's house in the country.

"Just one more minute and I'll be done," her mum replied as she struggled to zip up their one and only suitcase.

Their Brooklyn apartment near Prospect Park, with its grand Soldier's and Sailor's Arch and the Long Meadow with Carousel, was a must for Erin and her family when they decided to live in the city. Her need to be close to nature amid the grind of life in the Big Apple was an integral part of her very DNA and she knew she wouldn't be able to survive otherwise.

Their home was small but comfortable with French doors in two of the rooms that gave the somewhat cramped space an airier feel which all of them loved. With two bedrooms, a living room and eat-in kitchen and, of course, a decent sized bathroom, they managed and were very happy.

There was a definite chill in the air this November morning and both of them were excited to be getting away from the city for a week.

Erin and Lyric loved the hustle and bustle of New York but there was something intrinsically special about getting away from it all to the quiet of her parents house. The escape brought an exhilarating breath of fresh air into their otherwise busy lives and they both longed for this twice yearly trip with excited anticipation.

Lyric's daddy and grandpa were on a trip of mercy down south helping families recover from the devastation caused by a recent hurricane. Although the girls missed them, they were now looking forward to Thanksgiving so they could be reunited as a family again.

"I can't wait 'til Daddy and Grandpa get home," Lyric sighed out loud as she traced her finger down the bedroom window following a raindrop on its way to the puddle forming on the cracked windowsill.

"Me too!" her mum shouted back.

They finally finished packing and took a last look around their home to make sure everything was turned off. They grabbed their coats from the hall closet on the way out and locked the front door.

Before they could begin their journey they had to stop by Mrs. Seidman's apartment to drop off Lyric's beloved ginger cat, Duncan.

The old lady, who had lived in the building for thirty years, had promised Lyric on many occasions to look after Duncan, when they went out of town. As her mum knocked on the door to Mrs. Seidman's apartment, he meowed loudly declaring his disapproval.

"Oh don't worry sweetie pie;" Lyric reassured him, rubbing her button nose against his, "we won't be gone too long."

With that, the door swung open as the jolly, lived-in face of sweet Mrs. Seidman greeted them from within.

"Well hello ladies you're here at last, come on in," she exclaimed ruffling Lyric's hair as she stepped inside then added, "but what's all this noise about then, Mr. McLeod?"

Duncan McLeod was the full title Lyric had given to the great orange ball of fluff. She shrugged her shoulders, a little embarrassed at his apparent displeasure.

"He's a little spoiled I'm afraid, Mrs. Seidman, but he'll settle down once I've gone."

The apartment smelled of lavender and pot roast, with a dash of home-made bread in the mix giving it a distinct aroma of all that was wholesome. Lyric said a last goodbye to her kitty and they both thanked Mrs. Seidman and made their way down to the parking level.

The cold fall air caught them by surprise as they walked quickly towards the beaten up old Neon.

'Old Faithful' was what Lyric's mum called the old car they both loved.

For years now the girls had appreciated its willfulness in never giving up when the going got tough. They put its resilience down to its truly being of Scottish origin. True grit and determination were as much a part of their heritage as the names they had so lovingly acquired from a generational mix of Scots, Irish and Welsh.

As Erin struggled with a lock that seemed to be resisting every effort to be opened, she smiled at her daughter and sighed. It sprung open with a last twist of the key, and she packed everything in to the already overstuffed trunk as Lyric jumped into the back seat, face flushed and eyes sparkling.

It had finally stopped raining after the deluge of the overnight storm. As they set off on their grand adventure, pulling out onto the highway they began to sing "We'll tak' the high road," with a passion that sprung from deep in their souls.

Their love for the old country had been handed down from the very woman they were so eager to see and hug and Oh! Of course eat with.

The thought of the delicious Thanksgiving dinner that awaited them in a few days was already causing Lyric to salivate. As the car continued over the bridge taking them across the Hudson, Lyric asked her mum if she thought grandma would be making her special trifle this year.

"Well I can't remember a Thanksgiving or Christmas when we didn't have trifle sweetheart," Erin replied as her thoughts drifted back to the many times before when she had helped her mother prepare the favorite dessert.

Lyric loved the way her grandmother described the foods she was teaching her to prepare each time they visited. Her grandma could make even the plainest of dishes sound enticingly delectable with her soft lilting accent from a far off land Lyric wished with all her heart to visit one day.

She remembered when her mom had confirmed this thought to her when she was home from school one day with a fever. "You know Lyric, when I got sick, it used to make me feel much better just to hear grandma ask if I wanted some 'tea and buttered toast" and the thought of how her grandma sounded all her '***tees***' when she spoke made Lyric smile.

To Lyric, Scotland sounded romantic and full of exciting historical adventures. She loved to hear these old tales when she was alone with her grandma; the stories she told would take her to the place she longed for the most.

Lyric had already learned a great deal about her ancestry and how resilient and hardworking the Scottish people were. They were quite a force to be reckoned with in times of war she had come to realize.

She got her determination from that side of her family, she deemed, and this Thanksgiving eagerly looked forward to even more tales from back home.

"I love when Grandma teaches me how to cook," Lyric shared with her mom as they gradually left the city behind. "And when she tells me stories from back home in Scotland."

Erin smiled in agreement and glancing in the rear view mirror she watched Lyric's expression, suspecting her little girl was already with the grandma she loved so much.

"Well darling…" was how grandma Shy always started her cooking lessons. She rubbed her hands together as though dusting off imaginary flour dust then wiped them across her favorite tartan apron. The frayed but beloved relic looked as though it had come across the ocean with her twenty five years before!

Lyric loved that her grandma was so patient when she baked with her. She'd just laugh if Lyric made a mistake saying, "Och! Lassie, don't ye' worry now. That can easily be cleaned up!"

"Well now, it's a mixture of fruit jelly poured over cup cakes which have been broken up into little pieces. You then allow it to soak in and set with a few spoonfuls of sherry if ye' want," she would explain.

"Then fresh fruit and egg custard are layered, one on top of another, until almost to the top of the bowl, toppin' it off with cream that's been whipped light and fluffy."

Lyric would have the honor of spooning the thick cream over the ingredients already in the bowl, licking the spoon with relish when she was done.

"Finally it's topped off with some maraschino cherries for that extra special touch," her grandma would say with a nod of satisfaction as though happy with a job well done.

Every now and then Lyric would notice her grandma's brogue sounding heavier with a wee Scottish word sneaking in at times during the lesson and she'd just giggle and love her all the more.

Erin glanced in the mirror and noticed a far off look on her daughters face, teasing Lyric as she asked "And to where have you just drifted, little miss?"

"Oh I was just remembering the time grandma taught me how to make the trifle," she replied sharing the daydream with her mom and best friend.

"Ah yes, I remember that day too!" and they both laughed at the memory of Lyric throwing up all night long after eating too much.

A hushed silence then fell over the car as they returned to their own thoughts.

Erin sighed contentedly feeling sure, one day soon, her mum would share an even greater story with Lyric. She trusted her mum's judgment implicitly and felt it natural to leave the telling to her. She instinctively knew she would take as much care with her grandbaby as she had with her as they too shared the telling of life stories.

They journeyed towards their destination with the ever changing landscape gradually fading from the stark reality of the city to the lush green countryside of Bucks County Pennsylvania. There the grandest of oak trees cast great shadows across the fields, and vivid green rolling hills tumbled across the beautiful county that reminded Erin so much of home.

They traveled onwards through Newtown, and the sky above them turned ominous, dimming the morning light as great clouds merged into the blackened blanket of a storm engulfed sky.

Erin turned on the windshield wipers as fat spots of rain splattered against 'old faithful' making visibility difficult and quickly soaking the road ahead.

She leaned forward and gripped the steering wheel tightly as her heart quickened with the sudden change in the weather. .

"Mom shouldn't we stop for a while?" Lyric asked nervously.

"Oh darling I think it's going to blow over soon, but if I can find a place to stop I will, o.k.?"

Just as she spoke the rain began to lessen and the soft blue of the sky reappeared.

"Wow! Now that was a cloudburst if ever I saw one!" Lyric squealed with relief as they broke into laughter.

"See, we can make it through anything, sweetie, can't we?" Erin said with conviction as she glanced at the rear view mirror.

"Sure we can, Mom," Lyric answered with a nod.

Erin relaxed back in her seat and her mind drifted back to the many, many times when both she and her own mom had survived even greater adventures.

Unfortunately, not all of them had been as exciting, or as simple, as driving through a sudden storm.

Chapter 2
A Grandmother's Welcome

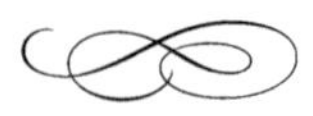

Shy was content that all the food was prepared and her home-made chicken pot pie was slowly turning golden brown in the oven, its delicious aroma threading its way throughout the beautiful old house. She walked slowly upstairs to sit at her favorite window and await the arrival of the two blessings that brought such a song to her heart.

Her eldest child Nathan lived in England with his wife and children, and she had ached for many years with missing them so much. However, he seemed to be happy and was doing incredibly well in his job with a national construction company so ultimately that was all that mattered.

Her youngest daughter Apryl, another apple of her eye, was living in Wyoming on a ranch. Apryl taught horse-riding lessons to underprivileged kids who came from situations of abuse and neglect. She'd had a heart for horses and children as long as Shy could remember.

Shy sighed with disappointment as she remembered the conversation she'd had with Apryl just the night before.

"I'm sorry I can't make it for Thanksgiving, Mom, but they're really pushed for help at this time of the year, and I said I'd work to let the married people have a break," she told her mom apologetically.

"Oh, of course I understand, sweetheart, but you'll be missed," Shy replied, loving her daughter's sweet spirit even more. "And make sure you have a good dinner!"

Apryl put down the phone shaking her head as she smiled with a mischievous glint in her eyes.

Being so proud of her children must surely be sinful, Shy mused as she waited at the window, knowing full well that particular sin would be forgiven.

She was alone in the home she shared with her beloved husband Paul, and although she missed him when he was away, she loved to spend these quiet times alone. Times to reflect on how far she had come in her life and how much she'd had to overcome to arrive at the blissful place she was in today.

They had prayed to be guided to the home they'd longed for just prior to their wedding and eventually, after many months of looking, they came upon this gem tucked away in a very unassuming corner of idyllic Yardley.

The house had two stories with an attic stretching its full width. It was made from grey brick that reminded Shy of some of the grand old houses back home in the city of Edinburgh. A weathered grey and reddish stone wall surrounded it, slightly crumbling in places. Forever reaching tendrils of dark green ivy crept over the wall and around the gate posts, giving the impression of an entrance into a secret garden, which in many ways it was.

Pretty wooden boxes which overflowed with blossoms of all colors adorned each window of the house, bringing an invitingly friendly appearance to an otherwise dark stoned exterior. The sweet and fragrant blooms reflected the loving hearts of the family within.

Shy had longed for her secret garden for many years and had known deep down in the quiet places of her heart that one day she would be blessed with such a gift. Of course, eventually she was, but only after years of making do, living in a tiny, cramped apartment with her two girls.

But it too had been their sanctuary of sorts for seven long years after surviving many years of heartache. Then she had found her garden.

The house was old, and more than a little run down, when they found it. Through many months of loving restoration it gradually became the home they all knew and loved.

Shy glanced down and watched the wind whip up leaves in the front yard as glorious hues of orange, red and brown created a ballet of nature's splendor around the house.

Like music to her ears the sound of her daughter's car wheels crunched over the gravel of the driveway and her heart skipped a beat with excitement.

"Oh! They're here" she said out loud as though still in deep conversation with someone; but that in itself wasn't too far from the truth.

Her life, she reflected, had been one long conversation with that voice of comfort only to be interrupted on occasion with the heartbeat of life itself. She stepped energetically down the long staircase with her little, white Maltese, Kylie, in hot pursuit. Shy stopped for a moment at the bottom to take a deep breath in anticipation of the wonderful few days that lay ahead.

Her cheeks flushed and her green eyes sparkled as she opened the front door and a joyous bundle of happiness threw herself into her grandmother's arms.

"Hi Grandma, I've missed you so much," Lyric cried as Shy held onto her tightly.

"Oh ma wee darling," she replied with a huge smile on her pretty, life- lined face cherishing every squeeze. "I've missed you too sweetheart and oh, look how much you've grown!" Shy answered stepping back to take in the sight before her.

"That mum of yours, where is she?" she asked and looking over Lyric's shoulder she saw Erin surface from under the trunk of her car.

"Hi Mum," Erin shouted but was almost knocked off her feet with a gust of wind as it swept around the corner of the house stirring up everything in its path.

"Oh, my gosh, where did that come from?" she spluttered as the strong gust forced her to run towards them. As Erin caught her breath Shy ushered them both indoors.

"We've been having lots of high winds lately but I guess it's the season for them eh, my love's?" Shy stated helping them with their coats and baggage.

Erin hadn't even had time to get her coat off when Lyric grabbed at Shy's hand pulling her towards the kitchen where the winding staircase led up to the attic.

"Grandma come on, come on, we have a lot of work to do," the excited high pitched voice urged as she tugged at her grandmas' hand. But the older lady was still spry and light on her feet, and in one swoop of her hand she twirled Lyric under her arm and swept her into a swirl around the hallway.

"Weeee!" Lyric squealed as Shy distracted her excitement and channeled it into a dance of delight as she welcomed her grandbaby home.

The dance ended as Shy bent down and whispered in her ear "Later, o.k.?" and then asked Lyric to take her things to her room and wash her hands as lunch was almost ready.

Lyric nodded and bounded up the stairs to the room that was once her mothers with Kylie close behind. The wee dog was excited at having her favorite playmate back.

The two women walked into the kitchen. "You look wonderful," Erin remarked as she wrapped an arm around her mother's waist and kissed her on the cheek.

However, suddenly noticing how labored her mum's breathing had become and catching just a glimpse of something in the older woman's eyes she asked, "Mum, are you o.k.?"

"I'm fine sweetheart; I just get a wee bit winded every now and then that's all.

"You look wonderful too, darling. Life in the city must suit you," Shy added marveling at the glow on her daughters beautiful face as she tried to distract her line of questioning.

But Erin would not be deterred. "Mum is there something you're not telling me?"

Her mom was not a complainer by nature and had plodded on for years struggling with asthma and arthritis always trying to keep her cheery disposition, especially when her children were around.

"Darling, I'm fine, honestly," she replied. "I'm just struggling with this arthritis as usual, so don't you be getting concerned. Okay?"

Erin nodded in agreement as she set the mugs out for their late morning treat.

Shy reached into the pantry for the teabags and just as she was about to turn towards the teapot a distant memory flashed across her thoughts forcing a smile.

She thought of when Erin and Nathan were young, playing games filled with imagination as they ran across the hills and braes of the Highlands with a freedom that city children rarely experience. Suddenly stopped in mid thought, she glanced over at Erin who was busying herself in the familiar kitchen and sighed.

That seemed so long ago. She reminded herself that Erin felt equally at home in New York, where she now shared her love of music and the arts with her own daughter Lyric. Lyric was also developing a love for both worlds.

Erin washed her hands and was about to roll up her sleeves to help with lunch when her mom assured her it was all done and asked if she could just check on the table setting instead.

The incredible aromatic delight of chicken pot pie wafting it's way throughout the house had not missed the attention of one excited little girl. Lyric was now playing with one of her mother's old dolls in her bedroom. Truth be told, her mind was mostly on the 'Aladdin's Cave' of undiscovered treasures in her grandma's attic.

The wonderment of what was to come seemed to override her normally insatiable appetite, but as she heard her grandma's voice calling her down for lunch the aroma of her favorite pie suddenly hit her senses. Immediately she felt warm and cozy inside with the mouth-watering smells beckoning her to come down and join the two women.

Lyric suddenly realized how hungry she was and answered Shy with a high pitched, "I'm coming," as she skipped down the stairs at a gallop, pretending to be one of the horses her Aunt Apryl worked with in Wyoming.

They sat down at the table and after saying grace began to enjoy lunch.

"As soon as the weather changes I start to eat like a horse," Erin admitted with a mouth full of food.

Lyric's eyes twinkled mischievously as she finished her first piece and asked for more, but then paused for a second. "Well on second thoughts maybe I should leave room for dessert," and turning to face the older woman she asked, "Should I Grandma?"

Before Shy could reply Lyric went on to question the topic of dessert without pausing for breath.

"Well, but perhaps I should be watching my figure just like Mommy?" she added with a grown up air forcing Erin to choke on her food, bringing a sudden eruption of riotous laughter to the table.

"My, my, someone **has** grown up in the last few months, I see," Shy remarked with a smile composing herself a little as she reached over to cut another piece of pie, winking at Erin in the process.

"But you know what, sweetie, you need all the healthy food you can eat because you're a growing girl," Shy confirmed to this little girl who was just starting to bloom and become aware of the woman waiting a few years around the corner of life.

"Would you like seconds too, Erin?" her mum asked making her feel as though she too was a little girl again,

"No, I'm fine thanks, Mum. I really don't need to grow anymore thank you very much," and Shy just smiled.

"Och get away with ye Erin, you're just as slim and beautiful as you've always been!"

They all relaxed into an easy banter of conversation catching up on the news in each other's lives.

It was so good to have them back home again and it would feel complete when the men came back home for Thanksgiving.

"Have you spoken to Dad today?" Erin asked having tried to call her husband, Greg, before they left.

"I did early this morning pet, before they went out and he told me not to expect to get through later, but they're both fine."

"I'm sure Greg will call tonight," Shy added to put Erin's mind at rest. As they finished the meal a certain little lady reminded everyone of an important job that needed to be done.

"Och! Do we really have to go up there today?" Shy teased with an exaggerated look of displeasure but Lyric knew her only too well to be disappointed.

"Awe grandma stop kidding," she replied, hands on her hips showing a determination of which they were already aware.

"Mum I'll clear up the kitchen so you guys can have some time together," Erin assured them, as she started to clear the dishes from the table. But they were already half way up the stairs sounding like two kids off on a secret adventure.

As she started to run the water and fill the sink full of fragrant bubbles, Erin gazed around taking in every part of the home she loved and had only actually lived in for two years with her Mum, Paul and sister, Apryl, before meeting Greg and getting married. She was twenty-four when they found it and as old as it was she loved it immediately and knew it was the home her mum had always dreamed of and, more importantly, deserved.

The rooms were spacious but cozy and the warm inviting shades they had chosen for décor reflected her mother's quiet but stylish nature.

A warm, toasty fire burned bright in the beautiful old fireplace which sat between two bookcases Paul had hand crafted. They were now packed with first editions and books on all subjects. Photographs of all the children in the family took pride of place in every nook and cranny in the family room. She loved to just sit and take in the years of cherished memories within those four walls. These musings created a true moment of thanksgiving for her.

It was the kind of room that could host a grand party or be a private retreat where one could curl up on the deep overstuffed sofa and lose oneself in a favorite book. In either setting, a glance through the French windows led you into a verdant wildflower garden outside.

Erin looked upwards with a smile as she heard the footsteps of the two people she loved and felt a sensation of perfect peace wash over her.

They climbed the stairs and heard the howl of the wind as it whipped around the eaves of the house adding an air of excitement to this predestined errand of discovery. With every step, Lyric's heartbeat quickened.

"Grandma what do you think we'll find up here?" she asked with wide eyed innocence hoping her grandma would tell of many precious treasures.

"Well, you know darling, I've all but forgotten all that's been put up here over the years, so your guess will be as good as mine, to tell the truth."

The next step took them into the pitch dark, dusty attic and as they breathed in the distinct musty odor of bygone years Shy groped to find the light switch.

Rain began to pitter patter against the roof creating an even greater atmosphere of mystery to this already exciting journey into the past. As Shy finally found the switch to the light, suddenly the attic was illuminated revealing piles of boxes and old books covered in cobwebs and dust just crying out to be discovered.

Lyric took a step towards a large box stuffed with old fashioned clothes, and something in the corner caught her eye, as dim light from the tiny window in the roof filtered through reflecting off something shiny. Stepping over a pile of well worn cushions to take a closer look, she discovered an old chest tucked away in a corner almost completely out of sight.

"Oh grandma, look what I've found over here," Lyric cried out losing her breath a little with the excitement of the discovery. As Shy approached a broad smile broke out over her face and she bent down to see what the child had found.

Lyric wiped her hand over the top of the chest to reveal a brass plate that had a name engraved on it and as her excitement grew she read the letters out one by one.

"Let me see now, it says **K I E R A N**, ***Kieran!***" she stated with satisfaction.

"I've never heard that name before do you know who she is, Grandma?" Without waiting for a reply she tried to open the lid.

Shy stood up to stretch her painful legs and looked around for somewhere to sit down.

"Oh! It seems to be stuck or rusty or something but it's really heavy, Grandma, so there must be lots of stuff inside, and, Grandma, you didn't answer my question, who's Kieran?"

"Hold on a moment sweetheart" Shy replied and remembering there was an old rocking chair tucked away behind the water tank; she dragged it over to where her Lyric was kneeling and sat down with effort, the pain in her knees forcing her to wince.

"Oh my wee lassie, grandma's a bit stiff today, but let me see," she said bending over to investigate.

"Who is Kieran are you asking?"

"Yes Grandma, who is she?" Lyric asked pushing at the lid with impatience.

"Well, let's open it up first and see what's inside, shall we?" Shy reached over to the chest from where she sat. She gave it a mighty tug and the lid flew open revealing the contents to the astonished little girl.

"Ah, ballet slippers!" Lyric cried with glee holding them up like a trophy she'd just won.

"And, Oh Look, Grandma, there's all sorts of letters and books and a funny old stuffed bear with one ear and, Oh! Grandma," she paused to take a breath and reached deep into the chest.

"A photo of a little girl but it's all worn and creased and ..."

Lyric sat back on her heels staring at the old picture and a fleeting glimmer of recognition passed over her big brown eyes as though she had just recognized someone she'd met a long time ago.

"Grandma, is this Kieran?" she asked turning to the woman who had been watching her expression, both amused and curious.

"Yes, my love, that's Kieran" Shy answered with a smile. Relaxing back in her chair once again with elbows on the arm rests and hands intertwined, she asked Lyric if she would like to hear Kieran's story.

"Oh! Boy a story! Yes please, Grandma" she answered reaching back into the chest to look for more evidence of this little girl's life, making it obvious as to how they would be spending the rest of their afternoon.

"Well it's a long story sweetheart so why don't you gather up those cushions," Shy said pointing to the pile Lyric had just stepped over. As the eager little girl created her comfy spot, the soft pitter patter of raindrops against the roof turned into a torrent once again battering against the outside of the house.

The droning howl of the wind rose to a crescendo as though accenting the lead up to the opening line and Shy looked down with a smile at a special little girl, wide eyed with anticipation of what was to come and said "Then I'll begin."

Shy paused for a moment then began the story of a wee Scottish lass.

Chapter 3
Kieran's Journey Begins

The story begins in Edinburgh, the beautiful capital of Scotland, and is set in the post war era of the mid fifties.

This beautiful city steeped in ancient history was lucky to have escaped the kind of devastation that cities like London had suffered during the hundreds of air-raid bombings of the blitz. After ten long years of the country, as a whole, getting back to 'normal life,' this majestic jewel of the north began a new season of growth.

Now, at the beginning of Britain's involvement in the war, in 1939, thousands of Scottish men had been called up to serve their country in the fight against Nazi Germany. The women had taken the place of their men folk on farms and in factories giving them a feeling of pride to be a part of the war effort. They were a country unified against a common enemy.

When the war finally came to an end displaced families from all over the country eventually found their way back home. Sometimes they brought new found love with them to create fresh beginnings and the hope for a brighter future with one less evil in the world.

"But when does Kieran come into the story Grandma?" Lyric asked impatiently not loving the history lesson so far.

"Well I thought you liked to hear about Scotland lassie," Shy replied playfully.

"Oh, you know I do Grandma but I want to know about Kieran too!"

"Aye I know ye' do ma' pet but all that comes before is important for you to really understand this wee lass."

"Well, OK then, Grandma you can carry on," Lyric agreed giving her grandma permission to tell the story her way.

"Well, thank you!" was the reply as Shy raised an eyebrow and smiled.

To this day Edinburgh is known as one of the most beautiful cities in the world and people travel from all over the globe to admire its magnificent buildings and architecture. For many of them it's a journey back home to fulfill the calling of a long lost heritage.

The city is steeped in history dating as far back as 1076. Edinburgh castle sits high on a rock right in its heart. At night the castle is lit up as though to enhance its majesty over its domain.

Many incredible examples of Scottish architecture line the Royal Mile which stretches from the castle all the way down to Holyrood Palace where the Royal family live when they come to visit the city. The Mile has maintained its original cobblestone streets and tall ancient tenements that seem like great formidable giants loom upwards into the typically grey sky. These buildings have been protected by the city because of their historical value and were renovated throughout the years into modern day flats and stores in drastic contrast to hundreds of years ago.

Back then families lived in cramped unsanitary conditions and children played in the gutters, digging in the dirt whilst their mothers hung the washing from one building to another on a long pulley, shouting greetings to their neighbors across the way.

"How's wee Charlie doin' today, Effie?" Lyric imagined two wifies hanging out their windows with wild, unkempt hair and shirt sleeves rolled up, shouting across the street to each other with thick Scottish brogues.

She could see ancient Edinburgh in her mind's eye with street vendors selling their wares and dogs running wild barking at the commotion of an ordinary day.

As she slipped deeper into her thoughts Lyric could almost smell the evidence of horse drawn carriages with their affluent patrons inside, whilst street urchins scurried out the way as they begged for just a ha'penny from passersby.

Lyric could hear the chaos that made up the throb of life in this ancient city and as she gradually left her daydream behind she turned to her grandma and smiled as though acknowledging that her heritage had given her the gift to sense this wonderful place so far away.

"You're getting lost in that world already aren't you pet?" Shy asked with a smile well aware of Lyric's vivid imagination.

"I know Grandma, but it's so easy and...hey! Wait a minute!" She said hesitating for a moment. "How could the children play in the gutters? Don't they belong on the roof?"

Her grandma laughed forgetting in her storytelling to explain the difference in language between the two continents. "Oh yes, you're right darling. I forgot. Gutters are what we call; where the sidewalk meets the road and I can remember as a child myself sitting in the gutter poking at the dirt or smushing the melted tar with an ice lolly stick on a hot summer day.

"You know, it's amazing lass, when living in an historical city like Edinburgh, how one gets so accustomed to living with the ancient and the new. How the bustle of a busy metropolis blends easily into the past as though proud to hold onto it.

"As I mentioned before the ancient tenements are now home to shops and eateries displaying their colorful wares. Pridefully, they show off the tartans of the Clan Chieftains with sporrans, dirks, and all the other regalia that depict the very essence of this beautiful country."

At the very foot of the castle rock lies 'Old Town' Edinburgh, where the ancient heart still bears evidence of squalor. Street people lie on benches drinking wine out of bottles hidden in brown paper bags. Amidst their destitution, the everyday bustle of city life rolls on.

The rich smells of beer and malt whisky permeate the twists and turns of the Tollbooth and Canongate. And in the nooks and crannies of this area you'll come upon pubs and restaurants serving traditional dishes like haggis, neeps and tatties, shepherds pie, and bangers and mash with the 'auld folk' of the city still loving to tell the tales of years gone by.

"Just like you do Grandma," Lyric remarked with a crinkle of her nose.

"Edinburgh sounds so beautiful" she added dreamily, wrapping her arms around her knees where she now rested her chin. "I hope I can go there one day...."

As the deluge continued, the rain dancing on the roof like a chorus of tap dancers, her grandma replied with a smile and a twinkle in her bright green eyes,

"Well, my love, anything is possible if we just believe."

Long before Kieran came along; her mum was what people back then referred to as a "war bride." Like many young women, she met her husband during the war and either married during or just after it ended.

Her dad had been in the Royal Navy and after doing his part serving on a minesweeper keeping the Atlantic Ocean safe for the allies to travel back and forth, his ship pulled ashore into the port of Swansea. Soon after he fell in love with a beautiful Welsh girl named May.

I'm only guessing, but I think it must have been hard for Kieran's mum to leave her own country behind, but then I've learned that love can often give you the courage to do things you'd otherwise never dream of doing. I'm more than sure her dad was quite the charmer with his handsome blue eyes and Scottish brogue.

Allan Stewart brought his bride back home to Edinburgh and their life together began at the end of 1945. Unfortunately, they had trouble finding somewhere to live straight away, so they had to live with Allan's mother, who turned out to be quite a force to be reckoned with.

The old woman had had a hard life bringing up five children on her own after the death of her husband. Life itself had made her a little hard and rough around the edges.

Poor May, on the other hand, was a quiet soul and had left a home where she'd been mistreated by her own mother. After months of battling with the feeling of being thrown 'out of the frying pan and into the fire', she was as happy as could be when they received the offer of a prefabricated home far enough away from her mother-in-law for life to become less of a trial.

By this time May had given birth to a bouncing baby boy they named William. When they moved into their new home she relaxed and began to enjoy their life together.

The city soon got back to normal and seemed even busier than before the war. Businesses evolved and a feeling of hope tinged the air bringing a new found vitality to a war torn Europe.

This energy brought about a brand new generation later to be known as baby boomers. Couples began to have more and more babies and the economy became healthier each year.

Eighteen months after the birth of Will, Joycie came along and three years after that, Drew. By the timer Drew reached his fourth birthday a new home was being built for the young family by Edinburgh Corporation, just across the road. It was called The Salvesens.

They were all extremely excited at the prospect of moving and watched in anticipation as construction got underway.

However, soon after learning of their new home another piece of news was shared with the children and nine months later as their house became ready to move into Kieran came along; a chubby baby girl. She looked nothing like the others, favoring her mother's coloring more with lots of dark brown curly hair and big hazel eyes.

Little Drew looked up at his mum after they brought Kieran home from the hospital with eyes full of question "Are we having any more babies Mum or is this the last one?"

His mum answered with a certainty to her reply that made everyone who heard sit up and listen, "Oh, this is definitely the last one laddie!"

The wind howled and rose again to yet another crescendo as though to celebrate the beginning of Kieran's story.

As she grew, little Kieran became closer to her sister Joycie and thought her big brothers to be more of an annoyance than anything else.

Joycie, which was eventually shortened to Jo, helped her mum with her new baby sister as though happy she now had an alliance within the family. It felt more balanced now with two girls and two boys, but there were eight years between the two sisters. As

Jo grew into her teenage years, little Kieran, as much as she was loved, became a little annoying too.

Kieran made it obvious she wanted to be with her big sister every minute of the day and loved when she sang to her at bedtimes, especially her favorite Scottish lullaby:

"Ally bally, ally, bally bee
Sitting on yer' mammies knee
Waiting for a wee bawbee
to buy some coulters candy."

"Oh, that was my bedtime lullaby! You and Mom used to sing that to me all the time Grandma!"

"I know darling... now isn't that a coincidence" Shy mused with a snigger watching as Lyric worked out the association in her mind.

As a tiny, wee thing Kieran would sit at the living room window, tears streaming down her face as she watched Jo and her friend Maureen turn the corner of the street. Kieran was just too young to understand she deserved a life without a baby sister trailing behind.

But she eventually came to understand that Jo needed her space and would watch in admiration as her sister got ready for a night out.

The fashion back then, in the late 50s and early 60's was a mixture of poodle skirts and pencil skirts that were worn with either flat moccasin shoes or high stiletto heels named 'winkle pickers'.

"What on earth are Winkle Pickers, Grandma?" Lyric asked screwing up her nose at the moniker.

Her grandma laughed and went on to explain it was slang for pointed toe shoes. "When I was wee my mum used to buy winkles from Leith, a small fishing town joined onto Edinburgh. Winkles are tiny shell fish preserved in jars of salted water. We'd fetch a needle from the sewing box and use it to spear the wee thing out of its shell."

"Yuck!" Lyric looked disgusted at the graphic image.

Shy laughed and agreed with her. "I know darling, I question my own judgment at that time too!" Anyway, that's where the name came from... ye' know, the needle being pointed and picking out the winkle."

"I don't know, Grandma, you certainly had some strange ways back then."

Kieran loved to watch Jo back comb her hair to the extreme. The teased mass would either be pinned up into a beehive, which was a high up do, or fall stiffly down to her shoulders, flipped up at the ends. The wee lass thought her big sister was just beautiful!

If Kieran was ever to choose one example of typical family life at that time it would be the night she and her family were settling down at tea time (Scottish for dinner) in their over-furnished living-room as they watched a favorite TV show.

The best mirror in the three bedroom house, which had begun to feel much smaller as the children grew, hung over the mantle in the living room. Jo stood right in front of everyone to put the finishing touches to her hair doo. Forcing them all to strain around her to see the television, Willy yelled with frustration, "Do ye' have to do that there?"

"Oh! Be quiet, for goodness sake, I'll just be a minute," Jo replied, totally ignoring her brother's tone of annoyance.

Willy hummed and hawed as he ate his food and tried to watch "Dr. Who." Just as he was about to enjoy the last of his dad's home-made chips, Jo sprayed her belle-aire hair lacquer on her beehive and all over him!

"Yuck! That was my last chip!" he screamed in disgust, his face turning red with outrage. "You and that blooming hair stuff nearly poisoned me!" he added for effect.

"Dad, are there anymore chips left?"

Drew almost choked on his tea with laughing so hard and Kieran just chuckled as she sat in the corner of the room swinging her legs feeling tickled at the goings on in her house.

Lyric laughed as she thought of the love/hate relationships between brothers and sisters.

Kieran's dad did most of the cooking on the weekends and for special holidays like Christmas and New Years Day.

He had been a cook in the Navy. After the war he found a job with Scot Lyons bakery as a master baker. Their family was often spoiled with delicious homemade scones and cakes.

Her mum was a good cook too, and made the best lentil soup.

Shy paused for a moment as Lyric noticed a frown appear across her brow.

As time went by, little Kieran seemed to acquire a sensitive awareness of life around her both inside and outside her home. Trying to deal with those feelings of growing confusion she turned more and more inward.

She became quiet and shy spending much of her time alone, aware of an emptiness of some kind that seemed to be growing inside that she couldn't quite understand.

Poor Kieran would blush at the drop of a hat and began to believe she was becoming an odd ball or a real 'query' as some Scots would say.

"What do you mean an emptiness grandma and what's a query?" Lyric asked with a frown.

"Well darling it's too soon to say but as Kieran's story unfolds you'll begin to understand what I mean. Enough to say at this time the wee lass was just an extremely sensitive child with a gift to sense things unspoken or unexplained that were part of the life around her."

Shy paused for breath.

"Now as for the word query; the Scots are a culture who seems to think they have permission to call anyone anything they like without considering their feelings. It's just part of their upbringing I guess but it was a part that saddened little Kieran. Query just means; a bit strange or not quite right"

Little Kieran was a thinker. She questioned a lot but not always vocally. She sensed that her sister had an easy going relationship with their dad but that unfortunately seemed to be something Kieran could never quite attain.

She'd been made aware, by Jo, on many occasions that their dad loved them all and had done a good job looking after them when their mum had gone to work at night as a cleaner with Ferranti's. That kind of parental shift work is hard on any family though, so it wasn't long before May gave up working and stayed at home.

Allan left the bakery and started at Ferranti's himself as a security policeman with better pay, so life became a little easier all around.

Nothing, however, seemed to have an effect on the obvious gulf between Kieran and her dad. She knew he was a good husband and provider, but she herself had few if any recollections of any kind of personal relationship with him.

She could recall distant vignettes of memory like dancing, standing on his feet when she was very little or watching him bake in the kitchen. She had a vague recollection of being taught to ride a bike, but couldn't remember conversations with him much, or ever going anywhere special with him, ye' know, just the two of them.

Kieran understood he worked long hours and tried to have compassion when he came home from work late looking tired, but yet she couldn't help but grieve over the relationship she longed for but couldn't quite attain. He was just there, working hard, but silently, in the garden or baking wonderful cakes and scones.

Unfortunately, the contrast between a full belly and an empty heart became so confusing for Kieran that she grew up to believe that's just who fathers were: silent providers, therefore she shouldn't expect any more. Watching him from afar and from a quiet place became her duty of sorts. Supporting his valiant efforts at working so hard for his family whilst denying that desperate longing she had to be closer to him.

She'd ask questions when he watched horse racing on the television every Saturday afternoon, trying hard to gain some kind of camaraderie with him. Yet it always felt awkward and the effort it took to try and create conversation began to emphasize the obvious silence and distance between them. Her sensitive soul reeled with hurt and disappointment. Gradually she learned to live with the truth of his aloofness, but the longing for closeness never left.

There was a time, when she was very young and before her sensitivity grew, that she was given a tiny gift of faith; a promise of another truth. A special man came into her life briefly and for the short time he was there, she was given a glimpse into what it truly felt like to be listened to and understood.

He was known to her as Uncle Geordie.

Many years later she was to find out that he wasn't her uncle at all, but merely a friend of her fathers who had been down on his luck, needing a place to stay for a while. But the memory of their moments together was lasting for wee Kieran and never to be forgotten.

The day Uncle Geordie took her down to Granton square became an indelible memory. She felt very special when they disembarked the number 16 double decker bus and as they walked towards the enormous red and black steam engines full of coal and oil she also felt safe, her tiny hand holding onto his tightly.

Before returning home after an exciting day of discovery, he bought her a packet of Maltesers, which were delicious balls of sugary honeycomb covered in smooth milk chocolate. She ate this favorite treat traveling back home on the top deck of the bus, somehow knowing she would remember that moment forever.

She loved the long conversations with him about ponies. Black and white ones like the Indians rode in the movies and Uncle Geordie promised to try and buy one for her birthday.

They discussed how they would keep it in the back yard and feed it hay and if it got too big for the yard they could board it in the stables up the road.

As young as she was, and as wonderful as it all sounded, Kieran seemed to have the sense to realize that this plan of theirs would never come to life, but wasn't it fun to dream!

She loved sharing her dreams and letting her imagination soar with a grown up who didn't laugh and call her silly or worse yet, not listen at all! Uncle Geordie listened to her heart and he dreamt with her. Unfortunately, it wasn't long after that he left.

She remembered vaguely hearing a heated discussion between her parents one night, and then he was gone. He left suddenly, without even a goodbye, and she grieved for the lost relationship that would never return. She kept her love for Uncle Geordie locked away in her heart knowing somehow that as fleeting as it was, she would cherish that time with him for the rest of her life.

"He left that soon?" Lyric asked, grabbing the one eared teddy for comfort.

"Oh, he was only there for a few months, sweetie," Shy answered.

"She couldn't help feel that her mum had something to do with his leaving and could remember being upset with her for quite some time without understanding why. Kieran was only a little girl who had lost a dear friend and couldn't be expected to understand grown up things." Shy stopped as though to ponder the thought.

"Much later in life she would gain a quiet understanding of what had probably transpired within her home at the time and forgave her mum quietly."

The important lesson little Kieran learned early in life was that she had to work at being noticed or talked to by her daddy. He was a man of very few words. Very rarely did he instigate any kind of meaningful conversation. As a result the learned behavior was: for her to be loved she had to try harder to win favor in his eyes.

Kieran played, she laughed, she loved life just like any other little girl and to those around her she was just 'the baby' of the family. She was there to tease, there to have fun with and not often listened to, but loved nonetheless. Love came silently, from a hard working daddy; in the form of pride by a mother who just loved to dress her up and by siblings who...well, she was never quite sure what she was to her siblings other than a baby sister.

She loved life, yet questioned the world around her. She breathed in the fragrance of every season as she discovered her world, yet constantly strove for love from her dad.

Chapter 4
Disillusioned

Another year or so passed and it soon came time for Kieran to start school. Children begin first grade at the age of five in Scotland and as she had stayed at home with her mum leading up to that time, she didn't take too kindly to being away from her all day long in a strange place with people she didn't know.

Of course she knew her older brothers and sister went to school and she'd played at pretend lessons for quite a while with her friends Kay and Janie, but this was different. This was real! The churning she felt inside when taken down to the Leith Provident store to buy her school uniform proved that to her.

What made it worse was that her mum insisted Kieran go to a fee paying school five miles away. She'd have to travel on a public bus with more strangers. That thought alone terrified her.

Her friends in the neighborhood were going to the local school and so this only added to her worry.

This decision would not only to take her to a place of anxiety and fear, but also isolate her from those friends.

It wasn't long before she started to feel different with them too and quickly she sensed them drawing away.

Disillusioned and fearful yet never to find out why her mum thought this to be so important, Kieran stood waiting at the bus stop on that first morning holding onto her hand tightly dreading to let go. Her mum had traveled with her to and from the school several days before, so she knew where to get on and off the bus, but the day for her to take the trip alone came all too soon.

Kieran was dressed in a starched white blouse with school tie, grey pleated skirt and black blazer. Her beret sported the school emblem on the front and she carried a large brown leather satchel that was obviously far too big for such a wee soul.

As she stood waiting her little heart beat so hard it made her tummy churn. She suddenly felt very small in this great big world.

Seeing the number eight bus in the distance she began to tremble.

"I don't want to go on that big bus all by myself, Mummy, I'm scared," she cried with tears staining her rosy cheeks.

"Please can I go with my friends to the other school?" she begged one more time, holding onto her mum's hand even tighter.

Unable to understand why the mum she trusted would force this on her she was to learn quickly to stuff her feelings. She tried really hard to be the big girl her mummy was asking her to be.

The bus came and she got on unwillingly forcing back tears unable to even look at her mum.

"Why are you doing this to me?" Kieran cried silently as she sat down and stared out the window. "I thought you loved me!" She questioned quietly trying hard to swallow the lump in her dry throat.

She felt abandoned!

The conductor of the bus was a friendly man and smiled at Kieran when he came to take her fare. In the days and weeks to come he would sometimes let her off with paying as he would just walk past and wink. Nonetheless, something inside told her not to trust him, and so she would look away shyly so as not to provoke conversation. She'd place her 'three penny bit' back into her leather purse with long strap which she wore slung across her body so as not to lose it.

As young as she was, she was learning to cry out to that unknown someone to help her get through this frightening experience. Although Kieran didn't understand it at the time she was beginning to develop a quiet trust in God.

"Poor Kieran, Grandma," Lyric said feeling sad for the little girl. "She must have felt terrified, but why did her mom think that was ok? Anything could have happened to her on that bus'."

"Oh darling I know it was scary for her, and it made her feel that no one cared about her fears," she explained. "But you know sweetie, sometimes parents do things for their children with the well being of their future in mind. Kieran's mom probably just felt she'd receive a better education at that school and times were different back then. Society as a whole seemed safer."

"But ye' know you were right, darlin'," Shy reflected on Lyrics concern. "It was definitely risky letting her ride on a public bus as young as she was. That was one of the many reasons Kieran became confused with the conflicting message of love she received," She added appreciating Lyric's tenderness towards another child's hurt.

"Anyway, back to the school..."

Within those first few years one particular teacher, a Mrs. Logan, brought a new level of fear into little Kieran's life on a daily basis. She was nothing short of evil and Kieran was absolutely terrified of her. In fact, she was so afraid of her that at times, when she desperately needed to use the bathroom during the lesson, rather than put her hand up to ask to be excused she would just wet herself.

She would suffer the pain of sitting there holding in the urge: rocking back and forward trying hard to listen to the lesson and convince herself she didn't need to go. The strain of this physical agony compared negligibly to her fear of asking Mrs. Logan to be excused. Kieran knew she would be subjected to heartless ridicule by this monstrous woman, so she chose to suffer the consequence of shame and embarrassment.

The janitor would come with his bucket and mop, shaking his head and muttering under his breath whilst the other kids sniggered and pointed fingers at her.

Kieran would keep her composure in front of everyone, but she was crying inside.

On the way home at lunch time she knelt up on the bus seat so as not to get it wet for the next person to sit down.

She arrived home feeling she'd disappointed her mum failing to be the 'big girl' she'd asked her to be and the shame deepened when she overheard Jo ask, "What's wrong with her? She shouldn't still be doing that at her age!"

Feeling she'd also let down the sister she loved and admired so much little Kieran was crushed.

A hug would have helped or at least a question or two of trying to understand why this kept happening, but instead she was left with the anguish and silence of coping on her own.

Bewildered and only six years old, she learned to cope by withdrawing.

Kieran was never taught that talking about fears or things that troubled her was an important part of supportive love from a family. She grew to fend for herself quietly accepting the injustice of life.

Mrs. Logan never missed an opportunity to ridicule any child in her class, but for some reason Kieran seemed to attract her rage more than most and for the smallest of things.

One day, within that first year of coping with this new season in her life, Kieran made the dire mistake of leaving her pencil case at home and asked a friend for a pencil. For that despicable crime she was convicted to two strokes of the belt on both hands placed one on top of the other.

That was Mrs. Logan's favorite instrument of torture! It was a long thick leather strap about thirty inches long with a forked tongue.

If the crime was really serious she would fold the belt in half to create a much bigger welt and the burning pain inflicted was almost too much for such a small child to bear.

Mrs. Logan raised her arm high above her head, making sure to create as much impact as possible as the belt bore down on Kieran's tiny hands. The expression on this woman's face was evidence to all of her evil intent.

Kieran's knees buckled with the force, searing pain and icy hot agony numbing her fingers. As she slowly walked back to her desk with hands tucked under her arm pits for comfort Kieran struggled to hold back the stinging tears which threatened to overflow from her big hazel eyes. She was determined not to allow this woman to get the better of her.

Little Kieran was gradually developing a resilience far beyond her natural years and took the pain with an inner strength and fortitude that would eventually carry her through most of what life was to throw at her in the years to come."

"Oh no! That mean teacher hurt her, Grandma," Lyric cried out as tears welled up.

Shy reached over and patted her grandbaby lovingly on her hands.

"Oh I know, darlin', but it was a different time and culture and schools had some harsh rules that were implemented with relish by some teachers.

"But you know Lyric, as cruel as that teacher was to Kieran her experience in that class taught her to be strong when going through life's trials. The very next year she was blessed with a kind teacher named Mrs. Holly whom she grew to love. She began to understand that people were different and she couldn't really judge all by just one person's actions.

"I wish she didn't have to learn that so early, Grandma," Lyric replied with a look of compassion in her eyes that seemed to far exceed her years.

Her mum complained to the school about Mrs. Logan's cruelty after seeing the welts left by the belt. Kieran felt a little more protected but it didn't really change matters much in class.

But at least her Mum had tried and in so many ways she was Kieran's hero.

A few years later she found out Mrs. Logan had been fired.

"Hallelujah!" Shy exclaimed praying she wasn't being too graphic in describing Kieran's earlier years. Lyric sighed with relief.

"Thank goodness Grandma!"

The following year Kieran began to thrive and develop a sense that someone was watching over her, smiling down on her strength. She could hear the whisper: "That's my girl!"

When Kieran turned eight, all that had been familiar to her was about to go through yet another season of change.

Her mum decided to look for work outside the home. She soon acquired a full time job in an old people's home just up the road from their house.

Kieran hated this new change in her life. She found it hard to adapt to coming home to a cold unwelcoming house with no warm fire burning in the hearth. All that greeted her now was a heavy silence that lay thick on the air; gone were the familiar voices from the afternoon plays on the radio.

The second paycheck soon made quite a difference to the family's finances though. But to Kieran, extra luxuries could not dispel the new-found loneliness which enveloped her every day as she let herself in the backdoor of her silent home.

She slowly started to understand; the only thing in life that was sure to remain consistent was that of change.

The way her mother dressed her was indicative of that era: puffy dresses with lots of underskirts just like Shirley Temple with white ankle socks and shoes. Her long chestnut hair tumbled down her back in bouncy ringlets.

As Kieran grew she never forgot the torture involved in making those beautiful curls, wincing at the pain the dreaded "rags" created.

"Hold still Kieran, it'll hurt more if ye' struggle!" Her mum would warn, as she wound a lock of the newly washed hair around a strip of material, usually torn off an old bed sheet, thus the name rags. She'd then wind it back up and pull it so tight it would make Kieran's eyes tear. The poor wee soul endured this process once a week wishing with all her might for straight hair minus the torture. She longed for a pony tail or some braided pigtails and hated those old fashioned ringlets.

"What we have tae suffer for beauty sake, eh lass?" Shy remarked as Lyric chuckled.

But Kieran, like any other little girl, liked to feel pretty, and most of the time she felt grateful for a mum who took the time to make her look nice. When they went shopping down to Leith on a Saturday afternoon in the winter, Kieran was expected to wear her white fur coat and hat to match feeling quite over dressed for such an ordinary outing. She cringed when people stared.

The town's claim to fame was the best pork butchers around. Mouth watering rissoles were Kieran's favorite and thick slices of stuffed pork were also top on her list. Another treat was a juicy pear from Rankin's fruit shop and as daylight turned to dark the two struggled home on the number 16 bus with bags full of groceries.

Gradually Kieran became aware that she was being spoiled by her mum and grew to hate that part of being the youngest in the family. She'd figured out herself it was likely because her parents could afford more after her mum had started to work. Nevertheless, she was never comfortable with reaping such benefits and longed to be a part of the family that was before she came along.

Kiernan's mum was ignorant of the rift she was creating between her older children and her youngest. She seemed driven to make a difference in her own life by making more of Kieran's. Unfortunately this felt to the wee lass that a quiet hostility was being created in the home.

Perhaps, little Kieran reminded her of herself as a child and so May was fulfilling her own heart's desire through her baby girl?

Or perhaps her mother just loved her and was showing that love the only way she knew how?

Kieran questioned life within and around her but had no idea how to put her feelings into words. She began to feel that no one would understand.

"Does Kieran ever find out if her Mum really did treat her differently from the others Grandma?" Lyric asked then added, "I mean much later on, of course."

Shy smiled and rocked back and forth her hands entwined and elbows resting on the arms of the chair.

"Well now, there's a question," she replied. "But I'm goin' tae' let you figure that out for yourself lass."

Lyric nodded in reply as the rain continued and the wind howled making the rafters of the old house creak and groan as though acknowledging the growing complexities of Kieran's story...

Slowly, she began to form friendships but none of them seemed deep or lasting. In years to come, when looking back at that time, she would come to realize; the moments she remembered that meant the most to her in primary school especially were visits to church, at Easter and Christmas.

'There is a green hill far away
Without a city wall
Where our dear Lord was crucified
He died to save us all.

He died that we might be forgiven
He died to make us good
That we might go at last to heaven
Saved by his precious blood.'

This was a hymn they sang in the ancient church, up the road from her school, during the lead up to Easter. It left an impact on Kieran for years as she remembered standing in the pew of the cold grey building beside her classmates with tears running down her face.

She sang with difficulty as the words strained through her trembling lips. Her tiny voice cracked. It broke her heart to think of the pain poor Jesus had suffered.

As young as she was, and without any proper education of a spiritual kind, Kieran seemed to sense His heart and pain for the world. There seemed to be an awakening taking place in her heart which she didn't understand and wouldn't for quite a while. Nonetheless, a seed was being planted by those trips to church with the school. Perhaps one day something great would grow out of that tiny little seed.

Like most children, Kieran's favorite time of the year was school break or holidays and a distant memory was when they shared a week during the summer on Owens farm in Ayrshire.

Her father's friend at the bakery owned a caravan on the farm and would allow Allan and his family to share it for a week every summer. Kieran could only remember little snapshots of those holidays as she was just a wee lass when the family enjoyed those times together.

"Do you mean vacations Grandma?" Lyric asked, once again confused by the language difference.

"Oh! Ye're right, sweetheart, I'm sorry you'd think I'd remember after all these years."

Kieran loved the distinct fragrances of farm life. The rich smell of hay bales stacked high in the barn where the black and white collies lived. And the not-so-fragrant odor from the milking shed as it wafted out to meet her in the early morning breeze, with the unfamiliar swooshing sound of milking machines sucking the warm delicious liquid from the patient cows chewing contentedly.

Many times her mum would warn her of the consequence of trying to play with the feral kittens under the abandoned truck, but to no avail. Inevitably wee Kieran would end the holiday covered in scratches. But something else was to happen one year that caused a sting of a different kind, leaving behind a lasting impression on little Kieran's conscience.

During the last few days of the holiday her dad heard news of a traveling fun fair that was due to visit the local town the last weekend of their stay. Although they didn't have transport, and knew it would be a bit of a walk, the decision was put to a vote, and everyone agreed to suffer the consequence of sore feet for the greater cause of having lots of fun.

When they started out it was a beautiful day and knowing it would take them at least half an hour to get there they walked at a steady pace along the pretty country lane, passing fields with cows and sheep and breathing in the wonderful fragrances of the countryside.

They must have looked like something out of The Broon's Family (a cartoon strip from the Sunday Post) as they walked in line down the narrow country road. Kieran soaked in the wonder of the day as she skipped feeling the warmth of midsummer sun on her face. Butterflies of all colors flitted to and fro with the wee lassie in hot pursuit as her mum shouted out for her to be careful.

"Don't you go too far ahead now, Kieran!"

The boys tormented Jo as usual and giggled with each evil deed as the poor girl became redder in the face with frustration.

"Dad will ye' tell them tae' leave me alone!" she yelled at the top of her voice scaring a few wood pigeon dozing under the hedgerow.

"Drew, Willy, if you two don't stop ye're nonsense we're goin' tae' turn around and ye'll go straight tae' bed when we get back ok?"

"Ok Dad," was the reply and the shamefaced duo hung their heads with a vain attempt at an apology, glancing sideways at each other whilst whispering revenge on their sister.

Poor unassuming Jo, innocently believing her torment was over!

They arrived at the fair and amidst the noise and excitement, they gathered to decide who was going on which ride and who wanted candy floss or an ice cream cone.

"Daddy can you win me a big stuffed dog with floppy ears?" Kieran shouted, jumping up and down with excitement.

"In a minute, lassie, but just calm down until we decide what we're going to do first," her dad replied digging into his pocket for loose change making sure everyone had something to spend.

Lots of fun was had by all, and as the long, hot afternoon slowly came to an end and dusk began to settle across a deep orange sky, little Kieran saw her brothers and sister walk back towards them. Disappointed that the day was almost over, and determined to squeeze one more thrill into an already incredible day, she begged her mum for one more go on the carousel.

"Kieran I only have one shilling left," her mum said, holding out her hand to show the shiny coin, trying to convince her daughter she'd had enough excitement for one day. In the blink of an eye wee Kieran snatched the last shilling out of her mum's hand and with a nonchalant air said, "Okay, that'll do," and skipped over to the man in charge of the ride.

In the years to come Kieran became convicted of her selfishness and the burning feeling of guilt remained.

She learned that day what it was like to have a conscience, and for all the years that lay ahead she would remember that moment with such a sour taste in her mouth.

Such a wee thing from a wee lass some would say, but it was a big lesson to learn and left an imprint on her for a very long time

Lyric looked at her grandma with a sheepish expression. "I can remember a few times of feeling like that. But I soon learned that getting my own way wasn't worth the guilt!"

Chapter 5
A Voice of Comfort Wrapped in Her Blanket

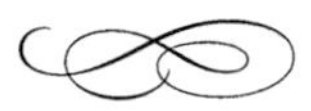

Kieran loved her neighborhood. The house overlooked the Firth of Forth giving an incredible view over the water to Fife.

It was a typical British three bedroom, with a living room, kitchen and only one bathroom. All the rooms were small and square in shape. The bedrooms were upstairs, with mum and dad's room facing the front garden and the boys and girls rooms facing the back.

Kieran shared a room with her sister and the boys shared the other room. She never knew whether straws had been pulled for the choice of bedrooms, but the boys must have won.

Kieran and Joycie's room was even smaller than the rest, but they made do. Looking back into their childhood, they all thought their house was big.

"Isn't it strange, when one goes back to a place we've known as a child, it always seems so much smaller and less significant?" Shy mused and Lyric smiled.

Her mum's taste in decor was unique as she tried always to add little touches of something different. Kieran loved her home, although she did prefer when they had a coal fire more than the new gas fire acquired later.

The coalman would come once a week to deliver the coal into a huge, concrete bunker in the back garden. Kieran loved to watch as he emptied the heavy bag from over his shoulder, causing a thick cloud of black dust to engulf everything around.

"No wonder he's got such a dirty face," she would think quickly getting out of the way.

The only thing she didn't like about the coal fire was how cold it was in the house first thing in the morning.

They only had one fire in the whole house so the bedrooms would literally freeze during the long winter months. Ice would form on the inside of the windows by morning.

Having to scrape the frozen glaze off the window so she could see out was no fun and dressing upstairs was done as quickly as possible so as not to prolong the deep freeze experience!

Kieran remembered being teased about being the coalman's daughter, because she was the only one of the children with dark hair and green eyes.

The others looked typically Scottish, with strawberry-blonde hair and blue eyes. It wasn't long before she came to realize, that they all took after her dad and she looked more like her mum and the Welsh side of the family.

Was this another reason why she felt so different from her brothers and sister? She didn't know but would ponder this question often throughout her life.

Of course, the different school and opportunities she'd been given may have factored into that difference, but deep down inside she felt it was much more. She actually felt at times that she may have been adopted. The feeling was overwhelmingly strong and yet at other times she felt somewhat included and happy; **but never quite complete.**

The house in which she grew up had a small front garden surrounded by a large, well manicured hedge. Added to his list of achievements Allan Stewart was a keen gardener and kept it looking neat and tidy.

The garden was split in two by the footpath which was edged with bricks to create a border. It was in that garden, where Kieran would develop her memory of sweet scents from her childhood.

Her dad grew incredibly beautiful roses of all colors imaginable. Two large bushes, one on either side of the pathway and smaller ones graced the outskirt of the grassy lawn. She loved the sweet fragrance the colorful blooms created, especially at night when walking up the pathway as she came home from class or shopping with her mum.

The front door was surrounded by a climbing honeysuckle bush. That wonderful fragrance, mixed with the beautiful rose blossoms was like an incredible aromatic glimpse into heaven itself.

Shy paused and took in a deep breath, as though smelling those very fragrances

"Isn't the sense of smell one of Gods amazing gifts, Lyric?

And as Lyric smiled and nodded in agreement Shy added, "A smell can take us back to days gone by in an instant opening familiar doors, sometimes bringing happy memories; sometimes pain and sorrow." As Shy continued Lyric couldn't help but notice that her grandma seemed lost somewhere back in a time that perhaps had caused her pain, but she stayed quiet as though sensing her need to talk.

"Some of those doors may have been closed for years under the pretense of keeping the interiors safe, but telling you these stories sweetheart I have come to realize that, more often than not, those doors need to be opened and the contents spring cleaned."

Shy slowly began to rock back and forward gazing up into the rafters. A soft smile grew at the corners of her mouth.

"To clean the rugs with a good old carpet beater and open the windows to let the pure fresh air of spring blow the staleness of time away, giving a lighter touch to precious, delicate treasures from a soft, feather duster," she added smiling at the picture she was creating and looking over at Lyric she went on.

"God wants us to go into these rooms but only when we can be completely sure that He is in there with us, holding our hand if the work becomes too arduous. We should never take our eyes off Him or close our ears to His perfect council." Suddenly as though waking up from a private daydream Shy sat up straighter in her chair and excused herself from going on too much.

"Grandma, don't apologize," Lyric assured her lovingly, adjusting one of the cushions she was sitting on. "I love to listen to you talk about God."

"I actually feel closer to Him when you do, because it sounds as though it's something He would say," she added making her grandma laugh.

"Well, I wouldn't ever aspire to know exactly what God wants to say, sweetie, but He has blessed me over the years with being able to feel His heart."

Shy went on…

Young Kieran was never able to figure out, whether it was the generation in which her parents grew up that made them lack in communication skills, or whether it was the Scottish culture itself, but nobody in her home ever discussed emotions, talked about loving one another or even hugged each other on a regular basis.

They came home, ate dinner, watched television and would usually only laugh or cry about something on T.V. But then that was normal wasn't it; to most perhaps, but not to Kieran?

Her parents would pay bills, buy groceries, and go shopping. They looked forward to holidays and special events like Christmas and Hogmany.

Kieran couldn't shake off that feeling of wonderment: there was something greater!

Instinctively, she seemed to sense there was more to life than what she had already experienced, but what?

Although there was always some kind of noise to be heard in her house, with the television or radio a constant. There were even times when her mum played the piano, but to the contrary Kieran was also aware of the presence of a deep silence; a silence that made her doubt whether she belonged in that family, or that place or even that time.

Maybe she just had a vivid imagination, she would wonder from time to time. Yet she could never deny the sense of being aware of her life going by as though witnessing it from a distance, almost as if she was seeing it through someone else's eyes.

Kieran loved to watch American films set around the forties and fifties. The characters seemed so full of life and eager to embrace and show love to one another.

Why did she feel more at home in this world of make believe?

Was she being given a glimpse into a future that was to prove to be far greater than her wildest dreams, or perhaps just the simple truth of what family could be?

Kieran thought she was loved. Perhaps just assumed it, but she was never completely sure because the words were rarely spoken, if in fact at all.

But life carried on and the years passed.

Her dad now worked long hours as a security officer with Ferranti's about two miles from their home and he would walk to work every day no matter what the weather.

He continued to make use of his baking skills, and Kieran never forgot the taste of wonderful cakes he baked as she was growing up. He'd let her lick the mixture of the spoon and she always thought it a special privilege to watch the master at work. Kieran thought he was the best baker in the world and as a little girl, looked up to him in awe with the yearning of a child wanting nothing more than to please her daddy.

The sultana- cake, scones, Cornish pasties and shortbread, coming out of the oven provided the most mouth-watering aromas imaginable. They wafted through the house creating an ever lasting memory for Kieran.

The concentration on her father's face as his strong hands mixed and kneaded the dough, was intense. He scrubbed the table brutally because he didn't like to use mixing bowls; but he would not tolerate germs.

She would watch. She'd sit on a chair and swing her legs being very careful not to disturb him at his work. Kieran was an excellent student and listened carefully to the lists of ingredients he would recite in answer to her questions. He was patient with her then, when he was doing something he loved.

She loved the intimacy of this quiet instruction. But for Kieran, what her heart truly cried out for was a close relationship with her Dad.

"Daddy, I want to know more about you and I want you to know more about me," she would hear her heart whisper. Sadly, she didn't know how to ask or what was stopping her from even trying.

Unfortunately, she also remembered the way she felt when she had no other option but to ask her father for help with her homework. She dreaded it, as more often than not he would lose patience with her if she didn't understand quickly enough and she'd feel the anger and frustration rise within him;

"Why can't you understand that you idiot!" He would bark, taking his frustration out on her.

On those nights Kieran's sadness was palpable. It could so easily have been a time of growth and positive development, but instead it became one of criticism and ridicule.

Kieran was to grow up thinking she was nothing, but an idiot!

The fear of sounding idiotic was the reason why she couldn't ask him those questions and in that place of disillusionment she would grow to accept the condemnation of those cruel words to be the truth of who she really was.

The mountain she saw before her that measured the distance she had to climb to gain her daddy's favor back from being 'nothing but an idiot' was too high for such a little girl who only wanted to hear the words; 'I love you and I'm proud of you.'

Kieran began to hear a tiny voice from deep within. This voice spoke a different truth to her. This voice was there especially when she felt judged wrongly by others.

She would hear the whisper but still suffer the pain from a child's heart when no one would listen....

Lyric sat hugging the teddy.

"Why would he have said that to her, Grandma?" she asked in all innocence, obviously upset by what she had just heard. "My Daddy would never say such things to me."

"I know, darlin', and those cruel words would haunt little Kieran all through her life and begin to create a deep broken place in her heart for many years to come," Shy explained, as Lyric tried to understand something alien to her.

Kieran was to wonder, in her silence, whether her other siblings had been told those words and if not, did that verify she was the only one to deserve them? Was it all her fault anyway? Was there something so terribly wrong with her and if so, what was it and what made her so different from the others?

Or, would this way of life just be an acceptable part of the culture in which she lived? Her confusion continued and with it the self doubt. The relationship she knew her sister had with her dad, seemed to compound the negative truth she was being forced to believe, making her feel even more inadequate.

"Ye' see lass, Kieran felt deep in her spirit throughout her life that both Joycie and Drew were favored by her dad and once again accepted it as failure on her part, always wondering what made them different in her daddy's eyes."

During those somewhat painful formative years she never did question, perhaps that was a failing on her father's part. After all she was just a little girl and didn't have the capacity to understand such things.

Idiot! One simple little word that yielded so much power.

In his eyes, she wasn't a princess. In his eyes she was just an idiot! Thus grew the void between them along with the ache in her heart.

"Grandma, I feel so sorry for wee Kieran, especially now she thinks everything's her fault," Lyric shared this sentiment with her grandma as the old woman listened to her granddaughter's heart.

"I know, darling, and what was even worse was the silence. She didn't share what she felt with anyone in case they agreed with her greatest fears," Shy added as she leaned forward to ease the dull ache in the base of her back.

"What fears, grandma?"

The rain continued to fall and the wind howled around the corners of the house causing the structure to groan as though in sympathy with wee Kieran's broken heart.

"The fear of discovering she truly was the idiot her daddy told her she was, honey." Her grandma unfolded the truth of how cruel words can crush a child's spirit and set her up for a lifetime of self doubt.

"You see, darling," Shy continued, "the bittersweet of Kieran's childhood was very difficult for her to understand and to feel cherished for all the wrong reasons was what caused most of her confusion.

"She felt that everyone thought they knew her by what was said about her, or how well dressed she was, or how spoiled she was compared to her siblings."

"Feeling that her self worth was measured on the superficial with no one having the time or inclination to find out more, she would just be there; as the 'baby' of the family with everyone thinking they knew her."

Was it natural to feel this confused with life and to constantly ask questions in her own mind? Did others question this much or was it just her?

And to whom did this whispering voice belong, that seemed to pull at her heart to confirm a different truth? A multitude of questions for such a little girl!

"Kieran did seem so full of silent questions, Grandma, but wasn't there anyone she could talk to?" Lyric asked.

"You're absolutely right, lass" her grandma replied. "And when she was older she did talk a lot with her sister, but not much when she was young. Jo began grown up life earlier than most, so she was probably consumed with her own issues most of the time. Kieran would never have wished to burden her sister with more"

She was most definitely an introverted child and spent many moments alone and most of the time content. There were times when she would sit on the doorstep of her home, wrapped in a blanket protected from the cold north wind that blew off the Firth of Forth, sensing she probably looked like an orphan to people walking by. She didn't care as an inexplicable longing kept her there.

Kieran loved to just sit and be still, feeling the wind and quietly observing all that was around her, listening to the rhythmic motion of the lawn mower as her father pushed it back and forth. She'd breathe in deeply the smell of newly cut grass, inhaling the wonderful fragrances from the rose garden and admire the glorious hues of the delicate petals of each flower.

She could hear the distant echo of the sea as the waves gently spilled onto the pebbly beach a mile in the distance. She heard the haunting cry of seagulls shattering the otherwise quiet of the afternoon as they followed ships making their way up the firth.

Her gaze followed the tracks of a beetle making its arduous journey through the jungle of nature, avoiding the deep chasms of cracks in the pavement. A beautiful butterfly with delicate wings of blues and yellows fluttered from one flower to another as Kieran sat motion less, transfixed with its playful dance. With all of nature quietly impinging on her senses, she'd feel a deep awareness of the intricate beauty of life, forever thankful for being a witness to all that had been created.

Then she would hear the voice. The one that told her how dear she was. For that moment she would feel a wave of unconditional love sweep over her.

At such an early age, she took the time to be thankful for all that was around her and felt the presence of something greater, yet simple, something so infinitely great that it made her still.

"I can't imagine living each day without knowing about God, Grandma." Lyric sighed as she drew her knees back up to her chin, wrapping her arms around them.

"But wasn't it cool that she was hearing His voice and seemed to sense Him even although she hadn't been taught much about him," she remarked with a bubbly flair that made Shy laugh.

"Yes, it was definitely cool, sweetheart, and a lesson to us all that we should always listen for His voice" she added feeling a shiver run through her tired body.

"Are you feeling okay, Grandma?" Lyric asked having noticed a change in Shy's demeanor.

"Oh I'm fine, sweetie pie; it's just listening to the howling wind that's making me think I'm cold. But let's get on" she insisted, as Lyric leaned against the old chest looking forward to the rest of the story...

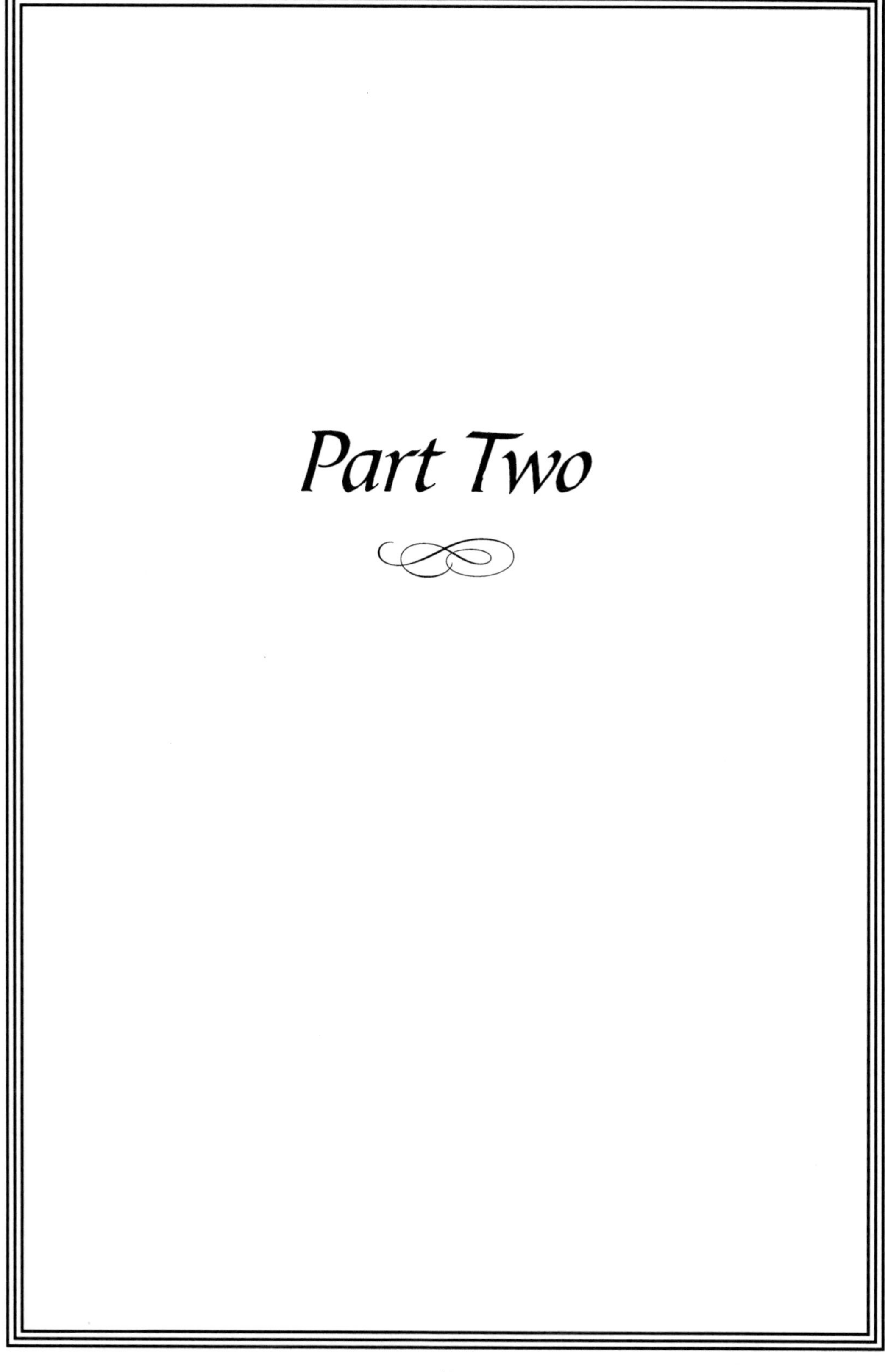

Part Two

Chapter 6
A Brand New Chapter Begins

"Mum what should I do?" Kieran agonized. "I really want to dance but I love horses too!"

This choice between taking dance or horse riding lessons was obviously too difficult for her to make on her own, but there had to be a choice. Her parents could only afford one extra activity given the monthly expense of the fee-paying school she attended.

Kieran was at the age of discovering her natural talents and desperately needed an outlet other than school so, after much deliberation, she chose dance.

"*Hardly a life changing decision*" do I hear you say? And maybe not in the history of the world but it was to become a big part of Kieran's future; as a great source of joy but heartache also.

She loved the lessons immediately and practiced constantly in their cramped home much to the annoyance of almost all family members, apart from her mum that was. She was Kieran's biggest fan and loved to play the piano as Kieran practiced. It would be during those times that Kieran felt her happiest and closest to her mum.

The rain continued to batter down on the roof, the wind whipped leaves into a tornado-like frenzy around the old house while Shy and Lyric snuggled in the cozy attic. This heightening crescendo of nature's elements brought an added air of intrigue into the musty room where Lyric now sat cross legged with face aglow.

She listened to the introduction of ballet class into young Kieran's life and her graceful hands stroked the soft satin of the shoes she had found in the chest. Lyric could picture the little girl tip toeing around a grand stage on point. She imagined how

Kieran would have felt free as a bird, jetteing and spinning around and around. As Lyrics thoughts wandered yet again Shy smiled and remarked on her expression.

"Hmm, perhaps someone I know with a very far-off look on her face would also like to take ballet lessons?"

Lyric shrugged her shoulders and slowly winding the faded ribbons around the worn shoes she replied, "Well maybe," then lowered her gaze as though disinterested but Shy knew her better.

"Now, let me see, where was I?" Shy pondered with an exaggerated look of question and a finger pointing to her chin.

"Ballet lessons Grandma!" Lyric answered more excited than she would have liked.

"Oh yes, yes of course ballet lessons, well let me see now"

Kieran's mum became increasingly proud of her little girl as she passed each exam with honors or highly commended. The wee lass seemed to do so with comparative ease.

On the other hand, Kieran usually found her mum's accolades embarrassing and cringed each time she was cornered into listening.

Kieran hated bragging and her own painful shyness, which led her to question the strange mixture of her personality. How could she be so shy around people hating the focus to be on her yet dance in front of an audience without a second thought?

After four years of taking just one class a week Kieran was encouraged by her dance teacher to take another class midweek which eventually led her to win a scholarship to one of the best schools in Edinburgh.

She appeared as an extra in a major movie at the age of twelve and went on to win a scholarship to study with the Scottish Theatre Ballet Company in Glasgow.

Kieran was living every little girl's dream and knew, without a doubt, that at least her mum was proud of her, yet she continued to question silently the deep sadness inside.

The extra ballet class began on a Tuesday night which meant Kieran had to take two buses to travel many miles across the Forth road bridge to Fife.

She didn't get home most Tuesday's until after ten o'clock making it harder for her to cope with school the next day. This weekly excursion eventually began to wear her down.

She was only twelve and loved to dance but hated the long trek to Fife. It terrified her to travel that distance on her own at night especially during the long, dark winter months. Each week she dreaded it more as she crossed the bridge and looked down into the deep black water below wishing to be back at home safe and sound.

Once again feeling thrust into a situation she believed herself to be too young to cope with she was forever thankful when this weekly experience came to an end.

Chapter 7
Life Lessons

In between those years of working hard at her studies and living for dance, she still endured loneliness at home. Her inability to communicate this emptiness to her parents drew her farther into herself and away from them.

Although Kieran was terribly shy she, like most children, just wanted to be accepted by her friends and piers.

She didn't find the encouragement she so desperately needed to build her confidence and self worth at home. During those pre-teen years when all children strive to find out where they fit in the world around them, Kieran fell short of her own expectations and inevitably found acceptance in the wrong place.

"Grandma, what do you mean she fell short of her own expectations?" Lyric asked, knowing somehow that trouble was brewing.

"Well darlin,' Kieran heard a voice deep down in her heart from very early on that gave her an unseen knowledge of who she was and was meant to be. But she didn't receive the kind of encouragement she needed to affirm it. Unfortunately, whenever we do anything in our lives that is not God centered, it sometimes means we step out of His will and what He wants for us. It's kind of like walking across a river on stepping stones but not quite making one of them." Shy explained, then asked, "So what do you think happens if we don't make the step onto the stone?"

Lyric replied with eyebrows raised, "We fall in!"

"Yep! We sure do, and that usually happens when we take our eyes off the rock."

"If we keep our eyes focused on God and what He wants for us we should never 'fall short' then should we Grandma?" Lyric concluded.

"Well yes, darlin', that's the way it should work in a perfect world, but we're not perfect and that's why we need Jesus every day," Shy replied, a soft smile appearing on her tired face, thankful she had learned so much to pass on to her daughter and grandbaby.

Kieran became friends with two girls at school who were obviously more mature in their world outlook than she was and who also had quite an interest in boys. Stepping quickly into the unknown, she began to discover a world outside the one she had known for eleven years. Her world of purity and innocence would soon become shattered, with new found carnal knowledge.

Her new friends talked her into going with them and a group of boys from their class to a playing field just up the road from the school. Since she never got used to going home to an empty house, she believed it would be o.k. to join her friends. She knew there was no one home to be overly concerned if she was late,

Naively, she thought they were just going to talk and hang out, but when they took her into a secluded part of the park away from prying eyes she felt overwhelmed by a sickly dread in the pit of her stomach and her heart began to race. Kieran knew instinctively this wasn't where she wanted or needed to be but at the same time she felt there was no way out; knowing that to leave now would mean ridicule and persecution. Her own knowledge of right and wrong was to be forsaken under the pressure from her peers.

"What happened to her Grandma?" Lyric asked, almost afraid of the answer.

"Well, darlin', they were still only children so nothing serious happened but curiosity got the better of them and I guess they explored a little and….."

Shy noticed Lyric's discomfort, so she concluded this part of the story with: "and kissed a little but it all felt awkward and embarrassing."

Kieran desperately wanted to get home and just put this awful experience behind her. She knew she had compromised her values and felt she'd not only let herself down, but someone else she didn't quite know. The voice that often told her how precious she was, was now disappointed with her also.

Now feeling as though she was no longer pure Kieran struggled with the guilt of what she had allowed to happen and once again withdrew deeper into her shell.

It became a deep dark secret this wee lass couldn't share with anyone. Although she kept a bright and somewhat happy countenance on the surface, Kieran struggled against the lie of which a darker more sinister voice was trying to convince her.

Shy watched as Lyric squirmed a little.

"Are ye' ok. lass?" Shy asked hoping she wasn't describing too much too soon for Lyric to handle.

"Yes, I'm fine grandma," She replied all of a sudden looking a little older.

"I understand that's the kind of subject that most children and parents find it hard to discuss, but I'm thankful my mom and dad brought me up to be able to talk about anything openly. I'm sad for Kieran though," she continued, "She sounded extremely lonely."

"You're right, sweetheart, and that loneliness felt like a prison. The wee lass felt desperate for the kind of family life that would have made it easier for her to cope with those kinds of life issues."

Shy sat back in her rocker and went on.

Now Kieran's father was a man of very few words to mostly everyone, that was, until he had been drinking.

Every Thursday was pay day. Although Kieran knew her daddy was a good provider, faithfully bringing his paycheck home every week for her mother and giving Kieran a pound pocket money, he would usually come home later than the normal 7:00 o'clock with the smell of beer and sometimes whisky on his breath.

Kieran hated Thursday nights.

Her mum seemed to accept that he deserved a pint after a long day at work; that was as long as he came home at a decent time. More often than not, the time would drag on and the later it got the more her mum's demeanor changed.

Kieran would watch the hands of the clock ticking past the acceptable time but with every minute that passed she began to feel more and more anxious. She knew the later it got the more upset her mum would become so why couldn't she just go to bed?

The wee lass felt responsible to keep the peace between her parents hoping that her very presence would stop them arguing but it never did.

Sometimes, unable to stay in the room another moment longer she'd sit on the third bottom step of the stairs in the darkened hallway and listen to the raised, angry voices of her parents arguing back and forth.

She was quite young so they may have assumed she was in bed and were probably oblivious to any trauma they were causing, but Kieran still felt drawn to be there nonetheless. She witnessed the turmoil within her home as though doing so would prevent it from happening yet feeling completely powerless to intervene.

Kieran had seen her dad come home one night with bloody knuckles and another with a deep gash on his forehead. From the tone in her mum's voice and the accusations hurled at him Kieran knew he'd been fighting with people in the pub.

Her mum's voice would take on a completely different tone to the otherwise sing-songy lilt of her homeland. This voice, full of rage and disappointment at how her father had behaved, scared her. It didn't sound like the gentle mummy she knew and all wee Kieran wanted to do was run in there and tell them to stop! Please stop the madness!

She'd sit on the third step from the bottom in that darkened hallway with her innocence for company and hope for what family life could be like if only....?

As the years went by, Kieran eventually realized the futility of her vigil on those nights. So she'd leave her post on the third bottom step to retreat to the distant quiet of her bedroom leaving them behind to sort it out for themselves.

Lyric's grandma paused for a moment noticing sadness in her granddaughter's eyes.

"Darlin,' I can stop if ye' want," Shy stated with concern.

Lyric shrugged her shoulders. "I'm just trying to understand how she must have felt, Grandma, but it's difficult 'cause I have tons of people in my life who make me feel loved and safe." Lyric explained as best she could.

"I know sweetheart."

"But God has such a tender way of healing us from all the stuff in our lives."

"Oh I know Grandma!" Shy was taken aback with Lyric's sudden input.

"Oh ye' do?" "Well pray tell." And the old woman sat back in her chair as though preparing to listen to an analytic truth from a learned scholar.

Lyric fidgeted to get more comfy. "Sometimes in Sunday school, or perhaps when I'm talking to you or Mum, we touch on something similar to what I've gone through with some of my friends and He reveals and heals a pain I didn't even know I had!" Lyric explained with an astonished look on her pretty face. "That's so cool how God works like that isn't it?" she added still with the innocence of a child but yet also with a growing awareness of how God heals.

"Well, ma' love, I think it's incredible that you're ready to receive that kind of healing, because many people much older than you aren't and, sad to say, waste many years of their lives struggling to figure things out for themselves or just live with hurts that mount up over the years," Shy encouraged her, feeling blessed with this time to share so much and as she glanced down at her wrist watch she asked Lyric if she wanted her to go on.

"Of course I do, Grandma, I can't wait to find out what happens next."

And with that assurance, her grandma continued as Lyric pulled her knees up to her chin readying herself for what was to come, looking every bit like the little girl again.

Just like when she watched horse racing with her dad, Kieran even pretended to love boxing so that they would have something in common. But it never felt natural. This desperate need to be recognized by the only man in her life, and a longing to please so that she could see even a glimmer of the love she never seemed to receive from him, was to take her down an extremely destructive path in the years that lay ahead.

"What's going to happen to her Grandma?" Lyric asked eager to find out more.

"Well sweetheart many trials lay in wait for Kieran in the years ahead, but many blessings were in store for her also. As we go through each season with her, you will begin to understand how much her past was to influence her future.

"However, it's good to remember that interwoven throughout those years there were also many happy family moments for Kieran: treasured holidays and long summer days when life felt just like everyone else's. More often than not Kieran just accepted her life as being a normal part of being Scottish.

Christmas day she especially loved just like any other little girl and would wake up in the morning much earlier than anyone else. She'd race downstairs to see what Santa had brought and brace herself for the bitter cold that greeted her before the fire was lit.

She'd have a look in her stocking, grab a treat to eat, and find at least one big present to open before retreating to the warmth of her bed to await the stirring of the household as dawn broke. She wasn't daft! And would much rather open the rest of her gifts engulfed in the warm glow of a toasty fire.

Life in general was good for Kieran and her brothers and sister compared to many children and she grew with a grateful awareness that her parents were decent, hard-working people who did their best for them.

Yet she couldn't deny the great sadness she felt inside longing for her parents to understand her and for the emptiness to be filled.

Another of the happier times from her childhood was when she and her parents were making preparations for a summer holiday.

Kieran would save most of her pocket money with excited anticipation of what was to come. As the time for the holiday drew near, she would empty her savings out onto the floor in the living room every night and count it just one more time making sure she had counted right the night before. Her parents would laugh at her antics and tease her when she counted yet again.

"Is there any more tonight Kieran?" They would ask playfully as she giggled and put her money away ready to be counted again.

Kiernan loved to travel by train. Her favorite holidays started at Waverley Station with its hustle and bustle of passengers rushing to find the right platform. The distinct sounds and smells of the trains as they discharged hot steamy clouds from under the huge shiny engines made Kieran's heart beat faster with excited anticipation.

As they climbed aboard struggling with their luggage, the conductor would blow his whistle to alert all passengers of the train's imminent departure. Kieran would run ahead to find an empty compartment. A delighted shriek would signal that she'd snagged one with a window seat all to herself.

Even as she got older, she could still remember how the prickly seat coverings made her bare legs itch. After an hour or so of gazing out the window watching the beautiful countryside go by with fields full of sheep and cows, they would unpack sandwiches her mum had prepared for the journey and enjoy an indoor traveling picnic. The juicy Scottish tomatoes made the thick white bread soggy. Thick slabs of cheddar cheese and tender roast beef from Sunday dinner were garnished with tiny silver skin pickles that made her tongue blister.

Those were the good times she recollected from the sweet corners of her mind. Everything seemed right in her world and her parents looked happy with each other. Rarely was a cross word spoken.

As Kieran grew older, however, the Thursday night ritual affected her in a different way and although she'd usually try to avoid being downstairs when her dad eventually got home, somehow she still felt drawn to be there.

Kieran still felt responsible somehow as though being there would act as a buffer against the argy bargy.

It was as though her father needed to make up for the whole week of not saying a word to anyone. He inevitably talked for hours about the world around him turning the night into a monologue of complaint.

Kieran sat there out of respect for the father she loved knowing the subject matter would always the same: what he hated most about the government, or religion, or the differences in cultures and, of course, his dislike for the royal family.

After many years of enduring the Thursday night lectures, and Kieran called them that because they were very rarely two way discussions, she began to feel extremely sad for her dad. She'd cringe inside with embarrassment for him, "Dad if only you knew how you sounded," but she'd also listen respectfully and try to ignore the anxiety those one-way conversations created in her.

As young as she was, she was more than aware that it probably didn't matter to him who was sitting on the sofa listening to him go on and on, and so the acute pain of invisibility continued to cut deep.

By the time Kieran had gone through years of Thursday nights, she had come to develop her own opinions on the topics he'd cover time and time again. Most of her views became the opposite of his. Whether those views were mere rebellion or not, she truly felt it was because she sensed there was a greater truth of which he never spoke. A truth for which her heart longed and if that meant she had to make a stand at times and question what was being preached in her home, then it had to be.

Kieran was slowly beginning to find her voice and was determined to use it. However, then there'd be the nights when she'd feel it was futile to argue. He never listened anyway so what was the use?

The rain lessened to a gentle pitter patter on the roof above them, the wind becoming a gentle breeze as it whistled down the old brick chimney.

"I can feel her frustration, Grandma," said Lyric, stretching her long graceful legs out before her. "Do you think her father was like that with her brothers and sister or did he change as he got older?"

"Well, ye' know, Lyric, that was never found out but even if he was, they may not have been affected the same way Kieran was because everyone's life journey is different."

"Remember sweetheart, she was a sensitive child with a tender heart and was actually like her dad in many ways, and because she didn't have the kind of relationship with him she longed for, she may have taken his curious behavior a little more to heart than her siblings."

"I'm confused when you say she was like her father, Grandma, how could that be if there was so much in their relationship that seemed to conflict?"

"Well now we're getting down to the real life stuff that affects us all, lass," Shy replied shifting back into her seat ready to explain.

"You see, darlin', sometimes people who have been wounded themselves are the first ones to lash out and wound others even though they may have forgotten what had caused them pain. Until we're healed, we don't forget hurts but rather stuff them into the dark recesses of our minds.

"And it happens a lot to the children who remind a parent so much of themselves."

"But why then Grandma?" Lyric asked listening intently.

"Because that very child who has so many of the parent's traits is a daily living reminder of the parent himself, and sometimes when the child is seen to make an error of judgment in a life choice, or doesn't learn quickly enough, those mistakes or failings feel like a direct reflection of the parent and his own inability to deal with that is what comes out in frustrated anger or harsh words."

"Hmm! I see," Lyric replied.

"Kieran's dad had a real soft spot for animals and for anyone who was hurting, but like an awful lot of men he tried hard to cover up that side of his nature, so as not to appear weak. He also had a heart of gold for anyone needing a favor or down on their luck. In fact, his favorite song he'd sing every Hogmany was "Buddy can ye' spare a dime."

He'd sing it with such passion he'd bring tears to the eyes of the folk listening. That's why wee Kieran hurt so much. She knew what a good man he was and loved him so much, it hurt for her to think he had no interest in her or, if he did, he didn't show it.

Shy looked off into the rafters and let out a deep sigh as though ready to be done with that part of the story.

"Well now let me see what else now..."

Kieran loved her home but hated how messy it had become since her mum began full time work. At times, when it got too much to bear the wee soul would get up in the middle of the night to tidy up. She hated to live with such disorder around her and hoped that tidying overnight would be a help to her mum who seemed so tired most of the time. But the tidied state didn't last long, and before she knew, clothes would be back on the chair in the corner and the mantel piece would become littered with bits and bobs.

In fact, apart from special occasions like Christmas and Hogmany, the house stayed in a state of permanent chaos.

Her midnight cleaning frenzy became a standing joke in the house. It also infuriated her brother Drew.

"Oh! No! Kieran's been cleaning up again," he would say with trepidation knowing full well what was in store for him.

"Well put ye're things away and ye'll know where to find them," she'd reply ignoring his plea for a return to perpetual chaos.

With all the up's and downs of an ordinary life, the gratitude of family values along with disagreements of family issues Kieran still had a special place in her heart for her mum.

She seemed to understand the yearnings her mother had for her homeland, Wales, and felt sorry that they didn't try to go back there more often, at least for her sake.

Her mum grew up in Swansea, Glamorganshire, in the southwest corner of the country. All that Kieran knew about her life was that her Welsh grandmother had preferred her mum's sister Rose to May. She had treated May very badly and on one occasion even hit her with a corset! The metal hook slashed her face leaving a permanent scar.

May seemed to have loved her father who was a quiet, kind man who probably had a hard life himself putting up with his harsh-natured wife.

He worked on the railways and her mum spoke of the times she had to wash his oily overalls by hand as a little girl but she did so with love.

She told Kieran how her heart had broken when he eventually went blind and died. But then she seemed reluctant to tell too much more about her childhood.

Sensing her mum's pain Kieran stopped asking more questions about growing up in Wales.

They did eventually visit Wales one summer. Kieran was about six and had not yet heard the story of her mum's childhood. Still when Kieran met her Aunt Rose for the first time, she knew instinctively there was something about her she didn't like.

But it was a holiday so they set out to enjoy themselves, and of course, her mum didn't miss the opportunity to dress Kieran in the Welsh National costume. When looking back at an old photo from that holiday, she had to admit to looking cute, boiling mad, but cute.

She had four cousins, two girls and two boys who were all older than she, so they naturally treated her as the baby.

Her cousins talked funny and very fast so it was difficult for her to understand much of what they said. However, kids have a way of understanding each other no matter what the language spoken, and before very long they were playing with frogs her cousins kept in a huge sink in the back yard. They had lots of fun scaring the grownups with them.

Although Kieran often saw glimmers of sadness and perhaps disappointment in her mother's eyes with the many problems of an ordinary family life, the only time she ever saw her cry with deep anguished sobs that broke Kieran's heart was when they heard news of the Aberfan disaster.

Aberfan was a small mining town in South Wales built at the bottom of a slag heap containing millions of tons of residue left over from the rich coal. On that fateful morning after many days of torrential rain the slag heap gave way and turned into a deadly avalanche of black sludge engulfing everything in its path.

At the bottom of the mountain of Black Death lay the Pantglas Junior School packed full of children and teachers busy with their morning lessons and nothing anyone could do was enough to prevent what happened next.

Before the alarm could be raised, half a million tons of black sludge tore down the valley swallowing up the school under a forty foot tidal wave suffocating all who was inside. Twenty nearby houses also took the brunt of the forty foot high wave of fury killing, in all, 144 people, including 116 children and 5 teachers.

Kieran's poor mum sobbed until her voice was nothing but a whisper and her breathing labored under the agony of such a loss.

"I'm sorry that happened, Mum," was all she could think to say as she comforted the heartbroken woman, witnessing for the first time her mother's vulnerable humanity for her suffering people.

Kieran was only eleven and on that day experienced the shocking reality of how quickly life could be snuffed out just like a flame. Full and rich and vibrant one moment, and gone in an instant.

She loved her mum with all her heart and sooner now rather than later began to think about life and the inevitability of death and immortality.

Aberfan left a haunting memory of the innocence that was lost so suddenly leaving an indelible imprint on the whole country forever.

Like most of us, Kieran's life consisted of happy moments and fond memories that more often than not would overshadow any prolonged feelings of sadness, but the hurt and existence of a deep void inside could not be denied serving as a daily reminder of who she was told she was, in her father's eyes, at least. As hard as she tried to ignore it, the sadness would not go away.

She constantly strived to prove her father wrong and longed for the day he would admit his error of judgment and ask for her forgiveness.

Chapter 8
Beyond Her Years

"Oh! No! What's happening?" Kieran cried, shocked to find the reason why she hadn't been feeling well all morning. She had just made it to the girl's bathroom after third bell and discovered something she was afraid to share with anyone. Kieran's thoughts run amok as shame and embarrassment engulfed her for three days until she couldn't hide it any longer.

Her ignorance was obvious due to her mum's negligence in preparing her for the changes that would soon be taking place in her body and so the wee lass became distraught with thoughts of the unknown.

"Uh! That's terrible Grandma," Lyric uttered saddened by what she'd just heard. "Why didn't they make sure she knew about that?" she added questioning the hearts and common sense of the family that surrounded Kieran.

"Oh, darlin', I know, it was traumatic for her to learn such an important life event by herself."

Back and forth she went in her mind for those three days practicing how she would eventually make her mother aware, knowing she couldn't keep it hidden much longer.

On the third evening just before bed time her mother came to ask for her laundry and Kieran began to cry. In between strained sobs it all came out.

Kieran's mum gave her a quick hug before discovering the laundry hidden under her bed and explained briefly that she was having a period. There was no tenderness or reassurance that everything was going to be ok and that this was nothing to be scared of. Kieran was given just enough information to get by.

Kieran longed for reassurance. Instead of that moment being one of celebration of becoming a young woman, she was made to feel awkward and embarrassed. Her mum remained standing in the doorway of her room keeping an obvious distance from her.

Kieran felt lost, almost drowning in what felt like a sea of unanswered questions. She tried to pull herself together, thinking this week couldn't get much worse.

Her mum stopped and turned back to look at her with a strange expression, "And Kieran, don't go near boys!"

"Huh!" she uttered quietly completely dumbfounded at her mother's remark. "What do boys have to do with what I'm going through?" and as she slid down between the sheets she tried to still her mind.

In that house of silent questions Kieran couldn't ask what her mum meant. Somehow the remark held an explanation far too deep and embarrassing for her to even want to discover.

The confusion of that night continued for many months as she struggled with the possibility of asking someone at school, but she couldn't risk being ridiculed even more. Kieran felt sure everyone else must already know the answer. So she kept to herself and just observed and listened to the conversations of others picking up little pieces of information here and there.

"My Mommy told me about that six months ago and I'm only eleven!" Lyric pointed out. She understood how traumatizing that lack of knowledge must have been for the little girl to whom she was gradually growing close.

"And that's the way it should be sweetheart." Shy agreed.

"If only she'd been prepared for such a huge change in her life, she wouldn't have suffered so and it would have been an incredible time of bonding for either of the women who should have taken on that responsibility," Shy added bringing to light the subject of close relationships within a family.

"I'm sure both you and your mom will always remember that particular conversation and also the change it made in your relationship with your mom."

"Well, Grandma, you know it really did," Lyric confirmed as she paused for a moment in thought. "It made me feel as though she was introducing me into the secrets of becoming a woman and not just talking about a kind of icky subject, where

some parents squirm with embarrassment," Lyric added sharing a glimpse into her deepest thoughts.

"I love that about my Mom, Grandma and you too," she said wistfully gazing into the older woman's eyes with a look that acknowledged the profound words spoken. "You've both made me feel that everything in my life is important to you, and you actually care to listen to what I have to say and not just tolerate me."

"Tolerate you! Oh no, ma' sweet, I've always thought of caring for you as a privilege I've been given. I feel honored that God would choose me as a caretaker of His precious daughter, and ye' know, Lyric, we all take our job very seriously," she ended with a twinkle in her bright green eyes that made her grandbaby giggle.

As the wind continued to whip up anything in its path, droning around the eves of the old house, Shy asked if Lyric could shout down to her mom to make sure she was o.k.

The young 'un jumped up and did as she was asked, and Shy rocked slowly back and forth reflecting on the conversation they'd just had as she heard Erin reply.

"Oh I'm just fine, you two take as long as you want and don't worry about me," her soft voice echoed through the rafters giving them the assurance they needed to continue with the story.

Lyric sat down on the cozy spot she had created and Shy continued.

"Well let's get back to the first two years of high school which were just as painful for her as primary school, apart from one thing."

"What was that, Grandma?"

"When Kieran started high school at the end of the long hot summer of '67, as a welcoming gift the school gave her a pocket sized version of The New Testament and her little world suddenly became brighter."

By reading a passage diligently every day, she slowly began to find some answers to the questions she had been asking for years.

Kieran gradually came to realize that some of the feelings of sadness and wonderment of something greater, that was never spoken about in her home and even of feeling different from everyone else, were all possible evidence of her search to know more about God.

She began to wonder if it had been God's whispering voice that seemed to have helped her through her challenges.

"Kieran, I am here and I love you, come closer."

But then, was that too all part of a vivid imagination? And how dare she presume that the God of the Universe was actually speaking to her.

Nevertheless Kieran felt the spiritual life in her begin to grow taking her in a different direction. She began to think about the world around her and to wonder whether she could possibly do anything to help those less fortunate than herself. She felt drawn to third world countries like Africa.

Kieran felt a stirring inside. She began to ask questions at school and found out about an organization called Voluntary Service Overseas or VSO. She became excited with the possibility. However, there seemed to be one important issue that would have to be faced. The majority of the people she saw in the advertising literature were nuns.

Did this mean she would have to change religion? That question alone spoke volumes about the lack of religious or spiritual education she'd received. Although this was no fault of her own, it made her wish she could have found out more.

The only time God was ever mentioned in her home was when there was a biblical epic showing on T.V. She loved those movies and it was still an education of sorts igniting an interest in finding out about God.

Kieran was never quite sure who taught her to pray, but she did so every night and would include everybody in her family. In a poetic childlike way she even included Gwynne her little white Sealyham terrier and Jenny the budgie.

She wanted to attend Sunday school at the church on the hill called The White Church, but couldn't go alone since her parents didn't attend church.

Her mum did make an effort on Easter Sunday and Christmas Eve. On occasion she spoke of the difference between the Church of Scotland and the one in which she grew up in Wales, so little Kieran knew her mum at least had some kind of faith upbringing.

She looked forward to going to church on those special occasions and it was those, albeit infrequent, services that made a lasting impression on her.

Christmas Eve, however, held more of a bittersweet taste.

Every year her mum would ask her dad to come to the midnight candlelight service, and every year he would promise to be there. Sadly to say he'd either turn up drunk or not come at all.

Kieran wasn't sure which scenario she hated most; to feel embarrassed at his behavior or worry about the consequence when they got home. She never did understand why it was so hard for him to keep a promise.

As young as she was Kieran sensed her father's disrespect for her mum's wishes and she began to wonder about relationships and marriage.

Was this what she should expect when the time came for her to have a husband? Was she to assume she'd just have to tolerate the bad points in a marriage to be able to embrace the good?

Reading her New Testament daily she tried to envision a life devoted to God instead of worrying about the inevitability of marriage, but the tidal wave of life in the world tugged at her.

Kieran slowly realized with a heavy heart that Leith Academy was going to be her life for the next four years. A few of the boys that had lured her to the park in primary school had transferred to the same High school.

The young lass was determined to begin this new season in her life with, true to her self, values and refused to have anything to do with them. Unfortunately they took that as rejection and began to spread nasty, vulgar rumors around school.

They'd continually taunt her with vicious name calling as she walked past them in the corridor making each transition to the next class a walk through the gauntlet of torment. And whenever a teacher left the class, they would seize the opportunity to embarrass her yet again, void of any compassion towards her. She detested this time in her life.

Kieran dragged herself to school every day knowing what lay ahead, but having no-one at home to confide in, she retreated into a place of self preservation.

She went to school and suffered the cruel taunts then returned home and kept to herself pretending to everyone that everything was just fine in her life. The only release from this cruel persecution was through her dance.

She would practice harder than ever determined to at least make the best of that part of her life and it became her shelter. Kieran tried to keep reading the Bible and praying, but thoughts of her VSO dream began to fade.

One morning, almost at the end of that painful first year she was walking down the stairs between first and second bell and she heard the familiar sound of sniggering just behind her. Suddenly she felt a hand on her back and before she could react she stumbled and fell head over heels down the stairs.

Feeling as though the fall was happening in slow motion she finally came to a halt with a thud at the bottom her leg twisted underneath. Excruciating pain throbbed in her left ankle and as she looked up she saw the face of the culprit. It was Norrie Roland, one of the boys responsible for causing even more pain of an emotional kind.

He didn't look that cool now. In fact, he looked kind of sheepish! To her dismay she found herself pitying him, sensing he knew he'd gone too far.

There were numerous witnesses to this terrible act of bullying. If she wanted to she could have had him expelled, but that wasn't the way her heart was to lead.

After visiting the school nurse, who advised her to go home, Kieran was called into the principal's office and asked if she knew who had pushed her.

Much to the surprise of the stern Miss Moffat Kieran spoke quietly and assured her that it was merely an accident. The principal knew it wasn't but rather than push the issue, she let Kieran go back to her class. She felt a mixed sense of admiration and sadness for this young lady. She seemed to understand Kieran was not acting out of fear but rather a deep sense of loyalty no matter how misguided it was and hard to comprehend.

Kieran didn't want to go home and limped around on the foot all day. By the time she eventually arrived home it was evident she had damaged her ankle badly.

Her mum insisted on taking Kieran to the emergency room after a disagreement with her dad about the severity of the injury. she and her mum grabbed a quick bite to eat and took the number 14 bus to the Western General Hospital.

Many hours later she hobbled into the house with crutches and a cast up to her knee. Her father looked surprised and a little sheepish.

"See, I told you her ankle was hurt badly," her mum retorted still mad at his stubborn attitude.

She was thankful for her mum.

Her dad had told them just to soak her foot and it would be fine. He didn't even consider the possibility of it needing an x-ray. Perhaps he was passing on the neglect he had endured as a child by his own mother, but his cavalier attitude hurt Kieran.

The only two stories from his childhood that he ever spoke of were about two horrendous accidents he'd had. His mother hadn't ensured proper medical attention and he never gave an explanation as to why she was so neglectful.

"Are you feeling OK?" Shy asked Lyric, who was beginning to look a little tired.

"I'm ok, Grandma, I'm just sad for Kieran. She seemed so lonely most of the time."

"She didn't feel able to talk about her problems because she hadn't been given that encouragement from early on," Shy continued. "And she felt so guilty and full of shame with what had happened to her in primary school that she probably felt everything was her fault anyway. She set herself up to become a victim of her own circumstance."

"Your mom and dad have made it easy for you to go to them with any concern you might have, as I did with your mom, sweetheart," she went on to explain the difference in the two lives. "But Kieran's home wasn't like that and that's why she kept everything to herself suffering silently." Shy looked down at her hands suddenly realizing her ring finger was hurting. She'd been squeezing her fingers too tightly and her ring had left a deep impression. Rubbing her finger back to life she looked up at Lyric.

"But you know, darling, sometimes when we cope with life situations on our own, without help from friends or relatives, we begin to grow stronger. Perhaps without even understanding it, Kieran was starting to trust in the voice she kept hearing from inside her heart. She would continue to feel terribly lonely for many years to come and make many wrong choices in the process. She had no clear understanding of how God can work in our lives if we know Him and allow Him to." Shy explained.

And as she was just about to ask if Lyric wanted her to continue, the bright eyed youngster made a suggestion.

"Well, Grandma, actually," Lyric said as she unwound her crossed legs and stood up to stretch. "I'm getting quite thirsty, do you mind if I get some water?"

"Absolutely not sweetie, in fact grab me some too please," Shy asked as she glanced backwards at the image of her graceful grandchild descending the attic stair.

In the quiet that followed Shy rested her weary head with its halo of snowy white against the back of the old chair. Rocking slowly back and forth she reminded herself of what lay ahead in the life of the wee lass named Kieran.

The rain had diminished to a faint pitter patter and the blustery wind had subsided bringing a gentle peace to the old house.

As she pondered over the story she was telling to her Lyric, Shy asked a silent question to the one who always listened,

"Where have all the years gone to, Papa?' she mused as her tired eyes glazed over with tears of reminiscent joy, "it seems like only yesterday when we danced and became lost in the melodies of Tchaikovsky and Debussy."

Her daydream was interrupted by a refreshed Lyric carrying two bottles of ice cold water. She reclaimed her cozy spot on the cushions, handing a bottle to her grandma. With the enthusiasm of a child lost in the story of another child's life, she asked "Are you ready, Grandma?"

Shy smiled and answered with, "Now let me see.....

Kieran stayed home from school for two weeks afraid to get on and off the bus with crutches. When she returned, with only an ankle support, she was called into the principal's office. Once more she was asked about the incident.

She adamantly stuck to her story of not knowing what had happened. This frustrated the patient woman immensely! Miss Moffat had been told by a few witnesses that it was definitely not an accident.

"Kieran, nothing can be done to prevent this from happening again unless you tell me who did it and file a complaint."

But Kieran wasn't afraid of the consequences of telling on Norrie Rolands. Somehow she just sensed that things would turn out better in the long run if she didn't, and her instincts proved to be correct.

The abusive behavior towards her stopped. The boys responsible started to treat her with a new respect. They talked to her kindly, and by the end of third year, she even started to date one of them. She became accepted on her terms and no-one else's. Kieran began to feel her character strengthen and life gradually became easier.

By this time, she was taking more ballet classes and her mum was pushing her into making a career of it. Although Kieran loved to dance, she felt inclined to agree with her father on this subject. He wanted her to keep her dance as a hobby, but to concentrate on another career so she could earn a living at the same time.

That sounded like a perfect compromise. Then Kieran's dance teacher informed her mother that to make it as a dancer, she'd need to take a full time stage course. That would of course, mean more cost to her parents and the likelihood that Kieran wouldn't be able to get even a part-time job, unless she danced all day and worked at nights.

It was terrible to be put in the centre of such a disagreement between her parents. Kieran felt she was in the middle of a no-win situation.

Ultimately she knew she would have to choose, and someone would feel let down. After agonizing over this dilemma Kieran knew eventually what the choice would have to be.

It boiled down to loyalty.

Her mum had been closer to her all her life, and although her dad helped pay for her tuition, he was never an element of support.

He very rarely attended any of her dance recitals. Kieran believed he thought of dance as a waste of time and money and was nothing to be taken seriously.

But did he even take Kieran seriously? Or was it more the fact that he felt out of his depth in his daughter's world? Perhaps he didn't know how to be supportive?

Kieran tried to give him the benefit of the doubt but then again supporting her was never a strength of his in any area of her life. Unless it was something he wanted her to do and excel in.

Kieran realized that seemed a harsh view of her father, the one who afforded her the ability to dance in the first place, but she couldn't deny the truth of what she had felt all through her life.

He'd never encouraged her in any way. The cruel words spoken to her as a young child made her feel like an idiot in his eyes,so how could she go against the mother who had encouraged her?

Kieran was quite unnerved at the prospect of actually being a full time dancer. She wondered if she indeed had what it would take to succeed and struggled with the reality of the choice she made.

Would it become perfect proof to her father that she was indeed the let down she already knew she was to him.

"Why must I always choose between them?" Kieran agonized. She felt instinctively that if her parents truly loved her, they would have listened to her heart and supported her in the decision she would want for herself and not out of loyalty to either one.

Reluctantly and almost with a sense of dread, she chose her mother.

She left high school at the age of sixteen, which was normal back then. Actually, she could have left at fifteen but she wanted to at least sit her 'O-Grade Exams', so that she would have some qualifications to fall back on.

The start of her stage course was to be exciting, but very hard work.

Kieran was disciplined and enjoyed feeling her body grow stronger and suppler with each class and throughout the years that lay ahead studying at the Theatre School of Dance and Drama was to become a wonderful experience for her but it would also have its ups and downs.

The school was in the centre of Edinburgh, which in itself was the centre of the arts industry in Scotland. During the International Arts Festival, in August, each year, famous people from all over the world would come to perform and sometimes teach at the school. This was a huge incentive for Kieran to excel and that she did. When she won a scholarship with the Scottish Theatre Ballet Company, she was elated.

Kieran took the train through to Glasgow every Saturday morning leaving from her beloved Waverley Station and practiced for two hours dreaming of being with the company one day.

Kieran was continually encouraged by a principal dancer in the company named Bronwyn Curry who thought she was extremely talented and had great potential, but something else was beginning to happen that would slowly begin to change Kieran's thoughts of what she would like to do with her life.

She met a boy when she was about sixteen and began to date and after a couple of years of dating, they became serious. He knew her choice of profession but didn't like it. Although she stood firm most of the time and was determined to finish the course, after the third year of dating she began to allow his opinions to affect her.

If she'd had the kind of affirmation and parental involvement that she needed and deserved growing up, especially from her father, she may not have been so easily swayed.

"Ye see darlin', if a little girl does without that kind of affirming love and nurture from her father and is not made to believe in the 'Princess' she truly is, as daughter of the King, she will accept the praise from the first male that comes into her life who makes her feel beautiful and worthy of being loved," Shy turned to the pretty face eagerly hanging on every word.

"As strange as it may sound, her father; is a little girl's first love. He's her first encounter with loving someone of the opposite gender. If that relationship isn't the positive and affirming experience it should be then she will grow up without the self esteem she needs and deserves to navigate through life.

She will grow to look for love in all the wrong places and you can be sure of one thing; there will be plenty men willing to step into that role. Saying the words she never heard as a child but usually with their own motives at heart.

"Words of encouragement will build a child's confidence. Words of insult and negativity will crush a child's spirit." Shy looked off into the rafters as though pleading for this simple truth to be heard by those who needed it most.

"Parents need to be an example of a loving and united relationship, Lyric, one that a child will relate to and identify with when she is looking for a spouse."

Lyric was listening intently.

"My Dad makes me feel like a princess, Grandma!" Lyric assured Shy. "And he's never yelled or said anything negative to me, ever!"

"I know, sweetheart and quite rightly so," she replied as she rocked gently on the comfy, old chair. "And we both know why he's a loving father don't we?" she added smiling at the precious little girl she loved so much with affirmation of a mutual family love for a loving Father in Heaven.

"Well, on that note, I think we should take a wee break don't you, ma pet, or else ye're mum'll think we've both fallen asleep up here?"

"OK, Grandma. I guess you're right, but can we continue at bedtime?" Lyric added already knowing the answer.

"Och! You know fine well we will, lassie." Shy replied getting up slowly trying hard to ignore the all too familiar pain in her joints.

Chapter 9
Why Won't They Listen?

Shy and Lyric walked into the family room together to find Erin curled up on the sofa sound asleep with a photo album draped across her lap.

"Oh! Oh! It looks as though we've been up there longer than either of us realized, sweetie pie," Shy said softly lifting the album off her daughter and with that Erin woke up.

"Oh my gosh! What time is it? How long have I been asleep?" she asked stretching her arms and rising up from the sofa.

"We're not sure ourselves, sleepyhead," Shy replied making her way to the kitchen to pop the kettle on for a cuppa.

"Mom, Grandma's been telling me a great story about this wee girl called Kieran from back home in Scotland, and I found a chest with all sorts of great stuff in it that's really old and...."

Erin interrupted Lyric with "Hold on a minute, Miss thousand-words-a-minute!" They both burst into laughter and flopped back down on the overstuffed sofa.

"What's all the commotion about in here?" Shy asked, coming back into the room with a tray full of mugs, milk and sugar and a plate full of warm homemade scones.

"That was quick," Erin commented turning as she got a whiff of the warm scones. She got up to help her mum with the tray, making a space on the coffee table.

"They smell as delicious as always, Grandma," Lyric remarked, her hand stretching over to grab the biggest one on the plate and biting into the fluffy scone dripping with butter she went on with her mouth full.

"Anyway Kieran had this really interesting but kinda' sad life and..." Lyric was once again interrupted by a well meaning mum. "Darlin', could you please not speak with your mouth full. I know the story about Kieran anyway." Erin stated, surprising Lyric as she stopped in mid bite.

"You do? But then why have you never mentioned her before?" Lyric asked beginning to feel a conspiracy coming on.

Shy and Erin glanced at each other and smiled one of those all-knowing smiles. Lyric was all too familiar with their behavior when they were up to something.

"Well, because it's a grandma story that can only be told by the woman herself." Erin stated with a satisfied nod knowing Lyric wasn't getting any more out of her.

"Oh, I see one of your conspiracies, huh?" Lyric smiled as she bit into another scone.

"Uh Huh something like that," replied Erin, her mouth now full of delicious warm memories of home.

Shy looked out into the garden. "It's actually still quite early girls. Now the rain's stopped would ye' like to go for a wee walk after tea? She asked well aware of how they all shared a love for the outdoors.

"Absolutely!" was the response with a mutual understanding that to eat delicious goodies one had a responsibility to one's waistline.

They cleared away the tea things and wrapped up warmly to begin a long walk down the country lanes that were thankfully quite deserted at that time of the year.

The trees swayed back and forth as though showing off the splendor of glorious colors they proudly displayed each one a different shade of orange, yellow and red. All three walked silently for a moment and looked up into the canopy where a cacophony of nature's brilliance burst across the clouded sky.

"When did Dad say he and Grandpa will be home?' Lyric asked breaking the comfortable silence as she kicked at mounds of leaves accumulating by the roadside.

"Well, hopefully on Wednesday, sweetie pie, so we have another three days to enjoy our walks and help Grandma prepare for Thanksgiving dinner," Erin replied, hands deep in the pockets of the warm ankle length coat she'd borrowed from her mum.

Shy had never had the heart to get rid of her favorite old wax Barbour which she wore on all their walks together. She had acquired it prior to coming over to America all those years ago. That, and her tweed skirts, and brogue shoes spoke volumes of the gentile woman she was and always had been. Erin smiled as she glanced at the woman of style who'd walked beside her all through her life.

The three of them, in fact, all had a distinct sense of their own style inheriting an eclectic mix of Scottish into the sophistication of American style.

"Well I already have everything we need for Thursday, so we don't need another trip to the grocery store," Shy announced as they continued down the lane.

Lyric had started to walk a bit farther ahead after finding a stick to poke at things she'd discovered.

"Lyric pay attention to the corner coming up, sweetie," Erin shouted knowing how easily she got distracted.

"Ok Mom!"

Erin curled her arm through her Mum's and asked her how far they'd got in the story.

"Well let me see, I stopped just after Kieran met her boyfriend, Danny, and was getting ready to begin her dance training full time," she replied then added, "But a certain pretty head was about to nod so I thought we should have a break."

Erin smiled as she remembered how quickly Lyric dozed off when she read her stories.

"I'm surprised you even got that far with that little sleepyhead!"

"Actually she's really taking it to heart, Erin, and asking lots of questions which, as I'd hoped, would begin to open up conversations about all sorts of issues," her mum assured her impressed at how wise her grandchild was for her years.

"Ye' do trust I'll only go into as much detail as I think she can handle, don't you?" Shy asked knowing full well how much her daughter trusted her.

Erin squeezed her arm tight and nodded, "I know Mum."

At that, the older woman looked up and spoke loud enough for Lyric to hear. "I think we'd better head home, ma' wee lamb, or we'll all be in for a good old drookin'," Both girls laughed as they quickened their steps to get back home before the downpour began.

"And what would you both be laughin' at now?" Shy asked as if she didn't already know.

It had always amused her loved ones when she threw a few authentic words into their every day conversation. Her natural lilting voice accentuated the brogue from another lifetime.

"Awe Grandma, you sound so cute when you talk like that."

They opened the door to the welcome of Kylie who had been limping for a few days after pulling a muscle in her back leg. She was wagging her tail furiously but looked a little disappointed at not having been included in the walk. "Och! Now don't be lookin' at me with those big sad eyes now, Kylie. Come on then lass we'll go to the kitchen and find a treat, o.k.?"

Shy had never lost her love for animals, Erin thought to herself with a smile as they struggled with their coats.

"I'll come and put the kettle on for a cup o' tea in a moment, Mum," Erin shouted as Shy disappeared into the kitchen, a fluffy white tail close behind.

"Okay, sweetheart!"

Lyric ran upstairs to her room to relax and play for a while before dinner.

As the two woman scuttled around the kitchen getting ready for another cup o' tea they soon fell into one of their easy conversations.

"Well, tell me now, lass, how are you all getting on in the big city and how's Lyric doing at school?" Shy enquired as she gave Kylie her favorite treat.

"Well... the city is much the same as it always was, and work is going well. And of course, you remember that Greg got that promotion, so we're enjoying a wee bit more money. Lyric is doing very well in school, so everything seems to be going just fine," Erin replied shrugging her shoulders as though having nothing more important to report.

"That's good then...that young'un is growing like a weed and blossoming into a beautiful flower, just like you did at that age," Shy stopped, lost in thought for a moment, drifting back many years to when Erin was twelve going on thirteen. Just as quickly, a dark cloud seemed to cover the sunlight of her daydream as she suddenly remembered where their lives had been at that time.

Erin instinctively knew what had clouded her Mum's thoughts, her face usually bearing evidence of perfect peace. She broke the sudden silence by changing the subject.

"Is Apryl coming home for Thanksgiving Mum?"

Shy snapped out of the bleak reverie that had transported her back to another time, and answered Erin with disappointment in her voice. "No pet, she called last night to explain she'd given her holiday up for the married people with families."

"Awe, sweetie pie that she is," Erin replied, with a swell of love rising up inside for her little sister. They had been through somewhat of a roller coaster of differences earlier on in their life together, but as Apryl began middle school they began to acquire a deeper appreciation for one another. This came from many years of witnessing their mother's determination to get them to understand that love for each other should override any frustration they had which, left unexamined, could have run the risk of lasting a lifetime.

Her mum sniggered as a memory of her having to act as referee on many occasions fluttered through her mind. She glanced over at Erin as they sat down at the kitchen table with mugs of steaming hot tea and began to reminisce about the happier times gone by.

"And how's Dad doing, Mum?"

"Oh, he's fine, and as strong as the ox he's always been." "I miss him a lot when he's away, but I also like my quiet times to read or write and just reflect.

"Well, you certainly deserve them after the life you've had," her daughter remarked as she stood up and cleared the mugs away.

"What are we doing for dinner tonight?" Erin then asked hoping her mum hadn't planned anything.

"Well I don't know yet sweetheart, what do you feel like?"

Erin jumped at the opportunity to steal her mum away for a nice dinner as a pre-Thanksgiving treat. After telling her not to bother cooking, she made reservations at the Briars Inn, a beautiful old carriage house that had been renovated a few years ago and turned into a restaurant with great food and reasonable prices.

Shy had never allowed her daughter to be over extravagant when treating her to anything apart from on her 50th birthday. For that special event, Erin had booked a table for four at another carriage house in Norfolk and presented her with a beautiful Anne Klein watch.

That night stuck in her memory for years to come as a milestone for the happier years that lay ahead. She smiled, once again losing herself in thought. When Erin came back she announced the reservation was booked for 7pm.

"You've been day dreaming again?" Erin teased.

"Can you remember my 50th birthday, when you sneaked a reservation at the most expensive place in town? Then you almost made me faint when you placed that little red velvet box in front of me without me noticing?!"

Erin laughed out loud at the memory of her mum's expression when she saw the box. "Yeah and although you loved every minute, you scolded me for quite some time for spending so much money!" Lyric walked into the kitchen to ask what was for dinner.

"Well, young lady, we are going out to dinner at The Briars. Why don't you freshen up a little and change into something nice."

"Sure!" Lyric squealed, her eyes suddenly bigger and brighter making the women laugh.

"Oh yes! She's definitely growing up," Shy announced as they both went upstairs to change.

The meal was delicious, the atmosphere just delightful, and the conversation light and easy going. When they got back home they agreed to call it a night.

"Are you too tired to tell more of the story, Grandma?" Lyric asked, hoping she wasn't but not wanting to make demands. "I can wait until tomorrow if you are."

Shy turned and grabbed her granddaughter's hand giving it a squeeze. "Are you kidding I'm never too tired for a story!"

They walked upstairs hand in hand feeling thankful for the wonderful day they'd spent together.

"Well let me see now," her grandma began after Lyric jumped into bed and settled down under the sheets. "I had finished off with Kieran starting at the dancing school hadn't I?" she asked and Lyric confirmed as she snuggled.

"Well now, when Kieran was sixteen she began to look for part-time work to give her a little extra income and so her mum offered to keep a look out. After a week or so of looking her mum noticed an ad in the local newspaper: "dancers wanted."

Instinctively Kieran knew what kind of dancing that meant but after a few days of relentless persuasion from her mum Kieran reluctantly gave in and agreed to at least go and find out. They turned up at the address given and her instinct was proven right. Kieran stood at the top of the steps that led down to a basement bar that seemed to look quite trendy for that part of uptown Edinburgh.

"Why don't you just find out what they want you to do?" her mother remarked completely oblivious to the shocked expression on her daughters face.

Kieran's heart broke with disappointment and disbelief. " It's a bar, Mum! I am not going to do that kind of dancing in front of a bar full of drunken men. What are you thinking?"

She felt devastated, her stomach turned over with the sudden reality of what her mum expected of her. How could she want her to do such a thing? Was she that naive or was she so desperate to make her daughter famous that it didn't matter what it took?

This experience only compounded what Kieran had been afraid of for years: that she was just a puppet living out someone else's dream having no right to a life of her own. All of a sudden the values she had been taught by her parents were being flushed down the toilet and compromised by her own mother. It hurt beyond belief!

Lyric drew a sharp breath in with shock. "You're kidding surely, Grandma?" was all she could think to say.

"Oh, if only I were, ma' pet, but no, I'm not. Of all the situations that had caused Kieran pain in her life so far, that day ranked close to the top."

Kieran felt herself retreat into her shell knowing the distance between her and her parents had now just widened. She continued to work hard and pass her exams, refusing to give up on anything she'd committed to. But her heart was no longer in her dance. Every ounce of passion she once had was now draining away and all that remained was a commitment to finish the course.

Standing at the top of those steps looking down at the terrible place her mum wanted her to work was glaring proof that her well being was being ignored. Kieran was crushed.

She didn't share her change of heart with anyone because she knew they just wouldn't understand. She'd be called ungrateful and selfish and be made to feel guilty for wasting so much of her parents' money! Kieran stayed quiet and kept on dancing.

Dancing all day, then spending most evenings with Danny became her life, rarely spending time with her family. Kieran knew that neither her mum nor her dad liked Danny. In their minds he wasn't good enough for her and sorely lacking in career prospects for the future. What they didn't understand was that Kieran had been told by Danny that she was loved for who she was and for that moment in time, at least, that was enough to fill the void of which they were completely unaware.

The saddest part was; Kieran sensed deep down, he was probably not the best choice of life partner for her. But she became caught up in yet another, which one do I please most, scenario. The relationship with Danny became familiar and comfortable to the point of expectations of marriage from his family, at least.

Positive now that her dancing career was more a dream of her mother's than of her own making, the relationship between Kieran and her parents became increasingly strained and the tension at home unbearable.

On a few occasions, when at Danny's house Kieran would accidentally miss her last bus home and have to spend the night on his parent's sofa.

It was wrong and she knew it but she desperately needed her parents to tell her so, when she arrived home the following morning. Once again, she cried out silently for compassionate support and guidance and probably even a way out of a relationship she wasn't sure she wanted to continue. Instead, all she got was an indignant grunt from her father when he opened the door in the morning.

That was his way of communicating his displeasure, but there'd be nothing else offered. No words of wisdom or advice or even outrage with concern for her safety!

"I could be lying in a ditch somewhere, raped or brutally murdered!" She often thought as the indignant silence met her with the harsh truth of a new day. She'd be better off out of this house.

The grunt spoke of so much more than mere disappointment. It told her they just didn't care.

All through her life, Kieran had felt her father's disdain for almost every choice she'd made, so she shouldn't have been surprised at his reaction now... but nevertheless it still hurt. To live at home, knowing her parents thought of her as a disappointment was painful enough, but to sense the seething declaration of the haunting words; you're nothing but an idiot," on a daily basis became almost too much for her to bear. Kieran felt she had little choice but to prepare for a life together with Danny.

Kieran went through the motions but her heart was empty of joy.

During one particularly cold winter, their family went through a season of worry and concern of a different kind. Her father was a proud and stubborn man, and unknown to anyone, he'd been sick for some time without saying a word.

He had caught the flu but kept getting up for work walking two miles to and fro every day in the freezing cold. After a week or so he developed a wracking cough that kept him up all night, but still he wouldn't stay off work or see the doctor.

By the end of three weeks of this personal neglect, he tried to get up for work one morning but collapsed and was rushed to hospital.

The family rallied around to hear the doctors diagnose: a collapsed lung with pleurisy and pneumonia. Even they were amazed at how he could have endured such an illness for that length of time and continue to work.

Allan Stewart endured appalling pain as his body fought to regain strength. Eventually he pulled through. He remained in the hospital for two weeks, and it was during that period that Kieran was to act in a way that totally bewildered her. When she wasn't at the hospital visiting her dad, instead of staying home to keep her mum company, she went to Danny's house as usual. She'd watch her mum sitting alone by the fire, obviously worried about her husband, but Kieran couldn't stay, feeling completely unable to comfort her.

Why Kieran? Why can't you console your own mother during her time of need? What the heck is wrong with you? She'd hear the voice of self condemnation screaming from inside. Ashamed, but no longer able to reach out, it seemed that Kieran didn't know who she was anymore. Desperately wanting to console her mum but unable to, she felt disgusted at herself yet powerless.

Too many unresolved conflicts and too little understanding, there was nothing left for her but to stay at home out of duty or obligation for the money they had spent throughout the years of fee paying school and dancing lessons. But wasn't that love meant to be unconditional? Who knew anymore! She was just tired of it all. All the analyzing and self judgment and condemnation, she was through!

She had run out of steam when climbing the mountain she saw before her and inevitably knew the only way out was down.

"What a horrible experience, Grandma." Lyric sat up a little rubbing her eyes and looking a little too sleepy to listen to much more.

"I know darlin'," Shy replied, "It was a time that magnified the complexities of her life, and to Kieran there was no other way out but to follow through with her next decision."

"And what was that Grandma?" Lyric asked before a full blown yawn and stretch gave evidence of much needed sleep.

"Well I'm not going to leave you with a cliff hanger because I know you won't be able to sleep but she and Danny began to make secret plans to get married within the few years to follow. Kieran would stay at home for at least three more years, now knowing that she'll eventually break free, but I think we should leave the next part until tomorrow, okay, sleepy?"

"Alright, Grandma, and thanks for today, it's been a great story so far," Lyric sighed as she slipped under the fluffy down comforter and drifted off.

Shy walked gingerly downstairs her knees hurting a little more because of the rain. She found Erin curled up on her favorite sofa watching a lifetime movie.

"I bet she didn't last long," Erin said turning towards her mum and best friend.

"Nope, and even I was beginning to wane a little," Shy replied as she veered towards the kitchen.

"De' ye' want some hot chocolate, darlin'?" Shy asked and as Erin's mouth salivated she replied, "Ooo! Yes please Mum," and shimmied down the sofa a little more feeling snug and content.

Erin loved being home with her mum again, just the two of them for a little while.

She was a mixed bag of introvert and extravert and through the years had sometimes found it difficult to talk at length with her mum. It may have taken a few years for Shy to understand that about her daughter but when she did it made all the difference in their relationship. There was never any pressure from Shy for Erin to be anything other than at perfect peace.

A few moments later Shy entered with a familiar tray and two hot steaming cups of rich creamy chocolate straight from heaven. Or at least that was always Erin's opinion.

"Mmm! Thanks mum."

As Shy took her seat, Erin asked if she wanted to talk or just watch the movie.

"Well darlin' we have days left to talk and, to be honest, I'm kind of all talked out for the day." She replied taking a sip of her cocoa.

"Good. That's what I thought and this is actually quite a good movie."

The two women finished their treat, watching the movie until the end…then both decided to call it a night. Erin got up and came over to give her mum a goodnight kiss never having grown too old for that particular love gift.

"Good night, darlin', it's so good to have ye' both home again."

"I know, Mum," Erin replied and walked upstairs to bed feeling happy and content.

Shy looked down at Kylie. "Well, I would say that was a pretty awesome first day wouldn't you, sweetie pie, and I suppose you'll be wanting out now?"

As soon as the wee dog heard the word 'out', she came to life wagging her tail furiously.

Shy stood at the open door to the back garden and breathed in the orchestral fragrance from the wild flower garden she so lovingly tended. Tenderly she whispered a prayer of thanks.

The following morning the sun was shining, the birds were singing up a storm of their own, and it felt more like spring than fall.

The girls were woken up with the smell of bacon frying and homemade biscuits baking. Erin stretched and pulled back the covers from her face feeling like a little girl again waking up on a Sunday morning.

"Oh, my! I'm gonna' have to jog around the whole of central park when I get home to ward off the after effects of all this home cooking," she sighed. She pulled herself out of bed, grabbed her dressing gown, and made her way down stairs via the bathroom.

Lyric had gotten up to open the door for Kylie who'd been scraping to get in. The little dog would not leave Shy's side through the night, but as soon as she remembered her favorite playmate was home, she left her post as valiant body guard, and ran upstairs to waken Lyric.

"Kylie, good morning, fluff ball!" And they both galloped downstairs to greet their Shy.

"Well, good morning, ma pet. How'd ye' sleep?" Lyric stood before Shy with legs crossed having forgotten to 'pay a visit' before she went downstairs.

"Really well Grandma, but hold on a minute..." And she skipped to the restroom just off the kitchen.

"My, my Kylie, some things just never change, do they?" And she cracked a couple of eggs into a bowl.

Lyric returned with a very important question. "What are we doing today Grandma?" "I mean after breakfast."

"Well now," Shy replied, whisking the eggs with one hand, and turning the gas on under the frying pan with the other. "I thought, once we get cleaned up, we could take a trip into town to have a look around the little antique shops you two like so much. After lunch, we could get the bikes out and go for a ride. How's that for starters?"

"Oh! There you go with your wee sayings again, Grandma," Lyric laughed. "Well, yes that does sound like fun, but........"

"Then I thought we could go back up to the attic to get on with a certain story I was telling."

A broad smile broke out across Lyric's face. "Sweet!" Was the response and she began to collect the knives and forks to set the table for breakfast.

A beautiful face under a mass of chestnut curls walked into the kitchen with a very contented smile. "Good morning," Erin sighed and stretched once again.

"How is everyone today?" she asked opening the door to the pantry just to stare inside.

"Fine, darlin', and what are ye' lookin' for?" Shy asked with fondness remembering another little habit Erin had obviously not lost.

"Oh nothing really Mum, it's just nice to be home that's all," she smiled well aware of the funny wee things she still liked to do.

"Greg called last night. They're both doing fine and hope to be back home by about 3:00 o'clock on Wednesday."

"Oh that's a blessing," Shy said as she bent down to retrieve the golden biscuits from the oven.

"Lyric, darlin', could you get the syrup from the pantry and Erin, could you get more butter from the fridge?"

"OK," they replied in unison.

Erin poured two mugs of fresh-brewed coffee and a glass of orange juice for Lyric and they sat down and said grace before enjoying their first holiday breakfast together.

They did a rundown of what they all wanted to do and after clearing away the breakfast things went off to shower and get ready for the day.

Shy got ready first, so she took Kylie out for her early morning walk and as she sauntered down the pathway that led to the lake not too far from the house, she looked up and gave thanks.

"Thank you, Papa, for your bountiful blessings. Thank you, Papa, for revealing the simple truth of who you made me to be."

Shy's heart was full to overflow with the gratitude she felt towards God and all he'd brought her through and revealed to her in the process.

As they arrived at the water's edge she looked out and remembered a similar scene from the dusty recess of a past life and a single tear trickled down her cheek. The water was still and the trees displayed a stark beauty of their own surrounding the little sanctuary as though hiding it from the outside world.

Little Kylie, sensing Shy was saddened suddenly, jumped up and down as though to distract her from the thought. "See me. See me, mama," the little dog twirled like a circus act. Shy's attention was drawn back to her sweet little antics.

"All right, honey bunch, I know." She stooped down to pick up the precious bundle of fur. "Ye're a wise one aren't ye', ma' wee guardian angel." And the wee dog snuggled into her arms for a moment then struggled to get down as she caught the scent of something intriguing in the woods. "Don't run too far now, Kylie," and Shy turned to follow her, retracing the path they had taken.

She got back to the house to find Lyric standing in the front yard with a ball in her hand ready to play fetch with Kylie.

"I wish I'd known you were going out, Grandma, I would've come with you."

"Oh darlin', we've not been long and you needed time to get ready."

As she passed she grabbed Lyric around the shoulders and gave her a squeeze. "Come on, let's go shopping."

They bundled into the car surprised at the change in the weather. As the car wound its way through the country roads excited chatter joined the spring like birdsong from outside.

It only took them ten minutes to arrive at their destination so they found a good parking space and readied themselves for a leisurely morning's shopping.

By the time noon struck from the old village green clock, they were all starving again so made their way to their favorite little deli/ café.

Lyric ordered a pile of blueberry pancakes topped with fresh whipped cream but the ladies were a little more conservative and ordered chicken salad on toasted rye.

"I honestly don't know where she puts it.' Erin sighed in amazement of how much food her tiny daughter could pack away without putting on an ounce.

"She's probably going through a growth spurt and will be tall like her dad." Shy smiled at the healthy little beauty beside her.

"Remember Erin you and Apryl were like that, too, worrying me to death sometimes because you hardly ate a thing and then you'd more than make up for it the very next month." Shy reflected on times when she'd just done grocery shopping and within a day or two would be out of supplies.

"Yeah, I remember," Erin replied smiling at the memory.

Finishing their meal and deciding to postpone bike riding until lunch had settled, they got back to the house and relaxed for an hour or so having no particular schedule to worry about.

Erin decided to play the piano that was tucked away in the corner of the room adjacent to the family room which they'd fondly named 'The Heritage' room. This beautiful room, decorated in rich, warm shades of red and gold had a collection of mementos from the Scottish and Irish cultures for all to see and appreciate. It was Shy and Paul's favorite place to spend time together.

Shy loved when Erin played, appreciating her self-taught ability as a very special gift. It had been a life-line for Erin, as they struggled through some particularly hard times and knowing how much her mum appreciated her playing, her fingers danced across the keys from one favorite melody to another. Erin had composed as well as played over the years and the music she'd brought to life had an ethereal quality to it like nothing else Shy had ever heard. Erin's gift was unique.

Both she and Lyric curled up beside each other on the deep overstuffed sofa and relaxed saying nothing but allowing the haunting strains to wash over them.

After a half hour of soothing relaxation they all felt recharged. Since the sun was still shining brightly outside they changed into sneakers and pulled the bikes out from the garage. Shy had a basket on the front of her bike so that Kylie could come with them and it never ceased to amaze her how much the wee dog loved sitting there, ears flapping in the wind, enjoying every bit of the experience without a fear in the world.

The bike ride was incredible and the girls felt carefree and refreshed. It was one of those special days when seasons in transition are unwilling to let go of the previous, holding on to the heat of summer like the last breath of something about to depart.

They got back around three o'clock and after putting the bikes back in the garage they settled down for a mid-afternoon cup o' tea.

"We're going back up to the attic Mum!" Lyric stated making sure she booked at least a few hours of private time with grandma.

Erin laughed and replied, "Oh I know, sweetheart. Grandma already informed me of your plans and I have something to pick up in Newton anyway, so you two enjoy."

Lyric didn't need any more encouragement.

"Are you ready Nana?" she asked Shy changing her beloved grandmothers title to the Scottish version at times.

"Well, I haven't heard that for a long time, ma' wee lamb junior." And after saying goodbye to her mum Lyric bounded up the attic stairs two by two.

The two women looked at each other, "Do you think she's excited or something?" Erin said turning to open the door.

"Well, I don't know, but I do know I won't be taking the steps two by two that's for sure!"

Erin laughed as she closed the front door behind her.

Shy climbed the stairs slowly feeling a little tired after the bike ride. After getting settled in her chair with Kylie now curled at her feet, she asked Lyric if she remembered where they'd finished off the night before.

"Well, Kieran was now about seventeen and was going through a tough time at home. She was making secret plans to marry Danny."

"Oh that's right darling. Remember; it was Kieran's inability to talk openly about anything in her life that had plagued her and was still hurting her the most."

The longing for an open relationship had never left her and it was around that age that she eventually gave into yet another one of her mother's dreams and enter the 'Miss Scotland' contest.

Ever since Kieran turned sixteen her mum tried to convince her to try out for the prestigious title which went completely against Kieran's will. Perhaps at that particular time she was feeling guilty about letting her parents down in other aspects of her life, but she relented and registered to enter the 'Miss Edinburgh North' contest. This was a qualifying round for the semi finals of Miss Scotland in Glasgow.

They bought her a new outfit for the contest but Kieran made it clear she didn't want any more money spent on something her heart wasn't in. She insisted on doing her own hair and makeup.

She was merely going through the motions just to please her mum so you can imagine her distress when at the end of the evening she was crowned "Miss Edinburgh"!

"Oh no! What did I get myself into?" was all she could think as the audience clapped and cheered. A deep sense of dread overtook her on the way home, conscious that she couldn't turn back.

The finals for the contest were to be held in Glasgow the following Saturday and the winner of this title would automatically qualify for the "Miss United Kingdom" contest then "Miss World!"

This was becoming seriously out of control.

The thought of parading around in front of a crowded ballroom felt demeaning. She could dance in front of an audience but that felt different. Dance was a gift and a safe place for her to retreat when the stuff of life had a choke hold.

Once again, reality set in and Saturday morning came all too quickly.

Kieran had to get up at the crack of dawn in order to catch the train to Glasgow. She wasn't a professional at this and didn't know how to prepare. Naively she got ready for the contest before leaving early in the morning. It was raining hard and she was alone. Her mum and sister were coming later.

When Kieran got there, she realized no one else was ready and each contestant seemed to have an entourage of help. By the time they had been put through their paces in rehearsal her makeup and hair looked awful.

The typical Scottish weather had done its worst and all the curls had fallen out of her hair. It was now a frizzy mess and her makeup wasn't much better. She couldn't remember why her mum and sister hadn't come with her? Was it because she hadn't wanted them there? At that point Kieran was so sick with nerves she couldn't remember anything. She became panicked and as the time for the contest to begin drew near Kieran tried to fix the remnant of curl that was left but made matters worse! She forgot, in her flustered state, how much hairspray she'd already sprayed on her hair, in the hope of it lasting all day. As she attempted to use a curling iron she'd borrowed from another girl, Kieran all too quickly realized her mistake. The pungent odor was the first evidence that something wasn't quite right and as she tried to unwind the singed strand she discovered it was tangled. Her only choice of action left was to cut it off.

The smell was nauseating and everyone began to complain, casting daggers at Kieran.

The poor lass was devastated and embarrassed beyond belief, feeling like an oddball compared to the pro's, but remaining true to her character and the promise she'd made her mum she didn't give up.

Kieran was number three to be called, and as the music started and the host for the evening began his introduction. Kieran took a deep breath and tried to ignore how much she was shaking. Stepping out onto the ballroom floor, she struck a pose while the host announced her name. Her heart was beating loud enough to hear, or so she imagined, then taking another deep breath she began to walk around the packed ballroom. She maintained the perfectly fake smile as her lips stuck to her teeth. How do I stop looking as though this is the last place I want to be? She thought as she circled the ballroom.

Kieran managed to complete the course, tottering in high heel pumps when her head began to swirl and a familiar gurgling sensation in her stomach warned her of imminent embarrassment ahead.

As soon as she left the main area, she made a dash for the dressing room just in time to address the nearest toilet bowl with a personal introduction! The smell of burning hair was still in her nostrils and that mixed with nerves and stress turned into an ugly combination.

There was no question of her being able to go back out so she gave up.

Her mum and sister consoled her and assured her they were proud of her. Their support was needed and appreciated, especially after what she'd just been through, but Kieran vowed never to put herself through such an ordeal again!

"Wow Grandma!" Lyric sat up straight in awe of Kieran's tenacity.

"Good for her, she won Miss Edinburgh, but I don't blame her for not wanting to go any further. I couldn't do that either."

"Well darlin', some girls have the ability and drive to do that kind of thing and actually enjoy the competitive nature of the whole process. I've always thought it would be a dull world if we all had the same likes and dislikes. Anyway, after that little encounter came the movie."

"Another movie?" Lyric replied not sure whether she'd heard right.

"Yes ma'm, can you believe it? You see, Lyric; the Theatre School of Dance and Drama was well known in the theatre and film industry. Whenever a film company was shooting in the area, they would contact the school for extras."

Kieran was actually excited about this, especially if it meant an opportunity to dance. She auditioned and got the part along with seven other girls from the school.

Her mum was obviously overjoyed and she supposed her dad was too. "As long as that's what you want Kieran." He replied as noncommittal as ever.

She still couldn't tell whether what he said came from the heart, or whether he'd retreated to a place of surrender, happier to remain in the background of Kieran's life. Refusing to dwell on anything negative she felt excited at the prospect of actually working with her dance.

The only one that was not happy was Danny, but she was determined not to allow his attitude to affect her decision.

Kieran was single minded about doing the movie and stood firm. She sensed that to give him the impression he was in charge of all her future plans, would be setting her self up for an unhealthy relationship. She began to create boundaries.

They were going on location for two weeks and would be traveling, by train, to a small village on the west coast of Scotland. Kieran had actually been chosen as chaperone for the group which showed a confidence in her by her school principal she truly appreciated. She began the trip resolute not to let him down. Within the next two weeks her faithfulness to that promise was to become tested..

"In what way, Grandma?" Lyric asked, intrigued with this exciting new event in Kieran's life.

"Well, after arriving at the place they'd be staying for the next two weeks of filming and later enjoying a get together with the cast and crew, Kieran was faced with a choice that would possibly compromise her values."

The following day they arrived on location at the crack of an extremely cold dawn and were told to meet with Miss Tripp, the wardrobe mistress, after breakfast.

During breakfast, they chatted excitedly about what the day held and after finishing a surprisingly delicious meal of bacon, eggs and English muffins, the group of girls went to find wardrobe.

They found the trailer and knocked on the door, only to be met with a gruff, impatient voice from within. "Come in.!" Miss Tripp barked loud enough for the whole crew to hear.

The girls stepped inside, the inviting warmth of the trailer greeting them. It was packed from wall to wall with clothing of all styles imaginable. Miss Tripp, who looked every bit like her impatient tone with unkempt hair and ruddy complexion, stepped forward to hand each of them a packet of stockings.

The girls looked down at what they'd been given with unified expression of query.

Flesh Colored, 30 Denier Body Stocking was written in bold lettering across the top of the packet.

"Well what are you waiting on, Christmas!" the now shrill voiced woman asked sarcastically, wondering why the girls were just standing there.

They were in complete shock! Each one looked at the other hoping someone would have an answer to what they were all thinking.

Kieran finally piped up. "I'm sorry ma'm, but where is the rest of the costume?"

Miss Tripp laughed with a loud guffaw that made the girls jump.

"That's it sweet peas, didn't you know?" "Now go on and get changed and stop wasting valuable time."

Kieran was distraught to say the least but tried to keep her composure and for the next few minutes felt overtaken by a force she'd never experienced before.

"Miss Tripp, I'm sorry but we are not going to dance in this freezing cold weather with next to nothing on! You'll need to come up with another solution."

Even Kieran couldn't believe she was being so brave, but she stood her ground. She felt super charged with a burst of energy and conviction. Miss Tripp almost blew a gasket, her face turning red and sweaty.

"The director's not going to like this one little bit young lady." And before the dreadful woman could get another word out Kieran took charge once again.

"With all due respect ma'am, I really don't care what the director will think, so please convey our concerns to him." The irate woman, with hair flying and eyes bulging, charged out the trailer mumbling under her breath as she went.

"Wow! You told her, Kieran, good for you!" one of the girls said. The others stood in awe. Just as Kieran let out a sigh of relief, the trailer door burst open and the director entered with Miss Tripp in hot pursuit.

"What's all this nonsense!" he yelled his hands planted on rotund hips. "Don't you realize you're holding up production?" he added with a pompous air, his neck turning red under the pretentious cravat he wore.

He sported one of those mustaches that curled up at the end with a twist that made Kieran baulk. It brought back memories of a retired major in her neighborhood who had a greasy face and stank of old spice after shave.

"Sir," Kieran said respectfully, stepping forward to assure him she was not afraid or intimidated. "As I told Miss Tripp, this is not a complete costume. We will need something with quite a bit more coverage, thank you."

The absurdity of the scene unfolding before their very eyes was almost comical as this feisty wee lass challenged the seasoned film director. In fact, he was so taken aback by Kieran's straight-forward attitude that he turned to Miss Tripp and ordered her to do something to make the costume more modest.

"But!" She began trying to convince him how impossible that task would be, but he held up a hand.

"Just get it done!" and with that he left the trailer leaving behind a not too happy wardrobe lady and a group of girls in awe of their chaperone.

"Oh my goodness Grandma, she was brave!" Lyric said, proud of the way Kieran had stood up for herself and the girls.

"Didn't she just!"

"Did anything else happen to her during the making of the film?"

"Oh, quite a few things 'darlin' but far too many to mention. I will talk about one more problem that arose where she had to stand her ground. Enough to say that in all, it was a wonderful and enlightening adventure and one she was glad to have had the opportunity to experience."

Shy rocked back and forth as Lyric began to rummage in the chest.

"I wonder if there's anything in here about the movie?"

"Oh, I doubt it, sweetie." And just as Shy was about to continue, Lyric sat back on her heels and turned around with a look of intent question on her face.

"Who is Kieran, Grandma? And why do you know so much about her? Why do you have all this stuff in your attic?"

Shy had known it wouldn't be long before that question came up. Shy took her time and rocked slowly. She intertwined her hands as the old chair squeaked and the rafters groaned. The wind outside picked up once again as though to enhance what was about to be revealed.

"Well honey, Kieran was someone very special to me. We were close all through our lives and the memories we shared were far too important for me to throw away. I tucked them inside this box knowing someday, I'd have the opportunity to tell her story."

"So Kieran was a friend?" Lyric asked well aware of how her grandma had given her a somewhat incomplete answer.

Shy smiled at her granddaughter's curiosity, knowing how much she loved mystery novels like Nancy Drew. Then, she laughed out loud and bumped her head on the back of the chair.

"Ouch!" she cried.

"Oh Grandma, are you ok?"

"Yes, I'm fine, darlin', you just looked so funny sitting there with that quizzical expression on your face determined to solve the riddle."

"I know! I'm sorry, I don't mean to spoil the story but Kieran sounds so real and….."

Shy interrupted her. "She was real, darlin', and that's all ye' need to know for right now don't ye' think?"

"I guess you're right grandma." Lyric sighed sitting back on the cushions.

"Well, what was the other problem that arose during the making of the movie?"

"Well, Kieran was a very pretty young lady and often had to fend off advances from men, even men much older than her. The assistant producer of the film was one of those men."

"Oh oh!" Lyric said drawing her knees up to her chin and wrapping her arms around them. Without taking her eyes off Shy she asked, "How much older Grandma?"

"He was double her age making him 34."

"That's disgusting!" Lyric said out loud, feeling anger rise up inside.

"I know sweetheart, but the world is full of predator types. They have very little social conscience and live their lives according to their own rules, quite happy to use people for their own pleasure.

And what made it even worse was that he told Kieran he was married and that his wife didn't mind him seeing other people. In fact, he admitted to having an 'open' marriage.

Kieran told him in no uncertain terms that she would never dream of going out with him. That was something he was obviously not used to hearing. He was an extremely handsome charmer.

In fact, even after the movie was over and Kieran was safely back home, he called her at the school on several occasions. What grieved Kieran most of all was what happened when her mum found out.

He called the school one day after Kieran had left and to her horror they gave him her home number. He called before Kieran got home and soft talked her mother into believing he was a nice guy who had some clout in the film business. When she arrived home Kieran was shocked at her mum's reaction.

"But Kieran he sounds like a nice man, and he's a film producer. For goodness sake, you never know where that could lead you."

She couldn't believe her mum was that naïve or would go that far.

"Mum, he's a married man and twice my age. What are you thinking?"

Once again her heart broke. Once again she felt abandoned by the one who was meant to love and protect her and once again it was evident that her welfare was less important than fame to her mother.

Trapped in an endless life of being manipulated into situations that went against her personal values, Kieran once again gave in to her mother's pleas and agreed to meet him for dinner.

The dinner was nerve racking and every bit as embarrassing as she imagined. Trying to create polite conversation knowing only too well what was on his mind was nauseating. Obviously, he wasn't stimulated by her intellect or worldly experience, even she knew that. So why was she there? Why had she given in? Kieran couldn't stand the pretense any longer and after finishing dinner she insisted on going home.

He realized he was getting nowhere with her. He finally gave up, ready to move on to the next little fish in the vast ocean of girls perfectly willing to compromise to get on.

Kieran was disgusted and disappointed. She vowed that she would work to create a life where no one would control her any more. She refused to be a puppet!

"Why was her mum willing to allow Kieran to go against her moral standards just to become famous?" Lyric asked Shy, confused with trying to understand why a parent that was meant to protect would risk putting her daughter in harm's way.

"Sweetheart that question took Kieran a lifetime to understand. As she grew older and wiser, no matter how often she explained it away as naivety on her mother's part, the disappointment she suffered because of it never left her. Eventually she forgave her mum, but often grieved that she would never be able to address those issues with her."

Chapter 10
Listen to the Voice

Life returned to normal. Her schedule got back to dancing during the day and seeing Danny every night. It was around that time Kieran made the difficult decision to give up the scholarship with the Scottish Theatre Ballet. She decided to get a job on Saturday, which would give her a little pocket money and help her mum out with supplies she needed to continue at the Theatre School.

That was what she told everybody anyway, and it was a truth of sorts. Truthfully Kieran knew in her heart that if she'd been completely committed to dance, she would never have given up such an opportunity. She was becoming bolder at taking charge of life decisions. She was trying to have a voice.

Kieran's mother was upset with her, but knew she couldn't force Kieran to remain in the scholarship program. The silence at home grew along with the tension.

"Now there's something you need to remember about all those years of Kieran's growing up, darlin'." Shy sat forward in her chair. "Kieran had believed in God, for many years, as a superior almighty force very far removed from such an insignificant Scottish lass. Without understanding why she believed, she refused to accept her father's explanation of the Bible. He believed it was just a book of stories handed down from generation to generation and that Jesus was only a man who liked to do good things for people."

"Somehow Kieran knew there was a greater truth, yet there was still no one in her life to teach her how to learn about God. To strive for a personal relationship with Jesus was completely alien to her and most of the people around her."

"Oh, I do remember that, Grandma, but why do you mention that now?" Lyric asked, curious as to the timing and relevance of Shy's last remark.

"Well honey, I think it's important you keep that in mind throughout the whole story. And it was around the age of seventeen that Kieran had a strange dream that seemed completely unrelated to anything in her life at that moment."

Kieran dreamt of having a baby and when she awoke, remembered every detail of that precious, chubby little face.

She never did understand the whole analysis of dreams and usually dismissed any she'd had in the past as just being a quirky side of her imagination. There was something about this dream that felt different.

Kieran continued to work hard at the Theatre School of Dance and Drama and passed all her exams. When she was twenty she graduated as an Associate of the Royal Academy of Dance.

She taught for a while but after studying for so many years decided that a change of job was needed, for a while at least. She applied for a position in Jenners, a reputable department store in the centre of the city.

The change was good for her and the paycheck was nice also. Her mum, on the other hand, was disappointed Kieran wasn't eagerly looking for dance-related work.

She was burned out after all those years of arduous training and desperately wanted a little time to herself just to think and contemplate her future.

Although no one ever said as much directly to her, Kieran felt her siblings thought she'd let her parents down badly. It hadn't dawned on any of them, of course, that it was she who had put in all those years of grueling physical work. She hadn't given up or even dropped out like many she had known, but had graduated with a degree!

Dancing is a tough business without many guarantees of work after graduation.

Kieran knew she was a good dancer with tremendous heart but she was also aware of her shortcomings. She had fought with her natural body frame for years; frustrated when teachers would continually tell her to lose weight but she couldn't. She was a muscular dancer known for her ability to jump higher than most men, but that wasn't what most companies were looking for. Kieran truly felt that her time in that world was limited. The rift she had felt between herself and the rest of her family widened.

Her boyfriend Danny was in complete agreement with her job change of course and after four years of dating they began to talk seriously about marriage. Her parents were furious with her and wouldn't discuss anything rationally. Kieran felt herself torn once again, forced into having to make a choice.

It was always either/or, in Kieran's life. Why couldn't she have a career and a personal life? Why did her parents always have to force her into a corner? She was hurt and frustrated and so desperately saddened by their constant expectations.

Instead of this being one of the happiest moments in her life it turned out to be one of the loneliest and most painful. Her parents would not accept her choice of husband to be. Instead of sitting down and talking with her about the situation with love and understanding, they nagged her about her choice. Kieran became withdrawn and even more dogmatic about her decision to marry. She desperately wanted to run from this home where she felt under so much scrutiny and obviously the cause of so much angst within her family.

Kieran cried out for her parents to stop nagging.

'Please help me to decide what's best for me, Mum and Dad. Tell me in a firm but loving way without name calling and belittling or worse still silence!' She begged from within her very soul. But they didn't understand her and obviously wouldn't even if she had tried to put it into words.

So marriage to Danny was to be the way out of a home she never truly felt part of anyway. Each day she felt the familiar lump in her throat with stress.

She wanted to plan her wedding with her mother; to help and guide her just like every little girl dreams. Instead she did everything on her own and felt forced to keep her plans to herself.

There was no joy. At home there was only the terrible accusatory silence.

How dare she choose to make this decision about her own life?

Quietly, Kieran saved as much as she could for a wedding dress. Alone, she went to shop for that dress eventually finding a white bridesmaids dress that was on sale. It was pretty and reminded her of the Edwardian era. It had short puffed sleeves, with a high waist which tightened just under her bust and a scooped neckline, which showed off her graceful neck.

She found a beautiful Anne Bolin style headdress which was a little too pricey, but the lady in the store told her she would hold it for a couple of weeks if Kieran gave her a deposit. She did and felt a rush of excitement as she handed over the few pounds.

The sales woman behind the counter was very sweet but she sensed something sad about this young woman with green eyes. It was apparent she couldn't afford much, but she was shopping wisely and most definitely had a sense of style. The woman wondered what Kieran's story was as she thanked her politely and promised to be back in two weeks to pick up the headdress.

Danny and Kieran decided to get married in January, which seemed to upset everyone even more. By this time she had had enough of the silent treatment at home and decided that no one was going to steal her joy, if in fact, that was what the bride to be was meant to be feeling.

Kieran was so confused. Feeling by this time, she was just going through the motions of yet another life, one she wasn't truly convinced she wanted either. She began to have serious doubts about getting married, but felt now she couldn't back out. There was no where to turn to.

As always during the most trying times in her life, Kieran felt completely alone. If she backed out now her parents would win. Did that then mean she was getting married out of some kind of rebellion against what had been forced on her most of her life?

Her mum and dad eventually came to understand that the wedding was going to happen whether they wanted it or not, so a truce was drawn.

The church and reception hall were booked, flowers were ordered and new clothes were purchased. Although things were a little less tense at home, there was still an edge to her parent's voices when they spoke to her. The underlying feeling of displeasure seeped throughout her home.

Kieran was glad when her wedding day came more than anything just to have it over and done with. They had bought a little flat in Stockbridge, an old area of Edinburgh not too far from the centre of town that had a certain charm to it Kieran loved. She couldn't wait to have a home of her own and make it into everything her parents' home was not.

If nothing else she was excited at the prospect of keeping her own house in order and having no one, other than a husband, to mess things up.

Chapter 11
The Big Bad World

The weather was cold but dry and when they left the church after being pronounced husband and wife, they were greeted with the haunting drone of bagpipes and a crowd of people throwing rice and confetti. A large bus had been booked to take everyone to the reception and Kieran and her new husband, Danny, were driven in a white car with ribbons on the front.

They arrived at the hotel reception hall and were all seated at their appropriate places. There were about one hundred and fifty guests at the reception and as the speeches were being given, Kieran became a little nervous thinking about what her father might say. His speech was short and to the point without many frills, but at least he didn't say anything confrontational. Kieran sighed with relief.

That over, the food was brought and everyone looked as though they were having a good time and enjoying the meal. As the tables were being cleared the DJ started to play some music. A few men began to move tables back to make room for dancing later on and the hall began to come to life with the rhythmic beat of the song 'My Girl.'

Some people started to join in with the words to the old favorite and as Kieran turned to smile at her new husband he was no longer beside her. She thought perhaps he had sneaked off to the men's room but after twenty minutes passed and there was still no sign of him, she felt her heart beat faster.

When the D.J. asked for the newlyweds to; 'please take the floor for the first dance', Kieran tried hard not to look as crushed as she felt, forcing back tears from spilling down her flushed face.

She casually tried to make a joke about losing her head if it wasn't attached and got up to see if she could find him. Sad to say it didn't take long. He was in a side room/bar getting drunk with a group of his friends.

"Wh.. what do you think you're doing?" Kieran stammered with disbelief! "Don't you realize the DJ's been calling us for the first dance?"

He didn't apologize or even look remorseful but muttered something under his breath about having fun with his friends!

"God, what have I done?" Kieran's heart sank to what felt like the bottom of an ocean drowning her in the reality of what she faced. That day was to be the most eye opening, heartbreaking day of her life.

How could she have been so blind? And why was she unable to see what everyone else had seen?

Her parents had told her but she didn't listen or was it that she couldn't? The nagging, the name calling and the cold silences were what she couldn't bear.

Things went from bad to worse after the wedding day as more and more of Danny's friends began to surface. Kieran was now faced with the reality of having made a horrendous mistake!

Shy stopped for a moment, wondering why Lyric had become so quiet and then she noticed the child was crying.

"Oh honey, I didn't mean to make you cry, I'll stop ok?"

Lyric wiped her tears with the back of her hand.

"Grandma, poor Kieran went from one sadness in her life to another. When is she ever going to find happiness?"

Shy dug into her pocket for a tissue and handing it to Lyric she said. "Come to a child with love and understanding and they will follow you the rest of their lives."

"As much as she loved her parents Kieran didn't get what she really needed from them. She did get love, but it was unspoken. She didn't get the understanding she needed to thrive." She felt lost most of her life, as though she never belonged no matter where she roved. She never felt understood by anyone because she was different. She was silently searching for the truth of life. She was searching for God without knowing." Shy stopped and looking down at her intertwined fingers, feeling the heartbeat of a lost lamb she turned to look at Lyric.

"Gods people are persecuted in many ways sweet girl. Even when they're still searching and don't quite understand the enormity of who He is."

Lyric was quiet and the stilled silence in the attic seemed to emphasize Shy's profound statement.

"But lass, on that note I think we need a break don't you?" Lyric agreed and after standing up, stretching and giving her grandma a hug they went downstairs to let Kylie out.

Erin was back from her trip to Newtown but didn't want to interrupt the story. She was pottering about in the kitchen when the two came downstairs. She saw the tear stains on Lyric's face and the look in her mother's eyes told her something had transpired.

"What's wrong sweetheart," she asked, taking Lyric into her arms and glancing over her shoulder at Shy.

"Oh, I'm ok Mum," Lyric replied with a sniff. Just before Lyric had a chance to wipe her nose with the back of her hand Shy grabbed a tissue.

"Here ye' go, wee lamb." And all of a sudden the gravity of the moment seemed funny.

"I forgot how tender hearted this wee soul is. I've probably focused too much on the heartache of the story so we're havin' a break for today."

Shy ruffled Lyric's hair assuring her they could stop but Lyric's immediate reaction displayed to the two women how involved she was in the story of this girl's life.

"No Grandma it's not the sadness of the story…well it is. But for some reason, I feel invested in her life now and I don't want you to give up. I'll just have to lighten up a little that's all." Shy hugged her in appreciation of all things that made up this precious bundle.

It was beginning to get dark and they hadn't decided what was for dinner yet.

"I have some of my homemade tomato soup in the freezer," Shy suggested.

"I can make some toasted cheese and we could have some hot chocolate for dessert."

"That sounds great!" both girls replied in unison and Erin went through to the family room to turn the fire on. Lyric fell down on the floor to wrestle with Kylie, quickly reverting to her playful self.

They enjoyed a hearty meal. Just as Erin and Lyric began to clear the dishes from the table the phone rang. Shy went into the kitchen to answer it. The girls couldn't hear what was being said but there was something about the tone in Shy's voice that told them something was wrong. The girls walked through to find out, Erin's arm wrapped around Lyric's shoulder.

"Oh no! But how is he now and where have they taken him?" Shy said her voice shaky and obviously disturbed with some bad news.

"What is it Mum?" Erin asked, the concern now rising in all of them.

Her Mum held up her hand and mouthing the words "Wait a minute" she listened intently to the voice on the other end.

"OK Greg, give me a call as soon as you get to the hospital, promise now?"

Greg agreed and Shy hung up and buried her face in her hands.

"Mum, come on and sit down. What happened?" "Lyric; put the kettle on' darling."

Erin helped Shy through to the family room where she composed herself taking a deep breath before letting the girls know what Greg had told her.

"Both he and Paul were finishing up work for the day, putting final touches to a house they were renovating. Paul had been working all day seeming in good spirits. Suddenly as their day was drawing to a close he felt a strange tightening across his chest. Within a few moments he was experiencing tingling in his left arm and immediately the medics were called. Someone on the team gave him an aspirin which helped stabilize him and the ambulance was there within five minutes. Greg says Paul remained lucid all the way to the hospital and the medics told him that was a good sign so he should be alright. Greg promised to call as soon as he found out more."

"Oh! Thank goodness!" Erin exhaled without realizing she had been holding her breath and Lyric went over to hold Shy's hand.

"Let's pray Grandma," the child said taking command of the situation.

"Oh of course, ma' sweet girl, of course we'll pray." All three sat holding hands asking God for Divine intervention and His miraculous healing grace over her husband, Paul.

"And God, give the doctors lots of wisdom to find out what's wrong with Grandpa Paul," Lyric added as Shy squeezed her grand baby's hand.

Tears began to stream down Shy's face but what had often, in the past, been tears of worry, were now replaced with those of joy. A perfect peace had washed over her during the prayer and she just knew God was keeping him safe. Erin made a cup o' tea for all and as they were sipping the brew that seemed to calm them all, Greg called back with good news.

Paul had suffered a minor heart attack that was just enough of a warning to alert the medical team to a problem that had probably been building up for some time. He had developed a slight blockage in one of the main arteries leading to the heart, and although it wasn't life threatening at the moment, if it wasn't addressed, it could become worse.

They put him on blood thinning medication and told him to stop all strenuous work and go home with at least a couple of day's bed rest.

Obviously, he'd have to see his own doctor and take it from there, but he was out of immediate danger and tomorrow they'd be on their way home.

"He's asleep right now, Mum, or I'd let you talk to him," Greg assured her.

"Oh thank you, honey," Shy said with relief. Telling Greg she'd call Paul in the morning she said goodnight, thanking him once again for being such a good son-in-law and handed the phone to Erin and Lyric.

The two girls chatted for a while and both squealed with surprise when they heard the men would be home the following day.

What had seemed like the possibility of their Thanksgiving being overshadowed by grief was now turned back around to celebrate the true meaning of the holiday.

They already knew they had much to be thankful for and never took anything in their life for granted. Within the last few hours the tidal wave of emotions they'd all just experienced made them feel like dancing with joy.

"Goodness! What a day!" Erin remarked as she collapsed on her favorite sofa. Everyone agreed and decided that to try and sleep after all that drama would be near impossible. The girls decided to choose a movie from "on demand" and Shy went to make her special hot chocolate.

They chose a movie all three agreed on and spent the rest of the evening relaxing, enjoying the calm that came after the storm.

Shy's mind kept drifting off to her honey lying in a hospital bed so far away, and although she was thankful it wasn't as serious as it could have been, she wanted him home. She wouldn't be completely at rest until he was tucked up in their bed and she was able to tend to him herself.

The movie ended and after letting Kylie out all three went to bed excited that Greg and Paul were coming home the next day.

Lyric read for a while, Erin listened to some of her favorite music and Shy entered the days' events in her journal.

She'd been keeping one for years now and had logged a lifetime of treasured memories, mostly good but some not so. As she unwound from that particular day's rollercoaster, she got into bed and curled up under cozy duck down thanking her Papa for His blessings.

Her eyes became heavy and Shy drifted into a realm of familiar yet unfamiliar, happy yet terribly sad with remorse amid discovery… She dreamed like she'd never dreamed before.

"And so you thought that leaving me at the table alone on our wedding day while you got drunk with friends was an appropriate way to act?" Kieran screamed at the man she'd pledged her life to just the day before, but he said nothing.

Kieran and Danny began their life together on a shaky footing but she was determined to make a go of it. As the days, weeks and months went by things got gradually worse.

She'd been conned by Danny throughout the five years of their courtship and was made to believe he was a nice guy who couldn't bear to be away from her. Now Kieran felt trapped unable to face an alternative her pride wouldn't allow; to admit to her parents they had been right.

She set her sights on being happy no matter what, and believing there was no way out settled down to the inevitable.

Within the first two months of their marriage Danny bought two puppies without talking it over with Kieran. He played on her soft heart and love for animals, and for the next few months all hell broke out in their home.

Every day she arrived home from work to witness complete destruction of their home. The adorable perpetrators had chewed the corners off each new piece of furniture in the bedroom. They chewed through the mattress and blankets and each day more and more stuffing was strewn all over the bedroom. It now stunk like a kennel with urine and feces soaked into the carpet and bed.

She had no laundry facilities in their flat so after arriving home from a full day at work she had to take the dogs out to exercise, walk back up three flights of stairs, gather together all the wet bedding and struggle back downstairs to walk at least three blocks to the nearest Laundromat.

Kieran would spend a couple of hours doing laundry, grieving over the money lost and time consumed with such unnecessary labor. Of course she complained. Of course she threatened. Of course she did and said all the inevitable things she could think of to get him to see! But nothing worked. The truth had dawned! She had married a selfish, self centered man/child. A man she thought she knew and loved. Kieran quickly came to realize that she'd swapped one unhappy life for another, but this one seemed destined to last a lifetime.

Once again, Kieran felt thrust into the secret world of coping with it all on her own.

She didn't feel able to share the tragic reality with her family just to be told "we told you so!" As often as she'd fought against the cruel words spoken by her dad so many years before, she now questioned whether there was actually some truth to them. Nothing but an idiot! Nothing but a bloody idiot! The words rattled around in her mind taunting her day and night.

"I can't take this one more day Danny!" she screamed when he came home from work after she had cleared up the mess one more time!

He promised yet again to talk to his mum about keeping the dogs during the day, but every day there was another excuse. She wasn't at home; I was too busy at work; my mum was sick so I couldn't bring it up. The list went on and on and on........and finally Kieran came to the end of her rope!

Danny had been out with his friends shooting rabbits. He used ferrets for this particular hobby and when he arrived home late on Sunday afternoon he announced he was too tired to take the ferrets back to his mum's house. They were kept in a large hutch in her back garden.

"I don't want those ferrets in the flat overnight Danny! Their odor is nauseating and the place smells bad enough so take them down to your mum's tonight!" Kieran insisted yelling at him from the bedroom. As usual he talked her round and promised to get up early the next morning.

The following day came and he slept in and so the little animals were destined to spend the day in the flat.

Kieran was understandably upset and barked at him! "At least make sure they're locked in the bathroom!"

She wasn't afraid to show him how frustrated he made her most of the time and when it came to an argument of words, she would usually win hands down. After an hour of silent preparation for the day ahead, they both set off for work, Kieran in a really bad mood.

Hating to start the day off with a fight Kieran relaxed a little on the bus ride to work fighting off emotional exhaustion. She was getting sick and tired of Danny's selfishness and knew her patience was wearing extremely thin.

She spent her day at work trying to focus on the positive aspects of her life. All Kieran wanted was peace and by the time she trudged wearily up the stairs to their flat she found her self looking forward to spending a quiet night with her husband.

Danny was supposed to have secured the ferrets in the shower room as Kieran had asked but when she came home from work she was met with a scene of complete devastation!

She opened the door to the flat and the rancid stench hit her senses making her reel backwards. Tears stung her tired eyes as she walked in to witness the chaos before her. The ferrets had broken loose and ransacked the bin. It was full of rabbit guts and fur which was now strewn all over the flat.

The smell was so nauseating she gagged and covered her mouth with her hand. The bedroom was in its usual state of destruction and she glanced in to see two happy faces looking up at her with mischief written all over them.

Something snapped in her that night and Kieran realized she couldn't take it anymore. Looking at the mess in her precious home, knowing that it was always left up to her to clear it up, a strange mixture of emotions overtook. She was drained with being taking for granted. Her heart began to pound with righteous rage. But then a strange sense of calm came over her and all of a sudden she knew exactly what to do.

Kieran closed the door to the living room and calmly put the leads on both dogs. She walked them for ten minutes and then climbed the stairs back up to her flat. After feeding the dogs she found a small case to pack enough clothes for a couple of days.

Kieran locked the dogs in the bedroom, ignoring the pleading expression in their eyes and descended the stairs. She felt bad locking them up again, their little faces wondering why mum was acting so strange but she had to make a stand. The number 22 bus came within five minutes of waiting and she took a window seat.

The bus ride up town took only fifteen minutes and when she arrived just outside Danny's shop she embarked with a sensation of purpose. Smiling at the assistant who greeted she asked politely where she would find her husband.

"Oh! Hello Mrs. Peterson, I think he's down in the staff lounge."

She thanked the young man and walked downstairs with quiet confidence. Walking into the lounge, Kieran was met with yet another little insight into her husband's double life. He was in the break room looking at pornographic magazines with two of his staff members. How appropriate, she thought to herself as yet another wave of discovery washed over her.

Who was this stranger she found herself married to? Disgust rose up like bile from the pit of her stomach. But then the irony of the revelation suddenly felt comical in a twisted way and she fought back the desire to laugh at the look on Danny's face when he realized his charade was up!

He sat silently and shame faced as she walked up to him. Dropping the house keys on the table in front of him she said quietly but firmly, "You clean it up!" And walked out of the store and out of his life!

Before getting on the bus Kieran found a phone box and called her sister to ask if she could stay with her for a couple of days, at least until she cleared her thoughts.

Jo sounded surprised as she listened to her little sister's story. Quietly reassuring Kieran that everything would be ok she told her to come straight over.

She arrived half an hour later and as soon as Jo opened the door, Kieran dissolved into tears. Jo wrapped her arms around her baby sister's weary shoulders and led her into the kitchen.

The kettle was put on for tea and the two women chatted long into the evening.

As the girls were coming to the end of the conversation Frank, Jo's husband, popped his head around the door just to say hello. He knew something was up but didn't want to interrupt the girls when they were talking, knowing that Jo would fill him in with the details later.

Jo listened but didn't take sides. What could she say that wasn't already obvious?

She sensed Kieran just needed to talk.

Just before she got into bed, Danny called and did what he would do time and time again. He begged forgiveness and promised to change his ways.

Kieran had made her stand and stayed at Jo's for two days.

After another long conversation with Danny she decided he'd stewed enough. Thanking Jo and Frank for being there for her she packed her bag and went back home.

Danny kept true to his word and began to talk of his dream to become a gamekeeper. Seemingly his grandfather had also had a love for country life and the more they spoke of it, the more Kieran came around to the possibility of making a new start in a different setting. The thought of bringing up children in the country compared to city life really began to appeal to her.

Not long after having their first big fall out, an opportunity of a different kind arose. The old lady in the flat above her in-laws had just died, and the family wanted to sell the flat quickly and at a price much lower than market.

They had to make their mind up fast. Kieran's senses screamed no, but then the common sense of it also pulled at her. They could renovate, sell at a huge profit and move out within a year and they knew how quickly a year could go by. With that plan in mind they decided to go for it. They were able to sell their own little flat for quite a good profit and that gave them a head start with renovation of the new place.

It was all going well, apart from the drawback of being that close to his mum and dad, but she liked them well enough and they liked her.

Within a month of moving and beginning work on their new home Kieran began to feel unwell. She thought perhaps it was the paint fumes that were causing the nausea, but then she remembered her monthly cycle! She'd been so busy working on the new flat she hadn't realized she was a week late.

"I'd better make an appointment with my doctor just to make sure everything's ok," she thought and feeling a little twinge of excitement she decided not to say anything to anyone until she was sure.

Wednesday morning came and Kieran got up for work or so her husband thought. She'd already called in sick for the day without telling anyone. She really wanted to do this on her own. After saying goodbye to Danny she walked down the road to catch the bus to the doctor's office.

She was the first one there so got taken straight away and within twenty minutes she had her answer. She was definitely pregnant!

Her head spun with all sorts of thoughts. She was excited but scared, elated but nervous, her heart raced and she wanted to run outside and scream out loud "I'm going to have a baby!"

There was a life growing inside her, a tiny little miracle. Only she and the doctor knew, but then there was that voice of comfort too. Kieran got back home and managed to sneak upstairs before her mum-in-law saw her and just rested all day and planned on how she was going to tell Danny.

She fixed a nice dinner and was carefully planning how she was going to divulge her secret, when she heard the key in the lock. All of a sudden Kieran found herself running to the door shouting "Hello Daddy!"

"What are ye' talking about and what's for dinner, I'm starvin'?" he asked without taking his eyes off the newspaper in his hand.

"Danny we're having a baby," she said with a whisper. You could hear a pin drop!

"You're kidding!" he stuttered with an odd look on his face. Sudden panic engulfed her.

"Aren't you happy?" She asked anxiously taking a step back as though to separate herself from the disappointment of his reaction.

"You're not kidding," he said this time with a large soppy grin.

"No," she replied sighing with relief. "You scared me there, you big donut," she added, giggling like a little girl and giving him a push for effect.

He grabbed a hold of her and swung her around the room, but then stopped just as quickly and sat her down to ask how she was feeling.

"Well, at the moment a little dizzy. But apart from that, if you can stop the room spinning, I'm fine and very happy," she sighed contentedly.

They ate dinner and talked for a while before eventually calling it a night. As Kieran was about to turn off the light a thought passed through her mind and with it a slight pang of fear.

How was she going to tell her parents and wasn't it odd that she should feel so fearful?

Kieran knew her parents still didn't think much of Danny. Instead of being thrilled to tell them the news most parents long for, Kieran agonized, feeling once again she'd done something wrong.

"Was she being made to feel like this; was it just her imagination; or was it a familiar learned trait from her childhood?"

It seemed that no matter what she did with her life, she sensed she was letting her family down. The void was just as prevalent now as it had been before.

They shared the news with everyone on Danny's side of the family and were greeted with elation and excited anticipation of the months ahead.

Quiet acceptance was the only way to describe the reaction from Kieran's family.

Part Three:

Chapter 12
Deceived

Kieran was about seven months pregnant and hadn't been feeling well for a few days. Initially she had low back pain and just put it down to the baby getting bigger but by day four of her illness she had a fever and the pain was getting so bad she could hardly walk. Danny came home from work and took her to the doctor.

The receptionist at the doctor's office was not very sympathetic. Since there were no appointments available she insisted they wait until everyone else had been seen. Kieran waited for an hour and a half slumped against Danny's shoulder. By the time the doctor eventually saw her she had a fever of 105.

Dr. Munroe called for an ambulance immediately and had diagnosed appendicitis or a serious kidney infection. Either way she was very ill. He was furious with the receptionist and threatened to fire her. Danny called Kieran's parents as soon as they'd settled her into the hospital bed and given her pain medication and something to bring the fever down. By that time it was late and he told them she was sleeping comfortably and that they should probably wait until the next day before coming to visit.

Kieran slept well for the first time in days. The next morning they found out that she had a bad kidney infection. She'd be in hospital until she was strong enough to go home.

Her parents came to visit that afternoon and were visibly shocked at the way she looked. She had an IV to help with extreme dehydration which made her look even worse. Kieran woke up from a nap when her parents entered the room and she felt touched when seeing the concern on her father's face.

He even tried to urge her to eat an orange.

"Kieran, you have to try and eat something," he said, with a note of worry in his voice. "You need to get your strength back for the baby too." Although she felt weak she smiled.

For all the years growing up at home Kieran could never remember such tenderness from her father. The tone in his voice displayed a love she'd never felt before. Upon reflection of that sweet moment Kieran came to realize she'd been given a glimpse into seeing the real man. This was the father she'd longed to be close to, but the stuff of life had gotten in the way. There were so many questions that just couldn't be asked. And even if they were, would the truth be told or would avoidance come into play yet again?

Kieran was in the hospital for nine days. She felt much better when she got back home. She couldn't go back to work after all she'd been through, so money became a little tight. But they managed and it began to feel as though Danny was trying to be a little more attentive.

After another two months of rest on the 27th of October, a bouncing baby boy was born weighing in at 8lb 13oz. They named him Daniel Thomas. Kieran knew somehow he'd be known as Thomas and after spending 10 days in hospital to recover from the c-section, mother and son went home.

Thomas was to prove to be a hungry baby who kept Kieran up all night for quite a few months, but in all she just loved being a mother. She was happier than she'd been most of her life and she quickly realized being a mum was a natural state for her. She tended to that baby boy as though life itself depended on it and for Kieran motherhood became everything.

When Thomas was about five months old Danny talked more of his dream to become a gamekeeper. They both agreed that to bring their son up in the country would mean a better life all round.

They began to look for job openings in that field and it wasn't very long before they found something not too far away from Edinburgh, in between Perth and Dundee. This location would prove to be a perfect fit for Kieran. She'd agreed to a life in the country but wanted to maintain close proximity to parents and family so Thomas could reap the best of both worlds.

They wrote a letter together, but since Danny believed his wife to be more eloquent with words he insisted she write the letter of application. Within a week they were called for an interview.

A gamekeeper's life is more of a vocation than just a simple job. It would involve his wife and children, so Kieran was required to attend the interview. Since Thomas was only a baby they decided to leave him with Nana and Grandpa.

It was only about an hour's drive from Edinburgh once they got on the highway which delighted them even more, feeling it was far enough away to have some peace but close enough not to miss home and family too much. It was perfect!

They got on well with the head gamekeeper during the interview and on their way home they chatted about the hope of a new beginning.

A few days later, Danny got a call to say that the job was his if he wanted it. Since both he and Kieran had discussed it thoroughly, they knew the answer and were overjoyed at the prospect of the move.

They were called back for a second meeting to go over details, like the pay rate. It wasn't great but the perks that came with the job more than made up for the poor hourly wage. They were shown the house that went with the position and although it wouldn't be theirs to own, it was a house, and Kieran loved it.

A pretty garden greeted visitors at the front of their new home. The larger garden at the back could be used to grow vegetables. More importantly, it was situated just off the main highway and bus route. Kieran could catch the bus easily into Dundee or Perth.

Everything seemed ideal. For the first time Kieran felt her marriage was becoming stable and their future bright. The next step was to tell her parents of their decision to move. With that came the familiar sense of dread. What she wished for more than anything was for them to be happy for her.

To hear them say just once, "If that's your choice Kieran, we're happy for you and we'll support you with it," was all she ever wanted to hear.

The following Sunday they took Thomas to visit Kieran's mum and dad. With a little apprehension she brought up the subject of the move. Kieran waited for their reaction having practiced counter arguments well in advance.

As she talked replying to each of their negative comments with a positive response, she began to feel confident they'd eventually come around. For once it felt as though she had taken charge, owning the decision she'd made. It was a good feeling.

With all that behind them they set their minds on selling their flat.

Kieran had stressed that it might be better to rent it, providing another source of income. But Danny wanted no ties to the city and was concerned with having to travel back and forth for maintenance issues. It seemed a legitimate argument, so Kieran agreed to sell especially as they made a sizable profit.

It was sold soon after going on the market so they were able to buy a few things they needed for the move and saved the rest.

Before they knew, it was time to pack and say goodbye to their families. Since they weren't moving too far away, Kieran was already looking forward to the family's first visit.

Chapter 13
Questions answered

Life in the country felt much more relaxing than in the city and Kieran soon fell in love with the perfect peace. Almost every day, she'd put Thomas in his pram and take off on a long walk down the country lanes that surrounded their home. She delighted in the fresh country air.

Thomas was a robust healthy baby with roses in his cheeks and big brown eyes. And with his soft brown curls, he could easily have passed for a Gerber baby. He was becoming extremely close to Kieran and as he grew old enough to walk he followed her every where she went.

She loved her baby boy and could no longer imagine life without him, but to have an afternoon to her self now and then would have been bliss.

Danny was a good provider but didn't feel the need to put too much energy into keeping their marriage alive and interesting. He didn't desire to have much say in his son's upbringing. Kieran did all the messy stuff. Trips to the doctor and getting up in the middle of the night were all considered her job, and to a certain degree that was understandable. She was a mother and a housewife and Danny went out to work. Still, she felt she deserved a break. To have a little time to just be would have been such a precious gift.

What happened to all the quiet intimate conversations? Where did that couple go? Kieran would try and communicate with Danny hoping her questions would trigger some inkling of regret in him, but the response was always the same.

"All you ever do is nag, Kieran. Wantin' tae' talk, talk, talk about feelings all the time!"

And so she'd be quiet and love on her baby boy, putting all her energy into keeping house and nurturing her child. Danny would never be able to understand her. Although in general she was happier with her life now compared to the beginning of the marriage, at times it felt all too familiar. Merely existing in a home with a void like a deep chasm between two mountains where the two are so close, yet so far apart reminded her of a painful longing as a child.

Kieran went on her walks with Thomas aware of the dull ache of loneliness. She asked herself the same question over and over again. Why is life such a disappointment no matter where we are? Am I just ungrateful and never satisfied with what I have or should there be more?

Thomas would watch her with his big brown eyes and wonder why his mummy seemed so sad sometimes. Kieran knew deep down she wasn't ungrateful.

She loved her new world, especially the trees. She loved trees. She didn't even mind the hard work involved in looking after her family, especially in the winter. She'd stand at the kitchen sink scrubbing clothes until her knuckles bled. Hanging wet clothes on a freezing line was a trial as the cold winter froze everything in its grasp.

During the washing she'd tend to the baby and start on lunch and often Kieran felt like a frontier woman. None of that grueling work bothered her. If only Danny considered what he had in her. If only he'd notice and make an effort to love her. Kieran's world seemed full of; if only's."

At least here, at Drimmie Lodge, Danny spent time in the garden planting flowers in the front and vegetables in the back. They enjoyed those vegetables all through the winter. He was a hard working man that fact was never in doubt and Kieran never complained about their actual lifestyle or what little they had in material wealth. She only longed for a deeper relationship with her husband.

They stayed in Perthshire for three years and, in all, it was a good life but when Danny began to listen to other gamekeepers talk of him furthering his work experience, their somewhat idyllic life became threatened. These do gooders convinced Danny he wouldn't be a seasoned professional until he'd gained experience on the high grounds of the Highlands and within a week he'd made arrangements for an interview with the head keeper of Lochinlea estate.

Kieran tried to make a stand but her efforts were futile. She knew once his mind was made up there was no talking him around, so she succumbed to his pleas. "At least go with me to the interview Kieran. If ye' don't like it we won't take the job ok?"

His parents came up to look after Tommy and reluctantly she waved goodbye.

As they traveled to the interview Kieran felt dread engulf her. The car seemed to climb up hill most of the way and the landscape quickly changed from the lush green rolling hills of Perthshire to a harsh and barren no man's land of grey rock.

The sky was overcast which made the terrain appear even more ominous. As she glanced out the car window Kieran tried to ignore the jagged grey crags of the mountains as the twists and turns of the road took them towards their destination.

All she could think was how relieved she would feel on their homeward journey. She couldn't bear to even imagine living this far away from civilization and her family. As the car climbed and wound around the narrow mountainous road, a suffocating fear numbed her senses.

After hours of driving they found the road that led to the loch itself and their final destination. (A loch is the Scottish name for lake.)

It was still winter and she was surprised that there was so little snow. The country as a whole had experienced one of the mildest winters in history, giving a false impression of this bleak and barren region. They turned a corner and suddenly the splendor of the loch came into view.

The ruins of a castle obviously hundreds of years old rose up in the middle of the loch commanding a presence of its own. They had found out prior to the trip that it was said to have been owned by a character called The Wolf of Baldernoch, and quite a character he was, so the story revealed.

In the distance and about a third of the way around the loch, she could see a small wooded area. As they turned yet another corner, Danny informed her that's where the lodge was and the place they'd be meeting the laird.

They bumped down the unpaved road. Kieran was jostled about in her seat, but remained deathly quiet. Danny was either completely oblivious to how panic stricken she was or he just didn't care. His eyes were fixed on the road and she could feel an air of excitement surround him.

"Well, we're here," he said with a satisfaction that forced fear to rise up once again. Kieran remained quiet and tried to control the sting of tears in her eyes. They parked the car outside a large house situated at the bottom of the bumpy driveway and were approached by two men and a very tall, elegant woman.

Both men were dressed like typical gamekeepers, with tweed plus four pants, heavy brogue shoes and tweed caps. One of the men was the laird and, of course, the lady was his wife. The other man was the head keeper.

They introduced themselves and ushered Kieran and Danny into the lodge. As they entered a beautiful sitting room with an enormous bay window that looked out onto the western side of the loch Kieran took a sharp intake of breath.

She had to admit that the view from the sitting room was spectacular! Just for a moment she could imagine sitting in that room after dinner, with a cup of tea listening to something on the radio and enjoying glorious sunsets.

She shook her self back to common sense thinking and quickly removed the idyllic picture from her mind, accepting their invitation to sit down. They were a pleasant couple, obviously from upper class back grounds and great wealth but relatively down to earth and the interview went very well.

Kieran had no option but to tell the truth when asked whether she could deal with the isolation of the place. She admitted candidly but politely that she wasn't sure.

She explained that she was a quiet girl who liked being at home and didn't need a lot of outside activities to keep her happy. Since she didn't drive she was concerned about the distance to the nearest town and being so far away from her family.

Danny, on the other hand, made a huge effort to convince them all, that he didn't think distance would be a problem. He stated his intention to teach Kieran to drive. With all that taken into consideration, he led them to believe they would be a good fit for the job.

Kieran could see he had his interview hat on so she wasn't too concerned with the enthusiastic tone in his voice but as they were driving home she discovered the energy of his countenance during the interview was genuine. Her mind began to race. She was furious and felt betrayed by him yet again and told him so pointedly leaving none of her true feelings to chance. On the other hand, Kieran was also aware deep down that disagreeing was futile. Feeling she had no choice but to accept her fate, Kieran knew Danny would eventually get his way so why drag out the inevitable.

He assured her they would only stay for a year and if she really hated it they would look for something else. That was his convincing argument, but she had heard it all before hadn't she, so why should this promise be any different? Danny knew her soft heart and her willingness to give so much for the man she loved. He used that knowledge to get his own way in everything.

Kieran agonized over her future. She wondered whether the fear that gripped her on the way up through the winding roads and ominous crags of the Highlands was to be an indication of what lay ahead for them.

When Tommy caught a glimpse of his mum and dad as they pulled into their driveway he went crazy, showering Kieran with hugs and kisses.

"Oh I missed you too, sweetie pie!"

They were no sooner back home from the long drive when the phone rang.

It was Hugh, the head-keeper of Lochinlea estate calling to offer them the position. To her complete surprise, she heard her husband explain that they'd just arrived home and would like a little longer to talk it through and think it over.

Hugh agreed and asked Danny to call him back as soon as they'd made up their mind.

For one of the first times in their marriage Kieran felt he had put her first and she appreciated the consideration he showed. However, throughout these last few years she'd become a bit of a skeptic. Realizing this could be evidence of yet another effort to win her over more than any sudden change of character, she pondered on that thought and waited to discover how he would broach the subject.

Her parents-in-law left the following morning and it wasn't long before Danny asked if they could discuss the job offer. Kieran began the conversation by reminding him of his promise to live in a somewhat populated area, not too far away from family and civilization. He knew those two criteria would not be met if they moved up to that forsaken wilderness.

The nearest town was nine miles away and goodness knows where the nearest doctor would be. Kieran explained to him that she felt panic stricken all the way there and was never so thankful to get back. Even here she felt isolated at times and this was suburbia compared to Lochinlea.

She fought long and hard thinking of all the worst case scenarios that could possibly happen, especially with such a young child, but Danny seemed to have an answer for everything.

Kieran gradually felt herself weaken.

He was smart enough to know that she wouldn't be able to live with the knowledge that she had deprived her husband of gaining the experience he needed to succeed in his career. He emphasized that point and drove it home to eventually win the argument.

Kieran dreaded telling her parents. This time she had no reason to debate anything with them. She knew what would be said and having no valid points with which to argue would have to agree with them. And in a quiet voice, so no one could hear she would also be in agreement with what they had said all along.

She was to have very little happiness or say in this marriage and trying to make the best of it was no consolation for knowing they had been right. Danny never did have his family's well being at heart. They were just along for the ride.

The move was going to be fairly quick, as the head keeper needed Danny up there to begin the pheasant rearing on the low ground. They had two weeks' notice to work and then they would be on their way. It was late in the season to change jobs. Usually by March in the game keeping world families would have already moved around, so in that respect they were getting a late start at Lochinlea.

Kieran began to pack up the things that weren't used much and as she worked away she started to feel a little strange.

To begin with it felt like a tummy bug. One day when having to scream at Thomas for unpacking toys she had already packed, she felt light headed and had to sit down with her head between her knees.

Thomas seemed upset with the way his mum was acting and Kieran suddenly felt bad for her baby boy. She had been losing her patience with him a lot lately and although she knew the reasons why it was still no reason to take it out on him.

After gaining her composure she gave him a hug and reassured him that Mummy was fine and asked if he would like to help. He smiled and ran to get a box from his bedroom.

And as though a light bulb suddenly switched on in her head something dawned on her. Kieran ran to her bedroom where she had packed the calendar and flicking back to the previous month she suddenly exclaimed, "Oh my!"

"What's wrong Mummy?" Thomas asked his eyes wide with question.

"Oh darling its ok, Mummy just remembered something that's all."

Kieran wanted another baby for many reasons. For company for Tommy; to keep her busy and distracted from her own thoughts; but most of all she wanted a little girl.

Danny wasn't too sure. He felt there wasn't enough money to care for the child they had, never mind another one, but Kieran felt a desperate need for another baby and especially since they were going to be living in the back of beyond.

She didn't trust Danny with the promise of staying only for a year, so if she had another baby to focus on it would keep her from going stir crazy.

Kieran knew she couldn't say for certain, but didn't want to visit a doctor before they left. She kept it to herself until they had moved and settled in. The last thing she wanted to do was add fuel to the fire as far as her parents were concerned.

So they packed up and with help from Danny's brother-in-law and a few friends they set off on yet another adventure.

Chapter 14
A Blessing

Kieran felt this time it would be better to sleep during the trip, she didn't want any more reason to feel sick, so she read to Tommy for a while and then both of them fell asleep.

Danny hadn't even noticed that she wasn't feeling well.

Once there Kieran didn't seem to mind the place too much. The house they'd been given was roomy with a coziness to it that surprised her.

The kitchen was enormous with a large window that overlooked the loch. It was furnished with a stove and a Raeburn cooker which ran the heat for the whole house. They had been allocated a log allowance and were told they could cut as much peat as they wanted, so they knew at least they would be warm.

The house had a good-sized living room, two bedrooms upstairs and one small one downstairs, with enough room for family to come and stay.

There was a small garden at the front of the house. A large piece of ground at the back held two sets of kennels, enough to house a number of dogs.

Kieran started to relax a little and tried to think of the positive aspects of the move. There were so many out buildings, which looked like empty crofter's cottages that had obviously been there for many years. She felt sure it would be a wonderland of discovery for her and Thomas. Although the journey emphasized the bleakness of the area, there were definitely ample places to walk, but no tree-lined country lanes.

The following morning was to bring reality back with a jolt when it came time for her family and friends to leave. Suddenly she felt a sensation of abandonment which overwhelmed her to the brink of tears. Kieran enjoyed her own company and didn't need to be surrounded by people to enjoy life, but to be left in such a desolate place with only Danny and Thomas for company panicked her beyond belief.

She reflected on her marriage and realized yet again, that if she'd had the kind of relationship with her husband she ached for, she more than likely wouldn't be feeling this sense of dread. Unfortunately, Kieran knew she couldn't trust him to keep to his word and began to feel she had made an enormous mistake in allowing herself to be talked into this move.

She started to unpack and Danny went out to inspect the rest of the property.

They were to be in charge of booking fishing on the Loch and the care and maintenance of the boats. Kieran was to be housekeeper to the lodge, which meant a lot of extra work. But she would definitely have enough time on her hands.

She unpacked necessities first and before long realized she was getting hungry. Kieran prepared a quick lunch and called for Tommy to come downstairs. He had already claimed his room and was eagerly unpacking and when he came down they went outside to find Danny.

"This place is ancient, Kieran," Danny said, when he eventually surfaced from one of the out buildings. He'd found old newspapers on the walls dating back to the 1920's.

It was definitely a place of discovery and intrigue, and Kieran kept drifting back and forth between feelings of dread and excitement. She was enamored with living in such a location of character and history, but the isolation of it still made her fearful. She couldn't shake the innate sense of foreboding in every fiber of her being.

Was there more to this place than was obvious at first glance? After lunch Danny helped her unpack the rest of the household items. She was thankful for his help and was feeling nauseous again. Danny asked what was wrong as it wasn't like her to get tired so easily. Kieran took a deep breath and decided to tell him.

"Danny, I'm late with my period and I've been feeling sick for days." she stated looking over to note his reaction.

"You don't think you could be pregnant do you?" he asked with an edge of nervousness to his voice.

"I think that's very possible," she replied, still watching him closely.

"Kieran, you've been carrying heavy stuff and cleaning and shouldn't you be resting a little?" Danny stressed with concern.

"You're not upset then?

He came over to give her a hug and Thomas looked up at them with curiosity, wondering what was going on.

"Kieran you know how I feel about the money situation but if you really want another baby then I'm happy," he sighed

"We're getting a baby?" shouted Tommy not quite sure whether he should be happy or upset. His eyes got very big and the look on his face made Kieran drop to her knees and embrace him.

"Yes, we are darling. Well, at least we think we are. Mummy will need to go to the doctor to find out for sure," she assured him with a new understanding of how this news will change all their lives.

"Thomas, this means you will have a little brother or sister to play with, so you won't get bored." "Being a big brother is one of the most important jobs in the whole world," Kieran stressed. She was trying to create excitement for him to distract from any negative thoughts he might be having.

The house soon began to look like home and feel like it too. Danny had set a fire in the living room and in the kitchen, so it was soon warm and cozy. As Kieran walked up stairs to make their beds, she reflected on the day and wondered about the new life being created inside her.

The rooms upstairs had comb ceilings and an incredible view of the loch. As she stood at the window of her bedroom and looked out, all too familiar dread and foreboding shuddered through her body.

She missed home terribly and asked the question to whoever was listening, "Will there ever be a time in my life when I will feel completely happy?"

Kieran wanted this baby and somehow knew it would be a little girl, but not the one she had dreamt of years before. She would call her Megan after a song she had fallen in love with as a child. The sweetly romantic refrain that came from a music box in the shape of a little Welsh cottage was called Megan's Song.

Kieran was a romantic at heart and was drawn to Cinderella type stories, where the downtrodden one finally succeeds in the end, to rise up like a phoenix rising from the ashes. Maybe she was still naïve but she didn't understand why people made life so hard.

She didn't understand why her husband could be so selfish and still profess to love her, but perhaps she was just an idealist and life could never be the way she dreamt. Or perhaps she was being told a secret; just a little whisper into her heart that the life she dreamt could be real.

From the bedroom she could hear that Thomas was starting to sound cranky, so she went downstairs to get him ready for bed.

They'd had soup for dinner and a large slab of her Dad's sultana cake with a cup of tea. As she'd taken a bite of the cake she had to gulp down a sob. Everything she did reminded her of home.

But she had a little one to put to bed and also had to make things fun for him. Just before putting Tommy down she dug out his big book of fairy tales and tucking him in she began to read about "Jack and the Beanstalk." Before long he was sound asleep.

Kieran left the door ajar, in case he woke up and felt scared in their new home and tip toed downstairs to make another cup of tea.

Danny was putting his guns away in a locked cupboard and said yes to another cup of tea.

They sat down at the kitchen table when the tea was made and talked about the new addition to their family and what they thought their parents would say.

Kieran already knew the answer and didn't even want to think of it, but Danny thought his parents would be happy. He told her she wasn't to worry about a thing. There was a doctor and small hospital in Grantown-on-Spey, the little town nine miles away. She wasn't sure of her due date yet and hoped the weather wouldn't be too bad. Even if it was they would know in advance and hopefully be able to make plenty arrangements.

Kieran was exhausted and decided to call it a night.

It was Friday, so they had the weekend to settle in before Danny began work and the first thing on the agenda, the following day, was to find the nearest grocery store and get stocked up. It was going to be far more difficult just to run to the store if they ran out so she'd need to make a detailed list, making sure she got plenty of everything.

As soon as her head hit the pillow Kieran was out like the proverbial light and had no, first-night-in-a-new-house problems in getting to sleep.

As she drifted she said her prayers quietly, asking God to bless this new home and help her survive whatever it was her instincts were warning her.

A new day dawned and when she opened her eyes she sensed a stillness that was completely alien to her. The soft light of the morning filtered through the lace curtains she had hurriedly put up the day before and as she got up an unfamiliar quiet pervaded. She was used to hearing cars on the highway and the early morning bustle of the world waking up. Here there was nothing. In fact the quiet screamed out to her with a deafening volume and she felt another wave of panic wash over her.

Dear God, please help me over this obstacle, I don't want to drown in this sea of silence, she prayed in the quiet of the dawn. I won't be able to survive each day with this crippling quiet so please give the silence a new meaning and allow me to focus on the life inside me and being the best wife and mother I can be.

Kieran's limited knowledge of God was that He was still a million light years away and far removed from her everyday life. She would never be good enough to understand Him. That kind of knowledge was reserved for Holy people.

"Mummy where are you?" a little panicked voice rang out from the other room interrupting Kieran's thought.

"I'm coming sweetheart."

Tommy's room was just across the landing and as she entered she could see he looked a little worried. She gave him a big hug relieved to see he'd had a good night in their new home.

Reassured he now seemed happy and excited to go off and explore.

"Can I go outside Mum?" "Well perhaps after breakfast, ok?

Danny slept in for a little while longer until he smelled the aroma of bacon sizzling in the pan. He walked into the kitchen scratching his head and yawning.

"I had a really good sleep, how about you?" he asked.

Kieran agreed and began to dish the food onto the plates as Danny turned to his son.

"Did you sleep well, wee man?" he asked, ruffling his boy's thick brown hair.

"Uh huh," Tommy replied with a mouthful of food,

"Thomas, don't speak with your mouth full!" Kieran reminded and he just giggled.

She loved her new kitchen so much that it made her forget the sensation of panic at the start of the day.

They still had a lot of unpacking to do, but decided to go into town first to stock up on supplies. They didn't know when they'd have another chance.

After clearing up breakfast Kieran got Thomas dressed and asked Danny if he would check on the dogs while she got ready.

Kieran loved her dogs and although most of them were working dogs and lived outside in the kennels, they were still part of the family. Honey and Lassie, their two pets from the start of their marriage were house dogs and now had a much better life in the country.

Like Kieran, both dogs had a rough start to their life together.

Kieran shared many a heartbreak with her little dogs especially Honey who seemed to sense when she was upset. Her big brown soulful eyes would look up at her mistress as though to say, "Never mind, Mum, everything's going to be ok."

Everyone finally ready they scrambled into the car and set off for town.

Grantown-on-Spey was a good sized town with everything they needed. Of course supplies would be more expensive than in the city. They'd have to make sure to do a big shopping at least once every couple of weeks.

The drive to town was a little more picturesque than the drive up so Kieran relaxed a bit more as she got her bearings of the surrounding area.

Thomas was almost four years of age so they wouldn't need to worry about school for another year. By then Kieran would have the baby at home for company and to keep her busy.

They picked up as many groceries as they could afford until pay day and took a short drive around town to get a feel for the layout. They soon realized it was quite pretty and Kieran began to relax. Living here might not be so bad after all.

When they got back to the house there was a big bunch of flowers and bowl of fruit on the doorstep along with a note welcoming them to their new home and job. It was from the head keeper and his wife and Kieran felt disappointed at having missed them. As soon as they got inside she called to thank them both.

Hugh's wife seemed really nice and their act of kindness and welcome made her feel better about everything.

She put the food away and started on lunch while Danny and Thomas took the dogs out for exercise. Danny didn't spend nearly enough time with his son which was another source of concern for Kieran but every now and then he made an effort.

Wasn't it ironic that she'd fallen for someone whose nature, in that respect, was close to her father's?

"Hi you two." Kieran said as the door swung open.

The look of sheer joy on Thomas's face when he came charging through the door was priceless.

Her mother's heart warmed when she looked down to listen to what he had to say and she laughed with him at his story. "That was funny Tommy. Can you go wash up for lunch now?" "Ok Mum!" And he skipped off happy as Larry, whoever Larry is. Kieran thought and giggled to herself.

Chapter 15
Idyllic Persuasion

All too soon, the weekend was over and their new life began.

As soon as Danny started work he began to make new friends and the unfortunate reality of her instincts was to dawn on Kieran once again. Very quickly it became the norm that if he wasn't out working all day, he was out shooting rabbits or deer in the evening with his newly acquired buddies.

Trips to the local pub became more and more frequent and Kieran slowly began to feel like the complete fool he obviously thought her to be. The betrayal of promises he'd made when talking her into moving to Lochinlea loomed up at her daily, pounding in her mind as she struggled to shake off the inevitable. Self condemnation was her greatest enemy and hurt more than anything he could have piled on her.

"How can you be such a fool," she'd hear the taunting voice say over and over, feeling completely powerless to think of a possible way out. Kieran felt trapped in a constant cycle of doubt and regret, every day feeling herself slip deeper into despair.

Within those first few months Kieran struggled to hold on to a healthy mind set. She took long walks in the woods with Thomas breathing in the wonders of nature after a sudden rain shower. Tears of anguish made tracks down her ravaged face, loneliness suffocating her under its powerful grip.

Finally, seeking only survival she cried out to God to help her get through this torment.

As she stood at the kitchen window looking out over the desolate loch, which she could see through the bare branches of the loveless trees that surrounded the house, she could see her self in the reflection. It was a haunting image forever forged in her mind like a ghost refusing to let go.

With no sound around her other than the beating of her breaking heart Kieran held on for dear life.

The summer was slow in appearing in that part of the country but when it finally arrived Kieran's spirit lifted. By the time her birthday came in August she was three and a half months pregnant and already showing.

Thomas was getting excited at the prospect of being a big brother but couldn't understand why it took so long.

Kieran suffered morning sickness until her fourth month but she had visited her doctor and was told everything was going well.

They had told both sets of parents and although they were understandably concerned, given Kieran's new location, they trusted she would take care of herself.

Then she met Danny's newest friend. He was a handsome man, well dressed and just well put together in general. He was polite and thanked her for her offer of a cup of tea, but he and Danny were heading off to shoot deer so needed to get underway.

How nice for you, Kieran thought to herself trying not to dislike this person for being the current reason for her husband's delinquency.

Danny had what most men would give their life for: a loyal wife and a beautiful healthy son and another on the way. Why did he not appreciate them? Why didn't he understand his behavior could eventually lead to the demise of their marriage?

Kieran wasn't always passive in her attempts to get Danny to understand her concerns. On many occasions there would be extremely heated arguments in their home which she hated Thomas to witness.

After a while one becomes exhausted with fighting and the constant battle to make a partner see what is so blatantly obvious to everyone.

Asking those questions of herself reminded her of a time gone by, a shadowy memory of when she sat on a doorstep appreciating all that surrounded her, but questioning why she didn't feel loved, especially by the daddy she knew.

Kieran knew she was back there, in the same vacuum as before, asking only to be loved the way she loved and the only way she knew how.

To keep focused she spent her days playing with her precious Thomas, feeding and exercising the dogs and cleaning out the kennels. She fed the chickens they had acquired and collected the eggs, cooked and cleaned keeping their home spic and span. She didn't have the lodge to worry about until it was shooting and fishing season, but it was hard work when she did.

In between all this she still had the laundry to wash by hand and as she got further along in her pregnancy that particular chore became impossible. Every now and then Danny would take her to the launderette a few miles away.

Kieran was the first one up in the morning to set the kitchen fire so the house would be warm for everyone else. She depended on Danny to chop logs and sticks. The summer months were a time of building up supplies for the long winter ahead and it felt good to see the sheds being packed with a stock pile of fuel.

They enjoyed a first summer at Lochinlea and a few of Danny's family came up to stay. It seemed life there wouldn't be too bad. But summers are short in that part of the country, and before they knew winter was upon them. By that time Kieran was getting tired easily.

It snowed early that year so their fuel was becoming somewhat depleted which unnerved Kieran.

Danny had been out late one night enjoying time with friends and when he eventually got home Kieran mentioned they'd run out of kindling for the fire in the morning. He promised faithfully to get up early and chop some for her before he went to work but morning came and he wouldn't get out of bed.

There was at least a foot of snow on the ground and by that time Kieran was seven months pregnant and extremely large. Thomas was 8lbs 13ozs at birth and the doctors thought this baby would be just as big.

She went downstairs and tried to set the fire with paper sticks, the way her father had taught her when she was a child, but to no avail. Then the phone rang making her jump. It was Danny's boss. There was some kind of emergency with the pheasant pen and he needed his help immediately.

Kieran called to Danny and he came running down the stairs and grabbed the phone from Kieran's hand. He tried to sound as though he'd been up for a while. She heard Danny tell his boss he'd already noticed the new fall of snow and would be there in fifteen minutes.

Without a word to Kieran, he got dressed came back down the stairs two by two, ran out of the house and was gone. She was left in a freezing cold house, heavily pregnant with a four year old child who was already up and complaining of the cold. Silently crying inside Kieran smiled down at the worried little face.

"What say we go on a search for hidden treasure in the wood sweetie pie?" The little face brightened up.

"Ok, Mum!"

She dressed Thomas warmly, gave him something to eat then they both put on their welly boots, heavy coats and gloves.

Kieran didn't think they would find sticks dry enough in the woods but they went to look anyway. Trying to make it a fun game for Thomas, the wee soul brought her every little twig he could find but the cold eventually got the better of them. The sticks were wet making them impossible to burn so Kieran had to quickly come up with an alternative solution.

She knew there were dry sticks in the woodshed down at the lodge but the only way to get down there was to walk. Kieran suggested they go on a treasure-seeking expedition and got the wheel barrow out of the shed.

Pushing a heavy wheel barrow through deep snow is hard enough for anyone but for Kieran it was torturous. With each step she took she struggled against exhaustion.

The woodshed was about 150 yards away. At any other time it would have taken five minutes to walk there, but with deep snow and Kieran's advanced pregnancy it seemed to take an eternity.

She had to keep going, knowing she'd only have the strength for one trip. They set off on their arduous journey with Kieran quietly praying all the way.

The ground was uneven with little potholes everywhere and every time she thought she had things under control she'd step down into a hole.

The heavy barrow tipped over and Kieran felt the tremendous strain against her swollen stomach and although desperate to give up, Kieran kept going for Thomas's sake.

The air was freezing but with the physical exertion Kieran's face became hot. She desperately wanted to take her coat off but knew that wouldn't be a smart move. If she fell, she might not be able to get back up and she'd need as much protection as possible against the frozen snow.

With every few steps they took she had to stop and after half an hour they were still only half way down the road.

In all it took over two hours for Kieran to struggle down that road to the lodge, load the barrow with enough sticks and logs to last a few hours and push it all the way back to the house. The homeward trip was even worse with the added weight of the logs. Kieran was drenched in sweat by the time she got home. The reality of what she'd just done suddenly hit her and she fought back tears of frustration.

Scots are a tough and resilient race and Kieran knew how strong she was, both physically and emotionally, but somehow she sensed there had to be a greater force at work enabling her to do what she'd just done.

After unloading the sticks she set the fire and it wasn't long before the house felt warm and cozy. Her baby was kicking and moving around a lot more than usual as though to give her mum affirmation of her well being. Kieran sighed with relief.

Thomas had loved their adventure, but knew his mummy was tired. After lunch he cuddled into her and asked if she was feeling ok.

Assuring him she was fine but just a little tired Kieran took a moment to enjoy the cuddle and be thankful they had survived the adventure.

They dozed for an hour, cozy on the sofa in front of the toasty fire, but the sudden chill of the air as the logs burned down woke her with a start.

"Sweetie mummy will need to chop some more logs." Kieran whispered to a sleepy little angel and squeezing out from under his embrace Kieran covered Thomas with a blanket and went outside to tackle some more logs.

She was still able to chop small ones and just as she was about to take a swing at one of them she heard the crunch of a car's tires against the rocky surface of the road.

At first she didn't recognize to whom the car belonged but as it pulled to a stop just outside the fence the door opened and she realized suddenly. Heat from embarrassment rushed to her already rosy cheeks.

Mark, the new friend of her husband, began to walk towards her and Kieran felt a bead of sweat run down her side. She was still extremely shy and didn't like to be alone with any man other than her husband or perhaps George the postman.

George was an older man and happily married. He was actually more like a father figure to Kieran and she enjoyed conversations with him when he came by with the mail.

As Mark got close, he realized what Kieran had been doing and couldn't quite grasp the scene.

"Hi Kieran," he said in disbelief. She smiled shyly and asked what he was doing way out there.

He told her he'd been driving past on his way back from a neighboring town and thought Danny might be home for lunch, but then Mark interrupted his explanation by asking her if she'd just been chopping logs.

"Well, er! Yes I was actually. We ran out and I had to put the fire on for Thomas, but I'm fine honest," she stammered, wiping sweaty palms against her coat.

Mark came over to her and grabbed the axe from her hands. "I'm desperate for a cup of tea, do you mind putting the kettle on?'

It was more of a command than a question but Kieran knew what he was doing and appreciated it greatly.

She was too exhausted to be concerned about the propriety of being in the house with him alone, and of course, Thomas was there and would be waking up at any moment. She took a deep breath and relaxed. Mark truly was a saving grace today.

As he chopped, Mark pondered on the scene that had met him as he drove down the road. A clearer picture of this otherwise perfect family was being revealed to him. As he gathered up an armful of logs, he shook his head in disbelief.

On the surface Danny seemed to be a great guy, the life and soul of the party in fact. He was willing to do anything for anybody and really good hearted with his friends, but Mark was starting to question: at whose expense? He was being given an insight that day into Danny's personality and what kind of man he really was.

On the other hand, he also saw Kieran for who she was, and his heart went out to her as he pictured her struggling with the axe, her big swollen belly pushing against the buttons of her Barbour coat. Although it infuriated him to think a man would leave his wife without the means to keep her and his child warm, she certainly made a very cute picture with welly boots and rosy cheeks.

Mark chopped enough logs to last for a couple of days. When he knocked on the door to let her know he had finished, she welcomed him in with a steaming cup of tea and a pile of hot buttered scones, just out the oven.

Kieran had become quite adept at throwing together a tasty bite.

"My! Those smell good Kieran," he said with appreciation. "I'll need to come over and chop logs more often if this is how you treat the help," he mumbled with a mouth full of scone.

He was aware of Kieran's shyness, which made her even more endearing, but he quickly reminded himself she was also Danny's wife, and he was respectful of that.

Kieran told him that Danny had rushed out that morning without taking lunch with him so he might be back. But then again she thought they were working over at the pheasant pens which usually meant they'd have lunch at Hugh's place.

"That's ok Kieran," Mark answered, aware she was making polite conversation. "I'm just glad I paid attention to that little voice telling me to stop by. You know you really shouldn't be chopping logs in your condition."

She smiled and lowered her gaze as she answered, "I know, but it was necessary today." And she looked away trying to disguise the hurt in her eyes.

It was hard not to like Mark, but she also found it embarrassing to converse with him at length. For some reason he unnerved her, even in her pregnant state. Although she was grateful to him for stocking them up with logs and felt obligated to do something for him in return, now she just wanted him to leave.

He sensed her discomfort and finished his tea, thanking her once again for the delicious scones.

He asked her to tell Danny to give him a call, thanked her again and left. As he walked towards his car he wondered what was wrong with Danny that he would neglect his family like that.

Maybe, he thought, trying to give his friend the benefit of the doubt, today was the exception rather than the rule. Perhaps he was usually on top of his responsibilities. He certainly hoped so for their sake.

Her husband spent the whole day at work. When he arrived home, she told him what she'd had to do to start the fire for the house.

"Didn't it dawn on you that we would be freezing? Did it slip your mind, Danny that I am very pregnant!" she cried, trying not to get too upset.

Thomas didn't like to hear them argue and she didn't want to upset her baby either.

"Kieran, I'm sorry, ok. I'll chop more logs and sticks tonight after dinner so that won't happen again," he said more defensively than apologetically.

But Kieran had become used to his lack of love and consideration and began to wonder whether one day she might be free from this marriage.

She also knew she could never be responsible for breaking up the marriage no matter how unhappy she was.

But then Kieran could see in her son's eyes that he understood her sadness.

Danny kept his word this time and was embarrassed to find out that Mark had witnessed the whole thing. Kieran knew he would concoct some excuse for his neglect.

She didn't want her marriage to be a game of covering up deep wounds with a band aid. She just wanted to be loved.

A simple truth overcomplicated by excuses and lies.

Chapter 16
Would Promises Be Kept?

Kieran's pregnancy continued to go well, and she was given an approximate due date of the end of March. She had prayed the weather would be kind to them that winter, and it was, compared to some of the stories she had heard from the locals.

The only people Kieran saw, apart from shopping trips, between October and May, were the men with whom Danny worked.

She still couldn't drive, and thought it wasn't good planning to try and learn during her pregnancy. She felt extremely isolated from the rest of the world. The head keeper's wife never came to visit, which disappointed Kieran, especially since she was pregnant.

She continued to take long walks, weather permitting, either around the loch or up the hill that rose steeply behind the house.

The hill walk was intriguing with a small wooded area half way up that opened out to reveal a flat grassy meadow. There, an old abandoned cottage dating back at least a hundred years stood abandoned with relics from the past scattered everywhere.

Thomas and Kieran were excited to have found this little gem hidden away from the beaten track and began to explore. They found an ancient kettle that hung on a metal hook attached to an arm that was probably used to swing the kettle over the fire for boiling. And a child's tiny black leather boot, which made her feel sad for some reason.

Kieran loved to imagine what people's lives were like. Who lived here? Were they happy or sad? Loved by family or alone and loved by no one?

On their walk back down the hill she reflected on life, comparing hers to its actual significance within the vastness of time and the world around her. As though to bring that thought to light she stopped in her tracks to take in the breathtaking view of the Loch down below.

She couldn't believe she actually lived in such a remote yet incredibly beautiful, setting and almost felt honored to do so.

Living here as a young family could have been such a wonderful, rewarding experience. They could have discovered the amazing history of the area together. So why did it have to be this way?

Danny slept in the same house and ate at the same table and talked about his work and what dog he wanted to buy next; or what new gun he was interested in. Kieran wanted to talk about the new life inside her and what kind of life they wanted for their children and what exciting adventure they were going on next.

She wanted to talk about believing in something greater. She wanted to talk about God.

At first Kieran thought she was imagining things when all of a sudden Mark began to visit more often instead of going out somewhere with Danny. He would usually turn up just before dinner and Kieran felt obliged to invite him to stay.

But then, after dinner was done, he would offer to help wash the dishes instead of retiring to the living room with Danny. Gradually Kieran became concerned.

Does her husband not think Mark's behavior odd? Or was she imagining it all? And if she mentioned anything to Danny would it be taken the wrong way? Her imagination or not, Kieran definitely sensed Mark was trying to get closer to her but she wasn't sure whether she felt disturbed by this or relieved that her husband was at least staying home more.

One evening they were watching a movie and she felt the baby kick. Kieran winced with discomfort, and Mark looked over and saw that she seemed in pain.

"Are you ok Kieran? " He asked obviously concerned.

She assured him she was fine but that the baby kicked and he asked if he could feel it. She immediately looked at Danny as if to ask for his approval and he smiled.

"I think it's going to be a football player."

Kieran took Mark's hand and placed it on her belly which was rising up and down as though the baby was doing summersaults.

Remembering how shy she was and how uncomfortable she normally felt in this man's company was a problem that seemed to fade for a split second. Her heart softened when she saw the look of wonder on his face. He reminded her of her own little boy when he laid his tiny hand on her huge stomach, asking to feel his baby brother or sister.

The reality of the moment returned just as quickly and Kieran suddenly felt embarrassed.

"Does anyone want a cup of tea?" she blurted out, getting to her feet with effort.

"Yes please," was the unanimous reply. "And some of that date and walnut loaf you made today" Danny added.

Thomas was already in bed so she went through to the kitchen, refusing the help that was offered by Mark and put the kettle on.

She sat down at the kitchen table to try and cool down and regain her composure. Maybe it was just her hormones, she wasn't sure, but she was feeling extremely sensitive lately and didn't like this weird situation.

She wanted to spend time alone with her husband to enjoy a film or a walk along the water's edge, but instead she was being made to feel like the third wheel to Danny's private life.

Kieran was so looking forward to the birth of her baby and the beginning of spring and summer again.

She had struggled through the harsh winter and had had her eyes opened by her husbands neglect so by the time March came she was thankful the pregnancy was coming to an end.

Danny arranged for his parents to come up for a couple of weeks just before Kieran's due date, and she actually appreciated their willingness to help.

Kieran was all prepared for the big day, and since she lived thirty miles away, the hospital had given her a specific book-in date, afraid to play chance with the unpredictable weather.

Thomas was understandably upset when the time came for his mum to leave, but after reassuring him she wouldn't be gone too long, he calmed down. Waving goodbye to her big boy was the hardest part for her.

They arrived at the hospital and apart from some kind of mix up with the booking she eventually got settled in and said her goodbyes to Danny.

Kieran was missing Thomas already but enjoying the rest.

She had never experienced labor before as Thomas was an elected 'C' section and so when she began to feel a dull ache in the base of her back that very evening she put it down to fatigue.

She was just as big as she had been with Tommy, but when the pain started to become worse in intervals she thought she'd better find a nurse.

When she eventually found one, Kieran was told it was too early to do anything and was told to go to sleep.

Sleep! How can anyone just go to sleep when they know they're in labor?

Kieran was shocked.

After an hour she talked to them again, and finally the staff nurse gave her a sleeping pill to keep her quiet and help her sleep.

Ok she thought to herself they must know what they're doing. She called home to let everyone know she had begun labor but assured them it may be a while yet. She tried to sleep, but the contractions wouldn't let her, and all through the night she tossed and turned. By the time morning came she was already completely exhausted.

The doctor examined her and decided to move her to a small room closer to the birthing room, and just as she stood up to transfer to the wheel chair her water broke and she got scared.

"Can someone let my husband know?" she asked as they wheeled her away.

"We'll do that straight away, Mrs. Peterson, so don't you worry about a thing."

The contractions suddenly became more frequent and extremely painful. When Kieran asked for some kind of medication to help with the pain she was told it was too late.

"Too late, I've been telling you since last night!" she screamed as she dug her finger nails into the nearest hand. They eventually gave her gas and air, and by the time they wheeled her into the birthing room she was writhing in agony.

When Danny finally arrived, she was already pushing and completely exhausted.

After twenty one hours of labor from start to finish, Kieran was spent and had nothing left to give. At one point she lifted her head to push and thought she was hallucinating when she saw at least a dozen people at the bottom of the bed.

She was later to find out the hospital staff had allowed a group of students in to witness the birth without her permission. At that point, Kieran couldn't have cared less if the whole of Inverness was throwing a party in there!

As the doctor monitored Kieran he became concerned with her exhausted state and the baby, so he asked for an episiotomy and by the last push the baby was out.

Baby Megan Peterson, weighed in at 8lb. 4oz., on March 22nd and a silent prayer of thanks was whispered to God.

Chapter 17
Another Blessing

Kieran was elated to have her little girl and to have one of each was truly a blessing.

When she found out that Danny had been called first thing in the morning and had gone to work for half a day before sauntering into the hospital, she was surprised at herself for feeling shocked and hurt.

Kieran still lived in hope that one day he would see the light and change, but it was obviously not going happen any time soon. Sadly, even when he came to visit them after the birth she felt let down by his lack of effort to look nice for her. As she watched other husbands visit their wives it only magnified what she didn't have.

She rested and enjoyed her baby girl, and finally it came time for them to take Megan home. Kieran had asked Danny if he could come alone to pick them up. She was grateful to her mother-in-law for all that she'd done for them, but on that special day she just wanted Danny to be there.

Her mother-in-law's face was the first she saw to come through the door, and Danny followed behind looking sheepish.

Kieran smiled but sighed at the same time and bent down to pick up her beautiful daughter.

"I'll take her, Kieran," Danny's mum commanded.

"No I'm sorry but you can't, the hospital has rules and the nurse will be carrying her out," Kieran stated with sudden gratitude for hospital rules. Danny's mum had proved herself to be a little controlling throughout their marriage and was actually one of the main reasons for Kieran's willingness to live in the country.

They arrived home and Danny's father greeted her with an observation that made her want to cry.

"Kieran you don't look as though you've had the baby!"

She could only look away with embarrassment.

Well thank you for helping me feel better about myself, father-in-law. The thought fluttered through her mind and quickly disregarding the ignorant remark she bent down to show Thomas his baby sister.

"Can I hold her Mummy?" he shouted with excitement as Megan jumped in Kieran's arms.

"Well I tell you what, sweetie, she has to have a nap after all that hard work coming into the world, but as soon as she wakes up you will be the first person to hold her. Ok?" she explained with a warmth that only a mum could give. Thomas seemed to understand and skipped off to fetch a drawing that he'd done for his mum when she was in hospital.

"Thomas," Kieran called after him and as he turned she added, "I love you, darling, Mummy missed you so much."

He ran at her and almost bowled her over with the biggest hug, and they stayed locked in that embrace for what seemed like ages. She loved her little boy so much and was so happy to be home to share their new blessing.

Determined to give Megan all the goodness of breast milk she tried to feed her as long as she could without prolonging the agony. She got Megan used to the bottle straight away to save her the emotional rollercoaster she'd been on with Thomas.

The summer was thankfully upon them at last and Kieran was happy to be able to take Megan down to visit everyone in her family. It had been three long months since her baby girl was born, and she hadn't seen anyone in her own family. What with dealing with the isolation and confusion in her mind prior to giving birth, Kieran felt on the brink of depression.

But it was June and Megan was three months old and as pretty as she could be. She was a daintier baby than Thomas and every bit a precious little girl. Kieran adored her. Her daddy would play with her, but when it came to feeding, changing nappies, and getting up during the night, Danny made it evident that was Kieran's domain.

When they were eventually able to visit her parents for a couple of days, Kieran's brother and sister came to see the baby. She was excited to finally be able to share her bundle of joy with her family, but also couldn't help but feel the pang of disappointment with them all.

She longed for a close knit family. A family that would make a special effort to visit no matter what the distance, but Kieran also understood the problem as being another symptom of living so far away.

Danny had actually booked a caravan for a week's holiday and after enjoying a couple of days at her mum's they packed for the trip to the caravan site. It was situated just outside Edinburgh and Kieran was so looking forward to some quiet time together as a family.

She was tired of feeling like a single parent and was hoping, albeit naively, that Danny might actually enjoy being with them. He did, for a couple of days at least but had failed to mention to Kieran on the third day that he'd invited friends from Edinburgh to shoot rabbits. The three men spent the whole day together and the rest of the evening in the local pub. It had rained off and on all day and Kieran was left alone again with her two children. The only difference between the caravan and Lochinlea was the conditions were even more intolerable. Kieran couldn't get Megan down to sleep, and Thomas was running around everywhere going stir crazy!

By the end of the day she'd come to the end of her tether and couldn't take it anymore!

When Danny eventually came back, she was in tears. She had packed their clothes and called for a cab to take them back to her mum's house. Once again Kieran was caught between a rock and a hard place.

She wanted to tell Danny what to do with his promises once and for all, but knew she would be robbing Thomas of his trip, and apart from witnessing another row, he was having a ball. Kieran's temper got the better of her and she blew! After an hour of arguing back and forth she succumbed once again for her children's sake and agreed to stay.

She hated herself for being so weak but was thankful they had a few more days to do some fun things with the children.

Although Kieran looked forward to watching her children grow and didn't ever want to wish those years away, she couldn't help but steal away into her private thoughts. She longed for a future free from continual turmoil. She longed for a future free from a marriage like this.

It made Kieran painfully sad to think of her marriage as a process, but Danny's selfishness had killed the desire she'd once had for him.

They actually sang on their way home to Lochinlea and Kieran smiled as Thomas pointed out cows and sheep. Those fleeting moments of joy were swallowed up by a woman starved of love.

As soon as they got back home Danny phoned a friend to arrange an evening's shooting. He had kept his promise for the rest of the holiday so his duty was fulfilled, and now it was back to the routine.

Mark came over that evening earlier than expected and asked them about their trip. They both said it was fun. Thomas jumped around, and poured out all the details of the wonderful time he'd had, but Mark could detect something in Kieran's demeanor that told of another story, but it wasn't his place to ask.

Danny and Mark were out until late, so Kieran fed the children and put them to bed. She made herself a cup of tea and stood at the kitchen window looking out over the loch as the sun went down. The stark beauty of the loch stood out against the incredible back drop of orange and blue as the sun sank behind the dark silhouette of the mountains.

And in the gloaming Kieran's thoughts drifted and she prayed.

"God if I have to endure this life with this man, please take away the yearning for a life so much greater. I would rather live in ignorance than bear this constant pain. I don't know if I will have the strength to survive this much longer, even for my children's sake."

The morning came and they only had that day together before Danny had to go back to work.

Kieran had lots of laundry to do, and the dogs needed attention after a week away from their masters. Danny had enlisted several people to help feed them while he and Kieran were gone, but the pups were all happy to see their family back home. Kieran took the children down to the loch to watch as the dogs played in the water.

As she watched, her thoughts drifted and she remembered an almost near death experience a few months prior just after Megan was born. She was at the loch's edge with her father-in-law one morning watching the dogs swim. She had thrown a stick into the water for them to fetch but only two of them went in, the large black Labrador, Brock, and Rusty, the little Lakeland terrier.

Brock, quite by accident, hit Rusty on the head with one of his huge paws and the terrier went down under the water. He finally surfaced but had obviously swallowed a lot of water and was starting to panic. Kieran screamed for Rusty to come out, but the wee dog began to panic. He thrashed around in the frigid water trying hard to keep his little nose above water. There was no doubt in Kieran's mind he was drowning. Without a moment's thought she began to wade into the ice cold water.

It was only April so the loch was still freezing from the winter temperatures. Her father-in-law tried to stop her but he was too late. The ice cold water crept higher and higher already taking her breath away but she kept going.

There was a shelf in the loch and as she waded Kieran prayed the little dog hadn't gone beyond that point. This time her prayer wasn't answered in the way she'd thought. The last step before reaching Rusty took her down under the bone chilling water, and as she surfaced choking and spluttering she grabbed at the little dog. For an instant Kieran felt elated but the ice cold water had done its damage and for a moment she felt panic rise within her. She was loosing feeling in her legs.

Suddenly she heard Danny's dad shout "Go Brock," and as she paddled with one hand to stay afloat she turned her head to see her faithful Lab swimming back towards her.

As he got close enough Kieran grabbed his collar and held on tight with one hand and to Rusty with the other. Her big black hero swam them to the shore.

Kieran lay on the hard stony beach and coughed up the loch water she had swallowed, while her father-in-law berated her for being so daft as to risk her life for a dog. Only then did Kieran realize the gravity of what she'd just done. But she also knew she couldn't have just stood there and watched the wee dog drown.

Kieran walked gingerly up to the house shaking as the ice cold water clung to her freezing body. She opened the door to the warm kitchen and her mum-in-law and Danny looked at her with shock.

"What happened to you?" they said in unison

She had held her composure long enough but then started to sob as she realized the miracle that had just taken place.

Danny's dad told them both what had transpired, and as Danny sat there in complete disbelief his mum put on the kettle and went to grab some dry clothes.

"What were you thinking Kieran" was all she heard for quite a while after.

Kieran sensed once again that something greater had saved her that day.

Chapter 18
Protecting Her Young

The summer passed by quickly and it came time for Thomas to attend school. It was a trying time for both Kieran and Thomas as her wee man struggled with mixed emotions. He was excited to meet friends and learn how to read and write but nervous to be away from his mum for so long. Kieran's heart was troubled for him. But that too passed, Tommy became accustomed to going to school and life slipped into an easy rhythm.

The days seemed longer for Kieran, but she took the time to enjoy her new baby and loved to take long walks along the water's edge. Sometimes she just wanted to enjoy the beauty of the water on a nice day, but mostly she would daydream of a time when they would be away from the solitude and bleakness of the landscape and back to a greener more hospitable location.

Unfortunately although she continued to fight through it, the depression still lingered and the months that lay ahead were to bring about a sequence of events that would gradually take her further down.

She visited her doctor for a post natal check up and described to him how melancholic she felt most of the time. Kieran was concerned she wouldn't get through the oncoming winter months.

Her doctor diagnosed her with probable post-natal depression and advised some mild anti-depressants, but Kieran refused. She worried about side effects and assured him she would come back if she felt things were getting worse. And so she struggled on.

Life around her went on as usual and there were many days when Kieran felt at peace and able to cope, but then fall came and with that the end of the fishing season. That meant the return of complete solitude once again.

Danny obviously thought Kieran was satisfied being occupied with the baby and so continued with his usual lifestyle. That's when a familiar feeling of confusion returned that would take Kieran on a journey of discovery she could've never imagined.

Mark, the friend who'd made Kieran a little uncomfortable at times, offered to drive her into the city whenever he was going there on business. He made the offer sound nothing more than a gesture of friendship. Of course, Kieran's natural reaction was to thank him kindly but refuse. and she looked to her husband for back up. To her horror Danny left it up to her saying he didn't mind and actually encouraged her to go and get away for the day.

Kieran began to panic and tried to think of every excuse imaginable but Mark wouldn't give up, so she eventually relented. All it took for the locals to take that piece of news and run with it was for someone from the local town to see Kieran in Marks car. Gossip ran like wildfire through every household, pub, and doctors waiting room in the area. Before long Kieran was branded.

For all that she'd been through, no one said a word. For all she had suffered with isolation and loneliness, no one said a word. And for being a faithful, hard working wife that took what most women couldn't even imagine, no one said a word. But as soon as she was even seen to fall from grace, everyone spoke up.

She saw it in their eyes when she went to the local town, and she heard the whispers stop whenever she'd walk into a store. The sideways glances and heads that turned away if she attempted to smile when passing someone familiar became her newest crushing reality.

It wasn't fair. Life wasn't fair, and she was so tired of people playing games. And then she got mad!

"Ok, if that's what they think of me why should I care about propriety anymore?" Every time Mark offered from then on she went and she dared to even have fun.

He talked to her, and he listened, and she ignored the nausea in the pit of her stomach when all that she was made of cried out to her to stop!

Kieran didn't know what was happening to her but she felt the despair deepen. The man she'd given her life to couldn't care less! He couldn't care about anything but himself, and their relationship was dying!

The real problem began when she stood on the bathroom scale one morning and felt disgusted by what it read.

"You're nothing but a fat disgusting idiot who can't do anything right!" The voice told her so she began to run from it. She would get through the day watching everything she ate and drank and stood on the scales after every mouthful.

Every day when Danny got home from work she would say she'd already eaten and went out for a run.

Run, run Kieran that's all you can do. Run away from the torment and become beautiful so no one can see the pain. She was suddenly running herself into the ground and even her husband began to see a difference in her.

The weight fell off but the lump in her throat wouldn't go away. The lump in her throat and the empty ache inside wouldn't go away.

Down, down she went spiraling downwards yet somehow still able to function for her children. Somehow feeling that to stay in control of her weight was to stay in control of her life.

Christmas came and went and she managed to keep herself occupied with the preparation making sure the children had fun. But she couldn't stand it if her husband came near.

And then came the storm!

Part Four:

Spirit Broken But Yet Survive

Chapter 19
Spiraling Downward

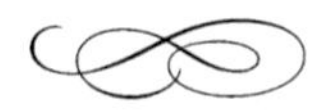

It was the worst storm they'd had in years, so the locals said, and Kieran believed it when she awoke one morning to witness a strange aura in the house.

She opened her eyes to the familiar dull ache in her stomach then noticed everything around her seemed surrounded by a pale blue hue. There was no sound at all.

Nothing stirred, not even a soft gust of wind or the screech of a crow.

At first it took her a moment to understand, and then when she got up and tried to look out of the kitchen window it dawned. There was snow everywhere, feet deep and covering everything.

Her heart began to race as she rushed to the back door, and when she opened it a quiet panic overtook curiosity. Kieran closed it gently and stood staring at the closed door unable to comprehend.

The whole house had been snowed over and they were literally buried alive!

Kieran walked slowly upstairs and sat down on the bed, shaking her husband's shoulder whilst still in shock.

He was in a sound sleep and she had to give him a harder shake before he opened his eyes. In a quiet voice she described the scene outside.

"That's not possible Kieran you're dreaming," he said with a note of skepticism. "You must have seen a drift," he added, but then something strange about how the room felt made him sit up.

He stood up to look out the window and prove her wrong, but couldn't see a thing. "The windows must have frozen up, that's all," he said determined to prove Kieran wrong.

"Alright, Danny, then you go downstairs and open the back door." She dismissed his know it all manner and went to check on the children.

They were still asleep so she went back downstairs to start the fire thankful she'd brought some sticks in the night before. As soon as the room felt warm Kieran went back upstairs to change into something suitable to face the day that lay ahead.

By this time her husband had come to his senses and was frantically trying to call Hugh to let him know their situation but the lines were down.

"Well that's just hunky dory, isn't it?" Kieran remarked as though today was just another ordinary day, and at that they both saw humor in the gravity of their predicament and began to laugh.

"What's the laughin' about down there?" a sleepy little voice echoed from the top of the stairs.

"Come here darlin'." Kieran beckoned to Thomas to come downstairs. When she took him to the back door to show him the wall of snow, his eyes almost bulged from his head! Somewhat resembling a little cartoon character Tommy asked "Are we buried, Mum?" That of course was the question of the day.

"Well I guess kind of sort of and maybe a wee bit," Kieran replied struggling with the truth so as not to panic her wee boy.

"Cool!" was the reply and he ran upstairs shouting; "We're in an igloo!"

Megan was woken up by her noisy big brother and as usual she greeted the day with a smile and a gurgle. Kieran heard Tommy talking to his baby sister so she went upstairs to get her up. "Mum when can I go ootside and play in the snaw?" Thomas asked jumping up and down as Kieran reached over the crib gate for Megan. "Good mornin' wee lamb," Kieran whispered softly then her attention quickly changed to the whirling dervish looking for something in the closet. "Tommy!" she said loudly, trying hard not to laugh.

"Since when do we say 'ootside' and 'snaw' in this house? Have you forgotten how to talk properly?"

"But Mummy, that's how everybody talks," he declared trying to justify the slip up.

"Well that may be how they talk up here, sweetheart, but that's not how Mummy taught you, and we won't be living up here forever. We need to remember that no matter where we go, we don't ever change who we are." He found whatever he was looking for and ran back downstairs. Kieran lifted her baby girl up high above her head.

"Good morning wee lamb," she repeated and blew into her tummy making her giggle.

Megan was a contented baby and hadn't given Kieran many sleepless nights even when she was a newborn. For such a wee thing she seemed to have a gentle peace about her that had nothing to do with anything bestowed upon her by her family making Kieran wonder.

Suddenly hearing raised and excited voices coming from downstairs, Kieran wrapped Megan in a blanket and went downstairs to start the day. They'd need to discuss what they were going to do about this predicament they now found themselves in.

Thomas was running around with excitement trying to put his coat and boots on when Kieran entered the kitchen.

"Now just hold on a minute young man," she said trying to hold on to Megan with one hand and the collar of Thomas's coat with the other.

"You haven't had breakfast yet and you couldn't get out the house if you tried anyway. Get yer' coat off, calm yourself down and sit up at the table," Kieran said with an authority that stopped her son in his tracks.

"Awe... Mum, but I was only..." he began to say but Kieran stopped him with a hand clapped over his mouth.

"I know only too well what you were going to do." And she sat Megan down in her playpen to start on breakfast.

There were still plenty of dry logs inside the back porch so at least they'd be warm for a while.

Kieran made a pot of porridge with cream and the bacon was sizzling on the Raeburn when Danny walked in.

"Well this is a turn up for the books isn't it?" he said understating the obvious. As they sat down to eat Kieran asked if he'd assessed how bad things were.

They still had electricity, so that was a blessing but the storm had caught them by surprise and Kieran was already questioning whether they had enough provisions to last.

After breakfast Danny changed into waterproofs. He was hoping the blocked doorway was just a drift he might be able to clear quite quickly but when he came back after ten minutes of digging he shared the bad news.

It was a drift but he guessed it was probably over ten feet and packed tightly and his shovels were in the shed. Who knows how long it would take to even get out the door.

"I want to help!" Thomas shouted as the adults wondered what to do next.

"Honey, no one can do much of anything at the moment, so you can best help by playing with your baby sister."

"Sissy stuff!" was the reply.

Kieran knew he wanted to be included in the mission albeit an impossible one. So, as a compromise, she asked him to get wrapped up warmly and stand in the porch behind his father as he began to dig.

All they had was the shovel for the ashes but it was enough to start with and before he knew Danny could actually see sky.

"I can see some sky mum!" was the latest report from the wee man who was diligently monitoring the situation.

"Well that's good darlin', maybe I should get my coat on."

"Kieran, I'm going to have to dig out the first little bit on my own," Danny shouted with a tone in his voice she'd never heard before. "The snow has drifted to at least ten feet in most places. I'm going to dig a pathway so that we can at least get out of the house."

There was a certain quiet urgency to his voice that told her to trust him and she did without question.

"All right then," she replied and caught Thomas by the scruff of the neck as he was just about to follow after his dad.

"Tommy, Dad says he's the only one that can get out at the moment," Kieran said to a little guy trying so hard to be grown up. "I need you to stand at the back door and watch him to make sure he's safe. We don't want the snow to fall down on him. Do you think you could do that for Mummy?"

"Sure Mum," he said puffing up his little chest. "I'll look after Dad."

Kieran had already resolved to stay calm as she did in most situations, realizing long ago that panicking was a fruitless indulgence. After all she'd had to put up with, she was geared to get on with the job in hand without complaint.

It took Danny a full hour before he even made a small dent in the enormous mound of snow that had accumulated overnight.

"Isn't it strange," Kieran thought to herself, "that whenever our little family goes through a crisis together, we actually feel like the family I always wished for."

Thomas shouted that his Dad had asked for the kettle to be put on and that he was making headway.

"Thanks darling" she replied to her son, feeling a twinge of pride. He was being such a good boy.

As the kettle boiled Kieran heard Danny stomp his boots in the porch.

"You won't believe how deep that stuff is, Kieran," he said in complete disbelief shaking the snow off his coat.

"I told you when I woke you up this morning, but you wouldn't believe me," she replied deliberately rubbing salt into the wounds.

"I know, I know, but who would have believed it could ever get that deep?"

More often now it became too painful for Kieran to voice how she was truly feeling. It took her back to years before when she was that wee lass who tried to have a voice but no one would listen.

But then she had her private conversations, as though her thoughts were now a secret between her and.... Well she wasn't sure yet who, but somehow she knew that someone was listening.

"Well it's going to be days before we're able to get out of the house alone, never mind getting to the road," Danny stated wiping his sweat soaked face with a towel.

"What will happen if we run short of supplies then?" Kieran asked.

"As long as we're fine for now, people will be checking on us, especially the ones who've experienced this before," he replied with a reassurance that comforted her somewhat.

Thomas asked his Dad how long it would be before he could help him dig and although Kieran realized he was trying to be a big boy, she could also see the danger in him being out there, as small as he was with such deep snow drifts all around.

She interrupted his father's answer by emphasizing the danger and reminded Thomas they had no phone. If anything happened to him she wouldn't be able to forgive herself for letting him go out.

Danny agreed and Thomas accepted his parents answer without argument. He seemed to sense that this was really serious and no time to be talking back and adding to the concern.

Lunch time came and Danny had made enough leeway to have them all help in the effort to dig a channel to the car. It was a good twenty yards away from the house and was also completely covered with snow.

They had discovered the snow was at least three or four feet deep all over, with drifts of up to fifteen feet and their main concern for the moment was the welfare of their dogs. The kennels were on the other side of the property and probably a good seventy five yards away from the house. From that distance it looked as though they had also been completely snowed over.

Even Kieran knew that it may take days before they could dig their way over to the dogs. But at least they' be warm and were strong enough to withstand a couple of days without food.

Thomas had joined them and was told to stay within the confines of the channel. Baby Megan was sitting in her pram wrapped up like an Egyptian mummy.

She was in the doorway of the house quite content just to watch and take in the new discovery of this white, powdery world.

Although it was cold everyone had quickly built up a sweat and all of them had rosy red cheeks. Although the situation was serious they maintained a light hearted banter determined to make this into an adventure.

Coming from the capital city, which was much farther down south Kieran and Danny had never witnessed anything like this before. Because they were becoming used to the more isolated life style in the highlands, they didn't seem too perturbed by a circumstance that would have put most lowlanders into a state of shock. Or perhaps it was the mode of survival that anyone would switch into under extreme situations.

Kieran's main concern was food. She had enough sense to stock up on canned and dry goods and thanks to her father Kieran could bake and turn her hand to almost anything. All depending on how long they were snowed in or even if another storm were to strike, they would definitely need supplies soon.

The first day was exhausting, and Kieran dug as much as she could, but she also had the children to look after and every now and then she'd have to stop to attend to Megan.

She had to feed the troops and still try to get housework and laundry done and so by the time eight o'clock came they were exhausted and decided to call it a night.

Kieran tucked the children into bed and thanked Thomas for being such a great help. "Are we going to get to the dogs tomorrow, Mum?" he asked, concern written all over his cherub like face.

"Oh! I'm sure we will, darlin', but you know even if we don't they'll be fine for a couple of days. They're warm and cozy in their little igloos too!" And they laughed as she ruffled his brown curls.

Morning of the second day was bright and sunny and looking out the window onto the splendor of the white blanket as the blue of the sky reflected off the frozen loch, Kieran reflected on how incredibly beautiful this world of theirs was.

It seemed so serene and welcoming, but at the same time, deadly. She pondered on how this sudden storm seemed to emphasize the contradiction that was her life.

"But enough dreaming," she thought as she reached over to grab her dressing gown.

She heard her children talking and without waking Danny she went to get them up.

Thomas was telling his baby sister about how much snow he had shoveled the day before and Megan was cooing back as though she understood every word.

"How she loved them both!" Kieran reflected with a sigh of gratitude and wasn't it strange how well she felt given their circumstances.

Her husband reached the car by the end of that morning and by the end of the day had dug a channel all the way through to the kennels. Danny was at least able to feed the poor dogs with frozen tripe which was nutrition at least and they seemed grateful to discover they hadn't been abandoned.

As each day came and went, the novelty of their situation wore off and they were gradually becoming a little stir crazy. At the same time there was a certain peace in the midst of their predicament.

Remembering how depressed Kieran had been prior to the storm, it was amazing she had endured this week without breaking down completely. She began to realize that because she had the urgent to focus on, her state of mind and her emotional well being took back stage to the events on hand. For that she was grateful. But then perhaps it had something to do with actually having her husband home, whether he wanted to be there or not.

By the ninth day, they had run out of milk, fresh and dry and if it wasn't for the fact that at least Megan was still on formula, Kieran would have been a little more than anxious. A rescue helicopter had dropped off emergency supplies to them the day before but the children were needing fresh fruit and vegetables and Kieran was really trying hard not to show her worry and concern.

It was then that Danny had an idea. He wanted to try and walk to the main road with the sledge, which was a four mile trip at the best of times. He thought if the main road was open at least he'd be able to get a ride into town to pick up supplies.

Kieran tried to talk sense into him but he wouldn't listen.

"Danny, you must know they're trying to get in to us so we just need to be patient," she said trying to convince him to stay. "What if something happens to you out there, then what will the children and I do?" she implored.

He wasn't being rational. Kieran was trying to look at the bigger picture and take into account the 'what ifs' of the situation, but Danny wouldn't listen. As soon as he'd gone Kieran felt dread wash over her.

"Dear God keep him safe and let him come back to us."

It took every ounce of strength for her not to completely fall apart with what her husband had so foolishly done. She understood he was trying to be the hero but at whose expense?

The negative thoughts rambled around in her mind. What if he fell and hurt himself? He could catch hypothermia? How am I going to get to him or anyone else for that matter with a baby and a five year old?

Coping through most of the day Kieran tried to keep the children amused and happy, fighting to keep panic from rising within.

After a very long day evening finally came. She fed the children with the last of the homemade soup and after dinner they played a game of Snap.

Throughout the game Kieran deflected questions of concern from Thomas with a promise of his daddy's return home the next day. "He's probably at Hugh's house by now stacking up the sledge with all of our favorite goodies," she said lightly determined not to show any signs of worry.

The game ended and she stood up and stretched weary legs.

"Well come on you two it's past your bedtime, and ye' know I think I feel a story coming on." Thomas hurriedly put the cards away and as Kieran followed behind him up the narrow stairs with an arm full of baby sister he urged, "Tell us the one about Hansel and Gretel, Mum."

Kieran finished the favorite story with the big build up that always tickled Tommy, and after tucking them both in turned off the light and went back downstairs.

Drained, Kieran eventually fell asleep on the sofa downstairs and woke up to hear the sound of her children's voices coming from their bedroom.

When she opened the door to say good morning Thomas immediately knew there was something wrong with his mum. "What's wrong, Mum," he asked with concern. "Your face looks as though you've been crying."

"Oh, I'm OK darling, I'm just a wee bit tired, that's all," she replied.

Tommy smiled sympathetically and gave her a big hug. "It'll be alright, Mum, we'll get out soon," he tried to reassure her.

When they went down stairs and Tommy found out that his dad wasn't back he looked a little panicked and asked why he hadn't come home yet.

"It's taking him a little longer, sweetheart, because the snow is so deep, but he'll be fine and we're not going to worry, OK?" she said squeezing his little hand.

He was trying so hard to be the big boy of the house and Kieran was so proud of him but that thought took an about turn when she had to tell him off for making faces at his wee sister. It's amazing how resilient children are she thought to herself with a smile.

They ate breakfast and Kieran dressed them both and set out some games and toys on the floor for them to play with. They were running out of clean clothes and she knew she had to wash some things, but she hadn't a clue how to dry them.

Amidst the concern for her husband's safety and the negative thoughts racing through her mind, she suddenly had an idea.

If she tied some string from the window to the cupboard on the other side of the room and wrung the clothes out really well the heat from the stove just might dry them, so she went to task and was amazed at how well it worked. Of course she couldn't do heavy articles of clothing, but small things of the children's would dry just fine.

The children were playing fine and Kieran was managing to juggle everything she had to do when she heard a noise outside and ran to the door. Pulling it open Kieran let out a gasp of relief, and threw her arms around Danny as he stood grinning from ear to ear with two large bags of groceries.

She was relieved, but furious, with him for putting them through such worry and the mixed rush of pent up emotions made her want to scream with relief.

But even Danny was gracious enough to admit that his boss was furious with him for leaving them alone and stranded and had agreed with every concern of Kieran's.

Danny remarked on how shocked he was when his boss picked him up on the road to town. "What if another storm had started, man, your family would have been snowed in with no means of survival at all and with two young children. What were you thinking Dan?"

Hugh was obviously upset with his lack of good judgment in such a serious situation.

But he was back and that's all that mattered now and the milk would be put to good use. Kieran put the kettle on and started to fix him something to eat asking him how long it would take for them to open the road.

"It doesn't look good Kieran," he replied shaking his head "They have all the big ploughs out to open the main roads and have told everybody else it may take weeks before they can get to the more remote places. I guess that includes us"

Kieran knew it would be a waste of energy to complain about something so out of their control, so she just lowered her gaze and carried on with what she was doing. Her silence and weariness of expression spoke volumes of how she truly felt.

Chapter 20
A Different Kind of Blanket

In all it took the road crew three weeks to open the road enabling them to get into town to buy their provisions. On their way back home it started to snow again, and they were snowed in for another week.

The only good thing that came out of this adventure or nightmare, whichever description comes to mind, was that they actually spent time together as a family. Kieran prayed quietly that it would make her husband appreciate them more and hopefully it would instigate happier times ahead! But that hope was short lived.

As soon as the road opened and it looked as though the bad weather had subsided for good, he slipped right back into his old ways and stayed out at night with friends shooting or going to the pub.

Kieran suspected it probably wouldn't last. But her survival had turned her into the eternal optimist, as she lived in hope of him seeing the error of his ways.

Mark came to visit them as soon as the road opened and could see something sad in Kieran's expression that worried him and asked if she was OK.

Kieran turned, ready as usual with a reassuring smile but the way he looked at her caused a twinge of something in her tummy she tried hard to ignore.

But the compassion in his eyes couldn't be denied.

Kieran wrestled with the thought that Mark liked her more than he should and she now felt guilty of having accepted the rides into the city with him, especially since it had brought about gossip with the local town folk.

Or were all those thoughts just flights of fancy and symptoms of an emotionally starved mind?

She had prided herself on being a good mother and wife, and the thought of her being talked about in such a way felt like another brick on the wall that seemed destined to crush her.

Internal torment reigned day and night as she grasped to remain in control of her thoughts and she turned once again to run.

"If I look perfect then I'll feel better," she thought her broken spirit creating a false sense of reality.

Weeks went by and Kieran felt herself spinning on an endless carousel of memories from her life forever dragging her downwards into oblivion.

"You're nothing but a bloody idiot Kieran, that's all you are."

The tormented voices kept telling her in her dreams day and night.

"You've gotten all you deserve for being such a fool, such an idiot!"

And every now and then she could feel herself slow down to gain a little strength or perhaps just a primitive need to survive.

Now that the external concerns for their safety were no longer an issue and the weather was behaving somewhat normally, Kieran's mind resumed its journey to where it had been consumed prior to the storm.

The deep white powdery cocoon that had embraced Kieran and her perfect family had given her a taste of a home life she constantly dreamt of and had a calming effect on her. It was only to be expected then, that when reality came back into play, her little dream was also brought back into prospective which served to magnify the contradiction of every day.

"It was only pretend, it was never real." Silly little Kieran had fooled herself once again into believing he loved her the way she deserved, and now the sting of truth hurt too much for her to bear.

She could no longer stand the pain she had stood for years in facing that truth once more and so she literally fell to pieces.

Kieran's sadness deepened, and day after day in the dark room of her mind vivid pictures developed. She saw herself clearly; lying at the foot of the stairs with her broken body reflecting the broken spirit within.

"It could be so easy to end the pain," the tormentor assured chasing her day and night.

The decent quickened its pace and try as she might to shake those images from her mind; she no longer had control.

On that final fateful morning Kieran opened her eyes to the dawn of a new day and she knew she couldn't do life anymore. She had no more fight left and was so very tired. She just wanted to sleep and sleep and be in a peaceful place away from the suffocating pain.

Kieran whimpered softly and just lay still. She had come to rest at the bottom of the hole, slipping quietly into self preservation.

After coping with depression for so long and dealing with the loneliness of a dead marriage Kieran could no longer tolerate the harshness of her life at Lochinlea. She lay down quietly and listened to a tiny Kieran deep down inside. An ever shrinking Kieran who had done all she could to survive those years of neglect.

Danny awoke to realize his wife was still lying beside him in the bed, which was unusual for a weekday. She was always up first to light the fire, start on breakfast, and see to the children. So what was wrong with her this morning?

"Are you feeling sick Kieran?' he asked but there was no reply.

He heard her crying softly and feeling panic rise within, he sat up and shook her gently by the shoulder. "Are you having a bad dream Kieran?" he whispered to her sensing there was something deeply wrong.

His wife still wouldn't answer him.

He got out of bed, walked around to her side and kneeled down beside her. The look he saw in her eyes sent a chill through his body, and he began to shake her harder.

"Come on now Kieran sit up and I'll make a cup o tea."

The tiny Kieran laughed inside. "A cup o tea ye' say, oh yes that'll make everything better." But her body wouldn't move, and she just wanted to sleep.

For a moment Kieran thought she heard another voice. A kind of demonic cackle which screamed at her husband, "Why are you so concerned now, dear Danny, don't you think you're a little late with your concern for her well being? But, better late than never eh?"

Kieran was aware of a battle going on inside of her and it was no longer just a fight for her sanity. Something dark and oppressive was trying to convince her that he had been in control all along and now he was winning.

Suddenly a sob caught in her throat causing her to choke and she coughed, forcing her to sit up right. Then she began to tremble.

Danny grabbed her dressing gown and wrapped it around her and as she felt a wave of warmth engulf her, Kieran was suddenly transported back to the doorstep.

She felt the warmth of a familiar blanket that cleared her mind for a moment and looking up at her husband she said, "I need the doctor."

Thomas heard voices coming from his parent's room, but the tone was different than anything he'd heard before, his instincts telling him there was something wrong. He knocked on the door softly and asked for his mum.

Danny shouted through the door. "Everything's fine Tommy. Mummy's not feeling very well. Can you keep Megan happy for a moment?"

Tommy knew by the tone in his father's voice that there was something very wrong, but he did what he was told without argument and went back to his room to play with Megan.

Kieran lay back down and listened to her children's laughter and every ounce of her instincts told her to get up and tend to them, but she couldn't move.

The dull pain she had suffered for months, in her stomach and throat, had spread to the rest of her body. She heard her husband come back up stairs and opened her eyes to see him holding a mug of steaming hot tea.

"The doctor will be here as soon as he's finished his morning appointments, Kieran. He told me to keep you warm and quiet," he added with definite concern.

"I'm going to get the children up now, and I've called Hugh to tell him I'm taking the day off, so you just go back to sleep or drink your tea and don't worry about a thing"

Kieran fell back into a restless sleep and dreamed of snow falling and never stopping. Digging her way out of a deep tunnel and walking up a hill with a brilliant white light at the top. Suddenly hearing her children shout "Mummy, where are you?" Kieran woke up crying to the sound of voices coming from downstairs.

Dr. Thomas came into the room and gestured for Danny to leave them alone.

He sat down on the bed next to Kieran and asked her how she was feeling but she couldn't speak for crying.

He lifted her hand to feel her pulse and asked her to try and take a deep breath so that he could listen to her heart.

Her pulse and heartrate were both a little fast and she looked much thinner than he remembered from her last office visit.

He knew Kieran to be a wonderful mother. She had always asked intelligent questions about her children's health. He also remembered she was from Edinburgh and, in his point of view, didn't belong out here in the middle of nowhere.

He often saw her husband in town at night and putting two and two together felt this young woman had fallen victim to severe depression.

She had probably suffered for many months with loneliness and isolation and was verging on the brink of a breakdown.

He was no psychiatrist, but he didn't think it was a complete breakdown yet. But he also knew she needed immediate help, and as he stood up he squeezed her hand and whispered softly, "We're going to get you some help, Kieran, and all you need to concentrate on is getting better OK?"

As he stood up he added, "I want to see the roses back in those cheeks the next time I see you?"

He was such a kind man. Kieran understood what he was saying and in between sobs she nodded and tried to give him a smile.

When he got downstairs Dr, Thomas told Danny she would need to go into hospital for a while and asked him if he could get help with the children.

Danny assured him he could and then asked what was wrong with his wife.

"I think she's suffering from acute depression Danny. This place is not for her, she's a city girl and you do seem to work long hours," he said trying to be as subtle as possible.

Danny's face turned beet red. "I know, Doctor," he admitted shaking his head. "I haven't helped her as much as I should have".

Doctor Thomas could have said a whole lot more, but knew he couldn't get personally involved with his patients lives.

He told Danny he would send out transportation that would take her to Raigmore Hospital in Inverness.

The Doctor left and Thomas looked up at his dad and asked, "What's wrong with Mum and where's she going?" The poor wee soul was so anxious about Kieran and sensed something serious was about to happen.

Danny told him she wasn't well and had to go into hospital for a wee while and assuring his son the best he could then went to call his parents.

His mother sounded shocked and reassured Danny they would get the train up to Inverness immediately, as long as he could pick them up at the station.

Danny sounded concerned, but was he truly worried about Kieran or was there also an element of panic on his own behalf?

He knew he'd taken her for granted for years, playing on her good nature and willingness to take on as much as he had piled on her. Broken promises were second nature to him.

But what if she doesn't get better? How would he cope with the children alone? The random thoughts raced around in his mind.

Every time they'd had a problem in the past his mother always bailed him out.

Kieran was thankful to her parents-in-law on many occasions for helping, but for years she had tried to make Danny see that to run to them every time they had an issue was not the right way to live. In fact Kieran believed Danny's mother enabled him to be less of the man he should have been by helping too much and too often.

Naturally, he dreaded calling Kieran's mum, knowing he would be in for an ear full of chastisement.

She had been completely opposed to her daughter moving up to Lochinlea, and if she'd had a clue how badly Danny had treated her she would have been furious to say the least.

Kieran had developed the habit of keeping most of her troubles to herself over the years, trying to take every possible route to solve her problems by herself before sharing them with any of her family.

She was ashamed of the choice she had made, but was determined to make the best of that choice and refused to allow her parents to suffer with worry.

But now it was inevitable.

Kieran felt heart sick leaving her children, but she knew she had to get better for their sakes.

"Mummy's going to be fine and I'll probably be gone for a couple of days at the most," she managed to tell her baby boy after he snuck into the bedroom when his dad was on the phone.

"Mummy hasn't been feeling well for quite a bit now," she declared, "And you and Megan need me to be well."

Kieran tried to explain but wasn't up to it.

"You've been crying a lot, Mum, 'cause your eyes get all puffy and you have this really sad look on your face and I don't like it when that happens," Thomas explained looking so very sad. Tears trickled down her face once again as she realized what she'd been putting her son through.

"I'm sorry I've made you worry Tommy," was all she could say and she held him tight.

When the car came Kieran had pulled herself together enough to dress and throw a few things in a case.

She went downstairs, and after hugging Thomas, gave Megan a kiss on the cheek as though to say she'd be back in a minute. But it didn't fool Megan.

As soon as Kieran turned to leave the tears now streaming, Megan started to scream to get away from her dad, stretching out her chubby wee arms towards her mum.

Kieran felt her heart was being ripped from her chest but couldn't stop or she would never go. Things would go right back to square one, and she would turn into a shell with nothing left to give either of them.

What she didn't realize was she was walking out that door for the very last time.

The drive to the hospital was completely silent. Kieran didn't recognize the driver and was thankful. She detested making small talk, and although part of her heart was left behind with her children at Lochinlea, the rest of her felt grateful to be going on her journey of recovery.

Part of the drive took her through some of the inhospitable terrain she recalled from her first trip up for the interview. The now, snow covered mountains looked spectacular in a foreboding way as they stretched up to meet the familiar overcast skies. In Kieran's opinion there was nothing pretty about this part of her country.

She didn't know what lay ahead in the process of her healing, and the anticipation was unnerving but she tried to stay calm and enjoy the quiet.

After thirty minutes the city of Inverness came into view, and she prepared herself for arrival. As they approached the hospital the driver took a different turn and veered down a road running along side Raigmore. Kieran knew the hospital since that was where Megan was born, and she leaned forward to ask the driver where he was taking her.

"I'm taking you down to the psychiatric wing, lass."

Her face flushed and her heart raced. That can't be right surely.

"I'm not crazy, I just need a break away from that place and my husband and the pain and loneliness and..." As quickly as she had denied her need to be there Kieran began to recognize the truth. Perhaps this was exactly where she needed to be.

When the car finally came to a stop, the driver got out and opened the door. Kieran tried to stand up but fell back into her seat. Her head felt light and dizzy and the kind man bent down and taking her by the hand he eased her out.

"There now, Miss, are you going to be alright to walk, or do you want me to get a wheelchair?"

He had seen a lot in the years he had worked for the hospital and as he'd watched Kieran in his rear view mirror on the ride to Raigmore, he noticed a deep sadness in her eyes that broke his heart. His instincts told him she wasn't the usual patient, but rather someone who just needed a little rest from what life had put her through.

He took Kieran to the reception desk in the front foyer and told her that he had to get back but wished her all the best. She thanked him for being so kind and stood alone looking like a wee girl who'd lost her way.

The lady at the desk asked for her name and told her to take a seat. "Someone will be with you shortly dear."

Kieran did what she was told. As she sat down a large group of people came out of a room close by and then entered what looked like some sort of cafeteria. They were quite a mixture. Some older men in their fifties, and a couple of middle aged women, and she was surprised at how many young people were straggling behind in a makeshift group of their own.

As she wondered what brought them all to a place like this a tall man in his thirties with a happy demeanor stopped and introduced himself as being a nurse in the hospital. He had kind eyes and a genuine smile and felt like one of those people Kieran just knew she would like. Her spirits raised a little. When he showed her into a very pretty room with two large windows that looked out onto the woods surrounding the hospital, they rose even more.

"Perhaps it's not going to be too bad here."

The friendly young, man's name was John, and he told her she was just in time for lunch. He explained Kieran had the option of either eating in the cafeteria or ordering something to be brought to her room. Kieran opted for staying in her room, insisting she wasn't really hungry. As John turned to leave he said he would send her something anyway.

Kieran picked up her weekend bag with the little she'd brought with her and started to unpack. She placed her belongings in the drawers he had suggested were hers and just as she was about to lie down on her bed, a knock came to the door.

"Come in," Kieran whispered with a tiny nervous voice.

It was John, with a plate full of sandwiches and a large glass of milk. "We have to keep your strength up, don't we now, Kieran?" he said his words tinged with a hint of mischievous.

"Thank you, John, I'll try to eat something."

"Kieran, dinner is at six o'clock, but I'll pop in just before I get off duty to see if you'd rather have it in your room, OK? You'll find that we're really laid back here. We want you to feel comfortable to come around in your own time, so just spend this afternoon relaxing." He smiled at her with a wink and then left, leaving Kieran to cool down from the blush he had induced but thankful to him for making her feel more at ease.

Kieran was amazed at how relaxed she was beginning to feel already, and spent the rest of the afternoon just looking out at the trees swaying gently in the early spring breeze. Although she missed her babies, she also felt a deep sense of affirmation that this was exactly where she needed to be. She felt no remorse at having agreed with the decision to come.

The very next day, however, the lack of remorse turned quickly to all consuming regret.

"What do you mean a minimum of three weeks," she cried out frantically to John after he gave her the news. "I can't stay here for that long I have a baby and a five year old, and they need me!"

"Kieran, wait one moment," he said softly and gently taking her by the hand he led her to a comfortable chair and encouraged her to sit.

"You have no choice in the matter Kieran." "When your doctor signed the papers to transfer you here, he knew the duration of the stay was mandatory. He probably didn't tell you because he knew you well enough to understand what your reaction would be."

"Kieran, you need to stay for the good of those children. If you had stayed there much longer, there's no telling what would have happened. You have to trust your doctor's judgment and mine also," he implored trying to ease the palpable anguish she was suffering.

She was crying uncontrollably and couldn't quite catch her breath. John got up and poured her some water from a jug on the sideboard. She sipped a little, then a little more and eventually took a deep breath in, her whole body shuddering as she exhaled.

She knew he was telling her the truth, but it was a hard truth. And looking up at him with a tear stained face Kieran explained she'd thought it would just be a weekend stay. "And I only brought enough clothes for a couple of days."

"I'll call your husband tonight before I leave OK?"

Kieran managed a faint smile as John left her room then turned to gaze out the window. The familiar lump returned to her throat and a lone tear slipped down her face as she wondered what her babies would do without her for three long weeks.

They didn't allow private phone calls until the patient had been evaluated, and she understood the hospital had to have strict rules.

Apart from wanting to know about her children, she had no reason to talk to her husband. Her heart knew that he was the cause of most of the depression apart from those brought on by hormonal changes after child birth, and she was glad to be as far away from him as possible.

For the first two days John was the only one she had any kind of contact with, and by the end of the second day, he began to encourage her to come out of her room and mix with the other patients. Kieran didn't feel ready to speak to people. It was hard enough dealing with her own problems without listening to other peoples. Believing she'd be completely unable to empathize with people she didn't know she stayed in her room and pondered. "Perhaps listening to the tragic stories of others might be exactly what she needed, to jolt her back to reality. But who's reality? And was this actually some kind of therapeutic healing process?" Kieran drifted off to sleep with muddled thoughts, praying her babies weren't missing her too much.

When morning came there was no one more surprised than John when he walked into the cafeteria and saw Kieran talking to Jennifer as they ate breakfast. Jennifer was a young girl of about twenty one who had found her boyfriend hanging by a rope he'd tied to the top of the stairs.

Kieran sat listening to her story unable to believe what she heard.

This young girl had gone through more in her twenty one years than most of us go through in a lifetime, and although Kieran's natural reaction was to reach out to her, she knew she wasn't able. What she could do was listen and that she did with compassion.

John came over to them and winked at Kieran who smiled and nodded in reply.

"Good morning, young ladies," he said, bowing deeply.

"Oh, away ye' go Johnnie ya' big eejit," Jennifer said digging him with her elbow. "I hope ye're no takin' him too seriously, Kieran, 'cause he's guilty of kissin' the blarney stone so he is," Jennifer giggled mischievously.

"I'll speak to you later, Kieran and Jennifer, you just stay out of mischief," he replied shaking a finger and feigning disapproval.

He was glad to see Kieran out of her room, and sensed a slight change in her demeanor already. There seemed to be a little more life in those green eyes than when she arrived, and he made a mental note to mention it to the doctor.

Chapter 21
Freedom of a Kind

John always seemed to have something encouraging or funny to say.

"What a breath of fresh air he is," Kieran thought to herself as she watched him leave the cafeteria and she sighed. "Some woman will be very blessed to marry that young man."

She returned her attention to Jennifer and asked her if they were allowed to go out for a walk. "You're not allowed to do anything here until you've been evaluated by the doctor."

"But this is my third day and I haven't seen any doctor yet," Kieran said trying not to sound too frustrated.

Jennifer told her that John would have been evaluating her from day one and have already passed on his notes to Dr. McLean who is the head psychiatrist here. "They usually give you a few days just to settle in before she speaks to you so you might be seeing her today."

Jennifer was such a nice girl, but a little rough around the edges, reflecting the life she'd had.

Kieran thanked her for all the information and noticed that people were starting to clear up. Jennifer explained that every morning after breakfast they have a group meeting, and she encouraged her to come along. As shy as she still was Kieran's first reaction was to refuse and go back to her room, but she reminded herself that she was there for a reason and had to face up to whatever they expected of her if she was going to get better.

She kept close to Jennifer and followed the group into the room she had seen them come out of the day of her arrival.

One of the older men made a joke of asking her if she wanted a drink to calm her nerves and Kieran took them seriously replying politely, "No thank you I don't drink." The group of men broke into uproarious laughter.

Kieran turned crimson red and was just about to turn and run when John walked in behind her. He had heard everything and holding on to her shoulders he took her to a seat and gently pushed her down.

"Kieran you've to pay no attention to these old coots because they think everyone is here for the same reason they are, which they've been told time and time again is not true," John commented his voice growing louder with every word. "So they need to be quiet and behave," he added glaring at the perpetrators. "Isn't that right, gentlemen?"

It had taken Kieran long enough to surface out of her room and these old geysers were quite happy to scare her back in.

He was mad at them and they knew it. They apologized in unison and welcomed Kieran to the meeting. "Don't mind us, Miss Kieran, we're really quite harmless," one of them piped up and she smiled back at him shyly.

She hadn't a clue what took place in the group meeting so tried to brace for the worse.

John explained that the group was completely voluntary and pointed out that no one would be forced to speak. He went on to explain that it had become a proven fact that people do feel more relaxed when sharing their stories in a common group setting. "Given that fact, I shall now call the meeting to order and ask who would like to speak first"

The first speaker was one of the old coots. After listening to what he had to say, Kieran felt herself warm to him amazed at how much more relaxed she felt. There seemed to be a certain camaraderie between everyone in the group, and Kieran somehow sensed they had all acquired a silent understanding of each other.

A younger man spoke next and then one of the middle aged ladies. Jennifer went next and after finally hearing all their stories Kieran began to feel less of an oddball.

Being with real people with heartaches and great sadness in their lives helped her realize she wasn't alone. She had a voice and people actually did care enough to listen.

As Kieran had listened to the others she was now encouraged to open up and talk. She nodded hesitantly and gazed down at intertwined hands, searching for the right words to begin her story. Sitting quietly for what seemed like an eternity she took a deep breath and began.

She started off by telling them who she was and where she lived and with whom and that she had been born and raised in Edinburgh but had moved to Lochinlea two years ago. She told them how she hadn't wanted to move up here and that after having her second baby she had fallen into a deep sadness.

Twenty minutes later Kieran wrapped up her story and thanked them all for listening. John brought the meeting to a close, and before Kieran left he told her how proud he was of her.

"Thank you John, but if you hadn't stopped me from running out I never would have had the opportunity to speak. Although I felt really embarrassed when I was talking, it felt good to get it all out, and I feel lighter somehow," she said with the first broad smile he'd seen since she arrived.

"You did great, Kieran, and I want you to tell Dr. McLean all about this morning when you see her later on today. I'll find out the time and let you know. Oh, and I did call your husband and he'll bring some more clothes tonight. He told me to tell you the children are fine and they all miss you," he said making it sound like a script he had memorized.

A great grey cloud passed over her thoughts as the sting of missing her babies was refreshed by the message. She thanked John once again and went off to her room to be alone with her thoughts.

Kieran had borrowed a book from one of the other ladies and tried to read but just couldn't get into it. She gave up and sat down by the window and relaxed, breathing in the peace and tranquility of her sanctuary.

Gradually becoming aware of a tiny spark of life returning to her otherwise bewildered senses Kieran marveled at this profound change. Still deep in thought she jumped as, a knock came to the door.

It was the lady from the front desk and she came to inform Kieran that she had a visitor. Assuming it was her husband with her change of clothes she thanked the friendly woman and asked her to let him in.

Kieran stood up with the familiar dull ache returning to the pit of her stomach, bracing herself to face the reason she was there, but as the door opened wider Kieran's next step was halted by the image before her.

It was Mark, not her husband, and as her face flushed she stood motionless with her mouth aghast. She wanted to turn and run, or just cry, or....she didn't know what she wanted to do, but she knew she didn't want him, of all people, there.

Unable to face any reminder of why she found herself in such a tragic season of her life a multitude of emotions coursed through her veins and she began to cry.

"What are you doing here Mark?" she asked trying to catch her breath.

"I'm sorry Kieran," he replied, "I didn't want to upset you, but Danny came into the store yesterday and told me what had happened and where they had taken you. " He stopped and looked down at the floor. "And I just wanted to make sure you were OK."

He didn't stop to think that seeing him might cause such a negative reaction, and he was mortified to think he was creating even more pain.

"Please, Kieran, don't feel embarrassed. Here, come and sit down and blow your nose," he said offering a tissue. "If you want me to go I'll go, but all I wanted to do was make sure you were alright." Kieran looked up and saw the genuine concern on his face and suddenly the irony of the situation seemed funny. She began to laugh hysterically. She laughed and laughed until she had no more strength left, and, eventually able, she took a deep breath in and exhaled. Kieran sat up tall and composed herself suddenly feeling empowered by the release.

"I'm sorry Mark, but you looked so dreadfully serious and you were talking so fast it sounded as though someone had wound you up. All of a sudden I just saw the funny side of it and, boy, that felt so good!" she replied wiping the tears away.

She actually felt better than she had for months or even years and almost felt guilty at the sudden rush of normalcy that had entered her day.

Kieran thanked Mark for coming, but at the same time admitted it was a shock. She apologized once again for her reaction, especially the hysterical laughter, imagining he must have really thought she'd lost it.

He told her apologies weren't necessary and admitted it felt good to hear her laugh. He felt there had been something wrong for quite some time but wasn't sure how to ask or even approach her about it, so he said nothing which he now felt guilty for.

"If only life were that simple, Mark," she replied reflecting on what he had just said. He looked confused so she continued. "Life's problems are never resolved by simply asking questions or answering them; it's never that easy, but sometimes it's a start," she said with a melancholy that made his heart break. "Sometimes it takes another lifetime to figure out the answers."

"I know, Kieran." Was all he could say in reply feeling hopeless.

He imagined being on the side lines of life watching a friend destroy a relationship he knew he would have given his life for, but there was nothing he could do.

Kieran looked so broken and almost bewildered, but yet Mark sensed a glimpse of hope in her eyes and the words she spoke seemed to momentarily break through the heartbreak.

Although he was embarrassed at his vain attempt to reach out to a woman who was so obviously deeply wounded by what life had placed on her plate, he now sensed the warrior in Kieran, the strong woman who seemed determined not to give up.

"I'm s--o sorry Kieran" he stammered, "I shouldn't have come here and, well I'm not sure what I thought I could do, I just knew I needed to make sure you were OK, or at least will be. I mm-mean."

As he spluttered over good intentions, Kieran smiled and went over to him.

Taking him by the hand she assured him that she was touched that he cared enough to come all this way to see her, and that his visit had actually given her hope. Hope that there are still some good guys out there.

"There are, Kieran," he said with a curious expression on his face. "You are worthy of a really good guy, all women are," he seemed to feel the need to add.

"I know but I need to concentrate on getting well for my children," she replied lowering her gaze. "I miss them so much."

Mark interrupted the silence that followed. "Well, I'm going to be going now Kieran, so take care of you," he said more reserved now as though trying hard not to say something he really wanted to say. And perhaps, she thought, she didn't need to hear it anyway.

She shook his hand, but then gave him a hug and thanked him with a whisper, leaving him standing for a moment as she took her place back at the window.

Hearing the door close quietly Kieran breathed a sigh of relief.

This was her time, she thought to herself minus the normal pang of guilt.

There had been too many years of living everyone else's life. Although she knew she would always give her children nothing but her very best, Kieran now understood she had to be good to herself. She had to pay closer attention to her wellness otherwise everyone suffers.

Kieran couldn't understand why Mark had come to visit her, but she refused to waste time trying to figure out anything that wasn't a part of her healing process.

Pulling herself together finally, she washed her tear-stained face to freshen up for lunch when there came another knock at the door.

It was John this time with a message from Dr. Mclean.

She would see Kieran in her office just after lunch. He told her the doctor was looking forward to meeting her, and that if she got there about 1:30 p.m. the doctor should be there, but if not just to wait outside.

After he gave the message she thanked him and expected him to leave but he stood for a moment as though hesitating.

"Was there anything else, John?" she asked.

"Well, I noticed you had a visitor and I wondered if it was your husband dropping of your clothes," he said, not quite sure if it was appropriate to ask. Kieran blushed and told him it wasn't. She went on to explain that Mark was a family friend who had found out from her husband that she was here so he came to ask if she needed anything.

John noticed she seemed a little unnerved by the question or perhaps the visit itself and asked if she was OK.

"Well, yes I guess," she replied unconvincingly, and because she looked a little less relaxed than before he asked if he could come in and talk.

Kieran stood back to allow him to enter and after closing the door, they took a seat. "You seem a little anxious, Kieran," he said with concern. "Is there something you want to talk about?"

He didn't want to pry and knew this line of questioning drew a fine line between professional concern and personal inquiry. With most of his patients he found it easy to keep his distance, but sometimes one would cross his path that left more of an impression on him.

"It was just such a shock to see him," she replied her green eyes wide with confusion.

"If you don't mind me asking Kieran who is he?" he asked treading very carefully.

"He's a friend of my husband's," she replied. "Mark used to go out with him all the time to shoot rabbits and deer, and at first I blamed him for taking my husband away too much. But then I realized it wasn't his fault, but Danny's," she tried to explain by condensing it as much as possible.

"Then what happened?" John asked sensing there was more to this story.

"Well through time things began to feel different. Instead of going out as much, Mark would come over to the house more and spend time with the family, and he'd usually stay for dinner," she said with big-eyed innocence. "And then one day he offered to drive me to Inverness with Megan so that I could enjoy a day out in the city," she added.

"And how did that make you feel, Kieran," he asked with concern.

She thought for a while and replied to his question with tears in her eyes.

"I refused because I thought it wouldn't be proper and I wanted my husband to agree with me and let Mark know how inappropriate it would be," Kieran explained as she began to cry. "But Danny would never stand up for me if he thought it was going to offend someone else."

Kieran looked up at John with a desperate longing in her eyes for someone to understand.

"You see, he did that all the time even with his family, and it always made me feel as though I was of little or no importance to him," she admitted feeling a sob catch in her throat. "If I ever had an issue with something his mother had done, he'd never contemplate approaching her about it, and I would be left to tolerate the problem. If I dared say anything, it would always get turned around on me and I'd look like the bad guy, so eventually I just got used to being quiet to keep the peace."

"That sounds like a sad existence, Kieran, and not the kind of relationship anyone deserves," he said sympathetically. "I've come to learn there are some couples who survive very strange marriages only because they are happy enough to live with their differences. But if one person is yearning for something deeper it becomes unbearable," he replied in a way that made Kieran wonder whether he was talking from personal experience.

John looked at her with an almost wistful expression and all she could do in return was smile sadly and whisper, "I know."

“Well,” he said getting up and pulling at his sweater. ”I really have to go now so don’t forget your appointment with Dr. Mclean. I hope you get on well with her. She can seem a little gruff sometimes but she’s really smart and doesn’t miss much, so just relax and tell her everything you told me.” He walked towards the door and let himself out leaving Kieran a little drained by the conversation.

Dr. McLean was on time and answered on the second knock. She was about Kieran’s height, around forty years old and looked a little severe but she managed to give Kieran a smile as she asked her to sit down.

The doctor told her what she was going to do and asked Kieran to answer the questions she was about to ask as precisely as possible.

She basically went over everything Kieran had spoken about with John so as nervous as she was initially Kieran slowly began to relax.

Dr. McLean then asked more specific questions about her husband and their relationship and what had happened before and after moving up to Lochinlea. By the end of the session she felt emotionally exhausted.

They had covered a lot of painful subjects, and although Kieran was drained she was also glad to finally get it all out.

As she entered her room and closed the door behind her, she heaved a heavy sigh of relief. Lying down on her bed she drifted off into a deep, restful sleep.

The session with Dr, Mclean must have tired her out even more than she realized as she slept for a couple of hours. She finally awoke to the sound of room doors closing and the delicious aroma of dinner being prepared.

Kieran freshened up and joined Jennifer at one of the tables in the cafeteria.

“Well, how did it go?” Jennifer asked getting straight to the point.

Kieran explained what went on and both girls got up to join the line.

“I told you it would be OK, Kieran. Dr. Mclean is a bit of a strange bird but she’s good at what she does and will give it to you straight, even if it makes you mad,” Jennifer admitted in a manner that spoke of tried and tested experience with that particular fact. After choosing their food they found their way back to their table.

Kieran picked up her knife and fork and was just about to cut into a pork sausage when her thoughts drifted back home to her babies and she wondered what they were having for dinner. The sudden reality of how much she missed them swept over her and she laid down her knife and fork as tears stung her eyes.

She’d lost what little appetite she’d had and as she pushed her plate away Jennifer asked what was wrong. Kieran just shook her head and stood up, pushing her chair back with the back of her leg. “I’m sorry,” Kieran cried to her new friend and ran out the cafeteria straight into John’s arms.

"Hey there young lady, where do you think you're going?" he asked trying to distract her from whatever had caused the tears.

"I ccan't ttalk right now John," she managed to blurt out and wriggling free from his hold, she escaped to her room. He looked over at Jennifer asking a silent question, and in reply Jennifer shook her head and gave a shrug of her shoulders.

John decided not to go after her with an understanding that giving a patient space is sometimes just as important to their well being as therapy.

Dr. Mclean had prescribed some medication that would probably make Kieran feel a little lethargic, hopefully inducing a good night's rest. It would be another two hours before her meds were ready anyway, so he sat down to chat with Jen.

Kieran was different from most people who came through Raigmore and he felt drawn to finding out what made her so. He was also well aware of the dangers of becoming emotionally involved with patients.

He was wise to give Kieran a little time to herself before checking on her, and when he eventually did he found her sitting at the window in her room, looking out at the woods she loved so much. A tear stained face told a thousand tales of the pain and broken promises she'd endured and it was obvious she had just returned from a visit to her past.

This was always the most difficult part of his job. To have compassion for his patients as the individuals they are, but to remain detached.

It took her a moment to realize he was standing in her room, and he apologized if he had startled her but assured her he had knocked before entering.

"Oh, that's OK, John," she replied in a tiny voice. "I was a million miles away."

"Dr. Mclean told me how your session went Kieran and she's written a prescription for something that'll help you feel a little more peaceful and relaxed."

She thanked him and asked if he wanted to have a seat giving him an answer to his next question. He wasn't sure whether she wanted to talk.

"Did the doctor give you any indication as to what her diagnosis was?" he asked having already been made aware of the answer but wanting to know if Kieran had understood.

She smiled and looked over at him.

"Yes, she did, and although I agreed with most of what she said, I'm afraid she might be a little biased against men in general."

John was surprised at Kieran's accurate assessment of the doctor and raising an eyebrow and suppressing a smile he asked, "And what made you think that, Kieran?"

"Well the way she talked about my husband gave me the impression she spoke from personal experience rather than just a professional view."

John laughed at Kieran's remarkable perception into the doctor's persona and told her she wasn't too far from the truth. He added that Dr. Mclean would never allow any personal issues to influence her diagnosis of a patient. It would be completely against her ethics, and although admitting her failing of social grace he couldn't praise her enough as a psychiatrist.

Kieran went on to tell him that basically the doctor thought she was just depressed and quite understandably so. What with having to live in such an isolated location and coping with a new baby and hardly any support. She told Kieran she was amazed she'd coped this long.

Dr, McLean shared as much with John but added another important detail. In her opinion Kieran should not go back to Lochinlea!

That instruction was to be passed on to Mr. Peterson himself, by John, as she still didn't trust Kieran's ability to be as assertive as she needed with that man. In fact the doctor even went as far as advising divorce as the best option with Kieran moving back to Edinburgh with her children.

Of course that thought had passed through Kieran's mind several times over the years she'd been married, but she was a women of integrity who'd taken her vows seriously. Coupled with the inability to admit she had made a life altering mistake with whom she had chosen as a husband, she felt she had no alternative but to stay in the marriage.

Kieran was given her first dose of medicine before going to sleep that night and woke up the next day feeling awful.

She tried to get out of bed amidst the fog in her confused mind but felt too light headed to stand. The room looked strange and everything seemed to be out of focus and fuzzy. When she eventually staggered over to look at herself in the mirror she began to cry. Her face looked puffy, and her eyes glazed. She could hardly recognize the reflection looking back at her.

But somewhere deep down inside she heard that tiny voice: "I'm still here Kieran so don't let go!"

She got dressed in whatever she could lay her hands on and made her way to the restroom.

The hallway seemed longer than she remembered and feeling her way along the wall it took forever to reach the ladies room. As she checked her reflection again Kieran still couldn't recognize the stranger staring back at her.

Making her way slowly back down the hallway she began to feel even more disoriented and had to stop at the little lounge just opposite the cafeteria. She sat down in a large comfy chair and laid her head against the wing and felt herself drift into a dream like haze. She heard life going on all around her in muted tones but couldn't distinguish between any of the voices.

"Kieran," said a voice somewhere off in the fog. "Kieran, what's wrong?" said the voice again but it was too far away for her to reply.

Noise seemed amplified yet muffled as though she was swimming under water in an indoor pool but then suddenly she heard a familiar name way off in the distance. "Go get John, something has really spaced her out."

He was there within a minute of being called and took Kieran's hand in his and looked into her eyes. "Kieran, its John, can you hear me?" he asked with concern. He lifted her chin and turned her face towards his. The glazed expression in those big green eyes told him immediately that something had gone wrong with the medication.

It was Jennifer who'd found her and called for John, and she asked him what was wrong.

"I think she's had an adverse reaction to the medication," he said, hoping that was all it was.

"I'm going to leave her here and Jennifer if you could sit with her until I get back?" He ordered calmly. "I'm going to check with the pharmacy to see if the dosage was correct".

He looked down at Kieran and making sure Jennifer understood he added, "I'll only be a few minutes so make sure she doesn't leave."

After all that Jennifer had seen and been through even she was a little unnerved at Kieran's condition. She hoped as she watched her new friend that she would be OK.

John was true to his word and came rushing down the corridor a few moments later. "She'll be fine," he reassured Jen. "It looks as though she was given a higher dose than she needed, but it wasn't enough to do her harm," he said with a smile. "She'll just feel very strange for a while, so, Jen, could you find Patsy, the staff nurse, and get her to bring a wheelchair. We'll get Kieran back to her room to sleep it off."

He delegated duties extremely well and made people feel they were doing something useful.

For Kieran, the rest of the day was spent in bed and as she slept, her husband came by with extra clothes for her. John thought this had been perfectly timed as, personally, he didn't think Kieran needed to see her husband until she was much stronger. She still needed to talk more and address those issues that had brought her down to the point of breaking. John even allowed himself to wonder whether divorce actually might be the better option, but he was wise enough to keep that opinion to himself.

John checked on her around three o'clock and she was up and sitting at the window, still feeling a little groggy but not nearly as vague as first thing that morning.

"John what hit me?" Kieran asked sounding like someone waking up from a coma. "I've never felt like that before, and I don't want to take that medicine if it's going to have that kind of effect on me," she added remembering only what she had seen in the mirror.

John walked over and sat down beside her. "Don't worry, Kieran, it won't have such a drastic effect on you in the future. You were given the stronger dose by mistake so it's no wonder you felt so strange."

They talked for a while and he mentioned her husband had dropped by with more clothes when she was sleeping but he didn't think it wise to waken her.

Kieran was grateful to him and decided she felt well enough to unpack the rest of her clothes before dinner. Just as he was about to leave she asked whether it was now possible for her to go out for a walk since she'd seen the doctor.

He smiled, knowing that she felt like a caged animal staying indoors when the woods were so close and calling out to her to walk in them.

"Probably tomorrow, Kieran" he replied with understanding. "You need to rest a wee bit more today after what happened with the medication. Tomorrow should be fine as long as the weather permits of course."

She nodded in agreement and began to unpack.

Kieran was starting to feel at peace again and the only thing that still caused her deep sadness was missing her babies. She had never been away from either of them apart from when she had Megan.

She did trust her mother-in-law in that respect and knew she would do the best she could for the children.

Chapter 22
A Twenty-One Day Weekend

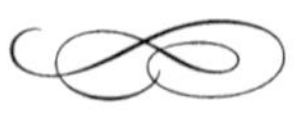

It was a beautiful day when Kieran awoke the next morning and she felt much better than the day before. Not quite herself but looking more like the Kieran she knew. Suddenly a rush of energy coursed through her once exhausted body and she felt like running outside to spin and spin just like a little girl loving life.

She showered and went to breakfast where everyone seemed glad to see her. Kieran sat down and began to eat as quickly as she could without choking.

"Hey where's the fire, lassie?" Jennifer asked unable to believe the change in her friend. Kieran laughed at her strong northern brogue and told her she was excited about going out for a walk.

"Jeez," Jennifer replied her eye brows raised. "I guess simple things amuse simple minds!"

Not enough people have an appreciation of the beauty around them. Kieran thought to herself sadly, but she did, and as she stood up to leave on her adventure she noticed John on his way to get coffee. Kieran said her farewells to those at the table and as she passed by John he gave her a wink. He sensed where she was going and felt like a co-conspirator in her delight.

She knew the sunshine was deceiving at that time of year so she dressed warmly in her thick coat and gloves and as she closed the large wooden door behind her, Kieran breathed in the crisp morning air. She looked upwards to see the vibrant blue of the sky peppered with puffy white clouds and then her gaze lowered to include the canopy above.

In all their glory swaying back and forth with the whisper of a gentle breeze rustling what leaves were left, her trees welcomed her.

Every time she felt relaxed enough to feel happy and glad to be alive, the longing for her children created a little tug on her heart, and she almost felt guilty to feel this way without them. Kieran shook that thought from her mind knowing full well that she loved them more than life itself and couldn't wait to get back to them. She also knew that she was starting to feel like her old self again and that this break was not only needed but deserved.

She walked down the path and along side the woods, feeling a little nervous to actually walk through them and just enjoyed the tingle of fresh air as it brought familiar roses back to her cheeks.

Kieran purposely stayed focused on her surroundings and celebrated just being one with nature and kept on walking until the path came to an end.

She turned around and walked back the way she had come and noticed John standing outside the front door watching her walk up the path.

"Well hello there," he said with a smile. "How are you enjoying this beautiful day?"

"Oh, it's so wonderful to be out, John, and on such a glorious day," she replied throwing her arms out and then giving herself a well deserved hug.

He laughed at the image before him and remarked, "You are unique Kieran did you know that?"

"Hmm, is that a polite way of saying I'm strange?" she asked, laughing with him as they walked back inside talking about nothing in particular.

The rest of her stay literally flew by as Kieran became stronger each day.

Her husband had come to visit on two more occasions before the three weeks' stay was up and he had actually impressed her on how seriously he had taken the doctor's advice.

Dr. McLean had had a meeting with Danny to discuss the reasons why Kieran had become ill with depression and assured him it would be dangerous for her to go back to Lochinlea.

Taking the doctor's advice, he secured another job on an estate just outside Edinburgh and had already made arrangements to move in a few days.

His whole family was rallying around trying to help out with the children and the packing and although Kieran was grateful to him for arranging all of this by himself, she knew him too well to believe this change of heart was solely for her benefit.

Kieran knew Danny was panic stricken with the possibility of being divorced by her. He was moving mountains to finally save the marriage.

She almost felt bad at feeling this skeptical especially knowing the effort he was making to do the right thing at last. Only time would tell whether the damage could be repaired.

When the day came for Kieran to leave she said her farewells to the people she'd become close to and was waiting in the foyer for her husband to pick her up. She had major butterflies in her tummy.

John said goodbye to her the night before as the following day was his day off. Knowing he wouldn't be seeing her again, he made her promise to be good to herself and not to forget to live **her** life and not everyone else's.

Kieran now understood she could only be a good mother to her children if she was well physically and emotionally. Thanking John with a hug for everything he'd done she reassured him she would never allow this to happen again.

She had learned so much in the past three weeks and would be forever grateful to all those who contributed to her recovery.

Her husband arrived on time and as she walked towards the car a sudden whoop of delight stopped her in her tracks. "Mummy!" a happy wee lad shouted. "Look Megan, there's Mummy," he cried out to his baby sister.

Danny opened the car door and Thomas jumped out and ran to his mum throwing himself into her arms. Kieran picked him up and swirled him around telling him how much she had missed him. Tears of joy streamed down her face.

Suddenly aware of another wee face staring out the car window, Kieran put Tommy down giving him a dozen sloppy kisses in the process.

Danny had lifted Megan from the car expecting her to copy her brother's reaction but Megan just stood and stared as though seeing a ghost.

Her baby stood motionless with a curious expression on her face and instead of running to her mum like her brother, she took a few steps back. A sharp twinge of guilt pierced Kieran's heart.

"She took it really hard Kieran," Danny said. "She kept walking around the house looking for you," he admitted sadly.

Kieran fell to her knees and coaxed her baby to come to her. "Come to Mummy, wee lamb, I've missed you so much." Megan didn't move.

She began to sing "Ally Bally Ally Bally bee, sitting on your Mummy's knee," and as she sang and cried tears of joy and heartbreak her wee lamb slowly walked towards her.

"Waiting for a wee bawbee, to buy some Coulters Candy," Kieran sang, the broken words catching in her throat and then she scooped her baby girl up into her arms and sobbed only the tears a mother can shed.

All the way home Megan kept looking up at her Mummy, touching her face as though to make sure she was real, and Kieran realized then how deeply this had affected her. Thomas was old enough to understand the meaning of illness and hospital and even the length of time she was away, but all her wee lamb knew was that her Mummy had gone somewhere and hadn't come back.

How devastating it must have been for her Kieran thought and she made a silent vow never to leave her children again.

Danny told her they'd be staying at the Loch for one more night then they'd travel down to the new estate tomorrow.

He described to her briefly where the estate was and who owned it, and he actually sounded quite excited to be closer to the city and family.

Kieran didn't say much, happy to rest in the news of a new beginning and as Danny and Tommy chatted away and Megan looked up at her mum with her big hazel eyes, Kieran stroked her precious face and whispered a silent prayer of hope.

A new day dawned and pulling out onto the winding road that led away from Lochinlea, Kieran didn't take one backward glance. Relief engulfed every inch of her grateful soul as the ominous grey mountainous crags shrank into the distance.

Looking forward, she could already see the green of the pastures and rolling hills they would be driving through on their way back home.

She had called her parents to tell them they would stop by briefly before driving to the new house and assured them she was feeling much better.

By the time they arrived in Edinburgh the children were cranky and they all looked forward to stretching their legs. It had been a long trip and they were relieved to be closer to home.

Kieran walked up the familiar pathway to her childhood home and looked down at the faded doorstep when memories of a distant childhood flooded back.

She had sat on the step as a wee girl, smelling the sweet scents of summer in appreciation of the world around her and listened to a reassuring voice.

As she knocked on the front door Kieran suddenly felt the fatigue of life bear down on her like a ton of bricks and she sighed heavily just as her mum opened the door.

"Kieran," her mum cried reaching out to give her daughter a big hug. "You look really thin lassie!" she said turning her around and looking her up and down. "Allan, will ye' put the soup on this lassie needs feeding!"

May looked past Kieran and glared at Danny but then was almost bowled over by Tommy's embrace. "Hello, Grandma," he shouted squeezing her tightly around her legs.

Jo and her husband were there and her dad and everyone remarked on how big the children had gotten and how thin Kieran was.

Before they could even get their coats off, Kieran's dad set out four steaming bowls of fresh lentil soup and Kieran just smiled thankful to beback home.

Well at least some things never change, she thought with a new appreciation of her parents. As she supped her soup a surge of guilt washed over her as she was suddenly reminded of all she'd put them through.

But that was Kieran at her best!

No matter what happened to her there was always some kind of guilt involved. The depression happened to her and through no fault of her own, but still she felt responsible for all the pain she'd caused others.

Kieran wondered if there would ever be a time when she'd feel at perfect peace with herself and relieved from the torment of self condemnation.

They ate the delicious soup and thanked her dad who stayed forever in the background, as silent as ever. And when they got ready to leave she kissed her parents, assuring them she was much better and happy to be moving closer to home.

"Yes, and not before time," her mum had to add casting daggers at Danny. "I know, I know, May, it was my fault for taking her up there in the first place, but things will be better now," he admitted

Kieran knew her parents would have been even more furious if they had known the whole story, but that would have to remain between Kieran, her husband and God.

They drove to the new house which took them about forty minutes and finally arrived to find Danny's sister and brother-in-law along with their children, waiting outside eating fish and chips.

"We're sorry we're late, Sandy, but we stopped in at Kieran's parent's house and they insisted we had some soup," Danny explained as Kieran went over to hug her sister-in-law.

"Thanks for helping so much, both of you," she said with genuine gratitude, knowing how much work it must have taken to pack up a house full of someone else's belongings.

Kieran had always liked them and they too seemed concerned at how thin she had become.

"Nae, problem," replied Sandy to Kieran's gesture of thanks, "You know me Kieran, I just love to roll up ma' sleeves and get stuck in," she said with her heavier Leith brogue.

They all laughed and decided to make a cup o' tea before doing anything else but after the welcomed break they got stuck in and most of the heavy work was done before dusk crept in through the woods.

Sandy and Alex decided to call it a day and as Kieran, Danny and the children stood outside their new home waving goodbye to their family, Kieran gave her husband a hug and a thank you for working so hard at making their marriage work and keeping the family together.

"Kieran" he said taking a hold of her shoulders, "I know it was all my fault, and I promise to try harder at being a better husband and father, so you don't need to worry anymore OK!" Danny said trying hard to reassure her that he meant it this time.

She smiled and just held him. It was touching to see their children look up at them and smile and it felt good to feel like a real family.

This time Kieran could see Danny was working at keeping his word and the time they spent on this new estate, was one of the happiest she could remember.

Deciding to keep the promise she'd made to the staff in Raigmore, Kieran treated herself to a haircut. She had her long hair cut into a bob and everybody liked it. Danny bought her a bike with a baby carrier so she could cycle into the local village with Tommy on his bike and Kieran felt she was taking back control of her life.

The first year flew by as they became acclimated to the new area. However before long they realized there was more to the landowner than originally met the eye.

He was Dutch and strange to say the least.

Within the first few months Danny had several disagreements with him which seemed to be increasing in severity as each one occurred.

He was a slave driver and seemed to have no compassion for an employee's homelife, calling Danny out at all hours of the day and night.

Kieran could see her husband was trying to endure for the sake of the family, but by the middle of the second year they both realized it was hopeless to stay.

Danny began to put feelers out to people he knew through the grapevine, and by Christmas of the second year they were called in for an interview for a job a little farther north but not too much so as to be a problem.

The estate wasn't far from Montrose; farther away than Perthshire but still quite central to towns and family.

Their relationship had improved, and the children seemed excited by another move. Once again, by the first weekend in February, they packed up their belongings and set out on yet another adventure.

It was a beautiful part of the country with glens and valleys, rolling hills and deep green pasture dotted with cows and sheep and for the first time in many years Kieran felt a tiny flame of hope ignite for the family she longed for.

Danny seemed happy with what they had offered as far as pay and perks, and they had already seen the house that came with the job. It was a picturesque little two bedroom surrounded by an acre of garden and situated at the edge of a wood.

Sitting at the foot of a hill covered in lush green grass the little house looked like the gatehouse to the entrance of a majestic castle with the slow incline behind rising upwards to reveal enormous rocks smoothed by years of inclement Scottish weather.

Kieran's heart skipped a beat when she first saw the house, thankful she had been given another hill to climb whenever she needed to just get away.

The estate contained both low and high ground which meant Danny would hopefully be satisfied working with pheasants, grouse, deer and salmon fishing, giving him a variety of work experience. It sounded perfect.

Kieran had been made aware of possible work opportunities during the shooting season which began in October. The extra income would help greatly with Christmas, and her only concern then would be to find someone trust worthy to look after the children for at least a couple of hours after school.

Megan would be turning five in a couple of months, and so it seemed pointless for Kieran to stay home alone all day long when she could be earning a little extra.

It looked as though this job could potentially allow them to finally set down some roots instead of wandering around Scotland year after year in search of that perfect somewhere to call home.

There was only one nagging doubt in Kieran's mind that continued to trouble her.

She just couldn't shake off an unsettled feeling. During the interview the head gamekeeper had disturbed her.

He was in his fifties with a wiry build and had the shiftiest eyes Kieran had ever seen. Although his words spoke of a family man who loved his wife and children, those eyes told Kieran another truth; something that made her extremely uncomfortable.

But they were all excited with the potential of this move, and Kieran wanted nothing to ruin what could be an ideal beginning. She tried to dismiss her underlying concern.

After yet another exhausting move they settled in and began their life in this idyllic setting full of excited anticipation.

Winter turned quickly into spring that year, and before they realized summer was upon them and family members from both sides came to visit.

The kids ran wild over the hills and braes of the beautiful countryside taking full advantage of their natural glen playground to the fullest.

The summer was long and unusually warm for Scotland and as it slowly drew to a close they faced yet another change in their life. It was time for Megan to start school.

Kieran couldn't believe where the years had gone, but her baby was now a big girl and excited about going to school with her brother.

The little school in the glen had only one teacher which meant all grade levels were in the same class together. It relieved Kieran to know that Megan would be with Thomas, and because she now had the whole day at home, she began to think about finding a part time job even before the shooting season began.

She found one almost immediately in a little restaurant in the village at the foot of the glen and so their life soon fell into an easy rhythm. The shooting season began in October and by then Kieran and Danny had made friends with Alex, the rabbit trapper, and his wife Maggie who lived a few miles further up the glen.

Kieran liked the couple as soon as they met and worked out an arrangement that suited perfectly. The children would be dropped of at Maggie's house after school and Danny could pick them up after the shoot. That meant Kieran would have to share a portion of her earnings to pay for childcare but she didn't mind. She was happy the kids loved Maggie and it also gave the older woman something to look forward to.

It quickly settled into an ideal easy going relationship of trust that suited all.

Danny and Kieran made friends easily with most of the folk involved with work of all kinds on the estate. Their life as a young family gradually became enriched with mutual relationships instead of the one sided kind Kieran had had to fight against throughout the earlier years of their marriage.

The people who had been raised in the glen or who had lived there most of their lives were a little harder to figure out and as Danny and Kieran tried to integrate into glen social life, the natives soon began to show their true colors.

Kieran had always taken pride in her appearance making sure she was suitably prepared for her day no matter what she had planned, and the women folk of the area apparently thought this an oddity.

Makeup was not something to save for special occasions in Kieran's mind, but rather an important part of who she was as a woman. She wore it every day even during the rugged outdoor world of beating.

Beating is the art, if it could be called that, of flushing game birds out of their natural habitat so that the paying guns would have something to shoot. Sounds barbaric I know but when one helps provide for their family needs must be met.

Throughout her life Kieran had shied away from women's groups and associations, preferring to be a loner of sorts, doing her own thing but yet loving to socialize at times.

Within that first year of their move the reasons for Kieran's preferred independence was to become unfortunately apparent.

Kieran became acutely aware of the looks and sideways glances whenever she came in contact with any of the women especially. Continuing to give them the benefit of the doubt she put that particular peculiarity down to the normal wariness of any newcomer into an already established community.

What she was not aware of was how her presence in the glen was about to automatically place her into a role of which she was completely ignorant and innocent.

The head gamekeeper had quite a reputation as a ladies' man, which is more than likely what Kieran had sensed during the interview. Because he had hired a new young keeper with a pretty wife, the gossip mongers waited in quiet anticipation of what might unfold in the glen's latest series of unfortunate events.

However, Kieran had a little one to prepare for a new season in her life and as she reflected back to her own first day at school many, many years prior she checked her list twice making sure she was giving Megan all the support and encouragement she felt she didn't get from her own mum.

Megan was just raring to go and it was different for her because she had the support of her big brother. Nonetheless, Kieran gave her baby girl some seasoned advice on what she might expect on her first day.

She had become quite astute at reading people through their eyes. Mrs. Thompson, the school teacher seemed pleasant enough on the surface but Kieran sensed an underlying something in her character that told her to remain alert.

The children enjoyed their first day at school and so the beginning of this new season seemed complete as her babies stepped boldly into carving their own place into life in the glen.

A few months passed and as every new day rolled around little instances began to happen at school. First it was one boy calling Thomas names. Then a girl picked on Megan forcing Thomas to intervene and stand up for his baby sister. Someone else's big brother then stepped in to sort Thomas out! A free for all broke out in the school yard and Kieran was called up to the school.

After that incident not a week would go by without something happening where Kieran would feel the need to have a word with one parent or another.

As the natives of the glen, by their indifference to outsiders, tried to pressure Kieran into compromising who she was she dug her heels in even more. She refused to trade in her personal values for an apron and house slippers or remain quiet in defending her young in the process.

Unfortunately, before even more time passed Kieran found it necessary to assert her personal values upon the school teacher when defending her children against the overspill of Mrs. Thompson's glaring disapproval.

School bullies are just as prevalent in remote glen life as in inner city, and when this acrid reality came to life within those first few months of the school year with the teacher herself being the perpetrator, the lioness in Kieran raged to the surface much to the astonishment of the glen pride.

The silly woman attempted to ridicule Kieran's children in front of the whole class: "Surely your mother can afford to buy pencils for you now she's working at the Tuck Inn in the village," she told Tommy and Megan after they both broke their last pencils.

Having to correct the behavior of the adult placed in charge of her children was disappointing for Kieran, to say the least, but she had no alternative but to make it clear to Mrs. Thompson what she would and would not tolerate when it involved her children.

"And if you **ever** speak to my children like that in front of the class again, I promise I will have you pulled up in front of the school board!" Kieran seethed through clenched teeth, a finger pointing as close to the woman's face as would permit without actually sticking it in her eye. "Do I make myself clear?"

The wrongs of the teacher's attitude were dutifully corrected leaving the poor woman shaking in her shoes. Now Kieran was able to establish a boundary in her family's life that she dared anyone else to cross. Finally life became easier on a daily basis for herself and her children.

She grew to realize the clan system of her country's heritage now bore evidence of a closed-minded mentality with bigoted people cut off from larger city life refusing to allow any new comer into the protection of their tiny worlds. They guarded that world with an ignorance Kieran actually felt sorry for.

But life went on and they began to associate with the good-hearted folk on the estate who had mostly come from cities and larger towns and hadn't become tainted with that ignorance.

Spontaneous parties would break out in each other's homes and all the kids from the respective families joined in the fun they created for themselves.

But Danny and Kieran also refused to isolate their family from glen get-togethers and actually had more fun because of the attitude of others.

They soon became the rebel "toon folk," refusing to dance to the fiddle of ancient mind sets and reveling in how their appearance at functions ruffled the feathers of the dowdy crowd.

Unfortunately throughout that year Kieran began to witness the reasons why her instincts had recoiled when meeting the head keeper during the interview. He soon began to take advantage of Danny's absence during the day.

He seemed to make tremendous effort to come up to the house on a regular basis even though his excuses for dropping by seemed vague. Although at first Kieran kept her concerns to herself, she finally felt the need to have a word with Danny.

"He's just a friendly guy, Kieran, and he's probably concerned that you're home alone this far up the glen."

Kieran looked at him amazed at his naivety.

"He gives me the creeps, Danny, and he always seems to appear when you're not around, now that can't be coincidence!" she tried to convince him.

Minimizing her fears as usual, Danny's reluctance to take her concerns seriously eventually led Kieran to question her own instincts. Gradually she talked herself into believing she may have over reacted.

The familiar sting of sadness still affected Kieran every now and then and when that came over her she'd ponder.

Always believing she had compromised who she was created to be Kieran longed for the day she would eventually find the perfect peace she strived for.

Chapter 23
Simple Things

Their family life as a whole had finally come to a place of quiet acceptance that their life in the glen was as average as the next person's. However, the veracity of the imbalance always evident in her marriage and the great personal sadness this continued to bring Kieran was to remain imbedded in her like the rancid after taste of bitter indulgence.

The effort it took to make their marriage appear somewhat normal on the surface softly killed her a little more each day like a self imposed life sentence.

Many a day, when the children were at school and she had finished her work, Kieran would climb the hill at the back of the house and sit on a large flat rock that jutted out like a balcony, giving her an incredible panoramic view of the glen as far as the eye could see.

Feeling the caress of a gentle breeze she'd close her eyes and would once again be transported back to her doorstep where under the warmth of her blanket she'd feel the embrace of a familiar voice.

"You can survive little Kieran, don't give up hope."

She adored her children and knew without a doubt that if she had been in a stronger marriage she would have wanted even more but her two blessings were more than enough, especially when she felt so alone.

As the summer drew to an end and fall announced itself with crisp winds whipping up the now empty glen road, they met a couple who had just recently started work on the estate. Rob and Marie had moved in a half mile up the road and were similar to Danny and Kieran in many ways. They had two children, a girl and a boy around the same age as Thomas and Megan with their youngest being a couple of years older. They had also come from a city upbringing.

They were roughly Danny and Kieran's age and as they got to know each other found they had a lot more in common with only one major difference; they were happily married. It was obvious they loved each other.

The first year came to and end under a soft blanket of pure white snow. The children spent the holidays sledging over the hills with their rosy cheeks permanent proof of a healthy life, and Kieran became resigned to a life of normal and placed her own heart's desire on hold for eternity.

The winter was long and cold, the picture perfect beauty of the glen inducing frustration akin to that of Lochinlea but the suffocation of isolation was nowhere to be found.

The roads got bad on a few occasions but they never got snowed in for more than a couple of days at a time, and there was something about not being the only ones to suffer that made the biggest difference for Kieran at least.

Kieran assumed she'd feel safer under her snow-covered blanket of protection feeling sure the head keeper wouldn't venture out in such terrible conditions, but it seemed that nothing would deter him from dropping by unannounced.

She remained polite but made her avoidance of anything inappropriate obvious, hoping he'd eventually get tired of the silly games.

Nonetheless she felt blessed with the life they now had compared to what seemed like an eternity ago.

During that first season Kieran and Marie both got jobs beating and Marie had also arranged for her children to be dropped off at Maggie's house.

Beaters walk in line through the woods and across the fields and countryside of the estate and truth be told Kieran let more birds hide than she did flush out, but we'll keep that to ourselves.

It was quite a challenge for Kieran especially since she now juggled two jobs and the running of the house. Although at the end of each day she was completely exhausted, she also felt exhilarated with life. She truly felt she was making a difference and it felt good.

Her day would start out at the crack of dawn by setting the fire for when they arrived home that night. She'd get the children up and ready for school and when they were both either in the school car or dropped off at another friends house she and her husband would make their way down to the meeting place for the shoot to begin.

They worked a full day, climbing hills, crawling through woods and wading through shallow rivers and by the end of the day Kieran felt tired but alive.

If the army truck carrying the beaters happened to pass their house first, Kieran would jump out at the kennels and feed the dogs before walking back to the house to light the fire and start on their tea, (Scottish for dinner).

By the end of the day she was spent and only had enough energy left to put the children to bed with a short story or a song.

This busier life style occupied Kieran's mind to the fullest, freeing her from concentrating on her personal sadness.

During the first winter of such a grueling schedule however, Kieran became gravely ill with pneumonia.

It had been a long and hard winter and the shooting season was drawing to a close. A particularly nasty flu virus had been going around and Kieran had just remarked on how thankful she was at having missed catching it when both she and Danny began to feel unwell.

It began with a head cold and quickly developed into a hacking cough. They were both trying to last out until the end of the season which was only a couple of days away but by the very next day Danny gave in asking Kieran if she could fill in for him.

"Danny I'm sick too and it's freezing outside," she stressed comparing in her mind the difference between earning fifteen pounds and being sensible with her health.

She wanted to stay at home too but Danny stressed that the shoot would really be affected if they had two people short.

Against her natural instincts, Kieran went out on one of the coldest days of the year and let Danny stay at home.

She struggled through the day knowing full well she should be at home cozy and warm just like her husband. As the day drew to a close Rutledge decided to change plans and finish the day off on the hill. That meant Kieran would be out in the open with no cover to shield her from the biting cold north east wind that had blown all day long.

By this time she had a searing pain in her back but there was no use in drawing attention to herself so late in the day. She knew she'd be home soon enough and imagined sitting beside a warm fire with a hot cup o' tea.

As the trucks took them up to the point of the last drive the beaters lined up and stood for what seemed like hours. Something was holding up the line and the way Kieran was placed meant she was higher up than anyone else. She suffered as the full blast of icy cold wind cut through every layer of clothing. Gathering all her strength just to hold on until the end of the day and stomping her feet to keep the circulation going, she promised never to listen to Danny again against her better judgment.

Finally after the last drive ended Kieran got home and lit the fire for the children. Danny had stayed in bed all day and after checking on him to make sure he wasn't feeling worse, she started on the tea then went down to the kennels to feed the dogs.

Her cough was getting worse and so was the pain in her back but she knew it was useless to complain.

After feeding everyone and doing the dishes Kieran drifted off to sleepon the chair by the fire her face flushed with the effort of the day and thankful to be home in the warm.

When she awoke it was eight o'clock and almost time for the children to have a bath before bed. Kieran managed to get to her feet but winced with the pain in her back.

Tucking them in warm and cozy Kieran bent down and kissed two precious foreheads hoping Thomas and Megan wouldn't mind going without a story that night and they both smiled and said in unison, "Night, night Mum we hope you feel better soon."

She smiled at them with gratitude and with all that done she went to bed. Danny was feeling a little better with the rest and actually thanked her for going out.

The following morning Kieran got up feeling worse. She started to set the fire to warm the house for Tommy and Megan and began to cough uncontrollably, the stabbing pain in her back now unbearable. She coughed and coughed unable to catch her breath, falling down to her knees with the exertion and a fluidic, gurgling rattled deep in her chest.

Kieran had had bronchitis as a child and knew how bad that felt but this was different and she felt a pang of fear run through her as the pain increased.

She was weak and extremely feverish but didn't want to scare her children and finally able to catch her breath she got them up and ready and off to school.

Her husband was feeling well enough to go to work and told her to call for a doctor's appointment later that day for herself. He said he would take her when he got home and as the day wore on Kieran felt herself weaken.

She hardly moved from her chair all day and by the time Danny got home even he had to admit she looked terrible. The children were dropped off by the school car and after having a quick bite to eat they piled into the car to take Kieran down to the village.

When she eventually saw the doctor and he found out how long she had been ill he was astonished she'd neglected herself for that long. The flu had turned into pneumonia. Kieran was seriously ill but refused to go to the hospital.

The doctor made sure her husband knew how ill she was and gave him strict instructions on how to take care of her. He promised to come by the following day to make sure she was responding to the medicine.

Kieran didn't sleep well and tossed and turned all night long, but when dawn broke she had finally drifted off.

Danny slipped out of bed quietly to set the fire and get the children ready for school. He was concerned about his wife and evidently felt guilty about forcing her out to work so that he could stay in bed.

After making sure the living room was warm enough he made a bed for her on the sofa.

He was a good man when it came down to it, she thought to herself when she was alone later that day but why did it always take a catastrophe to happen before he showed any kind of compassion.?

The illness lasted two weeks and left Kieran feeling extremely weak but her resilience was strong. She bounced back quickly and before too long she was back to her old self again and ready to go back to work at the restaurant. In her absence however something had happened to change all of that.

She called to tell her boss she was feeling better and wanted to come back to work but he sounded a bit strange and asked her to come down to see him. What he was about to tell her was to shock Kieran beyond belief.

Seemingly things had been going missing from the restaurant and when she wasn't around another employee pointed the finger of blame at Kieran!

Since she wasn't there to defend herself and her boss had known the other woman for years he took her word for it and told Kieran she was fired.

Unable to grasp what she'd just been told Kieran left the restaurant in tears. She made her way to the nearest call box and called Danny telling him as she sobbed, what had just transpired.

"I'll be there in ten minutes, Kieran, OK?" her husband assured her. "Just take a deep breath and try to calm down."

"OK." Was all she could say and taking a seat on the bench outside the phone box Kieran tried to pull herself together.

Danny couldn't believe it either. He knew the other woman and guessed that it was she who was the guilty party. By that time Kieran couldn't have cared less about the job. However, she was furious that her good name was at stake.

The money would be missed but Kieran almost felt relieved. She decided to buy a local paper the following day to see if there was anything else available in the area.

There was an interesting ad that caught her eye immediately on the joint Royal Air force/ American Naval Base just outside the village. They were advertising for a part time kennel person to be responsible for the police guard dogs on the base.

"Wow!" Kieran thought as possibilities soared then in an instant she second guessed that very thought.

"Yeah but they're not going to hire a woman surely."

Something inside of her suddenly came to life as though preparing for a silent battle of wills.

But on the other hand there's nothing to lose by at least trying. Her mind went back and forth reasoning the pro's and con's of what this opportunity might entail.

The base itself, Kieran later found out, had been there for a number of years and security on the base was run by the Ministry of Defense Police. When she called later on that day to enquire about the position she was told it included a two week training course with the Royal Army Veterinary Corps in England.

It was second nature for Kieran to put her family's well being first so her natural reaction was to dismiss it immediately, but then she paused and decided to at least talk it over with Danny.

At first her husband was dead against the idea, but the more he argued against it the more Kieran found she was defending her choice.

She had done enough of what he had wanted throughout their life together, and for everyone else to that matter. Kieran surprised herself with this new found determination.

She went by to pick up an application form the following morning and brought it home to fill it out. She felt exhilarated at the prospect of actually doing something for herself. Feeling empowered by the decision to stand up for her right to have a future Kieran filled out the form and daydreamed of the prospect of actually going on an adventure of her own.

The thought of missing her family, especially her children, engulfed her in between intervals of quiet anticipation. As those mixed feelings ebbed and flowed throughout the morning she finished the application and waited for Danny to pick her up. He promised to come back home for lunch and drive her to the base having realized Kieran's mind was set whether he disagreed or not.

Within a week of handing in her application she was called into the R.A.F. office for an interview. She dressed professionally but not overly feminine. She needed to let them know she was serious about this undertaking.

The interview went extremely well and although it went against Kieran's nature to self promote; she was aware she would need to, especially as a young woman in a man's world. She did and it felt positive as she took a step towards claiming her life back.

Kieran loved being Tommy and Megan's mum and even Danny's wife but somewhere amidst all of those titles she had lost her own identity.

It only took the defense police two days to make a decision and they had deliberately kept Kieran as the last interview to see if she would make the impact they needed her to make as the only woman to apply for the position.

They were very impressed with her and told her so when they called her back to offer her the job.

Kieran was elated and after accepting the position she found out all the information for her schooling and set about making plans for her families care when she was away.

Danny came back to pick her up and congratulated her with a little reservation. He wasn't quite sure how to handle this new assertiveness his wife had suddenly acquired amazed at how much it unnerved him.

On the way home Kieran chatted excitedly of the preparations she'd need to make, including the possibility of his parents coming up to stay. Both of them doubted he'd be able to take care of work and children and therefore they'd need help if this was going to work.

The date for her trip was only two weeks away, so she had to start making phone calls immediately and as she placed her hand on the phone to call her mum about the good news, it rang making her jump.

Kieran stood quietly and listened to the voice on the other end with her mouth open with surprise and Danny waited for a moment to find out who was responsible for Kieran's reaction.

"I'm sorry, Mr. Williams, and I'm grateful for the apology, but I have another job now and start in a couple of weeks." Kieran stated looking over at Danny.

"No! I won't be able to work for you, also, but thank you for calling and I hope you find someone soon," she said triumphantly placing the receiver back in its place with a smile of gratitude that the truth had been revealed.

"Well I was going to ask who it was on the phone but I guess I know now" Danny said smiling back at her. "It really is your day, Kieran!"

Kieran ignored the last remark that seemed tinged with a little hint of something she couldn't quite make out and as she plopped down on the sofa, kicking off her shoes she sighed, "Isn't that a turn up for the books."

"He said that he caught Elaine red handed one night when he had asked her to lock up. He forgot his keys and went in the back way so as not to scare her and she was filling her bag with stuff from the shed. When he walked in on her she almost died," she told Danny trying hard not to revel in the glory of vindication.

"Anyway he was extremely apologetic and tried everything to get me back" Kieran explained actually feeling sorry for him and Elaine.

But she was happy to be out of it and was now looking forward to her trip.

Before Kieran could plan anything else she knew she'd need to call home.

'I wonder what they'll think' she thought as she picked up the receiver but this time there was little dread.

This time she felt confident she'd given them something to be proud of and dialing her parents number Kieran's heart quickened with excitement and perhaps still a little trepidation.

"Mum, its Kieran, I got the job," was all she could think to say and the surprised delight in her mum's voice made her jump.

"Oh my gosh! You got the job?" her mum replied.

Kieran could tell by her tone she was happy and proud!

And as she tried to fill her in on more details she heard her mum shout to her dad, the beautiful soft Welsh lilt bringing tears to Kieran's eyes.

"Allan, Kieran got the job with the police and she's going to England to train with the Royal Army!"

A sudden wave of love and deep appreciation for her parents swelled up in her and she suddenly felt released from her self-imposed prison of guilt.

They actually sounded proud of her.

She couldn't say much more as the emotion of the moment overtook her and after saying goodbye and promising to call when she got down there, Kieran sat down by the window and breathed a sigh of relief.

The deep sadness birthed by years of letting them down was now diluted from the concentrate that had once crushed her to a dull ache of wishing it had never been there at all.

The "if only's" of her journey were now being washed downstream and under the bridge that would hopefully allow her to cross over from a life of condemnation to a new life of celebration.

"You're not; nothing but a bloody idiot Kieran, you're somebody who's doing something with her life!"

How sad it still seemed that it would take credit of some kind to feel worthy. Why hadn't that ever come from just being Kieran?

A truth that spoke of an unconditional love without trade off's or tallies taken. Medals won and certificates of merit with blue ribbons and sashes adorned were all conditions of the love received from her parents, or so it seemed to Kieran.

She shook her head and exhaled a deep sigh as though to dispel the ghosts of bygone years and went through to put the kettle on.

Chapter 24
Making the Most

When the children came home Kieran shared her good news and watched their mixed reactions. Of course they were happy for her and proud that their mum was going to train with the Royal Army but she definitely noted their sadness when realizing she'd be gone for two weeks. To a child it probably sounded like an eternity but she tried to get them to focus on the positive aspect of it.

The job was perfect, given that she didn't have to start until nine a.m. and would finish at one o'clock. She'd be able to see them off in the morning and would then be home for them in the afternoon and she'd also have weekends off.

When the kids heard that they seemed a little happier but Kieran knew that leaving them was going to be tough.

The two weeks of preparation for the trip went by quickly and Kieran waved goodbye to Danny and the children as they stood on the platform of the deserted station. A mixture of emotions was evident in her that day but she stifled any signs of sadness and found a seat by a window.

The journey took about five hours and she read most of the way. When she arrived at the station she was excited but definitely a little nervous, as the butterflies began to flutter.

She was able to find a taxi to take her to the hotel and after arriving at what seemed like a nice, homely establishment, she booked in and was shown to her room.

Kieran wasn't sure whether she'd be sharing with anyone and if there actually would be other women at the school. Her question was answered when the kind lady at the front desk assured her she was the only woman they'd had a booking for. There were four other men on the second floor belonging to the same school.

"Oh well," she thought. She was used to being in the company of men when she worked during the shooting season and although she was quiet, she could also handle herself quite well so she wasn't too worried.

Throughout many seasons of her life Kieran had come to realize she felt more comfortable in the company of men. Most of them accepted her readily and rarely treated her as any kind of threat. Women were different.

After Kieran finished settling in and freshening up from the long train ride she realized it was almost time for dinner and went down stairs to find the dining room full.

There was a table close to the door with four men of different ages, a middle aged couple sat at a table by the window and there were only two other tables in the room to choose from. She chose the one closest to the group of men. She didn't want to appear stand-offish and assumed that they were the ones the lady from the front desk had spoken about.

As Kieran began her meal she could feel the eyes of the men on her, as though trying to make up their minds to speak. She looked over at the group and said a polite hello. A conversation ensued and the evening became quite pleasant as they slowly got to know one another.

The school was within walking distance of the hotel and after a good breakfast the following morning they left together. It only took about fifteen minutes to get there and they signed in with the guard at the gate who gave them directions to the training barracks.

Kieran's excitement began to rise but fell just as quickly when arriving at the barracks. They walked into the class which was filled with about twenty five men of all different ages. The younger ones were apparently in the army and as Kieran glanced over she quickly assessed that they might also be trouble.

They were already elbowing each other, making comments under their breath and giggling like little school boys, but she was ready for them.

She hadn't come this far to become the victim of sexual harassment and knew if she was going to make it in this world of men, she would have to prove herself as an equal and create healthy boundaries.

Great just the extra pressure I needed, she thought as she found a seat beside her little group and prepared to listen to what the sergeant had to say.

He introduced himself as Sergeant Brewster, the man in charge of training new recruits. He pointed out that the course was mandatory for anyone planning to work with guard dogs and it was expected that all recruits pass the stringent tests whether they are military trained or civilian.

"As you can see gentlemen," he said with authority. "We have a lady present and although she will clearly be treated like everyone else as far as course procedures, we also expect respect towards her gender.

"That means gentlemen, you will curb your language and be aware at all times that a lady is present, do I make myself clear?" he barked. And the group of little boys dressed in soldiers uniforms sat up straight in their seats.

There was no reply to the sergeants' demands.

"Well! Do I?" he barked once again.

"Yes, Sir," was the unanimous reply and as he turned he looked over at Kieran and gave her a wink.

Well at least there's one gentleman here she thought as she too sat up ready to listen.

He gave out a list of what they would be covering that day and Kieran took lots of notes. She wanted to start well and finish even better, refusing to allow anything learned to chance.

That morning was spent in the classroom and at mid-day they were released for lunch. As they made their way to the mess hall the aroma of something delicious wafted towards them as they approached. The food was surprisingly good to Kieran's amazement and she wolfed down everything on her plate.

The afternoon went by quickly and they folded for the day by four o'clock.

"Tomorrow morning you'll be meeting your dogs so make sure you're dressed for outdoor work," the sergeant informed as they were about to leave.

"These dogs are extremely intelligent and have a regular turnover of recruits every two weeks, so they will test each one of you," he added with an all knowing smile.

"Unless you show them very quickly, who's in charge, they will walk all over you, and, trust me, they are vicious, so pay attention to what you are told and follow orders and you will be fine," he added putting the fear of death into everyone in the room. "See you tomorrow, recruits, you are dismissed for the day," he said walking out the room to leave everyone to wonder what they had gotten themselves into.

Kieran enjoyed a nice dinner and was eager to call home before spending a little time with her new friends in the lounge.

The children were so excited to hear from their mum and it turned out to be an emotional conversation for all of them.

She spoke to Thomas first which annoyed Megan no end and Kieran could hear her protest in the background.

"He's always getting everything first. It's not fair!"

Kieran smiled as she imagined her baby girl standing with arms folded, chin pressed down, big hazel eyes looking up through her long bangs and her bottom lip sticking out.

"Hello darling," she said to her son desperately wanting a hug. "How was your day at school?"

Thomas went off on a tirade of who had done what to who and then he told her that Grandma and Grandpa had helped feed the dogs and clean the kennels and almost as an afterthought told her he missed her and asked when she was coming home.

"Oh, darling, this is only Mummies second day, and that means I have quite a few to get through before coming home," she hated to admit.

Tommy went quiet. "O.K. Mum, I love you" he concluded and handed the phone to Megan.

Being that far away from her babies was even harder than Kieran thought and as she said hello to her daughter she fought back tears.

"Hello, wee lamb," she managed to squeeze out before a lone tear trickled down her face. "Hello Mum" a tiny wee voice replied. "Where are you and when are you coming home?"

Kieran was really trying to hold her emotions together and she gulped passed the familiar lump forming in her throat.

"I'm at the hotel darling and I'm going to start training with the guard dogs tomorrow. Then it will soon be the weekend and I'm sure you'll do something nice with Nana and Grandpa."

There was a long moment of silence. "Sweetie; are you OK?" Kieran urged her baby girl to talk.

Megan answered in a whisper. "It's not the same without you Mummy."

"I'll be home just one more week after this weekend darlin' so hold on to that big girl smile for me and don't be sad."

"OK Mum, I'll try." Kieran's wee lamb replied and she felt a familiar twinge of guilt as her little girl's voice tugged at her heart.

Kieran said a tearful goodbye to Megan and then Danny came on the phone. By that time Kieran was crying openly but trying hard to pull herself together.

"They'll be OK Kieran," Danny said as he tried in his own way to make them all feel better. "They just miss you a lot, but it's probably good for us all to miss you. We might appreciate you more."

Eloquent words of love were never amongst Danny's strong points but he was trying and she appreciated the extra work he was putting in to help her do what she really wanted to do. Just before she hung up the phone he said, "I love you, Kieran."

It sounded for a moment as though he really meant it and Kieran gulped passed yet another lump. "I love you too, Danny," she replied but something inside had died and Kieran knew she was no longer being completely truthful.

Knowing she was too emotional to spend time with her new friends in the lounge Kieran popped her head around the door and begged forgiveness. "I'm sorry guys but I'm really exhausted so I'm calling it a night."

"That's OK, Kieran, see you in the morning." They shouted in unison.

Kieran wished life with Danny could have been like this from the beginning and not only during the unusual circumstances of life. The last year had felt more like the relationship she had hoped for, but their marriage had been tinged with a permanent stain of painful disillusionment. As much as she tried, Kieran felt unable to rekindle a flame of any kind. She had felt it once but the embers had burned to a white powdery cool, leaving behind evidence of a fire that was, but seemed to be no more.

Perhaps she just needed to try harder at understanding him, she pondered as she walked wearily upstairs to her room.

The second day was going to be a trial for all of them. The sergeant had assured Kieran that the dog they had chosen for her loved women so she shouldn't have any trouble with him. Before they were even introduced to their dogs they were given a lesson on how to check them and bring them to heel. It all looked quite silly as they hooked the choke chains they'd been given onto the wire mesh fence and the sergeant walked up and down making sure everyone had the hang of it.

Unfortunately for Kieran it soon became all too obvious she did not and by the end of that week her legs were covered in black and blue pressure bites.

Feeling a little humiliated Kieran finally shared her discomfort with the sergeant and he looked down at her bruised legs with shock.

"Do you mean, young lady," he said with admiration for this girl's strength of character, "You have gone the whole week suffering like that without saying a word?"

She was a bit unsure how to answer.

"Yes sir," she said apologetically hanging her head as though ashamed at her lack of judgment and ability.

"I was trying to get the hang of it myself and didn't want to give up," Kieran added her green eyes fighting back tears.

"Gentlemen, keep walking your dogs at heel until you make a full circle then about turn and go around the other way," he instructed the rest of the class.

"Come over here, Kieran" Sergeant Brewster said in a gentle voice.

He took her to the side of the field and asked her to show him how she was checking Radar. She did and the dog actually did it right being wise enough to do so in front of the sergeant.

"Ye' wee bissum!" she thought, chastising the dog in her mind.

The sergeant started to laugh out loud. "Radar, you old coot," he said looking down at the German shepherd who now looked as though butter wouldn't melt in his mouth." Why are you messing with this young lass?"

He took the lead from Kieran and demonstrated how to do it so as to make the dog understand who was in charge. Kieran went next and to her surprise it seemed to work.

She went to bed that night determined not to let this animal get the better of her and fell asleep dreaming of ferocious dogs chasing her through fields.

After a restless night Kieran got up bright and early the following day and felt strong; her inner voice telling her she could do this and all that was needed was a little more assertion.

As she fed Radar before taking him out to exercise, she bent down and whispered in the dog's ear through clenched teeth determined to get her point over. "You are going to do it right today and give me no hassle or I'll kick your behind from here to Timbuktu, do I make myself clear?"

The dog turned to look at Kieran as though he understood every word and as she clipped the lead onto his collar he readied himself for his normal routine.

Kieran knew he got aggressive towards the other dogs when they were leaving the kennels together and so she waited until most of them had passed by before stepping out.

A handler came around the corner with another dog just as she stepped outside and Radar lunged at the dog, barking and foaming at the mouth with excitement. Kieran held the lead tight in her right hand and jerked his head to the side. Radar let out a high pitched yelp, "Yowl!" and looked up at Kieran with a new found respect. The look in his big brown eyes told Kieran his abuse toward her was over and from now on he knew who was boss.

"Radar walk," she said with authority, and they caught up with the rest of the group and followed them into the exercise field.

The sergeant looked over at her and winked. "That's my girl," he thought to himself admiring the gutsy determination of this wee lass from Scotland.

After another long but exhilarating day Kieran spent a relaxing evening reviewing with her friends for a written test the following day.

They'd be getting the results back on Monday and had the weekend free so after an hour or so of study they decided to discuss plans.

Some wanted to go farther afield to look for a nice restaurant for dinner while someone else suggested a movie. Truth be told, Kieran wanted neither.

They were given a per dium for food and Kieran decided she'd rather scrimp on spending extravagantly, so she'd have extra money to take home.

The test over with, and the weekend upon them, Kieran's first instinct was to stay at the hotel. However, the others had a different plan and coaxed her into going with them.

They went to a restaurant/pub and she was surprised at how much fun she had, and when they got back to the hotel she thanked them for the invitation and went to call home.

Thomas and Megan sounded a little better and were now focused on marking the days off on the calendar, until their mum came home. Kieran laughed a little and cried a little and made them laugh when she told them about Radar and what she had to do to get him to behave. And after saying goodbye she went upstairs to bed and fell into a deep sleep.

Saturday was reserved for shopping, and she managed to pick a little something up for everyone without spending too much. She wrote some postcards for the children and posted them hoping they would get them in a few days and then decided to take a walk around town.

Sunday came and went with most of them staying in the hotel. It rained all day and before they knew it Monday was here and so were the results of the test.

All of them had passed, but Kieran received the second highest mark and was pleased as punch.

Now if only the rest of the week goes this well, she thought but then the sergeant explained what they'd be doing.

The first two days would be spent in the classroom learning about medical care, and then on Wednesday they would experience chase and release training.

This part of the course was the physical, hands-on, training that most of them dreaded and literally meant dressing up in protective clothing and being chased and attacked by one of the dogs.

If they survived Wednesday, Thursday would be the five mile cross country run with their dogs and then Friday would be certificate ceremony day.

They were all praying Friday would come without too much mishap!

Kieran was excited and scared stiff all at once and wasn't too worried about the chase and release. She was more concerned about the run.

She was never that great at running but she had been working at the beating so was relatively fit. Not knowing what was expected of them was the biggest fear and most of them felt the same trepidation Kieran did.

They had another test on Wednesday morning and the afternoon was spent in the field.

All the men were picked to go first and although her adrenaline was pumping at what seemed like an unusually fast rate and her natural reaction was to turn and run in the opposite direction, Kieran began to get a bit annoyed at being left until last. Just as she was thinking, "He better not leave me out just because I'm a girl," the sergeant called her name to get fitted into the suit.

It which was much bigger on her than anyone else and off she went running as fast as she could. A moment later she heard the handlers command and felt the pounding of the dog's feet on the grassy field coming up behind her at an alarming rate.

WHAM! The force of the attack pulled Kieran off her feet and for a split second she felt herself airborne. She didn't quite understand how she landed on two feet and was more than happy to find she was still in one piece. The pressure of the dog's jaws on her arm as he began to shake his head was alarming but the handler was quickly on the scene and gave the command to LEAVE! And thank the Lord he did. It all happened so quickly, it took her breath away but then she heard the other men cheer. Kieran was elated!

"That was incredible," she said to someone who evidently thought she was crazy and by the time they all got back to the hotel they were exhausted and collapsed in the lounge. They had enough energy left to chat excitedly about the day, and laughed at some of the funny things they had all endured, but they all felt glad it was over and geared themselves up for the next day.

When she got up the sun was just starting to rise and it looked as though it was going to be a beautiful day. As they walked up the road to the barracks her thoughts were confirmed by the unusually warm sun beating down, and she was glad she had decided on a lighter jacket.

They had been told to dress sensibly but without a heavy coat as they would be running cross country. As the sergeant gave them a detailed account of how to handle their dogs during the run she listened intently, not wishing to miss a thing.

They lined up and the sergeant made a comment on whether she would really need the rain jacket she had chosen to wear over her white cotton turtle neck and since the comment seemed to provoke quite a bit of laughter among the rest of the class, she chose wisely and decided to keep it on. Later on she would truly appreciate the wise choice she'd made.

He told them he would be in front and there would be four other team leaders, one on each side and two keeping up the rear for safety reasons.

If they felt any kind of unnatural discomfort they were to tell one of the leaders immediately and not try to be heroes. If they had any questions they needed to be asked now as they would not be stopping, unless for an emergency.

Everyone seemed to understand what was expected of them and as they marched down the lane leading to the field where they would start. Kieran's stomach was in knots with both excitement and anxiety. She took a deep breath and decided to relax and just enjoy herself.

They started to run and to begin with it was difficult to get into a steady rhythm with all the dogs barking, but then they, too, settled down and quickly assumed a pace that seemed to fit everyone apart from one man. He was in Kieran's group. Poor Doug was quite a bit overweight and a wee bit older, and he had been worrying about this part of the course.

Kieran and another member of their group fell back a little to try and encourage Doug as his breathing was already sounding labored. They were really concerned about him and were considering calling to one of the team leaders when suddenly the group slowed down and came to a stop.

They had come to a fence and had to lift their dogs over it one by one and so this gave Doug a chance to catch his breath. Kieran bent down and lifted Radar over then crossed over herself and waited for Doug and Jimmy. After everyone had cleared the fence they took off again and Doug felt much better having caught his second wind.

They had run across fields and up and down braes and then they even crossed a shallow but wide stream. Slippery moss-covered stepping stones were the only way across, and as the last of the group survived the crossing, they began to run along the embankment until the river disappeared over a stone slab that looked like the remains of an ancient wall.

There was a large drainage pipe in the middle of the wall and all of a sudden Kieran became unnerved. This didn't look good!

Where were they meant to go now? She thought to herself and her question was answered immediately as the sergeant pushed his dog into the pipe and followed after him on all fours.

"Where does the pipe lead?" she asked one of the soldiers but he just shrugged his shoulders and replied, "I don't know but we're going to find out soon."

Kieran was about tenth in line and just behind the soldier she had just spoken to who had just disappeared into the pipe and as she bent down to push Radar in she could see the soldier vanish out the other end.

Kieran prayed the jump wouldn't be too high!

Along they crawled as Kieran encouraged her dog and as they approached the end he stopped and she soon found out why. There was a sheer drop sure enough and it must have been at least fifteen feet right into the freezing river!

Oh! My gosh, she thought for a split second but not wanting to hold up the line she hugged Radar and pushed him out. As Kieran looked down making sure Radar was OK she heard the class cheer.

"Come on Kieran you can do it," they all shouted, so she took a deep breath and jumped down into the icy cold water of an English river in the middle February and as she surfaced, spluttering and coughing she also smiled. She had done it!

When she struggled up the muddy embankment on the other side she suddenly realized the reason for laughter before they left on the run.

Someone had protected her from the embarrassment of having to surface from cold water in a white cotton shirt.

"Thanks I owe you big time for this," she smiled to herself and shook her head at the guys who were laughing, aware that they'd been found out.

But it felt that they were laughing with her and not at her and she realized then they had accepted her on her terms.

Chapter 25
A New Adventure

Kieran was so grateful she had survived the day and couldn't wait to get back to the hotel for a long hot soak, and to call her family and share her adventure. After her bath and then dinner she was the first in line for the phone eager to hear her children's voices.

She told her story and could hear the astonished gasps as the tale unfolded. Her children sounded so proud of her and after being on the phone for half an hour she said her goodnights and went upstairs to bed.

Kieran slept like a log and woke up aching from head to foot. She struggled out of bed when a sudden flash of realization made her stop. The next day she was going home! They ate a hearty breakfast and told stories of the experience the day before, and as they walked to the barracks they realized they had formed friendships they would remember forever.

It had been an incredibly enriching experience for Kieran and when waiting for the sergeant to arrive with their results, she just took a moment to appreciate being given this opportunity.

Sergeant Brewster arrived just after nine o'clock and most of the recruits were nervous, shifting around in their seats or strumming fingers on their desks.

As he took his place in front of the class and looked at them with his usual stern countenance he suddenly broke into laughter.

Sergeant Brewster shook his and without more ado assured them that everyone had passed!

He said he was going to call them out in order of marks scored as he had some comments for each one of them and felt that this was the best way to do it.

He started with the lowest scores first and told Doug that the only reason he passed at all was his willingness to try hard at everything he was asked to do. However, he did have to promise to train more and work on his weaker points.

Doug was relieved! He was afraid he'd failed and would be sent home in shame. Anyway, one down another twenty five to go and the sergeant kept reading out names, giving a little piece of advice here and there.

With every name read out Kieran expected hers to be the next. She didn't dream she'd be among the top ten. As almost everyone in the class had already been called Kieran's heart began to beat faster.

Maybe I was so bad he's going to leave me until last and dismiss the class, she thought to herself and then it came down to only two names; Kieran and a young soldier.

"Well as you can see we're down to the last two recruits," the sergeant said with a mischievous smile, aware he was playing with them a little. "And I have to say this is one of the first times we have had a lady in the top two. Mrs. Peterson only missed top marks because her boots were too big!" Everyone in the class laughed. Kieran's face went a deep shade of scarlet.

He continued to explain that she had received top marks in everything apart from the personal obedience one on one with her dog. She dropped two points there because she couldn't turn sharply enough with boots that were too big for her and she didn't want to risk standing on her dog's feet.

Everybody said "Awe" in unison to the comment and clapped in support of their wee Scots lass from Edinburgh.

Kieran was "fair chuffed" as they say back home in Scotland and still couldn't believe what she'd just been told. She looked down at her certificate and felt tears brim her green eyes, thankful she'd been given the strength to get through this incredible experience.

They were dismissed early and she raced back to the hotel to tell her family of her success but couldn't get a hold of her husband.

It was still early up north and she knew that her in-laws had to leave that day also so she called her mum and dad and was in tears by the end of the phone call. Her mum sounded proud enough to burst and once again the conversation helped Kieran come to terms with her private guilt.

She desperately wanted her parent's approval and to suddenly feel she had finally given them something to be proud of was in itself a victory.

Kieran couldn't wait to get to the station to catch the next available train back home. When she finally boarded the train Kieran was happy to find a window seat. She could watch the countryside go by and with the clickety clack of the wheels on the rails and the rhythmic motion of the train as it sped on to its destination, Kieran soon drifted off into a contented sleep. She dreamed of being back home with her family and sharing with them tales of her incredible adventure.

The train pulled into Waverly station in Edinburgh and Kieran desperately wanted to get off and visit her parents. But her own family was more important now and so she just sat and bathed in the memories of her childhood. The train and the station invoked those memories and when Kieran fell back to sleep they became vivid. She loved the smells and sounds of the train stations, but there was something special about Waverly.

She arrived in Montrose at around five o'clock and called home, surprising Danny.

Kieran heard him call to the children, "Hey, Mum's in Montrose, dae ye' want to go and pick her up?"

Lots of cheering and whoopin' was heard in the background and Kieran smiled. "Sounds like some wee ones are happy I'm home!" she remarked and Danny replied,

"Me too, Kieran, we've all missed you."

Literally before Kieran had much time to get her bags across the bridge to the other side of the track and settled in the waiting room she heard the familiar peep of a car horn and stood up to look out of the waiting room window. She saw her children waving frantically from the car with big eyes and smiles to match and she felt glad to be home.

Tommy and Megan rushed at their mum almost bowling her over and she held on to them with tears in her eyes.

"OK you two, let me have a hug," Danny said pretending to push through the masses. He had gained a new understanding of how much attention they both needed, even with help from his mother and he was glad to see his wife back home.

During the journey back home she was told many stories of things that had happened while she was away and she listened attentively to both versions. Kieran was just happy to just listen.

"Well it sounds as though you both had a good time while Mummy was away," she stated pretending to be a tad petulant, and they both laughed and assured her they missed her a lot and didn't want her to go away again.

Danny brought her up to date with the news on the estate and although she was happy to be home and wouldn't wish to be anywhere else, Kieran knew she had undergone a change. A change that had empowered her!

She now felt confident of having a voice and a value within this marriage and knew with absolute certainty she would never be undermined again.

Daylight filtered through the billowing lace curtains giving way to the gentle fall breeze that wafted softly through the open window in Shy's room.

The perfumed fragrance from the flower garden below was sheer heaven to wake up to and just as she stretched, displacing a little ball of fluff from her comfy spot, she suddenly realized it must be later than her normal time for rising.

As she reached over to check the clock, Shy had a sudden flash back of her vivid dream during the night which seemed of epic proportion.

She sat up in bed and reaching over to pet Kylie who was now wide awake she had to ask herself if it had been a dream or had she actually reached that far in the story.

"Well no, I'm positive I just got up to Kieran's wedding." she mumbled as she slid out of bed and walking over to the open window she looked out at the glorious day that awaited them. An air of excitement gripped her as she remembered Paul and Greg would be home today. Pulling on her robe she whispered, "Come on bonnie wee lass, let's get you outside," and an excited wee dog who loved her mistress so, did a dance of delight round and around.

The girls were still asleep so Shy put the coffee on and let Kylie back in from her time in the garden.

She loved this time of day.

As she pottered around her kitchen putting together the things she'd need to start breakfast, Shy's heart skipped a beat, reflecting on the joy she felt inside.

She couldn't thank God enough for all He had done throughout her life's journey. The abundant blessings He continued to shower down each and every day since kept her in a constant state of awe and gratefulness.

She took some homemade biscuits from the fridge and popped them in the oven and after pouring herself a cup of coffee she grabbed her bible and sat down in her favorite spot in the family room.

The air was a little too crisp to sit out, but the beautiful bay windows granted her the feel of actually being outside, sitting amongst the gladioli and snap dragons.

Shy found the place she left off from and read out loud her favorite verse; Rom 8:28

"All things come together for the good for those who love the Lord and are called according to His purpose."

How prevalent that verse had been all through her life even before she became familiar with it, and what a living testament her life was to the words of truth.

Just as she was about to read on she heard a familiar voice in the doorway. "Good morning, Mom," Erin sighed wrapping her robe around her feeling a little chilled with the morning air.

"Good morning, beautiful," Shy replied then added, "There's coffee made."

"I know! What do you think woke me up?" Erin answered as she went to fill her mug and when she came back she sat down on her favorite chair and curled her legs underneath.

"Did ye' sleep well darlin'?" Shy asked taking a sip of her second favorite brew.

"Mmm yes! I always forget how comfy my old bed is until I'm right back in it, and then the only trouble is I don't want to get up!"

They both laughed and turned their heads towards the doorway to see Kylie jump up and down like a circus dog celebrating the arrival of her favorite playmate.

"Well I guess you smelled the biscuits, honey bunch," Shy made the comment to a sleepy head that looked as though she got up completely against her will.

"Yes, I did and I tried to go back to sleep but my rumbling tummy wouldn't let me!"

"Someone's going through a growth spurt I think."

Lyric came over to hug her mom and grandma and disappeared into the kitchen.

Shy followed.

"Mom, do you need a hand with breakfast?" Erin asked both hands wrapped around the warm mug.

"Oh you're fine, darlin', I just need to put the bacon on, so it won't be long." And just before leaving the room she added, "Well maybe you could set the table when you're done with your coffee."

She loved when her girls were home.

As Shy pottered around the kitchen multitasking, Lyric asked about the story.

"I was thinking about Kieran when I woke up Grandma."

"And what were ye' thinkin'?" Shy asked placing the bacon in the pan.

"Well does her life get better or much worse after the wedding?"

Shy almost choked with surprise, marveling at how straight to the point thirteen year olds can be.

"Oh darlin', Kieran's life was like many people's; a real mixed bag of up's and down's, but she definitely went through some extremely trying periods."

Lyric jumped up on the counter top forcing a smile to break out on Shy's face.

"Ye' know ye're uncle used to talk to me when I was cooking, sitting on the counter top just like you. And we'd have long conversations about his day at school."

"My, my, would ye' believe!" Shy shook her head from side to side musing at the resemblance of two children cultures and decades apart. "I guess some things just never change."

"Did she stay married Grandma?"

Shy was a little taken aback once again by the candor of Lyric's question.

"Now what made ye' think she might not stay married sweetheart?"

"Well it didn't start off too well from the very first day, and I couldn't help but think it was sort of doomed from the beginning."

"Well there's no getting' anything by you, is there now?"

And Lyric laughed at Shy's remark.

"Well come on now Grandma it doesn't really leave a lot to the imagination does it!"

"If Danny could have done that to Kieran on their wedding day for goodness sake, there's no telling what else he had in store for her!"

Shy threw her head back and laughed out loud at her granddaughter's matter-of-fact way of sharing such a poignant truth, but then she became serious.

"Lyric, you're absolutely right! But ye' know, pet, I really don't think you need to be hearin' all the details of her misery."

Shy looked down and poked at the bacon sizzling in the pan.

"Suffice to say they had many ups and downs and some of them were definitely due to Danny's negligence. After fifteen long years of trying to make it work Kieran felt she was still struggling to keep the marriage from failing."

"I was kinda' thinking it might not last," Lyric stated with a shrug of her shoulders.

"Well, we haven't quite arrived at that place yet, but during those fifteen years of good times and bad, there were also many wonderful memories made. Kieran and Danny were blessed with two beautiful children; a boy named Thomas and a girl named Megan who Kieran doted on. They were her life!"

Erin walked in wondering what all the banter was about.

"You have an extremely astute young lady there, I hope ye' know," Shy remarked with a smile that spoke volumes of how proud she was of both girls, but she wanted to keep the story for Lyric and knew that some time later that day she might share more details of the tried and tested marriage.

Carefully getting off the subject for the time being she asked if anyone had any suggestions for the day and as she bent down to retrieve a tray full of fluffy golden biscuits from the oven, the girls thoughts were brought back to their stomachs.

"They smell delicious!" They both said in unison.

As they sat down and blessed the food, giving a prayer of thanks and safe journey for Paul and Greg, they chatted about their day and enjoyed a hearty home cooked breakfast.

The girls came to a joint decision. They wanted to take Shy to lunch in Newtown.

"We know as soon as the men get back you won't sit down for a moment so this is our treat," Erin stated as though she would consider no argument.

"Oh but!" Shy tried to tell them she had much preparation to make for the men coming home but the girls wouldn't take no for an answer.

"Well OK. But we can't be out too long now."

She had been shopping for a while and knew she had ample provisions to carry them well through the holiday and some, but ye' could never be too careful when it came tae' lookin' after the men folk!

They cleared away the dishes and Shy decided to forego her walk that morning.

She was too excited about her sweetheart coming home and was all a dither!

As she stood in the kitchen looking around, wondering what to do next without coming to any one conclusion Shy decided to go upstairs and get ready for the day.

She had just finished dressing when there came a gentle knock at the door with a soft voice accompanying it, "Grandma it's me, Lyric, can I come in?"

"Come on in, honeybunch!" Shy replied sitting down to brush her snow white hair.

Lyric sat down on the ottoman next to Shy's dresser.

"I was wondering, Grandma, since we're not going out for a couple of hours and there's nothing much else to do, could we continue with the story?"

And without waiting for a reply she went on, "I just can't get Kieran out of my head!"

"It's kind of like when you're reading a really good book and you just don't want to put it down but life keeps getting in the way!"

Shy laughed at the remark.

"Oh I know, honey, and it seems every time we leave the story there's a cliffhanger of some sorts."

"Exactly, Grandma, and of course I'm dying to see Dad and Grandpa, but I'm concerned we won't have much time for the story 'cause they'll be home early."

Lyric clamped a hand across her own mouth!

"Gosh I didn't mean that to sound the way it came out!"

"Its OK, darlin', I know what ye' mean, but don't you worry! Grandpa will need a bit of attention but he hates being fussed over so he'll probably be quite happy to leave us to our own devices."

Shy gave her grandbaby a wink and asked where she wanted to sit.

"Can we go back up to the attic?"

"Well I tell ye' what, you go and tell ye're mum where we'll be, and I'll be up there in two shakes of a lambs tail!"

"Awe thanks Grandma," Lyric cried throwing herself at Shy and giving her a great big hug.

That girl's definitely a hugger! Shy thought as Lyric disappeared out the door.

Erin was grateful for the extra time to get ready as her usual race in the mornings was always a bone of contention in their home, no matter how much preparation they made the night before.

She secretly longed for a bigger apartment or even a house but wouldn't think to share that with Greg.

New York was expensive and their little apartment had lots of charm and the more Erin thought the guiltier she felt.

Well, perhaps even one more bathroom would be a dream come true; but all in good time.

Erin was thankful she was happy and blessed with such a loving husband and quirky daughter who brought a smile to everyone's day.

"OK, darling, but don't you go tiring Grandma out too much now, and we're leaving at 12:00 so take your watch upstairs."

"OK, Mum," was the reply as the whirlwind left behind a wake of flurrying note paper that was once a neat pile on the dresser.

Shy made herself comfortable on her rocker as Lyric arrived out of breath after taking the stairs two by two.

"Well are ye' ready lass?"

"You bet Grandma!"

Lyric sat down on her makeshift sofa made of old cushions.

"Well I'm going to condense the story a wee bit darlin' so we can get more in, OK?"

"Sure, but don't leave anything out you know I'll want to know about."

"Well I'll try not to," Shy replied looking up at the rafters as her thoughts went back through the years to a wee lass and her journey.

Kieran struggled for years to keep the marriage alive but many events troubled her badly throughout their life together.

They left Edinburgh behind, when their son Thomas was only five months old, to spend the rest of their married life in the Highlands of Scotland. There, Kieran would be put through tests of endurance that most women would never have tolerated.

"What like Grandma?" Lyric asked insisting on more details.

"Well, as you realized very early on darlin' Kieran's husband was a selfish man at times.

"He took her up to the Highlands because he wanted a change of job and lifestyle., Although she agreed to live in the country, when they began their new life together, Danny changed even more, leaving Kieran alone whilst he went out with friends time and time again.

"At one point he left her in a freezing cold house, when she was pregnant with their second child, with no firewood to burn and she had to find some herself. She waded through a foot of snow with a wheelbarrow and her then four-year-old son and could have lost the baby with the extreme exertion!"

Lyric took a sharp intake of breath in shock. "Oh! My gosh how awful!"

"Well sweetie that was her life from the very beginning. He was self centered to the extreme, not all the time but enough to make Kieran so miserable that after the birth of their second child and surviving the storm of the century, she eventually had a mild breakdown, and had to spend a few weeks in hospital to recuperate from the terrible loneliness and isolation."

Lyric sat crossed legged with mouth aghast!

"But why was he like that, Grandma, and why did he get married if he didn't want to be with Kieran?"

"That's a very good question, lass, and one Kieran searched her soul for, for many years."

Shy looked pensive.

"There's just no tellin' some folk, sweetheart! He wanted to have Kieran and a family, but he also wanted freedom to enjoy his own life."

Danny had what most men would have given their life for yet he squandered it."

Shy sat back in the rocker and folded her hands one on top of the other.

"Instead of celebrating what he had in Kieran and the children, he took it all for granted and did so for years until Kieran could take no more."

"What did she do Grandma?" Lyric asked saddened deeply by Danny's folly.

"Well in the beginning she made a stand and after they moved to what could have been a permanent home for their little family, she found a job on a joint American Navy/Royal Air Force base.

"She became a kennel person on the base and had to go through rigorous training with the Royal Army Vetinary Corps to be able to handle the guard dogs."

"Wow! Grandma, she was tough!" Lyric exclaimed awed by Kieran's tenacity.

"Yes you could say that, honey," Shy smiled at the thought of tough little Kieran with her guard dogs.

"And her strong character is probably what helped her to keep going for as long as she did in that marriage, but after meeting a girl whose influence began to turn Kieran's head towards another possible alternative to her dilemma, her resolve to stay in the marriage began to weaken."

"What do you mean by another alternative Grandma?"

"Well, darlin', by that time Kieran was exhausted with trying to make the marriage work. In fact she truly felt there was no longer any hope for it to survive. Many years before she had resolved herself to the fact she would stay married for the children's sake, but when this friend came along, Kieran began to listen to advice to the contrary."

"You mean the opposite of what she'd believed all along?" Lyric asked her brows frowning with concern.

"That's right, pet. The friend was divorced and began to share with Kieran the possibility of her actually being happier without the bonds of married life.

Kieran was so disillusioned by that point she listened and began to dream. She went back and forth in her thoughts for months and months wondering if she could indeed be happier not married to Danny.

She could live on her own with the children and they would all get used to the new way of life surely? In fact the children might actually be happier to see their mum happy.

Kieran struggled to convince herself that this just might be a solution to her misery but her mother's heart wrestled with the truth. She knew the children would be devastated if divorce became an issue, however perhaps that was only half of the truth."

"What was the other half?" Lyric asked totally engrossed in the buildup of events.

"Well, one day after they moved yet again Megan came home from school and was helping her mum wash the dishes. Out of the blue the normally quiet wee soul said, 'Mum if you and Dad ever got divorced I would want to stay with you 'cause you do the lookin' after.'

"Kieran almost dropped the plate she was holding she was so shocked but regaining her composure she asked Megan why she had mentioned something like that. Megan just shrugged her shoulders and said, 'I don't know, I was just thinkin.'

"Kieran quickly became concerned the children were now being affected by the atmosphere in their home and felt desperate, not knowing which way to turn."

"I have a really bad feeling that something horrible is about to happen," Lyric stated as she fidgeted around on the cushions.

"Well there are quite a few rollercoaster events ahead darling."

"But if the negative things in our lives are not removed or atleast dealt with the true purpose of what God has in store for us can't be revealed, even when we don't yet recognize Him."

Shy shifted back in her chair as though reflecting on what to say next when she suddenly noticed the time.

"Oh my goodness look at the time, sweetie! Didn't your mom say we'd be leaving at 12:00 noon?"

"Oh! Yes she did." Lyric admitted a little disappointed the story was being cut short.

"Sweetheart, we'll make time over the next few days to finish the story, I promise?" Lyric nodded as she helped Shy up from the rocker.

"I know Grandma."

The two walked slowly down the narrow steps suddenly excited about going to lunch and the thought that Greg and Paul would be home soon.

The men left at the crack of dawn or even before and would hopefully be home around seven that evening.

Erin drove them to the restaurant that served a mixture of European and Asian food and everyone seemed happy with the choice.

Lyric loved Chinese food and so did Shy but she had to be careful about MSG. She was highly allergic to "that poison" as she called it and would swell up almost immediately if she ate it by mistake.

They all three enjoyed the food and as what seemed 'the norm' that day the time flew by. It was only two days till Thanksgiving and the girls were happy Paul and Greg would be home in a few hours.

Erin had missed her husband a lot and Lyric was eager to find out what the men had been doing down south, including all the details!

She was definitely a detail girl and never happy until all subjects had been covered. Her dad was a quiet man and not one to draw attention to work he'd done for others but he was a nurturer by nature, also, and encouraged his little girl's curiosity to the fullest.

"I've really missed Dad this time," Lyric said softly as they rose from the table.

"Me too!" Erin added as she slung an arm around her daughter's shoulder and gave her a hug. All three walked out the restaurant arm in arm and on the drive home they chatted excitedly about Thanksgiving and Christmas.

"Is Apryl going to at least make it home for Christmas Mum?" Erin asked hoping her sister wasn't going to miss out on two family get-togethers.

"I hope so! But if she tries to bow out again I'll be the first one out to Wyoming to fetch her home," Shy stated with a definitive tone of conviction.

The girls laughed knowing full well Shy meant what she said.

She had defrosted a pot roast for dinner knowing the boys would be starving when they arrived home.

After speaking to Paul first thing that morning and feeling that he sounded fine and in light spirits the air of concern that had hovered over her in the last 24hrs had finally dispersed. Shy knew Paul hated her to worry about him, especially when he was off on one of his errands of mercy.

"There's no point in me being led to do Our Lord's work if I have to be concerned about you worrying about me, Shy, so stop it, please!"

He had only said that once to her and she felt a little ashamed that it had come across as though she wasn't putting her full trust in God to watch over him.

"I'm sorry, sweetheart, I promise not to harp on at you anymore." "I do put all my trust in Papa to look after you, ye' know," she added knowing Paul could trust her word.

They were a good fit for each other and had been given the blessing of an almost perfectly balanced relationship. Every quirky side of one personality complemented the calmer side of the other. As the two were getting to know each other before they married, the girls often giggled at how they interacted with each other.

When they got home Shy got stuck into preparing the evening meal and as she reached for flour, confectioners' sugar and chocolate Lyric's mouth began to water.

"Grandma! Are you making chocolate éclairs?"

Shy smiled knowing full well everyone in the house had a sweet tooth, especially for home made éclairs.

"Oh I thought I'd give the boys a wee treat since they've been working so hard."

"But after Thanksgiving Grandpa and I are going to be cutting down a lot!"

Lyric smirked knowing full well she'd heard that before.

"And I mean it this time!" Shy added.

"Grandma I really do think you have eyes in the back of your head!" Lyric stated shaking her head and wondering how her grandma and mom did that.

"Oh it's just a Mom thing honey and just another extra blessing from Papa!"

It had turned out a pretty day, and Lyric was feeling a little bored staying inside.

She decided to take Kylie out into the garden and grabbed one of her balls.

"Come on, girl, let's play!"

As the two bundles of energy disappeared into the garden Erin walked into the kitchen.

"Greg just called, Mum. They've been making really good time and should be home around five o'clock."

She leaned back against the counter top and grabbed a handful of pistachios from a bowl Shy kept in the kitchen.

"Well that means I have a couple of hours left to get everything done; that sounds perfect!"

"Can I do anything?" Erin asked knowing what the answer would be.

"Darlin', you go and relax in the garden and stop fussing, this is your break!"

Erin reached over and gave her mum a kiss on the cheek. "OK, I'm going."

The girls relaxed and Shy pottered and two hours sped by.

The crunch of a car's wheels on the gravel in the driveway was the first sign the boys were home and Kylie ran around the corner of the house barking with excitement.

All three girls piled outside to welcome their men home.

Paul was moving a little slower than normal for him, but he didn't look gravely ill, thank the Lord!

And Greg had lost a bit weight. But the women looked at each with an affirming nod that neither of them would nag. They'd just be thankful the two of them were home safe.

By the end of the evening everyone was caught up with the news and information on what the doctors had said.

They all enjoyed dinner and Paul remarked that nothing was gonna' keep him from having a chocolate éclair! Greg and Lyric finished off what was left on the plate so that grandpa couldn't over indulge and Shy smiled at them both with silent gratitude.

Although Greg was tired from driving, he offered to clear up the dishes with Erin so they could have a little alone time and Shy, Paul and Lyric retired to the family room where Shy had lit a fire.

It was that time of year where, although it could be nice during the day, a definite chill would tinge the evening air. A fire in the hearth made everyone look forward to the winter months. Curling up beside the fire with hot chocolate and a good book was a mutual treat.

"My, my, it's good to be home, sweetie pie!" Paul remarked as he sat down on the sofa beside his beautiful bride. He called her that often and it made Shy giggle like a school girl.

"Och! Away with ye' laddie!" She would say attempting to chastise, but she loved it!

"Grandpa, tell me what you and Daddy did down there," Lyric asked her eyes big with anticipation.

Paul went on to describe, in as much detail as his energy level would allow, what they had done and who they'd helped without giving themselves any praise whatsoever and Lyric listened in awe.

She knew she wanted to do missionary work when she was old enough and just soaked in the richness of her grandpa's story.

But Paul kept it as short as possible as humble as he was.

"Well but enough about me, what have you three been up to while the cats have been away?"

"Well, Grandpa, we mice have been having tons of fun and this one in particular has been enjoying her grandma tell her a story about a wee Scottish girl named Kieran!"

"Really!" Paul said giving Shy a quick sideways glance.

"And how did you two get around to that story?" He asked Lyric eager to hear why Shy had decided to tell her that particular story at this time.

"Well you know how I always love Grandma's stories from back home in Scotland?"

"Uh, huh," he answered with a nod.

"Well we went up to the attic on a dark and stormy day with the wind howling and the rain battering down against the roof and...."

"My goodness it sounds like the build up to a suspense thriller already!" And all three laughed.

"And I spotted an old chest hidden in the corner covered in dust and cobwebs!"

"Ooo! It's getting eerie!"

"Oh, Grandpa, stop it and be serious for a minute!" Lyric frowned as Paul feigned a deadly serious look.

"OK honey I'm sorry."

"Well anyway as I was saying. We opened the chest and it was full of stuff from this little girl's life and so Grandma began to tell me her story. However, I've got a distinct feeling there's more to this story than meets the eye!" The two adults looked at each other and laughed.

"Oh Ye' do now well pray tell?" Shy asked.

"Well we've covered a lot of her childhood and now she's all grown up and not really doing so well but…" And Lyric looked up as though in deep thought, "I've got a feeling there's more that Grandma's not telling me!"

Shy smiled and looked down at her folded hands.

"Yes, but we came to an agreement that she would be patient and trust me and in all good time the mystery might be revealed."

Lyric got off the subject quickly knowing she'd been found out and came to snuggle in with her grandpa. "I'm having lots of fun, but I did miss you and Daddy."

The three enjoyed each other's company amidst the glow of the cozy fire and it felt good to be together.

"It must have been a terrible shock for you, honey, when Paul collapsed?" Erin asked knowing how close the two men are.

"Yeah, well it was kind of, but the ambulance was there in a few minutes and as soon as he was on his way to the hospital I relaxed," Greg shared.

"It'll take much more than that to keep that old dog down!" And Erin smiled giving her husband a hug around his waist.

"Munchkin sounds as though she's been enjoying herself," Greg reflected thankful to be home to the family he loved.

"Mm! She is, and Mum's telling her a special story about a wee Scottish girl!"

Greg's head turned to acknowledge what he'd just heard.

"You know, my mum's special story that she was waiting to tell Lyric."

"Well your mum's a smart woman and I think we both trust her enough to know best."

"I knew you'd say that."

And they chatted away until all the dishes were done and then joined the rest of the family.

Everyone had gone quiet but in a place of perfect peace and it wasn't long before Paul called it a night.

"Me too guys!" Greg agreed and after letting Kylie out they turned off the lights and retired to their rooms.

Just before Lyric closed her bedroom door Shy slipped in to give her a hug.

"We'll find some time for the story tomorrow sweetheart, I promise."

"OK Grandma, I love you!"

"Love you too darlin' goodnight."

Shy and Paul talked for a few minutes more and she asked him to promise her one thing.

"I'm not going to nag but I love you Paul. Ye're not going to ignore this now, are ye'?"

Before slipping under the covers Paul took his brides hand.

"Darling; do you honestly think I'm going to ignore my Papa when I know full well He was giving me a little warning of what might lie ahead?"

"I've already called the best cardiologist in the area and I have an appointment tomorrow. How does that suit you?" He asked smug with his own common sense for once.

"That's what I'm talkin' about," Shy replied and gave him a kiss.

She didn't want to tell Paul about the vivid dreams she'd been having ever since beginning the story. She didn't want to worry him even more.

Before falling asleep Shy prayed that God would place a hedge of protection around her subconscious so she wouldn't dream and disturb her husband.

Try as she might Shy couldn't fall off to sleep.

She'd struggled for days with the question of when and how to share the most difficult part of the story with Lyric.

As troubled thoughts bounced back and forth in her mind Shy fought against the return of a familiar spirit, that of shame.

How would her dear sweet grandbaby take the news that Kieran was by no means perfect and now on the verge of committing one of the greatest sins!

Shy's heart broke for the young woman that had been all those years ago but just as tears of a painful past were about to spill over yet again onto a soft down pillow, Shy gathered her strength and prayed for her joy to return.

"God help me through this once again. Help me translate the hurts and trials of Kieran's life into a walk to remember for our little Lyric.

"Help me be a good steward of your mercy and grace and bless me with the perfect words to teach and nurture and help her to understand the difference between a life spent with or without you.

"Thank you Papa for the Blessing of Redemption!"

Shy cuddled into her beloved's side and drifted once again into the familiar but this time feeling completely safe.

After a restful night, Shy opened her eyes to the dawn of Paul's first day home and as she listened to natures' chorus just outside her window on this crisp fall morning she rolled over and gave her husband a hug.

She loved her times alone just to be with Papa, but was always happy when her beloved came home and nuzzling into his arm she watched as his eye lids flickered, his soft breath evidence of a peaceful sleep.

It looked as though he had a restful night she thought to herself and then it suddenly dawned on her! I didn't dream last night!

Her prayer had been answered!

Reluctant to waken him, Shy rolled out of bed quietly and put on her robe.

The temperature had definitely gone down overnight and even Kylie was a little reticent to face the morning chill.

"Go on then, lass. Ye'll need to go out sooner or later!" Shy coaxed gently thankful she wasn't a pooch.

Making the coffee was one of her favorite things to do in the morning, the enticing aroma of the percolating brew being the best alarm clock in the world!

The second was thick slices of bacon sizzling in the pan, but Shy loved her quiet time and so breakfast underway she grabbed her bible and headed for the family room.

Shy threw one of the cozy throws over her legs and found her place with the book mark Apryl had given her many years before. As she tried to read the nagging thought of the last few days suddenly gripped her.

Closing her eyes to calm her senses Shy breathed in the knowledge that her God was there. He never left she reminded herself and with Blessed Assurance Shy suddenly felt at peace.

"How silly I still can be after all these years!" she mused scolding herself for falling into the bait time and time again. "Ye'd think I would've learned after all this time, Papa?"

Sensing in her spirit that this was the day she'd be sharing with Lyric evidence of how Kieran had survived the most deeply painful wound of her life so far, Shy pondered on how her granddaughter was going to react to Kieran's plight.

She was taken aback by how this part of the story was actually affecting her and as she sipped her coffee and gazed out at her floral sanctuary, a lone tear trickled down Shy's face.

"She'll be OK!" the voice of comfort caressed the older woman's broken heart.

"She's my daughter!"

Waking up to the aroma of Shy's homemade biscuits and fresh brewed coffee wafting upstairs, tantalizing his taste buds Paul turned over and swung his legs out of bed. "I must have been a really good boy to have deserved such blessings!" He shared with His Papa.

Kylie had sensed the movement upstairs and ran to greet her daddy.

All of a sudden the whole house was awake, and so the day began with excited good mornings and chatter about what the day would hold.

Breakfast was delicious but Paul felt the need to scold his wife.

"Sweetheart, you can't keep feeding me like this and expect me to lose a few pounds, now can you?"

Everyone laughed but agreed with the sentiment and Shy piped up with only one request.

"Alright I can take a hint, but come on now, it's Thanksgiving! Ye'll all have to start the health commitment on Friday OK?"

Paul made sure everyone knew that Erin and Greg were taking him to the doctor. Then they'd probably have lunch out somewhere. "So," and he looked over at Lyric, "You, young lady, and Grandma will have most of the day to do whatever you want. How's that?"

"Well that's great, I guess." Lyric replied and looking at Shy she asked, "Is that OK with you Grandma?"

"You bet, ma' bonnie lass!" Shy replied feeling her husband was in cahoots with God Himself and just before he left the table he looked over at Shy and winked.

Thankful they'd all been given grace over indulgence for one more day they dispersed to their rooms to get ready for the day.

Paul, Erin and Greg left around nine and Shy and Lyric decided to take Kylie out for a long walk before they began the story. They realized the opportunity they'd been given to spend lots of time together and so were determined to make the most of it.

It was another beautiful day with the sun shining brightly through the canopy of brilliant colors and as the two walked, they discussed what Lyric had benefited from the story so far.

"Well, I think overall, Grandma, when I hear stories about anyone who's going through tough times, it makes me thankful for what I have in my life. But with Kieran I've found it harder to relate personally with her. I've received everything she seemed to have done without and longed for as a child."

"Do you mean the kind of relationship you've had with your parents?" Shy asked.

"Yes and you and Grandpa of course but even more important than all of that, I've known God!"

A broad smile broke out across Shy's face as she looked at Lyric and nodded as though in complete agreement with a poignant truth.

"That's right darlin'."

And they walked for only a few moments more before deciding to go back home and return to another lifetime.

The two conspirators fixed a few snacks with plenty of water to drink and ascended the attic stairs to their favorite spot.

After getting comfy Shy asked Lyric a favor.

"Darlin' the next part will take a while if I'm going to tell it all."

"Oh I want you to tell it all, Grandma!" an excited young lady answered. "Well OK, but I'd like to go into even more detail with this part of the story and I thought, unless it's a question that you're biting your lip to get out, could we perhaps just leave the not so important questions until the end?

"Ye' see lass I really need ye' to listen to Kieran's heart more than ever now?"

"You're making it all sound even more intriguing than ever Grandma, but of course I can do that."

"Thank you, pet. Well now let me see."

"Kieran had just come back from training with the guard dogs and she was keen to start her new job."

"Yup that's it," Lyric agreed and got herself situated amongst her cushions.

Kieran immersed herself in her new job loving every moment she spent with her four-legged friends. Even when she was attacked by the Rottweiler, Bruce, she took up where she'd left off, after a quick trip to the emergency room and returned to work the very next day.

She was made of hardy stock and seemed to be driven by challenges, as though always having something to prove to someone.

But it was exhausting.

She strived to prove her father wrong from the title she'd been branded with so long ago yet forever fresh in her heart.

Living under that pressure was a recipe for disaster.

Eventually, no matter how hard Kieran tried to make everything in her life work, she began to feel as though she was failing miserably.

The exhilaration of the course with the Royal Army soon faded and her life became mundane as she strained against the bit of freedom.

Interwoven in and out of her now complicated life Kieran struggled to hold onto a simple truth. The simple truth that whispered to her of loyalty and commitment, no matter what situation she found herself in and unknown to Kieran, somewhere, in the vastness of this universe, there was a battle being waged for her soul.

"Uh!" Lyric exclaimed but clamped both hands over her mouth.

Shy went on....

Thomas was entering into an awkward stage of life when he needed guidance from his father, but Danny was to prove delinquent in that department also. He'd never aspired to be a good husband let alone a good father and as the year wore on Kieran began to worry about her son.

He hadn't made close friends at the glen school and as he entered into his twelfth year, when bodies begin to change Kieran became aware of an unsettling in him.

She was extremely close to Tommy and always had been and although he had shared many intimate thoughts with her growing up she sensed he was now having difficulty relating his problems to her.

He needed a man in his life. One who would listen with a compassionate heart and not one who would mock or make light of his concerns.

Thomas was a sensitive soul and needed that sensitivity nurtured, not crushed. Kieran agonized for her son, wondering if she could find someone else to talk with him.

Chapter 26
A New Chapter - Going Home

Kieran pondered carefully the question of finding help for her son and life on the estate went on with its usual slow pace, at least for some.

As they left behind the last long hot days of summer that'd turned Kieran's skin golden brown the familiar crunch of unwelcomed wheels creeping slowly up the drive way made that skin crawl one day when Danny was even farther away from home.

The head keeper just wouldn't give up and as often as she complained to Danny he continued to ignore her pleas for support.

She was left to deal with a situation of sexual harassment alone and this time her heart quickened as she gingerly locked the back door and hid behind the curtain.

She heard his footsteps on the gravel and felt her hands grow damp and clammy, feeling sure he would detect she was inside.

"Please let him go away," she cried silently as her heart raced and her breathing became fast and shallow and as she stood praying for his departure she suddenly saw something move out the corner of her eye.

He had walked around to the side of the house and was looking in the kitchen window.

Kieran's face flushed and knowing she had been discovered she slowly opened the back door and awaited the outcome of this embarrassing scenario as it unfolded before her."Are you OK Kieran," he asked pretending innocence. "You looked a little scared when I saw you through the window. I didn't mean to frighten you."

"Well I wasn't expecting anyone and for some reason I didn't recognize your Land Rover and..." She spluttered out a makeshift reply.

"Why don't you put the kettle on and I'll make us a cup of tea, lass."

"Well, no thanks, and I'm fine now and actually, I'm not sure how appropriate that would be with Danny not being here."

He told her she was being silly and dismissed her discomfort. He refused to leave making her feel awkward and Kieran took a step back to create as much distance between them as possible.

A lone trickle of sweat made its way down her back as he began to ask her personal questions about her life and her relationship with Danny. Kieran wanted desperately for the ground to open up and swallow her. Praying that Danny would come back at any moment she tried hard to skirt around the answers to his inappropriate conversations. He stepped closer and Kieran backed into the counter top.

"Please leave, Mr. Rutledge, I really don't think it's right that you keep calling when my husband isn't here." She managed to get the words out at last hoping it would defuse any notions he had but he was obviously intent on making the most of this visit. As his lust full eyes took in the golden satin of Kieran's shoulders he took another step and grabbed a hold of her arms.

Before he could do much else Kieran struggled to break free and lifting her knee up to block his vain attempt to get closer she pushed him back against the wall and ran out the back door.

She ran down the road tears streaming down her flushed face and made her way to the kennels directly adjacent to the house, knowing he wouldn't be stupid enough to follow her down to the dogs.

Kieran stepped inside the kennel that housed her biggest Labrador, Brock, and squatted down beside him, holding on to him for dear life. She closed her eyes and listened as the screech of tires on the gravel made it obvious he was leaving at high speed and as the sound of the Land Rover disappeared into the distance Kieran slowly stood up and wiped her tear stained face. Brock looked up at her with his big brown eyes full of question and she hugged her valiant hero for once again saving her from yet another potential disaster.

Pulling herself together Kieran closed the kennel door behind her. Walking slowly back up to the house her thoughts raced, reliving the terrible drama she'd just survived.

Was it all her fault? She questioned reliving the echo of distant memories and feeling the crush of a spirit broken. Why couldn't people just leave her alone?

Kieran's thoughts raced trying to make sense of how to handle what had just transpired. If she told her husband what had just happened he might get mad enough at his boss to do something violent, and then they'd be out of a job and a home. But if she didn't breathe a word to anyone Rutledge might just try again.

Kieran was tormented day and night not knowing what way to turn and finally after having no more unannounced visits she decided to protect her family and put it all behind her.

Shy glanced over at Lyric and asked if she was OK.

"I'm fine, go on, Grandma."

The respective families had come to visit over the summer and after a well deserved trip to Edinburgh in early September they settled in once again for the beginning of a new school year and shooting season.

Danny's boss kept his distance and Kieran's memory of that day began to fade until the season ended in mid January and with it the end of Danny's employment.

They were shocked!

As they reeled against the dizzying whirlwind of such terrible news the couple took a deep breath and considered their options.

Rutledge had no valid reason for firing Danny as his work had been exemplary throughout the two years working there.

Although Danny had been mouthing off at his boss a little more recently when disagreeing with work related issues, in general he was known as a hard worker.

Kieran sensed Rutledge had decided to cut to the chase before the dogs of wrath devoured him. Without knowing whether she had told anyone about his advances on her he was obviously trying to get rid of the damaging evidence before it destroyed him.

He probably thought that Danny's big mouth would be enough proof for dismissal, but didn't bank on the couple taking legal action.

Their lawyer was convinced they could at least get a severance package due to unfair dismissal and before it even got as far as court they settled on an amount that would get the family through a few months of having to look for a new job and home.

The search for a new home proved to be harder than they'd expected and after the first week they still hadn't found anything and Kieran was starting to get worried.

By the middle of the second week someone at work told her about a place he thought he'd seen not too far from the village.

After work that day, instead of going straight home she went to check out the house, and when she found it she was amazed at how pretty it was.

It was on a farm not too far from the village and had a huge front garden that could be made to look really pretty, but at the moment was overgrown.

It looked empty so she had a peek in the huge bay window at the front and was excited to see how large the living room was. She walked all the way around the house and tried to count the rooms. If she was correct it looked like a three bedroom with a roomy kitchen at the back.

Her heart pounded as she decided to try and find out who the house belonged to. She walked down the lane and knocked on the door of the nearest neighbor.

It was answered by a pretty lady probably in her sixties and Kieran asked politely if she knew anything about the house on the corner.

She was told it belonged to Mr. Brown, the farmer, and had been vacant for quite a while. The lady added that it would be nice to have someone living there again. Kieran found out where the farmer lived but it was getting late.

She needed to get home for the children, so thanking the lady Kieran drove back home trying hard not to get too excited.

She decided not to say anything to Thomas or Megan until she'd spoken to Danny. She didn't want to build their hopes up. Instead, she listened attentively, whilst starting on the tea, as both Megan and Tommy told her about their day.

When Danny got home she shared her news. Danny was just as excited as Kieran and after dinner they told the children they were going to look at a house.

They all piled into the car and off they went on their adventure. Kieran prayed silently all the way down the road and by the time they arrived at the little house it was dark. They found it hard to see clearly but what they could see they loved.

Danny found the farm house and knocked on the door hoping to find the farmer home and he did, but he was having dinner. He gave Danny his phone number and asked him to call the next day when he'd have more time to let them look inside the house and discuss details.

This was really starting to look positive and as they drove back home the children chatted excitedly about living on a farm.

"Hey you two," said Kieran understanding their excitement completely. "Don't get too worked up now, we don't even know if we have it yet!"

When they got back home it was already time for bed. Thomas at least was too old for the bedtime routine of the past and shouted a general goodnight from his room but Megan loved to be tucked in and Kieran bent down to give her a kiss on the forehead.

"Do you think we'll get the house on the farm, Mum?" Megan asked her big hazel eyes full of hope. "Oh, sweetheart, if it's the house for us then we'll get it. If not, something else will come along soon. But don't you worry about a thing."

Kieran squeezed her baby girls hand with reassurance.

When she went to bed she prayed quietly.

"Dear God please let this house be the one. We don't have much time left before we have to leave and I don't want the children to suffer."

A multitude of thoughts coursed through her mind and as she lay quietly and contemplated, she wondered where this new phase of their life would take them.

Danny called Mr. Brown the next day and they were told the house was available for rent and if they wanted to see it they could come back around two o'clock. They were both hopeful and when two o'clock came Mr. Brown was outside waiting for them.

They were showed into the house which was incredible inside and just what they were looking for. All the rooms were spacious and she had been right with how many there were. The only thing that concerned her was the dampness, especially in one of the bedrooms. Mr. Brown assured her they were aware of the problem and were already looking into doing something about it.

They discussed the rent and what they'd be expected to pay in utilities etc. and on the whole it sounded like a good deal. They shook hands on it and asked if they could start painting before they actually moved in.

Kieran explained that Tommy had asthma and the fumes might irritate the problem unless they had time to ventilate before he moved into his room.

Mr. Brown handed them the key and told them they could do what they wanted, as long as they informed him of the date they were actually moving in so he could make sure the power was turned on.

They shook hands once again and left just in time for the children to arrive home from school.

They shared the good news with the children amidst whoops of joy and excitement and were astonished when the two hugged each other.

It was Friday so they were all looking forward to exploring their new house over the weekend and suddenly it felt that things might possibly start getting better. Kieran hoped that included the marriage.

The only thing they had to be concerned about now was finding Danny a new job which was going to be hard in that area. But they had moved before and would do so again if need be.

They were enjoying a busy weekend, cleaning and preparing the house for painting but when Danny came back from borrowing a few tools from Rob and Marie he looked more than a little glum.

"What's wrong with you?" Kieran asked sensing his change of mood.

He sat down shaking his head. "Kieran you're not going to believe what they just told me.

"Well go on then" she replied impatiently.

Danny went on to explain that Rob and Marie had applied for and accepted the job at Lochinlea. The very job they'd left behind three years prior.

Kieran couldn't believe her ears and sat down in complete shock, her mind racing. Why would they go to a place like that after all the stories they had told them. Were they crazy? She thought to herself and then vocalized her thoughts to Danny.

"I know Kieran and you can bet that's exactly what I told them!"

What Kieran didn't understand was why she was feeling so betrayed by her friend?

Why hadn't they mentioned any of this to them?

She wasn't only shocked at their decision but was also concerned with the way she had reacted to it and she tried for days to figure it out. Finally Kieran came to the same conclusion as her husband.

"Kieran, it's their life and we've nothing to do with what they decide to do with it."

Her excitement with the new house had faded memories of another time in that dreadful place. She refused to allow the decision Rob and Marie had made to influence their own.

The two weeks they'd spent preparing the house for moving in seemed to fly by. Within a couple more days they would be moving and they were exhausted but thankful they'd found something so pretty.

The children had a room each, but Kieran was still worried about the dampness in Thomas's. It was the larger of the two and he was thirteen now so deserved to have his choice. She worried so much about his asthma and reminded her husband about the farmers promise to do something about it.

With the money they received from the settlement they bought some new furniture and the place started to look like home.

Megan had a pretty little room which Kieran spent a long time decorating. Tommy's larger room was definitely all boy.

Everyone was exhausted with the move but Kieran seemed extra drained of energy.

"I wish we were all going out for Chinese food!" Thomas complained adding to Kieran's guilt of going out with Dana.

It was three weeks after having moved to the new house and Kieran was worn out. She hadn't taken any time off for the move so was working whilst painting and packing. When everything finally settled down she accepted an invitation by the new friend she'd met, to go out for a quick bite to eat.

"Well maybe we can save up and all go out next pay day, sweetheart." Kieran replied, hoping to be able to keep her promise.

"I'm really tired after all the work getting the house ready and I need a little time to relax, Tommy."

"Oh, I know Mum, I'm sorry," he added knowing how hard his mum worked for the family and when she told him it was mince and tatties for tea, he brightened up.

"Awe Great! Ma' favorite!" he exclaimed forgetting all about Chinese.

How she loved her children! She would do anything to make sure they were taken care of. That truth had been her heart's delight for all the years they were together, and she truly believed she would never feel any different.

But life has a habit of throwing curve balls more often than we'd ever wish to admit, and before too much longer one of those balls would hit them all straight on at ninety miles an hour!

When Friday came Kieran didn't feel well and was considering canceling her arrangements with Dana. When she called, Dana sounded so excited about getting out for a few hours Kieran didn't have the heart to cancel.

It was cold and wet and they decided to just run into Brechin to pick up a curry and eat it in the car. Not much of an evening out but to a single parent and an over worked mum it was joy!

They didn't stay out long. The struggle to keep warm in the car was suddenly no longer fun and on arriving home Kieran invited Dana in for a cup of tea.

"Oh I'd love one, thank you, I have the chills," she added and they ran inside to avoid a drookin.

They must have been really quiet because no one heard them come in.

A fact that became all too obvious when Danny and Tommy jumped when the living room door opened!

Guilt was written all over both faces when Kieran realized what they'd been watching on TV.

She stood for a moment unable to quite take in what she saw and as her temper rose like a tidal wave Kieran turned slowly to Dana and asked if she would mind taking a raincheck on the tea.

When they had moved in and had a little extra money on hand, Danny had insisted, against Kieran's wishes, to have satellite TV installed.

That evening she understood why.

The disgust and contempt she felt towards her husband at that moment washed over her drowning any resolve she'd had to stay in the marriage.

They were watching a raunchy, Italian, topless game show!

When the door opened and Tommy saw his mum standing there he bolted for the remote. He was embarrassed she'd discovered what they were watching and out of respect to her made the obvious effort to get rid of the offensive images.

Kieran could have cried and honestly felt that she would have felt less disgust if she'd walked in on Danny with another woman.

At least there might have been a positive outcome to that indiscretion!

To involve his child in such a despicable pleasure teaching him that it's permissible to keep secrets in their home, was completely beyond her understanding.

Kieran told Thomas to go to bed after thanking him for turning off the show.

"Don't worry, sweetheart" she reassured her boy." I know it wasn't your fault," she added, giving him a hug.

Tommy walked out the room with his shoulders slumped knowing that his parents would be having one of their disagreements and wishing that he hadn't been watching that show with his dad.

There was no argument but rather, a chilled silence. It was broken when Kieran told Danny she didn't ever think she could feel more disappointed with him.

He had stooped to a new low in her mind, and she refused once and for all, to bring her children up in a home where her moral standards were constantly being undermined.

"It has been bad enough to accept your disrespect for me over and over again in our marriage, Danny, in all possible ways!" she declared her head held high. "But I won't stand by and watch while you train our son to disrespect women!" she added and walked out of the room.

Kieran couldn't take it anymore. She knew she was done with this poor excuse for a marriage and now it all became clear.

Her children were suffering anyway so why should she worry that divorce would cause them any more pain! She was exhausted and wanted to leave more than ever. That night she made a promise to begin the process of finding out how to survive on her own.

A month had passed and her husband still hadn't found a job and that was adding to her concerns. When one of the police officers on the base told her they were looking for security guards she picked up an application form and took it home to Danny.

He was feeling down and had been much quieter of late.

Kieran wondered if he was concerned that if he accepted this job, his days of being a gamekeeper would probably be numbered.

He had always been a responsible provider and since nothing else had come up he knew he had no other option but to apply for the job.

Kieran actually felt bad for him but sometimes she also felt he was his own worse enemy! Most of the problems that had come his way were usually the result of his own actions, but he never seemed to learn.

He was offered the job and accepted it, and for the next six months she watched as Danny went downhill.

He would come home from work, plank himself down in a chair, and stare into space. Kieran went back and forth from being concerned for him and downright mad.

The effort he promised to make to turn the overgrown garden into a beautiful wild flower garden fell by the wayside, and she watched as he indulged in a mire of self pity. This last chance pit stop of making their family life together work was now falling apart at every seam and Kieran finally came to a place of no return!

Throughout the whole of their life together, it was he who had made the career choices. Kieran and the children were always expected to just accept it and follow.

Uprooting lives constantly without a thought of how it was affecting them all as a family was second nature to Danny, but when life threw him a curve ball leaving him with little choice, he took it badly, like a spoilt child unable to get his way.

Of course Kieran understood his concerns but gradually she lost all ability to be as supportive as she had been for the fourteen years of their life together.

It was a particularly beautiful summer and it was breaking Kieran's heart to see what could have been a beautiful home, go to ruin.

The children, although sensing the ever-increasing distance between their parents, were enjoying life on the farm and loved living so close to the cows, which they began to call by name. They would go out first thing in the morning and not come back until lunch time, always starving with roses in their cheeks, but they too noticed the difference in their dad.

Although he had never really made an effort to be that close to them, apart from the occasional wrestle on the rug and gift giving at Christmas, they could see he seemed sad all the time and had even less to do with them than before.

"What's wrong with Dad, Mum?" Thomas asked one day after arriving home from school in early summer.

"He misses being a gamekeeper, pet, and I'm not sure he loves what he's doing now," Kieran shared.

"But life's not all about what we want to do, ye' know Tommy. Sometimes we just have to buckle under and get on with what comes our way, especially if there are children to look out for." She added stating a simple truth and giving her son a hug.

"Don't you worry, he'll get over it and ye' never know what might come up soon!"

She hated to see her children worry but knew she couldn't shield them from everything.

The summer passed and just around the corner was her birthday. Kieran never was one for great celebrations. It was different for the children but she didn't care for herself.

The atmosphere at home was more or less the same every day and as each week went by and nothing was done in the bedraggled garden, Kieran began to look at it as a symbol of their life. Worn out and overgrown with choking weeds so deep rooted that nothing else was able to flourish. Promises for their life had fallen by the wayside just like the garden, crushed under foot with no chance of survival.

How sad to see something die. To watch the life blood drain out of whatever was left of their life together Kieran felt powerless and sick to her stomach with hopelessness.

The battle she'd fought for years trying to hold onto the dream of what could have been was slowly running out of will and ammunition and a little girl's innocent remark, riddled with a profound truth began to resonate in Kieran's mind.

"If you and Dad ever got divorced I would want to live with you, Mum, 'cause you do the lookin' after!"

Where did that thought come from, in one so young? Did her children have a greater understanding of her sorrow than she'd realized?'

Shy stopped for a moment and looked over at Lyric who looked deep in thought, as though in a trance almost, transported back into Kieran's life.

"What are ye' thinkin', darlin'?" She asked praying the story wasn't too much for one still so young.

"It's finally coming to an end isn't? Or if it isn't, it downright should be!" Lyric stated with indignant outrage that even surprised Shy.

She sat back in the rocker.

"But Lyric, isn't marriage meant to be forever? And after all didn't Kieran make a vow before God?"

"Well of course it is, Grandma, but Kieran had put up with enough over the years and I feel she had every right to break off that dead end relationship. He was hopeless! And she and her children deserved more!"

Lyric's big hazel eyes were full of indignation for the injustices of Kieran's life.

"So you don't think they could have worked it out and perhaps gone through counseling?"

Lyric shrugged her shoulders and her expression softened a little.

"Maybe, I dunno', but to be honest, Grandma, there's been something telling me all along that the whole relationship was doomed. They just weren't right for each other from the start were they?"

Shy rocked back and forth hanging on every word the child said and she replied. "Sweetheart you hit the nail on the head! It wasn't right from the start because Kieran hadn't been taught how to look for a partner. She had been left to her own devices all through her life growing up in that house of silence and so when someone, and it could have been anyone, came along and told her he loved her she believed him and thought that was all there was to it!"

"She couldn't ever remember being told the words 'I love you' from the only man in her life she needed to hear them from!"

Shy looked down at her hands as though to take a moment to ponder.

"So she married the first one to say, 'I love you.'"

A sudden stillness entered the dusty attic where the two women young and old shared a legacy of a lifetime and as though to break the silent heartbreak Shy sat up in her chair.

"You've been blessed with parents who have taught you about God's unconditional love for all His children. They've nurtured you to believe in who God made you to be and to expect nothing less than what He has planned for you. That includes the man He's preparing for you right now, sweetheart."

"I know Grandma, I know." Was all Lyric could reply. She seemed to sense it wasn't the right time to say more.

"Well let's get back to Kieran shall we?

A few days before her birthday, sensing it wouldn't be spoiling anyone else's plans, Kieran accepted an invitation to the club on the local base as a birthday treat from her friend Dana.

With that invitation came an avalanche of unfortunate events; a downwards spiral towards the destruction of her true life values that would eventually take on a life force of its own.

She met someone that night who was to take her on a journey into a world she had always despised. One full of lies and deceit, ultimately destroying the purity of the character she had held onto dearly all through her life.

Lyric looked bewildered yet engrossed in the mystery; but she sensed not to interrupt.

He was handsome and charming. A world traveler with a unique sense of style that quickened Kieran's heartbeat the first time she laid eyes on him. He had huge brown eyes that made any resolve she'd been clinging to melt away like a light fall of snow after the sun's rays warmed the dawn of a new day.

He danced with a rhythmic sway of his lean muscular body Kieran tried hard to ignore but a flicker of woman was being reignited. The woman that had been buried alive under the blanket of responsibility with the titles she'd so willingly adorned all through her life; Dancer and Beauty Queen, Wife and Mother, Head Cook and Bottle

Washer, Dog Handler and more. And last but not least 'Nothing but an Idiot." Not so willingly adorned.

"I'm sorry I can't dance with you. I'm married," Kieran answered to his offer to dance as a last ditch attempt to hold on to sanity.

"That's nice but I only asked for a dance!" was his reply that broke the ice, that broke her resolve, which ultimately broke the very core of decent woman she believed herself to be.

Kieran knew with every ounce of who she was that a quickened heart usually meant danger! This is not healthy for you! Alert! Alert! Pay Attention, Danger!

Deprived from love and respect within the bonds of Holy Matrimony how was Kieran to react?

She'd held onto the note he slipped her before she left that night, knowing it was wrong to do so.

Suddenly she felt the surge of blood run through her veins as though every cell in her body had been brought back to life, but she was aware she was treading on treacherous ground.

Every moment of every day, no matter how hard she tried to shake it off, was filled with memories of that one dance. The intoxicating fragrance of his cologne had attached itself to her very senses driving her crazy for one more dance. Just one more dance.

He'd asked her to call him the following Saturday and Kieran fought a battle of wills all through the week leading up to that day, struggling to remain true to her vows. How could she be such a hypocrite, especially after all she'd said to her husband about moral values within the home.

As the day drew near she almost got through it until a taunting voice convinced her she should call to put an end to her torture.

Just call to let him know you're married and as nice as he seems, you won't be calling him again because it's just not right. Go on Kieran a phone call's harmless enough.'

She gave in and called five minutes before the end of the window of time he'd given her and she felt nauseous telling that first lie to her family!

"I'm just running down to the store!" she cried out to whomever was listening.

"Get some more milk while you're there, Mum," Thomas called and her senses seethed with self loathing.

"OK, darlin', I won't be long."

The night they met he pretended he wouldn't let go of her hand until she promised to call and so she did.

I'll just call to let him know I won't be calling again.

Oh yeah, that sounds like an excuse if ever I heard one! Her true self railed back against whatever was overtaking her.

But when she picked up the receiver in the pay phone across from the village grocery store, her decent self and the woman she always knew herself to be won the battle.

"Hi Martin it's Kieran from the club last Friday."

There was a long pause on the other end. "Well I didn't think you were going to call," he said sounding surprised.

"Martin, I have to be honest. I wasn't going to but you made me promise, so I'm only keeping that promise to tell you I won't be calling again."

"OK... Well that doesn't sound logical, but if that's what you want Kieran, I'm not going to force you, even if it is just to talk."

His charming voice was just as alluring, but Kieran forged on with the commitment to remain faithful, her heart pounding with fear.

"Well even I find that a little naïve but nevertheless I just wanted to say I enjoyed meeting you but I won't be calling again."

"Kieran you're a sweet lady, and I understand but if there's anything you need at any time please feel free to call, OK?"

He tried one last time to smooth talk her into.....well she wasn't sure what. But what she was certain of was her conscience forcing her to stop before the madness started!

Shy looked over at Lyric, feeling more like the child herself.

Lyric's expression was soft and full of grace.

"What else was it about him that caused all those emotions to rise up in you, Grandma?

"Well she...!" Shy was about to answer when she stopped.

"Did you say 'Kieran'?" she asked Lyric heat suddenly rushing to her face and fighting to keep tears at bay Shy fidgeted in her seat.

"No, Grandma, I said you." And suddenly the tears flowed and Lyric was in her arms and Shy wept like she never had before.

"Grandma, it's OK!" Lyric assured the woman who had been there for her all through her young life no matter what.

"It's OK," and she held Shy in her arms feeling her pain.

Shy's emotions were spent and as she raised her face she looked into Lyric's eyes. "How did you know?"

Lyric took a tissue from her pocket and wiped her grandma's tear stained face.

"I've suspected for a little while but today I felt something deep down that confirmed to me the pain you have kept inside all this time, and it's time to let it go Grandma."

"I thought I had. I thought I'd given it all over to God a very long time ago but..." And Lyric finished Shy's sentence. "You were worrying about my response to that part of the story. You were concerned about what I would think of the grandma I love and the enemy tried to make you feel ashamed."

Shy sat up and leaned back a little in the chair. Holding on tight to Lyric's hand she asked, "But; how could you know all of that, darlin'?"

"Grandma: Do you think God only talks to adults?" And without waiting for an answer Lyric continued. "Do you honestly think that grownups have all the answers and can't learn from the young?"

Shy smiled and slowly shook her head, "Well of course not to both questions sweet girl. I've learned simple but profound truths many times through the years from all my children and others!" Shy replied finally letting go of Lyric's crushed hand and as the child shook the blood back into her limp fingers her grandma apologized.

"Oh darlin' I'm sorry." And she grabbed Lyrics hand and kissed it all better.

They both laughed and couldn't stop for what seemed like ages and when they eventually did they were exhausted.

"I feel wonderful all of a sudden!" Shy remarked. Realizing a huge burden had just been lifted she looked to her Lyric and said, "Thank you, ma' pet. You're just incredible; do ye' know that?"

"Well........." Lyric drawled the mischief returning to her cherub face.

"I don't know about you lass but I suddenly feel a bit stuffy in this attic."

"What about a walk in the fall breeze to blow all the cobwebs away?"

"That sounds like a plan, Grandma." And both girls young and old all but skipped down the attic stairs feeling as though they'd just been drenched in God's Healing Rain.

They stopped by the kitchen to have a quick snack of fruit before leashing Kylie and grabbing their coats.

It had turned out to be a beautiful day and for some reason everything seemed fresher.

"Is it my imagination or has something changed between us Lyric, I mean in a good way?" And then Shy added, "Because I feel at perfect peace."

Lyric smiled.

"Well I feel Grandma; that as close as we've always been, something was stopping us from being as close as we are right now, and that something was what you had been holding onto," Lyric stated, kicking at a pile of leaves with her hands deep in her pockets.

"Oh there ye' go again, little miss, ministering to your old grandma!"

They both laughed out loud.

"Well I'm not sure about all that, but don't you think that's true?" Lyric asked.

"Well of course I do, silly! Isn't God absolutely great?"

"Absolutely, He is Grandma!"

The two walked and talked about a multitude of things and the fall breeze blew an untold amount of cobwebs away that afternoon.

"So did you begin to have a relationship with that man, kinda' like a boyfriend, Grandma?"

Even given what they'd just experienced that question grated on Shy's nerve endings but instead of retreating she ran into the roar!

"Yes, darlin', unfortunately I did," Shy admitted feeling it easier to say than she'd expected.

"The irony being of course that I'd made up my mind to leave Danny anyway as we've spoken off before. I'd been looking in the paper for somewhere to live, but, of course that didn't vindicate me from the sin!

"Actually I came to realize many years later that I may have never had the courage to leave the marriage had I not followed through with the relationship.

"Sad to say, interwoven within the web of emotions at that time there must have been some kind of subconscious push to do something radical enough to get me out of the marriage for good."

Shy talked as they walked and Lyric was quiet and listened.

"I've learned that many people and, unfortunately, more so girls, cut themselves to release a deep rooted pain from their past they've been unable to face or heal from. It sounds impossible to believe that someone would inflict even more pain when already suffering, but unfortunately that seems part of the human condition.

"We do things in an effort to cry out for help or sometimes just to dull the pain of the tragic reality in our lives. I think that's sort of what happened to me."

Shy walked, eyes lowered to gaze at the road covered in brightly colored leaves, with her hands deep in her pockets. She was concentrating on every word.

"I think I was done with trying to make things work. I was done with all that I'd put up with over the years from a husband who couldn't care less. I was done with the pretense. And that man began to fill in almost all of the blanks of my life."

"What like?" Lyric asked intrigued but desperately sad for Kieran.

Sometimes it was still simpler to relate to her as Kieran.

"Well sweetheart I loved the wonders of nature, especially at this time of the year when the rainbows of glorious autumn shades played out the romantic side of my nature. I truly was and still am a romantic at heart, but I had been starved from all romance throughout my life with Danny, and so Martin romanced me.

"He wrote me poems, in the beginning and I became lost in a whirlwind of beautiful words that fed me what I was desperate for; the nourishment of knowing I was truly loved by another."

"He showed compassion towards Thomas and expressed a desire to help. And eventually he bought me wonderful fragrances I'd never been exposed to before personally and all of a sudden I felt vibrant and alive!"

Shy looked at Lyric who had a somewhat intrigued expression on her face.

"But darlin', all of that was a lure to drag me down and into the snares of sin.

As wonderful as it all made me feel, filling a terrible emptiness I'd suffered for years, it was nothing more than a bait of Satan!"

"Yes, I see, Grandma. Satan knew all along that God had been calling your name and so he was out to destroy you!"

Shy stopped walking and looked at Lyric completely aghast at what the child had just said and tears flowed.

No words can describe what Shy felt like at that moment so she took Lyric in her arms and they hugged in the middle of the road.

"You get it, sweetheart, you get it!"

Shy released her arms reluctantly as they heard a car coming down the lane and as Lyric linked her arm through Shy's they looked up at the dark clouds beginning to gather.

They were getting hungry anyway so turned around to retrace their footsteps back to the house.

Shy felt elated with the conversation that morning and didn't ever think she could feel closer to her Lyric, but she did!

It had suddenly become a lot cooler so, when they arrived home, Shy first went to turn up the heat and then set the fire in the family room.

It had been a blessed morning and after all the talking that had taken place Shy and Lyric were now in a somewhat contentedly quiet place.

Lyric asked if she could put on some classical music and then they met in the kitchen to discuss lunch.

"Well, I know I'm hungry but it almost feels surreal, after our conversation of another lifetime, to do something ordinary like have lunch!" Lyric remarked always a genius at describing exactly how things are!

Shy laughed.

"I know you're absolutely right, sweetie pie, you're absolutely right!" she repeated shaking her head. "But what do you feel like to eat nonetheless?"

"Hmm! I'm not quite sure," Lyric answered Shy and then just as quickly changed her mind. "Oo! Wait a minute though do you have any Branston Pickle?"

"Oh! Ye' know I always keep a stock for ye're mum coming now, don't ye'?"

"OK then I'll have a cheese and pickle sandwich with a glass of milk please."

"That's ma' girl!" Shy answered thankful Lyric still had her appetite.

They enjoyed a relaxing lunch and after clearing away the dishes Shy asked if Lyric would like to watch a movie.

They walked into the warm and inviting family room and sat down on the overstuffed sofa and as they cuddled in together a distant rumble of thunder announced the definite arrival of the thunderstorm that had been forecast.

Lyric looked up at Shy and said, "Grandma, there's no movie we could watch that would intrigue me more than your story."

They chatted away for half an hour, Lyric asking question upon question and then they heard a commotion at the front door. They hadn't heard the car because of the thunder but suddenly the front door flew open and the rest of the family struggled in, soaking wet and fighting with stubborn umbrellas.

Shy turned to Lyric. "Looks like our time together is over, honey bunch." And Lyric just smiled and ran to help with soggy coats.

The kettle was put on and over a familiar cup o' tea Paul explained to Shy the report given by the cardiologist.

"He said that what happened to me was more of a little episode rather than a minor heart attack, and as long as I stay on the medication and check in regularly with him, I should be good to go for some time!"

Shy relaxed into her seat and with a look of slight distain she asked for verification of said report from Erin and Greg.

"Well, that's nice I'm sure!" Paul said pretending to be insulted.

"Mum, we went in with him to ask questions if necessary and that's exactly what the doctor said."

"Well OK then but you better keep taking that medicine or I'll turn into a nag!"

"What do you mean turn into!" was the reply and Shy swatted him with her napkin.

Greg had brought a movie home so for the rest of the afternoon the family shared time together and relaxed.

"Do you want to go out to eat tonight honey?" Paul asked as the film drew to an end.

"Not particularly but we could stay home with Lyric and let Erin and Greg have some time together," Shy suggested as usual thinking wisely about everyone's welfare.

Lyric over heard the discussion and chimed in. "Hey! We could play the game of Life and I really feel like Chinese!" The two grownups looked at each.

"Well I think we have tonight planned!" Paul remarked giving Lyric a bone crushing hug. "Ooo! Grandpa your hugs hurt!"

Erin loved the idea of having her husband all to herself and Greg didn't complain either. Paul ordered Chinese food from their special little place in Newtown that didn't use MSG and they all enjoyed the evening.

The young folks arrived home around ten and by that time they were all exhausted and decided to call it a night.

As Shy was just about to enter her room Lyric stopped her in the hallway.

"Thanks again for today, Grandma. You've no idea how much it means to me, or any child for that matter, for a grown up to tell them the whole truth. Most adults just don't get that, but you definitely do, so thanks!" And she threw her arms around the woman she loved so very much.

"It's my honor sweetheart and remember, there's a lot more."

Lyric bounded away with Kylie hot on her heels as she shouted, "Oh! I know, goodnight Grandma, goodnight Grandpa."

Paul turned as Shy closed the bedroom door. "Well sounds like you made quite an impression today! That's one grateful young lady, sweetheart."

Shy sat down at her dresser and sighed.

"I had a really difficult part to tell her today but ye' know, I shouldn't have got myself all tied up in knots, as well as we know our Lyric."

Shy sometimes talked to Paul as though drifting in and out of questions she was actually asking herself. That particular little quirky side of her had amused him for years, and he just shook his head and sighed.

"Honey, you will just never understand how much you are loved by all of us, but especially your girls." Then he added; "There's not much you could have ever done or experienced that would make them feel anything other than more love for you, so you'd just better get used to it!"

Paul always had a way of making her feel better, minimizing monsters she had created in her mind and turning them all into puppy dogs.

She loved him so.

They got into bed and snuggled into each other's arms. Listening to the storm still raging outside whilst under the covers all comfy cozy was a treat and they lay together and prayed a simple prayer of thanks to their Papa.

Part Five:

Chapter 27
As The Mirror Cracked

A sudden crack of thunder seemed to jolt Shy out of a realm of peace and tranquility and back into a place of torment. As the storm threatened the safety of her sanctuary outside, yet another nightmare threatened her peace within.

When Kieran told Martin it was over; he turned up at the house one night after Danny left for work. He came to plead with her not to end the relationship which had now developed into a full blown affair. But Kieran could no longer bear the lies and deceit, refusing to live in the shadows where she felt tormented day and night.

The children had gone to bed and Danny was on night shift.

Martin was smart enough to watch for her husband's arrival on base then he took the opportunity to try and convince Kieran to change her mind.

She had tried to be strong and even stopped answering the phone at work, but every time she saw him her will power would all but melt, and she'd give in to the magnetism that had drawn her to him in the first place.

An emotional conversation ensued and try as she might she couldn't resist.

Surrendering her will yet again Kieran fell into a passionate embrace with the man who had captured her heart and she returned the desire that raged from his kiss. Just at that moment the living room door opened and there stood her son.

"What are you doing Mum!" Tommy screamed.

All Kieran could do was run. Run out of the house and as far away from her sin as possible. She heard Martin call her name from the driveway but she couldn't face the shame and disappointment she'd witnessed in her son's eyes. So she ran like a coward into the dark.

God help me! She cried out as she ran and stumbled in the pitch dark of the night. How low had she stooped? What had she done to her family and herself? The torment of the sordid reality tore into every fiber of her being.

Kieran stopped and hid behind a shed, exhaustion burning her chest as she waited for Martins car to pull away from the house. What seemed like an eternity went by when she finally saw the headlights of his car and listened as it disappeared down the lane. She rose to her feet and went back to the house to face her son.

At that moment Kieran felt ugly! Like a soiled remnant of her former self and as she approached the front door she swallowed past the enormous lump in her throat induced by the shame of that night.

All the years of fighting for happiness for herself and her children had just been flushed down the toilet! She was now the villain!

Causing more pain in the last fifteen minutes than Danny had caused in a lifetime of being together, Kieran realized she truly was 'nothing but a bloody idiot!'

He'd been right!

She tapped softly on Tommy's bedroom door hearing whimpering from inside and she entered. Walking over to his bed her head hung in shame. She no longer felt worthy to be a mother.

"Tommy, I'm sorry you witnessed that," she said in a tiny voice suddenly afraid she'd lost her son forever.

"I don't know what happened to me Tommy. That woman is not who I've known myself to be."

Tommy was silent apart from stifled sobs.

"I feel so ashamed. I beg your forgiveness Tommy!"

Thomas didn't move and Kieran laid her hand on his shoulder. He flinched and drew away as though offended by the touch.

With that gesture Kieran suddenly felt righteous anger rise up inside at the injustice of her tragic circumstance.

"Tommy, I understand how hurt you feel just now. I understand how angry you are with me. All I ask is that you don't judge me on one terrible indiscretion! No, let's call it what it really is; one terrible sin."

Thomas sat up in bed his face ravaged with disappointment and pain towards the mother he loved and had held in such high regard.

"How could you do that in our house and when Dad's at work?"

Kieran recoiled at the reality of her child's accusation and all of a sudden her actions of the last few months seemed illuminated from the dark shadows, revealing the gravity of what she'd done.

Tears streamed down her face as her resolve to stay strong for her boy broke!

"I don't know what happened, Tommy!" Her shattered voice struggled to explain and in between heart rendering sobs Kieran went on.

"I tried to be a good wife and mother but life with your dad has been a constant uphill battle, and I just ran out of steam!" Kieran lowered her eyes. "I just ran out of all hope!"

Every word that came out felt like a miserable excuse and she knew there was nothing she could say that would ever excuse what she'd become.

"I didn't mean to hurt you or Megan or even your dad, Tommy. I didn't mean to let you down. I'm so sorry, I'm so sorry Tommy!" Kieran wailed as a lifetime of broken dreams crumbled before her. She got up and left her child, knowing she didn't have the right to ask for his forgiveness.

The following weeks were agonizing to live through. Kieran felt unclean in her son's eyes and no amount of tears, no amount of woeful admissions of guilt could release her from her self imposed prison. She had committed the unforgivable sin and destroyed her relationship with her son, in the process.

She couldn't possibly feel more ashamed than she already did. But, now Kieran lived with the added guilt of involving her child in her terrible secret.

She knew she had put her son in a painful no-win situation. He couldn't tell his father because of fear of the consequences! Yet keeping the sordid truth to himself was eating him up!

She could see the pain in Tommy's eyes every time they were home together and she wished with all her heart that she could turn back the clock. But turn it back to when though? Turn it back to when she was the only one to suffer. Turn it back to when she was the one defending her young like the lioness she was. Turn it back to when Danny had hurt his son yet again but it was Kieran who had picked up the pieces. Turn it back to when she struggled to believe she was much more than 'nothing but a bloody idiot!'

Danny had done nothing worse than this!

To end the torment for everyone she had no choice left but to find somewhere else to live. She set about looking with even more conviction.

A month or so passed and the atmosphere at home was morbid to say the least, but she didn't stop being the caregiver.

Then, out of the blue, Danny received terrible news that his father had suffered a massive heart attack. By the time he got down to Edinburgh he had died.

Another crushing blow to enter his life!

The cycle of tragic events their little family was now experiencing seemed to be on some crazed track down a treacherous slope, gaining momentum as each day passed and Kieran knew she had to get out soon.

But her conscience began to attack! 'Oh yeah! Why don't you kick the poor guy when he's already down, Kieran?' The tormentor bombarded her thoughts and she knew she was in an unresolvable situation.

As hard as she tried to have compassion for her husband Kieran almost felt devoid of any emotions towards him and she continued to question who she had become.

Danny was to be gone for a few days at least and she struggled with many questions.

Does she stay and put the past behind her and remain living with the hypocrisy of this marriage. And the guilt of what she'd done to her children?

Or does she stay on the crazed track downhill and continue to search for somewhere to live, hoping the destination at the bottom wouldn't be worse?

Kieran searched the local paper for rental properties and even drove around the country lanes hoping to come upon a little cottage tucked away, but her search was in vain.

Sunday came and she'd been out searching yet again when Danny arrived home early. He sensed something was wrong and had done for quite some time but now, with the addition of his personal grief, his senses had become heightened.

He got in the car and went to look for her. He took a left into the village just as Kieran was about to turn into the road leading to the house and he stopped her in the middle of the road. He had a crazed look in his eyes as he got out the car and Kieran froze.

"Where have you been Kieran?" he asked his face now scarlet with rage!

"If you really want to know where I've been, Danny, here in the middle of the street for everyone to hear, then I'll tell you," she said with a conviction that surprised her.

She waited for a moment then proceeded.

"I was looking for somewhere else to live because I'm leaving you! I'm sorry to tell you at this time, Danny. I'm sorry about your Dad, but that doesn't change us!"

He lowered his eyes, his shoulders slumped and he looked defeated.

But as though a switch had suddenly been turned on in his mind, he looked up and what Kieran saw in his eyes sent a chill through her veins.

"It's him isn't it?" He spat out between clenched teeth the vein in his neck bulging. "The good friend who was taking Tommy to football games, it's him isn't it?" he raged, grabbing her by the shoulders and shaking her violently!

The weight of her helmet caused a piercing pain in her neck and for an instant Kieran thought she was about to lose consciousness. He let go and ordered her into the car.

"But what about my bike?" she asked, her voice barely a whisper.

"We'll pick it up later,"

He slammed the door on his side and burned rubber as he sped up the road.

When they arrived he dragged Kieran out of the car by her hair, pulled her up the path and into the house.

Kieran's heart pounded in her chest, and her scalp throbbed as hair was torn from the roots! The pain was excruciating but she tried not to scream! Her panicked thoughts were for her children, but as he burst into the living room, she saw her precious babies standing together looking completely terrified at the violent scene unfolding before them.

He threw her to the ground and screamed vile accusations and picked her up and shook her, his fingers digging into her flesh.

She begged him to stop in front of the children, but he screamed back; "You couldn't have cared less about the children when you were carousing with your boyfriend!"

Tommy and Megan didn't know whether to run and hide or stay to save their mother from their fathers' rage. The terror in their eyes caused Kieran even more pain! She thought she would throw up.

Suddenly Danny dropped her on the floor and left the room and both Thomas and Megan ran over to help her to her feet.

"I'm so- sorry," she managed to blurt out in between sobs, tears streaming and her hair a tangled mess. "I didn't want to hurt either of you," she added trying to catch her breath.

As they held her tight and rocked her in their arms Megan said, "It's alright Mummy, we know you're a good mum."

But the truth was she had shattered their world and would never forgive herself for the anguish she had caused. Kieran tried to compose herself, reassuring her children that their dad would be ok.

"I'll go in and talk to him in a moment. But you two should just go to your rooms."

The children looked reluctant to leave her. "Go on now I'll be fine and your dad will be too," Kieran tried to reassure them. They went off to their rooms both stupefied with what had just happened to their family.

The atmosphere was heavy with anguish and deep hurt on all sides. Kieran couldn't believe what had just transpired. Knowing only too well that her marriage had been a sham for years, she also knew she should have left a long time ago, before falling from grace, before shaming her children and herself.

Now, it was too late. It was she who had brought about this tragic turn of events.

"Can we talk Danny?" she asked softly after knocking on their bedroom door. There was no reply so she entered with trepidation. She was trembling with fear after the assault on her earlier, but knew that she had to face him and better sooner than later.

He just sat there dazed and confused ignoring her question. He seemed completely broken and Kieran felt drenched with remorse.

What in the name of God had she done! She was worthless! An adulteress! A murderess of family unity and more, much more! The appalling shame crushing she found it hard to breath but dared to speak.

"I don't know what happened," she went on hesitantly.

He didn't respond so she sat down on the bed beside him.

"One moment it was an innocent friendship because he was helping Thomas get through stuff he was dealing with at school, and then it became more, without planning or even realizing it," Kieran tried to explain something unexplainable.

"I can't believe you've done this Kieran; you of all people! And to the children too," he said as though the pain of hurting him wasn't enough.

"You of all people" he repeated his tone rising and torment returning to his eyes.

She ignored the fear and took a deep breath.

"Danny, the pain I have caused everyone is obvious and to say sorry seems so inadequate; it's useless and pointless, but I am nonetheless and I wish I could turn back time. I know it hurts too much to talk just now, but all I ask is that we try and keep it as low key as possible for the children's sake, please Danny!" Kieran pleaded.

"I'll try," was his reply.

Danny kept to his word whenever the children were within hearing distance but for the next twenty four hours Kieran was put through the mill. She honestly felt she deserved everything she got by that point, but by the next morning the situation took a turn for the worse.

The children woke up reluctantly as usual but that was the only evidence of 'normal' that morning. They looked as though they hadn't had much sleep and once again the pain of conviction thrust a knife through Kieran's heart.

She felt that school was the best thing for them both and so she prepared breakfast and encouraged them to eat. The proverbial pin could have been heard dropping amidst the pained silence at the table as Tommy and Megan pushed the food around on their plates. Kieran wanted to die!

Megan's attitude towards her mum hadn't changed any apart from an obvious sadness. But as hurt as the child was, she glanced up at Kieran and gave her one of those endearing; "I'm really sorry this is happening" smiles. But then that was typical Megan, Kieran's Wee Lamb.

Thomas, on the other hand, looked crushed and desperately disappointed with her. Kieran even sensed his upper lip flinch as though to look upon her was now disgusting.

As though the pain of all the times his father had let him down in his life, had been condensed into one giant ball of putrid, agonizing, torment had imploded , tearing him up and dragging him down into a nothingness of denial.

She had spoken to them both the night before and did what she'd always done when suffering within herself. She talked to her children trying to get them to understand as much as they needed to know, trying to ease their pain.

But this time it was different. This time she was the betrayer of their trust!

Reluctantly the children left for school and as Kieran was getting dressed Danny came in to the bedroom to ask what she was doing. She jumped when he entered! He'd been nowhere to be found earlier.

"I'm getting ready for work, Danny," Kieran replied determined to keep calm and centered.

"I don't think so Kieran!" was his reply and he left the room, slamming the door behind him.

She heard him pick up the phone in the hallway and listened as he told someone they were both sick and wouldn't be at work for a few days.

Terror suddenly gripped her!

When he came back through to the bedroom Danny spoke in a strained unfamiliar voice that caused nauseous bile to rise up inside as Kieran began to fear for her life. There was something ominous in the way he was acting and Kieran realized the best thing to do was remain calm and quiet and still her pounding heart!

He was going to keep her hostage in her own home!

The day passed and they talked as Danny's temperament changed from moment to moment. Kieran began to realize that nothing she could say would heal the pain that seemed to be pushing him over the edge.

Remorse, regret, shame, and confusion ran havoc with her all through the day, but then her mind became suddenly lucid as a crystal, clear thought came to her.

"Ok you're going to have to make a run for it!"

Danny had locked them both in so she knew the only means of escape would be through the bedroom window. It was level with the road outside the house so Kieran bided her time and when Danny finally left the room to use the bathroom she made a bid for freedom!

After climbing out of the window Kieran took off like the wind, running faster than she'd ever done before. The ground was covered with gravel and she went over on her ankles a couple of times but she didn't stop! A few moments passed and the end of the driveway was in sight! She heard a car door slam and turning her head as she ran Kieran saw their car approach.

Her heart thumping she got to the end of the road and just as she turned the corner she saw Peter Rose coming down the road towards her in his jeep. Peter was a good friend of the family along with his wife Margaret, and when he saw Kieran running towards him with a look of terror on her face, he stopped and got out the vehicle.

Kieran turned to see Danny close the distance between them and then she ran right into Peters arms.

The flood gates opened and Kieran fell apart unable to catch her breath.

"Peter thank God, please help me!" she gasped. Catching her breath and trembling with fear-filled exhaustion, she stammered, "Danny's after me!"

"Kieran calm down! What do you mean he's after you? Have you two had a fight?"

"It's much more than that Peter." And as she looked up their car had pulled to a stop about twenty or so yards away.

Danny got out the car with a relatively calm countenance and tried to assure Peter they'd just had a little falling out.

He listened but knew it was more than a "little falling out."

"Well let me take Kieran over to spend the afternoon with Margaret, and when things calm down I can bring her home, OK?" Peter insisted pushing Kieran into the passenger side of the jeep.

Tension from Kieran's panic bore evidence of the gravity of the situation and Paul knew the best thing to do was keep her safe for right now.

Danny resisted Peter's suggestion trying to make light of the predicament, but the family friend was no fool and stood his ground.

"I think it best the two women talk, Danny, so I'll call you later."

Without further question he got into the jeep and turned to make sure Kieran was OK.

As the jeep pulled away increasing the distance between terror and freedom, she could see Danny in the rear view mirror.

"Thank you, God!" Kieran prayed quietly knowing she'd just been saved from something terrible.

Peter and Margaret saved more than Kieran's physical well being that day. During the two weeks that followed they would prove themselves to be dear, dear friends.

After listening to Kieran's candid story, including the culmination of events that led up to the tragic happenings of the last twenty four hours, they insisted Kieran stay with them for a few days.

She had been completely truthful with them, admitting her guilt in detail. But what she hadn't realized was that nothing had come as a complete surprise to either Peter or Margaret. They had known Kieran and Danny for over two years and were wise enough to discern the imbalance in their marriage from very early on. They shared that fact with Kieran without condoning her actions.

Margaret was ten years older than Peter who was around Kieran's age, but they were deeply in love and she could see easily why Peter had fallen for his sweetheart. She was a gentle woman with so much wisdom and a zest for life that would put anyone younger to shame.

Kieran knew she had been blessed with their friendship and felt that it was much more than coincidence that had brought Peter down that road at precisely the right time to save her.

After many hours of talk and cups 'o' tea Margaret looked at the clock on her mantle.

"Come on then, lass! Who do we pick up first?" and they laughed a little at the ironic tragedy of life. Kieran exhaled a long sigh and wiped yet another stream of tears from her face.

They picked up both Megan and Tommy from school and brought them back to their house.

Megan was relieved to see her mum, but Thomas still looked furious with her and when he heard they weren't going home he became outraged!

"I want to go home and make sure dad's OK," he said adamantly looking daggers at Kieran.

"Thomas we have to stay at Margaret's for a little while," she insisted then explained.

"Peter's gone over to check on your dad and if he's feeling better, we might let you go back to see him tonight."

Thomas agreed reluctantly hardly looking at his mother or sister.

She daren't even think of what would have transpired if Peter hadn't been there to save her that morning and when he got back home she thanked him profusely once again.

After talking to Danny Peter convinced Kieran her husband was in no state of mind to look after Tommy, so she had to share the news with her son.

"Perhaps in a couple of days, Tommy," she added realizing the chasm between them had widened.

Not long after dinner they decided to call it a night. Kieran felt awkward suddenly feeling they'd taking over someone's home and dumped her garbage on their doorstep. But the couple had offered and she truly felt their concern for her and the children.

After a trip to the bathroom Kieran went to say goodnight to the children.

"How are you both doing?" she asked as she entered the room looking from one to another.

As she walked over to kiss Megan on the head her wee lamb said, "We're fine, Mummy," but she replied for both of them, smiling up at the woman she knew and loved no matter what. She was four years younger than Thomas but showing a maturity that far exceeded her years.

Thomas didn't even raise his eyes from what he was busy with as though trying to deny the existence of the one who'd shattered their lives. Kieran sighed as she stroked Tommy's curls knowing it would take him a long time to forgive her, if ever.

He was like his dad in more ways than she wished to admit, and she wondered, as she stood in the doorway, whether her male child would ever survive the heartache.

She said, "I love you," and left, closing the door quietly behind her.

After wearily slumping into bed Kieran drifted off to sleep unable to believe how incredible her friends were. She'd never known anyone to have done so much for no other reason than to help someone in need.

Feeling completely drained by the events of the last few days Kieran knew without a doubt there was no going back. As she slowly surrendered to the exhaustion of the day she remembered something Danny had said as she'd tried to explain her demise into unfaithfulness.

"Trying to turn this around on me now, are you, with your pathetic need for conversation?" he mocked her attempt to communicate just like he'd done for years and yet was shocked when she'd been drawn into a relationship that had began as a crying out for……! Everything that made a relationship complete.

Within the two weeks that followed Tommy was eventually able to see his dad which seemed to lighten his spirits slightly.

When it came time for Kieran to go back to the house to pick up more of their personal belongings Peter went with her to ensure her safety. As she looked at Danny on that sad day, she noticed he looked grey as though haunted by the ghosts of a lifetime. He was much thinner than before and Kieran's heart broke as she struggled to keep her resolve.

She gathered her belongings and left quietly with Peter.

There was nothing more to be said.

Chapter 28
Picking up the Pieces

By the end of that week Kieran was able to return to work, but life was still unsettled and she felt a burden to her friends.

She hadn't heard a word from Martin which was a good thing, and in the silence of her room at Peter and Margaret's house she reflected on how she felt. She tried hard to unravel the tangled complexities of her life.

Kieran soon came to realize that even though it was the affair that had finally ended her marriage; this new phase of her life wasn't about that relationship. She resigned herself to the fact that Martin had intoxicated her senses for months gradually luring her into believing she couldn't live without him, but being apart from him Kieran began to understand that wasn't true.

She had just needed to break free from that dead marriage.

The relationship with Martin was more like a drug she had stumbled upon that, albeit fleetingly, had felt like an antidote for years of emotional malnourishment.

She had been starved of all the ingredients that make up a wholesome marriage.

"I know Dad's missing us and I want to go home, not look for a separate home away from him," Thomas raged at Kieran when he found her looking through ads for rental properties.

Before Kieran could reply Megan answered her brother's rant.

"I'd rather see my Mum happy and live in a separate house than sad all the time living with Dad," she stated with wisdom and maturity far beyond her years. "Why can't you see that Tommy?" she added attempting some convincing of her own.

"She doesn't care about our happiness so why should I care about hers?" he added with a fury that emphasized where her son's heart was at that time.

He felt nothing but hatred towards Kieran for what she'd done, but she refused to allow that kind of anger into Peter and Margaret's home or to influence the future she was now trying to create for them all.

"Thomas I can't change how you feel about me, but you have to understand right now." And she paused for breath. "I am not going back to your father and that's final!" Kieran looked at her son and felt his pain cut deep into her heart, but she knew he didn't want her to console him.

"Sooner or later you will have to accept it Thomas. As painful as it may be right now, time has a habit of healing all pain."

She left the children to talk things over allowing them to release any pent up frustrations. After calling it a night she prayed that she'd find somewhere to live soon.

The hardest part of all of this was to stay strong and true to her convictions. Excluding her recent guilt, her greatest drawback had always been to give into other peoples demands. By going along with what others wanted from her, she had denied herself chance to have a voice. Now she did but she had to stay strong at all costs.

The following morning Margaret told her she had to work, but she'd still be able to drop the children off at school. This situation wasn't ideal for anyone and Kieran longed to find that perfect home.

By the end of that day her prayers were answered!

Peter had found out from a friend that there was a pretty flat for rent in Brechin. It was in a great neighborhood and actually the upper floor of a beautiful old nurse's home. It was on Infirmary Street and only about fifty yards away from the town's hospital and Kieran felt positive even before seeing it.

After work the following day Peter took her to see it having made prior arrangements with the landlord. It was everything Kieran dreamed her new place would be. It had a nice size living room, two large bedrooms, one big enough for Megan and Tommy to share and a huge kitchen and bathroom. It was light and sunny and more important it had a peace within its walls.

Kieran knew when she found her new home she would feel it in her spirit. And she did immediately. Peter watched as she walked from room to room, her face a beacon of hope, but then suddenly her demeanor changed and she turned to him defeated.

"But I don't have any money! I can't afford it."

Peter turned to the landlord and asked, "Have you advertised it yet Mrs. Scott?"

"Well, no actually. I was waiting until we cleaned it up a little but that shouldn't take long."

"Can we get back to you tomorrow?"

Mrs. Scott said she'd hold it until the end of the week which gave them four days to decide.

"Thank you, we'll call tomorrow."

Kieran looked at Peter, sensing he was up to something. On the way back home she sat quietly, scared to get too excited about the pretty flat.

"You liked the place didn't you Kieran?" Peter asked as she lowered her eyes.

"It's absolutely perfect. I'm just not sure I'll be able to afford it."

"Well, let's not get disheartened until we find out, OK?"

Kieran smiled trying hard to hold onto hope.

The following few days flew by like a whirlwind and Kieran could hardly catch her breath!

Peter and Margaret offered to help her with the two hundred pounds deposit, which at first she refused, but they insisted. Assuring them she'd pay it back little by little she eventually and gratefully accepted.

She found out from the local Housing Department that; now being classed as a single parent, working only a part time job, she was eligible to claim for assistance, which meant she'd have help with seventy-five percent of the rent!

Kieran couldn't believe it!

Piece by piece everything fell into place. She worked out a budget for food and utilities and all of a sudden her new life of freedom became possible. She was elated!

The children were still sad understandably so, especially Thomas, but when she took them to see the new flat Megan fell in love with it.

Tommy said it was stupid and nowhere near as nice as their house.

She realized he was not only furious with her, but in denial. He refused to believe that the break up was real and seemed determined to hate everything his mother was trying to do, but she left him alone. There was no point in trying to convince him of anything other than what he'd already made up in his own mind.

His mother destroyed their life and he was not going to accept it without a fight.

By the end of that week the contract was signed, and the keys were handed over. Kieran was happy with the flat the way it was, so she assured the landlord she would do the cleaning. Since Mrs. Scott didn't have the expense of hiring a cleaning person she took fifty pounds off the first month's rent.

That little extra was enough to buy groceries and a few bits and bobs to cheer the place up, and when Friday night came they were ready to move.

It didn't take them long. All they had was personal belongings but when everything was finally unpacked they collapsed on the beaten up old sofa in the living room.

The furnishings weren't really Kieran's style but she didn't care.

It was a beautiful old building that stood at the top of a brae which led up from the little town square and looked out over an expanse of Brechin itself. There were trees everywhere and Kieran finally felt she'd come home. She had found her sanctuary. A place she could call home.

This old house was a place to reflect on what life now held and somewhere to begin building a new life.

Chapter 29
The Perfect Place

She grieved for a few moments when she saw the beautiful furniture she and Danny had bought together and tears welled up in her eyes as she came to terms with what could have been.

Peter had taken her over to the house on the farm to pick up the last of her things and her heartbreak was more than obvious to him.

As he went over to ask if she was OK, the door opened and Danny walked in looking grey and withdrawn. He had a gaunt look in his eyes like a dead man walking and seemed almost like a shell of his former self. Kieran felt solely responsible for his demise.

"We did knock, but there was no reply and the door was open," she explained.

Three weeks had passed since that fateful Sunday but it felt more like an eternity. Peter had called Danny the day before to ask if he could bring Kieran over and he'd agreed. He knew it was over. He knew he had lost her for good this time. He knew there was nothing he could do to get her back.

"How're you doing Danny?" was all Kieran could think to say, although it was more than obvious.

He could hardly get the energy together to whisper "OK" before heaving a deep sigh with a heavy shrug of his shoulders. He was in his work clothes and looked as though he'd lost even more weight.

"You look thinner Danny. I hope you're looking after yourself," she added feeling the statement had a hint of pathetic.

Every fiber of who she was fought against the guilt she struggled with on a daily basis, but to see what she'd done to someone she'd once loved crippled her. She struggled to shake it off, knowing if she stood there one moment longer she'd cave.

She excused herself, first asking permission to collect the rest of her clothes as though she was now an intruder. But she was. And this was no longer her home. She went from room to room stacking clothes on the beds and looking through drawers trying hard to hold on to her emotions.

She hadn't realized how hard this would be and as she packed away the remnants of a lifetime, she became aware that she was stripping Danny of all the years they'd shared together. She left behind all the furniture they'd bought together and asked him for nothing. How could she, he had nothing left to give.

Kieran's heart ached for the man she had thought her husband to be when they were courting all those years ago. She cursed the spirit of selfishness that had increasingly devoured him over the years, ultimately bringing them to this destination of regrets.

She prayed he would be OK, and only wished for him to try harder to be a better father to his children so that they could at least get through this as unscathed as possible.

The trip to town was silent. Peter instinctively knew Kieran didn't want to share niceties. She was heavily burdened and probably would be for quite a while wondering whether she had done the right thing. But then that was normal and like the end of any life there had to be a grieving process.

The sun was shining and a gentle breeze drifted down the hallway of her new home. Peter helped her unpack and smiled as he watched her come to life. It was apparent she'd shed the ghosts of the past that had haunted her on the trip back from the farm, and he was thankful he was able to help her with the transition.

He knew, also, he would try to be there as much as he could for Danny, but he assumed that it might be more difficult, given how much they'd already helped Kieran. However, he'd already spoken to him and he felt that Danny had resigned himself to the break up. He even admitted that it was more than likely his neglect that had chased Kieran into the arms of another man.

Peter had been taken aback by his confession, but had also gained a new found respect for him with the candor he displayed.

After finishing most of the unpacking Kieran just had enough time to run to the store to pick up a few things for their first night. She didn't want Thomas to have any more reason to complain about the move so she bought a few of their favorite goodies.

Peter and Margaret offered to come by with fish and chips for teatime and so after unloading the groceries and treats she walked to Megan's school. It was nice to live in a town again and be within walking distance of everything. Even the High school wasn't that far away.

The school bell rang just as Kieran arrived and within a few moments the children came running out screaming and laughing and jostling one another. Kieran searched the crowd for Megan and then she saw the familiar face with big brown eyes and long hair all the way down her back. Try as she might to wave and shout her name, Kieran's voice was lost in the racket of the end of the day.

Her bonnie wee lass looked like an orphan standing all alone, and Kieran felt a pang of concern run through her. Suddenly another little girl with blonde hair ran up to Megan, and the two began to chatter and laugh like long lost friends. "There's my mum. Mum!" Megan shouted waving excitedly and the fear Kieran felt a second earlier dissipated quickly and she hugged her wee lamb grateful that she'd made a friend on the first day.

They walked with Megan's new friend until she said "Well this is where I live but I'll meet you here tomorrow morning at 8:30, and we can walk the rest of the way together."

"That would be great, Ailsa!" Megan replied with a huge grin.

They sauntered along and chatted about the day, and when they arrived home Megan ran to her room and squealed with delight when she saw all her favorite things.

Quickly realizing her mum must have gone back to the farm Megan came to ask about her dad.

"Well he's lost a bit of weight which isn't surprising, but I think he's well enough, darlin', just really sad." Kieran had no intention of candy coating anything and was determined never to lie to her children again.

"Maybe Tommy and I could go and see him at the weekend, Mum?" Her wee lamb asked and Kieran gave her a hug.

"That sounds quite possible."

Tommy arrived home and didn't offer much more than a disgruntled snort.

Kieran followed him into the bedroom.

"How was your day darlin'?" she asked desperate to recreate their afternoon banters. But how would that be possible? Could she ever expect him to be the same towards her?

"Fine," was his reply without as much as a glance.

"Margaret and Paul are coming over with fish and chips, Tommy."

"That's nice, but I don't like them. In fact I'm not even hungry so I'm goin' out with ma pals!"

Kieran's heart beat quickened and she felt heat rise to her face, but she tried to play it cool.

"Have you done your homework yet?" she asked as calmly as possible forgetting which day of the week it was.

"I don't have any; it's the weekend remember!" He almost spat the words at her and she flinched from the venom in his voice.

"Don't talk to me with that tone young man!" Kieran replied returning quickly to the lioness.

Tommy recognized the roar and quickly softened his attitude a little.

"I'm sorry, but I'm not hungry and I don't want to be here when *they* get here."

It was obvious Thomas regarded *them* as accomplices to his families break up.

Kieran backed off. "Ok then but be back by nine at the latest. We don't know this neighborhood yet."

Her son left and Kieran's heart sank. What was their life going to be like with this perpetual poison of unforgiveness? Had she left one miserable existence for another?

Perhaps it's just because it's still so real for him, and she had a sudden flash back of that terrible night. The night it had become all too real to Tommy, and she felt remorse and shame flood back like a gift from hell that kept on giving.

As the days wore on, time began to heal.

Every now and then she'd catch Tommy playing with Megan in their room and even a burst of laughter could be heard down the hallway at times.

Within a few weeks of them moving in Danny called to suggest the children spend the weekend with him at the farm.

He sounded a little better than the last time they spoke, and Kieran hoped that this effort by him to reach out would be a turning point in their lives.

She hadn't spoken to Martin in weeks now and had found out through the base grapevine that he'd been ordered to stay on base until his command investigated the claims made against him by Kieran's husband.

Was that the reason Danny suddenly sounded well?

Kieran desperately wanted to move on with her life, but all of a sudden she felt she was being dragged down into a cess-pit of revenge and desperation by her husband. Was Danny trying to get even?

Chapter 30
Guilty as Charged

Danny was bent on revenge!

Martin was ordered not to leave the base or communicate with Kieran, at least until her divorce was final and this new turn of events now enraged her to the point of; turning her compassion for Danny's pain into a battle of wills.

She tried to figure out his game plan. Was Danny's effort to destroy his adversary designed to show Martin up as the only bad guy? Perhaps in the hope of gaining Kieran's trust he thought she just might go back to him? If that was his intention he obviously didn't know her. She wouldn't have gone back to Danny if her life depended on it! And his vain attempt to prove redemption in her eyes was pathetic.

But Kieran atleast was determined to keep their life on as even ground as possible for Tommy and Megan's sake and they eventually fell into a rhythm of sharing the well being of their children. Kieran kept the children during the week and on the weekends they visited their Dad.

Remaining true to his colors, however Danny inevitably let them all down miserably. More often than not Tommy and Megan would come back from their father's house stressed, describing how sad their father was and how desperately he wanted them all back. Instead of him being a supportive father encouraging his children to accept the situation and heal, he bombarded them with questions about Kieran's life. He used them as informers and go betweens towards his vain attempts at getting her to return.

Kieran confronted him on his diabolical behavior when she called after a heartbreaking conversation with Tommy.

His final attempt to bring even more heartache into the situation was to convince Tommy he was lonely. Her son made a decision that was to tear Kieran apart.

"Mum, I can't stand to see Dad so sad, missing us so much. I've decided to live with him, and I can come here at the weekends."

Kieran was shattered and tried to convince Tommy of the reality of his father's ploy. It was a balancing act though. She didn't want to drag Danny down in Tommy's eyes, ultimately hurting her child in the process. She knew she had to choose her words carefully.

"Sweetheart, I understand why you're doing this because I know your heart. I know you've been desperate for a close relationship with your dad, but this is not the time," Kieran went on treading carefully. "Yes; he's still hurting but you are not the adult, he is, and you're the one who needs looking after, not him."

"But he seems so sad every time we go over and I just thought..."

Kieran interrupted. "I know what you thought sweetheart and I commend you for it, but not at the risk of your well being. I'm afraid you won't be looked after properly." Thomas stood tall and dug in his heels.

"Mum, I'll be fine. I need to do this!"

Kieran felt defeated and then something else took over. She felt betrayed! As much as she understood the reasons why Tommy had made his decision Kieran remembered how she'd been there for him all through his life and she felt let down.

Tommy had turned his back on her and was now looking towards the parent who'd belittled him, the parent who'd broken an untold amount of promises and guided him down many a wrong path. Tommy was choosing the parent who never got up in the middle of the night when he was desperately sick and the one who never listened to his chatter about his day.

Flash backs of fond memories played out in Kieran's mind like a family movie and after Tommy left she broke down and wept. He was going to be neglected! She could feel it.

Within a month Kieran's dread came true but Thomas wouldn't admit his error of judgment. He'd turn up at the weekends with unwashed and unkempt clothes. He was always starving, but she'd put that at least down to him being a teenager.

Kieran only had a tiny budget to feed her little family for the week and Tommy would eat almost all the fruit over the weekend, as though he was building up a stock pile of nutrients. Kieran bought him boots, she could ill afford, because his shoes were thread bare and she felt worried sick with concern.

But then her husband called one day and asked if he could come over and talk.

Kieran had just arrived home from work when Danny knocked at the door. She was taken aback at the sight before her!

He'd lost a lot of weight, which he'd needed to do for a long time and was trim and quite handsome. He had obviously bought new clothes and looked the way she'd longed him to look throughout the fifteen years of their marriage. She invited him in as she struggled with internal rage.

His son looked bedraggled, but Danny was dressed up. All she'd dreaded that terrible day when Tommy left, seemed to be coming true.

Basically Danny came over to impress her with his new look and ask her to come back. He made the same promises he'd made for years, but she could see straight through the façade.

Kieran listened to what he had to say and sat quietly. She didn't need to interrupt because she knew exactly what was going on and she knew exactly what her response was going to be.

"I'm happy to see you're getting your life together, Danny, and I must say you look really well, but our only concern now should be the welfare of our children and not the mending of a broken marriage. That had many a chance to heal throughout the years we were together, but it didn't so there's no use treading over old ground." Kieran sighed and looked at Danny with purpose.

"Thomas concerns me. He looks terrible when he comes over here at the weekends." She chose her words carefully, although she wanted to rage at him.

"Kieran I'm doing the best I can." And he stood up realizing finally the reason for his visit was futile. Danny left defeated and Kieran wondered if he would ever get it.

Just after He left the phone rang and when she answered her heart jumped.

"Martin you shouldn't be calling me! What if the phone lines are monitored?"

"I don't care, Kieran, I'm going crazy missing you so much! I want to come and see you," he added sounding desperate.

"Don't do it, Martin, you'll be seen and it's going against the orders of your command!"

She was outraged he would put himself and his career on the line just to come and see her. She didn't even take it as a compliment and just thought it downright stupid!

Kieran was beginning to see Martin in a different light, also. She put the receiver down after begging him not to come over and decided to take a long hot shower. She hoped it would relax her and take away the pressures of the day.

An hour later the door bell rang. It was Martin.

Kieran was furious but when he took her into his arms she melted, just like she always had. They hadn't seen each other for months and so their passion heightened to a crazed crescendo of desire. One thing led to another and before she realized they were in the bedroom and Megan was standing at the open door!

Her innocent baby girl witnessed something that afternoon she didn't need to see. Kieran screamed and rushed to cover her shame whilst her wee lamb just stood transfixed unable to move.

"Go away Megan. Go away!" Kieran screamed, and she fell trying to get to the door.

Megan just stood there seemingly in shock, but then she ran!

Grabbing at her robe Kieran followed Megan to her room and in a split second of craziness her initial reaction was to spank her for not turning away from the shameful scene. Kieran was mortified and wanted it to be gone. She desperately needed that horrendous scene from her tragic life to be gone.

Just as quickly she felt even more ashamed. She was punishing her wee lamb for something that wasn't her fault. What the hell was she doing!

Kieran collapsed beside the bed and both of them cried gut wrenching rivers of shock and shame. She held her baby and rocked her in her arms.

"I'm sorry darlin'. I'm so-so-sorry!"

She felt so embarrassed, wishing with all her heart to erase the image from her daughter's mind.

Martin was discrete enough to leave quietly. Mother and daughter just held each other for what felt like hours.

It seemed like every time Kieran had a legitimate complaint against Danny she herself would fall by the way side and into the snare of sin. And it always seemed magnified.

Two days after that terrible afternoon Kieran found out that Martin was going to court. Someone had seen him at the house that day and reported him to his command. A week later he was stripped of two stripes and ordered to house arrest for three months.

He wasn't allowed to see her until after the divorce and Kieran felt she was losing her mind with the drama of ever-mounting problems.

Ever since she'd laid eyes on Martin her life had been a travesty. One tragic event followed another. Aware that her life had turned into a soap opera, Kieran withdrew into a shell of protection. She didn't go anywhere apart from work and home and her neighbor downstairs began to worry.

Susan was a nice woman, who liked to drink a little too much for Kieran. Although she had passed the time of day with her on occasion, Kieran didn't know her that well. Susan had two daughters who played with Megan occasionally but other than that Kieran kept to herself.

It's strange how people react to a relatively young woman on her own who's trying to make a life for herself and her children. In most peoples mind a woman can't possibly be happy unless she has a man in her life and they seem inclined to matchmake with every possible eligible bachelor they know. That's exactly what her neighbor friend Susan had in mind.

Unknown to Kieran she'd been talking about her to Kevin, her divorced cousin, for some time. The closer she got to Kieran the more she became convinced they'd make a nice couple. She broached the subject with Kieran one day when she was hanging out washing in the back garden. Kieran's reaction was to laugh.

"Thank you Susan, but no thanks!" she replied then added, "I'm sure your cousin is a sweet guy, but I'm all burned out of relationships; thank you very much. I just want to enjoy life on my own, peacefully, with my children."

But Susan would not be deterred. Within a week she'd made it possible for Kevin to 'accidently' bump into Kieran when she arrived home from work. Yet another chapter in Kieran's life was about to step into the soaps.

"Kieran, I don't mean to sound forward but Susan's description of you, albeit a great one, pales to the real thing."

Her skin crawled with the compliment!

He seemed like a nice guy and was quite good looking too, but she just wasn't interested. Far too much had gone on in her life within this last year and she needed a complete timeout from any kind of social activity. She especially did not need to become involved with another man.

She said as much to Kevin and he gracefully accepted her answer but not before giving her his number.

"Just give me a call if you need anything, OK?"

Chapter 31
Message from Home

After her "chance" meeting with Kevin, Kieran went about her chores to fill in the rest of the day. She called down to Edinburgh to say hi to her parents and after hanging up decided to run a bath. She loved her bathroom. It had once been another bedroom that had been converted into a bright and airy room of relaxation and she looked forward to this time after a long, hard morning at work.

Her mum and dad were getting on in years and she hadn't liked the way they both looked the last time she'd visited. They only had each other now and Kieran was thankful Jo and Drew were still in Edinburgh and could visit them on a regular basis. But she had missed her parents for years and felt a constant sense of guilt for not being able to do her part in helping care for them.

It wasn't possible for her to go home that often, her life just wouldn't allow it. When she did manage to get home it was hard to ignore the change in them.

Kieran knew they'd worried about her with all that had gone on in her life, and it was difficult to shake off the nagging impression that everything was her fault. Compared to her brothers and sister, Kieran's life was a shambles, and the cruel words from her childhood constantly haunted her.

Her mum had developed cataracts in both eyes and her sight had been failing her for some time now. She'd also had problems with high blood pressure for years, and Kieran felt concerned with the lifestyle they'd chosen for themselves.

When they retired neither of them had developed a hobby or interest that would ensure their good health and general well being. Instead they seemed happy with their daily routine of walking over to the shops and watching television.

Her father hadn't had the wisdom to buy their home when the price was low so as a result they struggled with a high rent on their meager pension. That was until Jo and her husband Frank made the sacrifice to buy their home for them and pay the mortgage themselves. That meant their mum and dad would live rent free for the rest of their lives.

She admired her sister's sacrifice and loved her all the more for doing for their parents what she could only have dreamed of doing.

After her bath she put her feet up on the footstool in the cozy living room she'd created and looked out the tall window that gave her a view of the square at the bottom of the hill.

Martin had only called one more time since he'd been restricted to the base, and Kieran knew he was upset at her attitude. She had tried to convince him he was doing neither of them a favor by constantly disobeying his command, and she insisted he stop calling her. She'd had enough of his determination to create even more problems for himself and felt if he didn't care about his well being then at least she could make a stand.

She tried to read but couldn't concentrate. She put down her book and rested her eyes. Her thoughts whirled around in her mind and as she closed her eyes thankful for the peace and quiet of the day, the phone rang again.

It was Dana, the friend who'd encouraged Kieran's bid for freedom. She hadn't heard from her in a while but knew how busy she was and Kieran was surprised at how nice it was to hear her friends' voice.

"Do you want some company?" Dana asked and she accepted. To talk about nothing in particular might just be exactly what she needed.

Dana arrived half an hour later and they sat in the kitchen and enjoyed some tea and delicious cakes she had brought with her.

"Wow! Kieran, they seem to be lining up outside your door," her friend stated with astonishment. She'd just given Dana a condensed version of what had been happening in her life.

"No they're not," Kieran replied shaking her head. "It's just coincidence that everything seems to happen at the same time. It's like everything in life, you know that Dana. It's either feast or famine!"

"Well I'd like a taste of the feast," her friend added forcing Kieran to choke on her éclair!

The girls talked for hours and just before Dana left Kieran thanked her for the cake and conversation. "I was actually feeling a little bored without Megan here."

Megan was on a trip down to Edinburgh with her dad and Tommy and Kieran missed her wee lamb.

"I'll give you a call next week and maybe we could go out," Dana suggested as she left.

After fifteen years of heartache sprinkled with moments of happiness here and there, Kieran couldn't believe how much her life had changed.

There had been and still was an insurmountable amount of grief attached to the breakup and she prayed that through time it would diminish.

She pondered on the possibility that something just might come out of meeting Kevin but for some reason she was aware that her heart was being drawn elsewhere and that did not necessarily include staying in Brechin.

Red flags had begun to surface with Martin. Kieran acknowledged that she felt so much more at peace when he wasn't around. Why was that, she wondered. She admitted to herself that occasionally she missed the electricity of his touch. Still she could not dismiss these new signs of warning, nor the way they unnerved her.

Kieran made use of her time alone that weekend to clean and make her little sanctuary even prettier. She had found some cheap pieces of porcelain up town and used them to brighten her home. As she dusted and caught up on laundry, she tried to work out the mixed thoughts in her mind.

Was the love she felt for Martin, more like an addictive drug of sorts or was it the kind that would last a lifetime?

Unfortunately Kieran sensed the answer almost immediately. She had indeed succumbed to an addictive love. But then why did she feel a distinct pull to leave her homeland? What other reason could there be to leave, other than to be with Martin?

Was there such a thing as a pull of destiny?

Kieran dismissed the thoughts as romantic daydreams that held no basis of truth for the reality of her life. But then why did she feel so familiar and comfortable with the places spoken of in her books?

She liked to read Danielle Steele novels. She lost herself in the lives of people from as far apart as New York to the Californian coastline unabashedly taking comfort in this diversion.

Was what she was feeling just an escape from reality? Or was someone giving her a glimpse into what the future held for her?

She didn't attend church on a regular basis but still searched diligently for a greater truth.

In the square at the foot of the brae was a very old Church of Scotland but sadly enough, although the church was pretty the services themselves were downright boring!

Her flat was her sanctuary. Kieran embraced that perfect peace she found when just reading or listening to Mozart and Debussy. The music brought a quiet time of thought and reflection, stilling her heart from the chaos of life. Just like when she was a wee girl sitting on her doorstep, wrapped in a blanket and feeling grateful for all that surrounded her.

Sunday went by quickly and as she stood at the kitchen sink peeling potatoes for dinner that night she heard a car pull up outside. Some excited voices told her that her children were back from their trip. When she answered the door Megan staggered in, laden with bags of stuff her Nana had given her for her new bedroom.

Thomas was standing at the foot of the stairs so Kieran went down to give him a hug and thank Danny for taking them down.

"Nae'bother Kieran," he said in return, opening the car door and stepping out. "How are you doing?"

"Oh! I'm fine, just catching up on some cleaning, so I was able to keep myself busy with the weekend free."

There was still awkwardness between them but Kieran was happy he was making an effort to be a better dad.

They said their goodbyes and Danny and Thomas drove off to leave the two girls alone but content with their life together. Kieran sensed Tommy was in a calmer state of mind although she still saw deep sadness in his eyes. At least now she knew he was being looked after. Danny was doing his best and a relationship between Tommy and his dad was finally being forged.

"So you had a good time in Edinburgh?" Kieran asked her wee lamb.

Wee Lamb went on to tell her mum all they had done, including singing along to "Queen" all the way down the road. Sudden sadness tugged on Kieran's heart at the almost complete family picture Megan painted. But then she smiled, with the knowledge that more childhood memories were being created for her children even though they were no longer together.

They enjoyed dinner and just as Kieran was filling the sink with hot soapy water the phone rang. Thinking it might be Tommy for some reason she said 'hi sweetie,' expecting her son's voice to reply, but it wasn't.

"Kieran its Jo." There was a long pause, as though her sister was trying to catch her breath.

Immediately Kieran panicked.

"Jo what's wrong?" she asked but there was still no answer and Kieran felt a surge of adrenaline rush through her body.

"Jo what's wrong!?" she screamed into the phone and suddenly the dam broke. In between heart rendering sobs, her sister told her their mother had been taken to hospital suffering from a massive stroke!

"Oh my God! Oh Nooo!" Kieran fell to her knees and curled up in a ball, still holding the phone to her ear. Minutes went by and the two women sobbed uncontrollably on each end of the phone. Megan was now holding onto Kieran listening to the reason for her mother's sudden collapse and she wept along with her.

Ten minutes or so went by and eventually the two sisters pulled themselves together and tried to come to some understanding of what to do next.

Kieran had no savings and knew Danny would be just as broke so when she finally got off the phone to Jo, she took a deep breath and called Peter and Margaret. They'd saved her before, and because Kieran had managed to pay them back all of what she owed she felt they were now her only hope.

She composed herself but as soon as Peter asked what was wrong she fell apart once again. Little by little he gained an understanding of what had just happened, and he reassured her without hesitation that they'd be able to help.

It was still early evening so they came straight over.

"Thank you both yet again!" Kieran cried to the dear couple who'd been there for her no matter what. She wasn't able to give anything in return for their kindness to her, and she felt so humbled by the experiences of the last eighteen months.

It had been hard for her to swallow her pride and accept help when it was offered. She had spent so many years doing life all on her own, even when she was married!

They didn't stay long appreciating her need to calm and get herself together.

Before Peter and Margaret arrived she'd called Danny and had cried another river as she shared the news from Edinburgh.

"I'll come by in the morning and take Megan to school, Kieran, so don't worry about that. If you can pack a bag of clothes to do her for a few days, I'll pick her up after school, and she can stay here until you get back."

"Thanks Danny. I didn't know how I was going to cope with worrying about Megan's school and all."

Kieran packed enough clothes for a week or so, just in case and made sure everything was packed for Megan also.

By that time it was ten o'clock and she'd already found out there was a train for Edinburgh at 10:30 the following morning. That would give them enough time to see to the children and get to the railway station in Montrose.

Kieran tried to sleep amidst the turmoil of her thoughts. She eventually drifted off and dreamt about dance lessons, piano playing and hospitals; with a multitude of faces from the past and present laughing, crying and talking all at once, a reminder of the travesty that was her life.

Kieran was woken up with the impatient screech of the alarm clock. It sounded as though it had been ringing for some time and she felt drenched with sweat. She got through the motions of the morning almost robot like whilst trying to make sure her wee lamb's mind was somewhat at peace.

"Whatever happens I'll be fine, darlin', so don't you worry OK?"

Danny picked them up right on time, and after dropping Megan and Tommy off at school they drove to the train station.

Once again she felt humbled but this time it felt painful. After all she'd done to her, soon to be, ex-husband, he was showing compassion and being there in her time of need.

Tears flowed as she sat quietly and hid her face with her long chestnut hair. And as though sensing her grief he took hold of her hand and said, "She'll be fine Kieran. May's as strong as an ox!"

They arrived at the station just in time to board the train, and as Kieran was about to climb the steps Danny gave her a quick hug. "Take care of yourself, Kieran, and give us a call when you're able."

"Thanks Danny," she replied, holding herself together by a thread. "Thanks for everything," she added, and disappeared into the crowded train.

Kieran was lucky enough to find a window seat farther up the train and after loading her bags into the space between the seats she sat down and sighed.

It would take about an hour and she held onto every emotion as though her life depended on it. She didn't want to cry in a train full of people, but it was hard to stop her mind from wandering to the obvious.

It had been three weeks since her mums' cataract operation. May was so happy she could see clearly for the first time in a while, but now the rejoicing had turned to fear for her life. Kieran fought to keep her mind on anything other than her mum!

Jo had explained that she had mentioned having a bad headache for a couple of days but hadn't felt the need to call the doctor or worry anyone.

Drew had dropped by one night on his way home from a friends' house, and his parents were both asleep as usual in front of the television. His dad woke up immediately, but not his mum. When they tried to waken her and couldn't, they called for an ambulance.

She'd had a massive stroke.

Kieran gazed out the window at the beautiful, lush countryside, wincing at the extreme contrast between the glorious scenery and how woeful she felt inside.

Her mum! The only one who knew her like no one else did! It was a thought that would have surprised her many years ago, but on her last visit home, when May was still blinded with cataracts she said something to Kieran that shocked her.

Jo had put a plate of food down in front of her mum as she sat at the tiny kitchen table, but didn't think to help her with the knife and fork.

It was an immediate reaction for Kieran to hold her mum's hand, letting her know where everything was and then she cut her meat into bite size pieces.

It was no big deal! But as she bent down her mum whispered in her ear, "You're the only one who'd think to do that for me, Kieran."

How did she know? How did this woman who, it seemed, had never understood Kieran's feeling or thoughts about anything through the years, how did she know her that well now? Why did you leave it so long to tell me Mum?

Fat tears welled up in her eyes and spilt over to form tracks down her ashen face and she blinked to clear them away.

A middle aged man sitting across from her noticed her sadness and leaned forward to pat her on the hand. "Are ye' ok sweetie?" he asked with concern evident in his tone.

Kieran sat up and pulled her jacket around her nervously and wiping more tears from her face she replied, "Yes, thanks, I'm fine."

She didn't want to say more. She didn't want to talk to anyone. She just wanted to be with her mum.

Chapter 32
Too late for Sorry

Kieran was still scared to live without her mum, feeling like a little girl again abandoned at a bus stop. Could she please just have a few more years to be the daughter she'd always wanted to be?

There were never conversations from two hearts. There were never days of going to lunch and talking about silly things. Why didn't you want those moments Mum? Why didn't you make sure they happened? She prayed she'd be given the chance to at least say something even if it was only sorry!

When the train arrived she hailed a taxi that took her home to the Salvesens. When she arrived she noticed her sisters' car outside.

Kieran walked up the familiar path lined with bricks now worn with weathered age, breathing in the familiar fragrance of honeysuckle and roses. She tried to shake fond memories from her mind, to keep her composure. Looking down at her faded doorstep she knocked on the door and waited.

Jo answered within moments and they fell into each other's arms. The two sisters tried to catch a breath of welcome and happiness to see each other amidst the crushing pain of sorrow.

As Kieran walked into the living room she caught a glimpse of her dad before he saw her, his small stature looking even smaller and his raven hair now grey.

"Oh Kieran's here!" He said in a trumped up jolly voice.

"How are you doing?" she asked, giving her dad a hug, knowing what the answer would be.

"Oh I'm fine, love," he answered as though he was just getting over a cold.

The pretense and cover up of real human emotions still enraged Kieran. Let's pretend everything's OK when it's not and it might just all go away!

She heard the irony of her rebellious self rear up its ugly head and she herself stuffed it back into wherever it belonged. It wasn't the time or the place or the right situation to invite the battle into play.

Why did everything have to be this way? She couldn't stand feeling like an alien in what should feel like her home. Why am I so different or do I just dare to question? It was the same question that had haunted Kieran for years.

"Dae' ye' want something tae' eat before we go to the hospital, Kieran?" Her dad asked, still concerned with everyone's stomach.

Reminding herself that that was the way he showed love, she replied, "No thanks, Dad, I just want to see Mum." And tears welled up yet again.

The smell of antiseptic and floor wax hit them as the double doors opened and the family took the lift to the fourth floor. As they entered May's room, Kieran stopped. A sharp intake of breathe made her feel lightheaded.

That wasn't her mum lying in that bed. It was a shell she almost didn't recognize. Was her mum still in there somewhere? Could she even hear Kieran's voice and feel her touch?

Familiar tears overflowed as she leaned over to kiss the face of the woman who'd given her life. The woman who'd taken her to dance recitals and whose eyes sparkled when watching her on stage; the woman who was so proud of her little girl when she won the beauty contest; the woman whose heart broke when watching her little girl make so many mistakes!

The family had gathered round, and her older brother was on his way from South Africa where he'd made his home many years before. There was quiet in the room; each of them spending personal time of reflection with the woman that lay so still.

Each of them with their own version of memories from a life spent together. Very rarely togetherness memories; but perhaps that was only for Kieran. She was the baby and had felt like an only child for years after they'd all left the nest.

Her mum was grey and lifeless against the snow white of the bed sheets and it was hard to hold onto hope. Hope of a few more years to fill with what should have been. Hope that Kieran would have the time to say all the words left unspoken because she hadn't known how to give them life.

She couldn't leave her side now. She didn't want her to leave for those green hills of home, lying in a hospital bed all alone. May hated hospitals and Kieran didn't want her to be afraid. The family tried to convince Kieran there was no point in staying but she wouldn't leave. She couldn't leave.

Kieran braved two weeks of hospital visits and many hours of whispering words of love and encouragement: May held on. The doctors were shocked at her resilience. They kept giving the family a diagnosis of permanent brain damage even if she survived but they didn't give much hope for her recovery.

Kieran was proud of her mum's valiant fight to stay with them, and she prayed night and day for a miracle.

After receiving a call from her job, however, she had yet another painful decision to make.

She only had two weeks grace from work. They tried to be compassionate but more or less told her they couldn't extend her time off. She'd have to make up her mind whether she was coming back to work or not.

"I'm sorry Kieran; trust me we understand how hard it must be," the secretary at human resource said, sympathizing with her as much as possible.

"I know. It's OK, Jen, I'll be back on Monday so if you could let the kennel staff know, I'd be grateful."

It was Friday and Kieran had to get back home, or to Brechin, or wherever home was.

She gave her family the news and then caught the bus up to the hospital to visit with her mum, praying it wouldn't be the last time. She wanted to be alone with her. She wanted that special mum and daughter time to chat about silly things.

It was a breezy day and Kieran fondly remembered her mum's little word to her many times when growing up, especially when she was bored or a little sad.

"Go outside, pet. The wind will blow all those cobwebs away."

Perhaps that's why she always loved windy days.

Walking into that hospital room for what could possibly be the last time was hard. To see the motionless figure on the bed where her mum should be was heartbreaking, and Kieran felt both she and her mum were now ready to leave.

"I don't know if you're in there, Mum," she whispered, her bottom lip quivering as she took hold of her ice-cold hand. "But all I have left to say is I love you. I always have and I always will, and I knew you were the best Mum you could be."

More familiar tears followed more familiar tracks in the all too-familiar heartbreak of a little girl who had missed her mum all through her life.

She'd missed the relationship she'd longed for, and she'd missed special times together as her mum had grown old because her life had been such a mess!

"I'm sorry for making you sad Mum. I'm sorry if I let you down."

Kieran couldn't say another word as she watched her mum lying still. She just hoped she'd heard the regrets of a lifetime, and she hoped she'd forgive her baby girl.

Kieran went back to the house she once knew as home for a season and packed for an early rise the following morning.

There was nothing left for Kieran in that house anymore, and sad as it was to realize, she felt the life had gone from number 68 Salvesen Gardens. It had always been her mum who'd kept the house lively with beautiful music and her special prowess for décor. Little touches of unique flavor here and there, was her mum's motif, even when it was untidy.

It was her mum who pushed to go on holidays every year. It was her mum who'd pushed her children to excel, and, as painful as it felt sometimes, Kieran knew she did it out of love.

She was going to miss sitting by her mum's bedside but Kieran held on to that flicker of hope that she'd recover, no matter what the doctors said to the contrary.

She said her goodbyes and was thankful her brother-in-law had offered to drive her to the station.

"I'll call, Kieran, as soon as there's any change!" Jo shouted as the train began to pull out, and Kieran lowered the window to wave goodbye.

She claimed another window seat and as the train's motion jiggled her gently back and forth like a baby being rocked, she closed her eyes and pondered on the thought of moving back down to Edinburgh.

The journey was short this time, or so it seemed, and she was glad she'd called Danny the night before. He offered to pick her up at the station, and she was looking forward to seeing the children.

It was the summer holidays and school was out for eight weeks.

She'd hoped to spend some time down in Edinburgh that summer as a treat for Megan and Tommy if he wanted to come, but she'd used up all her holiday time with the visit. The train slowly pulled into the station in Montrose, and Kieran could see Tommy and Megan on the platform with Danny.

As she disembarked and dragged her heavy case over the little bridge Megan ran when she caught a glimpse of her mum. She ran into her arms and the tears flowed freely!

Kieran wasn't afraid or ashamed to show her feelings and as she wiped her face one more time Tommy caught up with the two and gave his mum a hug.

"Are ye' ok Mum?" he asked feeling a little awkward with the display of emotion in public. It wasn't cool!

As Kieran pulled herself together she stretched up and ruffled Tommy's hair. He was growing so tall and looked more like an adult than a child now, but every now and then Kieran still saw her baby boy in those eyes.

The new week started without any news of change from Edinburgh and when Wednesday came Kieran decided to call.

"There's been no change apart from Mum getting some bed sores but the doctors are still amazed that she's holding on," Jo said sounding a little weary.

"Miracles do happen, Jo," Kieran insisted, praying her sister wouldn't give up hope.

There's wasn't a whole lot more to say, so they said their goodbyes and Jo promised to call with any news.

Kieran got through the rest of the week trying to remain as busy as possible and before she knew it Friday arrived and Megan began packing for her weekend trip to her dad's.

"Mum I could stay here this weekend if you'd like the company?" Her wee lamb asked, thinking only of her mums' well being.

"That's OK sweetheart. You go and have fun on the farm with your friends' I'll be fine, honest."

A car horn blew announcing the arrival of Danny and Thomas, and Kieran walked Megan downstairs to say goodbye. Danny asked if she needed anything before they left but she declined, feeling that to interact too much with him might give the wrong impression.

As she waved and watched the car drive down the brae with a funny little face pressed against the window she heard the phone and ran back upstairs. Grabbing the receiver she said a breathless hello, but didn't recognize the voice on the other end.

"Hello, Kieran, I hope you don't mind me calling, but I'd been speaking to Susan yesterday just after coming back from the rig, and she told me about your mum. Is there anything I can do?" the voice asked as Kieran struggled to recognize it.

Then suddenly it dawned. "Kevin is that you?"

"Oh I'm sorry, I should've said but I guess I'm a little nervous. I-I-I hope you didn't mind Susan giving me your number," he stammered.

Kieran was still a little startled not knowing quite what to say. Her mind was confused and her emotions were a wreck.

"No I guess I don't mind but…."

"You don't need to say anything, Kieran, I just wanted to make sure you're OK," Kevin assured her, feeling stupid for calling.

But then her heart softened and she allowed the drawbridge to her re-enforced castle to slowly come down. Kieran sat down on the floor and crossed her legs like a little girl.

Perhaps it would be nice to have someone to talk to, someone who wasn't a part of the turmoil of the last year and a half, someone who might just listen without wanting anything from her.

"To be honest, Kieran, I kicked myself for not asking for your number when we met before, but somehow I felt you wouldn't have given it anyway."

He was being honest and Kieran appreciated that. She hated the games people played.

They talked for over an hour and Kieran almost had to admit she'd enjoyed the conversation. There was no guilt, no shame or remorse for pain inflicted, there was just casual conversation and it felt like a breath of fresh air.

"Kieran, I don't want to pressure you in any way, but I'd really like to see you again," Kevin said after taking a deep breath.

There was something about this woman with green eyes that had haunted him from the first time they'd met. He'd asked his cousin Susan more about her when he got back from the off-shore oil rigs where he worked. He was intrigued by the deep sadness he'd seen in her, but there was more, much more.

"I understand you've been through a lot. I don't want you to feel that seeing me would bring even more confusion into your life right now, but I'd still like to see you."

Kieran suddenly felt saddened, wondering now whether he too just wanted a piece of her.

"Kevin, it was really nice to talk to you. But you're right, I have gone through a lot in the past year or so and, well, I've told you about Martin and...." She lowered her eyes unsure of what to say next. "I'm not sure what's going to come of that, if anything at all."

There was a long moment of silence then Kevin spoke.

"Kieran, I know, I know but I just feel in my gut that, that guy isn't right for you!"

Kieran was quiet but felt a twinge of anger inside. How did he know and what business was it of his anyway?

"I'm sorry I shouldn't have said that, it's none of my business, but just know that I like you a lot, and if you've kept my number I'd really like to hear from you, even if it is just to talk."

It was Kevin's turn to go quiet and Kieran just thanked him for calling and asked him to give her a little time.

"I'll try and call you next week, Kevin."

She laid down the phone and wondered what the heck was she doing? She was beginning to feel she'd had it with all men! Relationships were too draining.

Kieran spent the weekend cleaning and using that time to mull things over in her mind.

She'd thought she was in love with Martin, but so much tragedy had come out of that relationship and she wasn't sure whether she had the courage to continue with it. Since he was American, there was so much more at stake.

If she and Martin did decide to be together and eventually marry she'd need all the courage she could muster to leave her family and country behind. And how would the children take to living in America?

The thought was daunting but she didn't need to put herself through that yet at least. There were other issues about that relationship that needed more thought before she made any firm decision.

Kieran also knew the children weren't crazy about Martin and Tommy had recently been showing signs of contempt towards him. She had a nagging feeling that his father was as much to do with that mindset as anyone, but she didn't want to continually bring it up when Tommy came over. His visits seemed to be less frequent now, since the weekend was when Megan went to see her dad, but when she did see her son Kieran wanted peace just to be with him.

Saturday was spent enjoying the beautiful weather and hanging laundry out to dry. Kieran felt at peace during her busy day, but as night fell the turmoil returned.

Could I live in Edinburgh again? She asked herself once again and then she dissolved into tears wondering whether her mum would pull through. If she didn't survive the massive stroke would she be able to move down to the city to be closer to her dad?

Sad to say she wasn't sure.

Kieran's heart ached for him all alone in the house, fearing for his wife.

She couldn't get rid of the image of him, sitting on his chair looking tiny and frail. The vision filled her with despair. Paralyzed almost with the inability to reach out to him, Kieran blamed herself and grieved the relationship she'd never had with him.

She had called a couple of times just to hear the same thing, "I'm fine."

But she also understood or at least just accepted.

Chapter 33
End of an Era

"Shy! Shy sweetie, are you ok?" Paul shook his wife's shoulder gently, afraid to waken her too quickly.

She'd had these nightmares for years and his heart went out to her that morning. She looked troubled and desperately wanting to take her pain away he shook a little harder.

Shy awoke with a start.

As she gradually grew accustomed to the quiet of their room she knew exactly where she'd just returned from.

"It was a bad one Huh?" Paul asked tenderly.

Shy sat up in bed and rubbed her eyes.

"Yes, I guess." And then she remembered. "I'm more vulnerable in my dream state apparently. The enemy attempts to attack me there as I continue through the story with Lyric. But he can't get through the hedge of protection I know the Lord has around me honey. I'm OK honestly darlin'."" She grabbed his hand and squeezed. "It doesn't bother me when I'm awake and you know as well as I do, the Lord healed all the pain many years ago, so please don't worry." Shy assured him. "This story is important. Lyric needs to know."

"I know, I know honey but I hurt for you. You seem to go through so much torment in those dreams," he said with empathy.

Shy leaned over to kiss his cheek. "Well, I've never heard of anyone dying from a dream." And she giggled like a little girl as she slid out of bed.

Paul just shook his head and smiled.

Healed indeed! He thought to himself as he too got up to start their day.

It was a warm and sunny day before Thanksgiving and the house was soon bustling. Shy let Kylie out into the backyard and stepped outside to breathe in the, day-after-a-storm, fragrance.

How amazing is God's earth! The thought stirred her as she wrapped her robe around her waist and tied a knot in the belt.

Little Kylie was foraging around in the undergrowth having caught the scent of some little unassuming creature. Shy wiped down one of the wrought iron garden chairs and sat down. She felt a surge of sheer joy rush through every ounce of her body and she felt vibrant and alive. That's Papa's joy, she mused.

Shy loved the incredible delight of nature just after a rain shower and felt it was like a special little gift remembered and renewed afresh, time after time.

Shy called Kylie who looked as though she was just getting ready to disappear after her quarry and they went back inside.

She started on breakfast and before long aromas of the edible kind were drifting upwards to solidly confirm everyone's wakeup call.

At the breakfast table there was a hub of chatter about the day that stretched out before them. The men were talking about football and the women were going over a check list of everything they'd need for Thanksgiving dinner.

"Are we going to start on the trifle today, Grandma?" Lyric asked with anticipation.

"Oh yes we surely are, ma' pet!"

Breakfast over, the men folk retired to the family room to read the morning papers, and Erin and Lyric cleared the dishes away. "Thanks, ma' darlin's," Shy remarked as she was ushered out of the kitchen by her willing helpers.

"Well I guess I'll just jump in the shower then," she added but no one was listening. They were all busy about their tasks, and Shy sighed contentedly as she climbed the stairs to her room.

She wondered when they'd have the time in the next few days to continue with the story. But with what lay ahead, perhaps a couple of days of family time and relaxation would benefit them all.

Shy stepped into the shower allowing the hot water to wash away any concerns she may have had about the next chapter in a lifetime. She closed her eyes and began to sing her favorite hymn;

Amazing Grace how sweet the sound that saved a wretch like me,
I once was lost but now I'm found, was blind but now I see!

The family spent the whole day just enjoying the down time and not doing much of anything. The women began to prepare for the following days dinner.

Erin sensed Lyric might just enjoy time with her grandma in the kitchen so she offered to run to the store to pick up a few last minute additions to the menu.

Just as Lyric was about to add the special ingredient to the trifle Kylie began to bark frantically and then the door bell rang. Shy and Lyric met Paul in the hallway as all three went to see who was at the door and when it opened they screamed with surprise!

"Apryl!" they all cried in unison.

They fell into each other's arms amidst hugs and kisses and tears of joy.

Greg came in to join the happy group and the front door flew open as Erin arrived back from the store.

"As soon as I saw the cab driving down the driveway I knew it was you ya' toe-rag!" Erin remarked giving her baby sister a bear hug!

"Oh! There you go with your unique terms of endearment," Apryl replied catching her breath from all the loving!

Shy couldn't take the excitement and suddenly escaped to the kitchen in tears. Apryl and Erin gave each other an all-knowing glance.

"She'll be fine," Erin told her sister noticing she looked a little sheepish.

"Go on in and speak to her, lassie, she's just missed you so much!"

Everyone caught their breath and the two girls helped Greg to take Apryl's bags upstairs.

"I'm sorry I played a trick on you, Mum," Apryl admitted giving Shy a hug.

"Oh! Darlin' don't be silly now. Ye' don't need to apologize I'm just a wee bit emotional that's all. I'm so glad your home."

More tears began to flow.

"I couldn't stay away for another day Mum. I've really been missing home lately," Apryl confessed and the two women chatted, catching up on all the news in each other's life.

They were soon joined by the other two and after an hour of catch up and a few cups-o'-tea Apryl and Lyric went upstairs.

"I'll help you unpack!" an excited little girl had offered. Lyric hoped to spend the rest of the afternoon talking about horses, and her aunt was more than willing.

"Those two are like two peas in a pod," Shy remarked as the two horse lovers left the kitchen.

"Oh! I know. Lyric had been praying Apryl would be here this Thanksgiving so that was one prayer answered," Erin sighed knowing how desperate her daughter was to visit her aunt on the ranch.

The excitement of the last few hours eventually died down and Erin busied herself rinsing out the tea cups. With slight hesitation she turned to Shy.

"How's Lyric coping with the story so far, Mum?"

Without taking her eyes off what she was doing Shy shook her head, smiled and sighed, "She is taking it amazingly well." Shy looked up at her wee lamb with pride evident in her green eyes.

"You and Greg are doing an awesome job with that young' un. I'm so proud of you!" Shy went on. "Do you know she's even witnessed to me through one of the hardest parts of the story?"

Shy paused for a moment to breathe in the truth of the words: "out of the mouth of babes comes much wisdom."

"We've had more than a few tearful moments, but she's just taking it all in her stride." And as though to confirm a few concerns Erin had had she added, "And I'm still being careful, pet, so don't you worry!"

Erin dried the tea mugs and smiled, "Mum, I'm not worried."

The silence that followed reflected the trust between the two women of God who both listened intently to their Papa's voice.

The day passed quickly and when evening came they decided to spend the time playing one board game after another amidst constant chatter and laughter. By the time ten o'clock arrived they were all exhausted and decided to call it a night.

Shy considered explaining to Lyric that tomorrow should be story free, but she obviously needn't have been concerned. As she looked up the stairway she saw Lyric disappear into her Aunt Apryl's room and she knew where little miss's thoughts would be until Apryl left.

Thankful she didn't have to say a word, Shy retired to her room with her honey bunch. With a quick goodnight kiss on his cheek she drifted off into a deep and peaceful sleep.

Almost all of her babies were home so all was well indeed!

Thanksgiving Day was spent like most families: eating and relaxing, watching the parade in the morning and football in the afternoon.

The food was incredible and the trifle was its usual big hit. Everyone ate too much, waistbands expanded and the family knew they had plenty to be thankful for, especially that year.

Apryl had to leave early the following morning and Greg offered to take her to the airport.

"Can I come with you?" Lyric asked her dad before they called it a night.

Normally Erin would have been reluctant to allow her to get up that early, but Lyric was growing and needed to start making decisions for herself.

"As long as you won't be too tired the rest of the day sweetheart, you can go."

"Are ye' going tae' be able to stay longer at Christmas, Apryl?" Shy asked her baby girl, missing her already.

"I've already put in for a whole week, Mom, and they said that was fine."

Apryl felt torn sometimes between the job she loved and missing home, but getting home every now and then for a wee break made all the difference.

Shy set her alarm for 4:00 a.m. and got up willingly the following morning to fix breakfast before they left for the airport.

Apryl had said goodbye to everyone else the night before and true to form Shy still got teary eyed.

"You looked a wee bit thinner this visit, Apryl, so I've made up a box of your favorite goodies to take with you."

She smiled and thanked her mom with a huge lump in her throat.

"It won't be long until Christmas, Mom."

"I know sweetie pie." And her horse-loving baby was gone.

They never grow up in a mother's heart, Shy thought to herself as she sat down in her favorite chair overlooking her garden. Unable to see much apart from shadows Shy opened her bible but didn't get very far. Her eyes soon became heavy and her head fell back against the soft cushion. She fell into a peaceful sleep with Kylie curled at her feet.

Shy awoke with a start as a slash of lightening preceded a thunderous rumble.

"Oh Lord! That scared me," she said out loud to no one in particular and Kylie, her protector, jumped up on her lap.

Suddenly the front door opened and in stumbled two soggy figures, stamping water off their feet.

"My gosh! What a gulley washer!" Lyric spluttered as she emerged from under a dripping hood.

Shy stood up, displacing her little pooch from her comfy spot.

Kylie didn't seem to mind and ran to the door to greet her playmate.

"Well that came out of nowhere, didn't it?" Shy stated as Greg struggled with his coat.

"Actually, I think it was forecast for a bit later but it's really bad now."

"Thank goodness it was dry when Apryl's flight left or it might have been cancelled," Greg added.

"Well that wouldn't have been a bad thing," both Shy and Lyric said in unison and they laughed.

Shy fixed another pot of coffee but since it was still dark outside Greg went back up to bed.

Lyric wasn't deterred with the gloomy weather, and since Shy had napped she was bright too. The two decided to curl up in the family room and continue with the story.

"Well now, let me see," Shy once again pondered on where she'd left off. A dark shadow seemed to cross her face as she remembered.

"We don't need to continue if you don't want to, Grandma." Lyric said softly reluctant to cause her grandma more pain.

"Oh, Honey, I want to, and more than that, I need to carry on, OK? I'm fine honest. Shy paused for a moment. "But ye' know lass, I think I just might condense quite a bit of the story before I continue in more detail."

"Ok, Grandma. But can I ask just one question?"

"Surely sweetheart."

"Why did you call yourself Kieran?"

Shy smiled.

"Well darlin', I've never mentioned it before but that's my middle name."

"Really!" Was the reply and just before Shy began Lyric had one more request. "Would you still tell the story using that name then?"

Shy looked over at Lyric with a troubled expression and before she could answer the wise wee lass interrupted.

"But not for any other reason than I've become so used to hearing the name, Kieran, it will help me to keep focused."

With a thankful smile relief washed over Shy and she took a deep breath and continued from where she'd left off.

Kieran did have an affair with the man she'd met and began to detest who she had become. One lie soon turned into a diabolical web of deceit and for Kieran, it may have even been worst than most.

Before that time she'd always held her self accountable, having high standards for her own behavior and her family's, but now her very character was in question. She'd become flawed and tarnished with a terrible sin that destroys one's soul and Kieran could literally feel herself being poisoned from it.

It was all culminating into an extremely tragic season in Kieran's life and what came next was to hit her with a force that made her reel. Her mother had a massive stroke!

Three weeks later and just one week after Kieran had returned from visiting her in Edinburgh she awoke on Sunday morning to the sound of the phone ringing in the hallway. She was just coming round from that in between state when not quite sure whether it's dream or reality and then all of a sudden she knew. She bolted out of bed catching her foot on the bed sheet and just made it to the phone before it stopped ringing.

"Oh, hello Kieran, I was just about to hang up. Did I wake you up?" Her sister asked, and dread engulfed her.

"Yes, well no, I mean it doesn't matter, Jo, what's wrong?"

It was strange of her to ask and assume it was bad news but something inside had already prepared her.

"Is it Mum?" "Oh No! It's Mum isn't it?" and before Jo could share the news Kieran began to wail.

"Kieran calm down now. Take a deep breath," Jo tried to calm her baby sister but it was no use. Kieran collapsed on the floor and cried gut wrenching sobs that broke Jo's heart.

"Kieran, she went peacefully in her sleep, sweetie, and it was probably for the best," Jo explained but she wasn't really listening.

Kieran held on to the phone like a life line. She was alone and needed to hold on to something or someone. The loss was unbearable. Minutes passed as the two sisters cried together but finally Jo caught her breath.

"Is there anyone there with you, Kieran?" she asked with concern.

Kieran slowly began to breathe deeply and every breath brought her a little more calm.

Exhausted, Kieran finally answered. "No, but it's OK, Jo. I'll be OK." And in between those hiccupy, breathless sobs she took a final deep breath and relaxed.

"Megan's at her dad's house but she's meant to come back home today."

Her mind was crazed with grief and she struggled to keep her thoughts clear.

"I guess I'd better call Danny to let him know and I'll get the train down straight away."

"No. Don't do that," Jo interrupted. "We're not quite sure when the funeral will be yet, so just hold tight, and I'll call as soon as we know more."

"OK, Jo."

Her head was spinning and she went back into the bedroom and cried an ocean.

It seemed like hours had passed but in truth it was only about thirty minutes. Kieran wiped her blotchy eyes and sat for a moment feeling drained. She struggled with the reality. Her mum had gone!

She decided to take a warm bath to relax and it filled up with soapy bubbles quickly. Kieran stepped in and slid down into the warm water, it wrapping around her like a familiar blanket, comforting and helping her feel safe. She lay soaking in the warm bath water and tried to focus on the wonderful memories they'd shared together and her spirits lifted.

But grief is a respecter of no man or woman and knowing her mum had gone with so many words left unspoken, regret crushed her suddenly making it difficult to breathe.

She could feel despair in every cell of her body and she wondered if she would ever be the same? The same as yesterday, or the same as six months ago, or perhaps the same as thirty years ago when she had just started to dance?

She would never be the same.

Half an hour passed and the bath water turned cold and Kieran lay limp and unable to move. Thinking that life was almost too painful to go on with, the cold of the water suddenly caught her by surprise and she sat upright, shivering from head to toe. The cold snapped her back into reality and Kieran grabbed her robe.

She took a deep breath and went to call Danny.

There were no more tears left. She just told him and kept her composure talking past the lump in her throat.

Danny was saddened by the news. As much as May had complained about his bad decisions throughout his life with Kieran, he liked her a lot and knew the whole family would miss her terribly.

"Kieran I'm so sorry." "When will you be going down?"

She paused for a moment and tried to clear her thoughts.

"I'm waiting on a call back from Jo."

Kieran felt her stomach ache. Her mum had died!

Desperate to end the conversation she asked him one more favor.

"Could you keep Megan until after the funeral, Danny?"

"Of course, Kieran, that goes without saying. Just let me know when you need to be taken to the train station, OK?"

She thanked him, feeling guilt wash over her once again and after getting off the phone she lay down on her bed. She was drained with the events of the last month or so and wondered as she drifted off to sleep whether her life would ever gain a steadier rhythm.

When Kieran awoke from her nap aware of the perfect silence in her room, the sudden reality of tragedy hit her like a ton of bricks. Deep, painful grief numbed her senses, she broke down and wept until she felt sick.

Her voice was hoarse and gravelly and feeling a stirring deep inside Kieran just got to the bathroom in time. She hadn't eaten hardly anything at all for days and she felt weak.

"Kieran, you have to eat to keep up your strength for the children," she heard her mother's voice resonate in the recesses of her aching heart.

Tears spilled over once again and she said in a whisper, "I know Mum, I know."

That day was the hardest to get through and her sleep that night was troubled.

When she eventually woke the following morning she felt a little more like herself but still with the terrible ache of missing in her core.

She felt abandoned. An integral part of her very being had been stolen from her. As she forced down her mum's remedy for all ailments; a cup o' tea and a slice of buttered toast, she turned on the television.

Why? She did not know. She hardly watched it when life was somewhat normal. But for some reason, this morning, she felt compelled to flip over the channels, as though purposely searching for something to ease the pain.

And then suddenly she stopped!

"Do you have emptiness inside this morning?

"Have you suffered terrible loss or experienced tragedy in your life, making you feel unloved? And do you feel that no one cares enough to listen?

"Well I have the answer for you. It lies in the redemptive, healing and unconditional love of Jesus Christ."

Kieran stared at the screen. She was transfixed on an angel with beautiful blue eyes who seemed to be talking directly to her, as though she knew everything she had suffered. She even seemed to be aware of Kieran's grieving heart.

"He is the only one who can heal you from anything life has brought to your table and He's waiting for you to call out to Him."

Time had stopped! Or at least it felt it had. All Kieran could see or hear was the vision before her. What strange words she spoke. If I give my life over to Jesus and ask for his forgiveness I will be saved? What does that mean and what will I be saved from? The pain I brought into my own life and inflicted on others? Will I be saved from this unbearable grief and regret?

Kieran didn't know the answer to any of these questions but felt drawn to do exactly what the angelic host told her. Kieran said the sinners' prayer that day and accepted Jesus as her Lord and Savior.

She'd never seen the show before and she never saw it again. How bizarre!

They were Americans and everything about them felt foreign, yet familiar. How was that possible? Kieran pondered on her morning experience throughout the rest of the day.

That night her sister called and gave her the information on the funeral.

It would give her a day to pack and prepare clean clothes for Megan and when she slid into bed she reflected on what she'd done.

I don't understand much of what they were saying but suddenly I feel more at peace. Sliding down between the sheets her mind meandered through past and present. Was the peace just coincidence or was that prayer the possible beginning of the answer to a lifelong prayer? One that she could never even put into words but had felt deep in her heart.

Her thoughts drifted back to her doorstep and she remembered that peace she'd felt as a child when just being still. A stillness she felt when wrapped in a blanket protecting her from the chill of the cool, salty breeze from the ocean just a mile or so away. A stillness to take in the wonders around her as she listened to the voice that whispered comfort; was it Jesus she'd been listening to?

Shy snapped out of her daydream aware of someone holding her hand and looking down at her feet she saw her Lyric sitting crossed legged on the floor. The child had compassion in her eyes for a daughter's pain.

"I didn't ever imagine you as a daughter before hearing the story Grandma."

Realizing how that must have sounded she quickly tried to explain.

"Well, I mean….!" Shy squeezed her hand gently and smiled.

"I know what you mean sweetheart."

"Perhaps that's another reason why I needed to tell you the story. Ye' know," she said giving Lyric a pat on the hands, "so that when you grow, you'll have a greater understanding of how everyone feels in any given situation, especially when going through tough times. You'll even be able to see your mum and dad and hopefully Grandpa and I in a different light; like we're people with feelings, too, and life experiences worth listening to."

Shy gave her a wry smile and crinkled her nose.

"Oh, Grandma, I already know all that!" Lyric stated a little miffed at the leg pull.

Shy paused and looked out at the flower garden through the rain spattered window.

"I think because of what you've told me today Grandma, I'm gonna' try harder to remember how important time is and not take anything for granted."

Shy nodded and smiled appreciating Lyric's willingness to understand.

"I know how words can crush because there are some silly boys at school who upset kids all the time with name calling and they never say sorry." A look of defiance crossed Lyric's face. "But I don't let them off with it and try to stand up for anyone their picking on." She looked off into the distance as though checking off a mental laundry list of things learned from Shy's story.

It was a precious moment and Shy remained quiet allowing her granddaughter time to reflect.

"I'll try harder to share more with all of you and promise never to feel anything is too unimportant to talk about. I don't want to have regrets, Grandma!"

Fat tears swelled up in Lyric's eyes and she stretched up to give Shy a hug that would last a lifetime.

Shy understood that the child meant when she and perhaps her mother were no longer here with her. They held the embrace for a long time unwilling to surrender such a priceless exchange.

Lyric pulled back suddenly as though a light bulb had suddenly lit up the room.

"Grandma; Kieran gave her life to Jesus!"

Shy relaxed back in her chair and Lyric regained her spot on the soft rug.

"Well, yes she did. But she didn't quite understand what she had done, and there was no one around her at that time to encourage and help her understand the full depth and meaning of surrender to Him. Nevertheless it helped her continue the search for that greater truth." Shy looked down at her hands intertwined. "Kieran was suddenly aware that there was something more to faith than what she'd already experienced in the Church of Scotland."

And so she wondered.

There was a silent moment between them suddenly broken by a thirsty grandma.

"I don't know about you, pet, but I'm parched," Shy said, bringing them both back to the now!

"Want a cup o' tea?"

Lyric sat back on her heels and sprung to her feet without a smidgeon of effort, making Shy slightly envious of her youth.

"You bet Grandma! I'll put the kettle on."

There had been movement upstairs and Shy followed Lyric into the kitchen to start on breakfast.

As they began to potter around the kitchen Paul walked in with ruffled hair, yawning and scratching his belly at the same time.

"Well good mornin' tae ye, honey bunch, and what a bonnie sight ye' are for sore eyes!" Shy stated the obvious always ready to have fun with her best guy.

"Mm good morning, sweetie, I'm sorry! I must look like a bear coming out of hibernation."

"Yep! Kinda' sorta', but still as handsome as the day I met ye'," Shy added giving him a kiss.

"Good morning Grandpa," Lyric piped up waiting her turn for affection and she gave him a great big bear hug which seemed quite appropriate.

"How are my bonnie lasses this morning?" Both Lyric and Shy said "fine" and looked at each like co-conspirators.

"How long have you been up?" Paul asked addressing both young ladies.

"Well, I got up to make breakfast before they left for the airport. Then I had a wee nap," Shy replied.

"And Grandma has been telling me more of the story."

Paul leaned against the counter top and crossed his legs at the ankles.

"And how are you enjoying the story honey?"

"Well, at the beginning I was really interested in this wee girl called Kieran."

Lyric replied looking a little older somehow to Paul.

"But then after a while I began to feel her story was familiar somehow, even though I'd never heard it before. Then I slowly began to think that Kieran might actually be Grandma! And…." she paused for effect, "I was right!"

Paul stood upright with a look of surprise.

"Really?" And he looked at Shy amazed she hadn't told him.

Shy smiled with acknowledgement and glanced over at Lyric.

She stepped towards her grandbaby and put an arm around her shoulder.

"We've truly been blessed with this one, honey, don't ye' think?"

"Absolutely we have!" Paul stated which instantly instigated a group hug!

The rest of the day was spent enjoying each other's company and relaxing. The weather had calmed enough in the morning for the men to knock a few golf balls around on the nearby driving range and the girls went into Newtown for a few hours shopping.

Shy wanted to get more of the story out to Lyric before she left and asked Erin permission to take her back up to the attic in the afternoon. Another thunderstorm had been forecast later that day, so there wouldn't be much else they could do as a family together anyway.

"Mum, we have all the time in the world with Lyric and the story is important to both of you," Erin reassured Shy.

"Thanks darlin', I'm not quite sure how to put the next part into words, but I know the Lord will guide me," Shy admitted knowing this part was going to be difficult to tell.

"I'm sure too," Erin replied. She had always been sure of her mother's determination to listen astutely to God. Especially when faced with a difficult situation and she knew this was one of those times.

Their life together within the first six or so years of living in this country was by no means a bed of roses and there were many dimensions of it that needed to be explained. But Erin knew how wise her mum was and how good she was at telling enough of a truth to get the message home without shocking the listener.

In bringing up Lyric she herself had hinted that life was difficult for them, many years before. She was also aware of the deeper messages behind all those trials. Knowing that at some point in the future Shy wanted to share those life lessons with her grandbaby Erin willingly left it up to her.

The men came back from the range and had already had lunch. Paul decided he wanted to get on with putting the finishing touches to a desk he'd been building and knowing how much Lyric loved to help he asked if she wanted to, be his assistant for an hour or so.

His real intention behind this gesture, apart from the obvious of loving to share time with Lyric, was to give Shy a break from the story so she could breathe in what the Lord had to say.

He knew his sweet darling intricately and felt she'd need a little time alone just to be still with Him.

"Sure I'd love to, Grandpa," and she bolted out the doorway ahead of him.

Paul turned just before leaving. "That OK with you honey?" He asked already sure of the answer.

Shy smiled. "That's fine with me, darlin'. Take as long as you want 'cause I've kinda' hogged our Lyric most of the holiday anyway. You go have fun!"

Shy knew it wasn't about having fun as much as he loved Lyric and sharing quality time with her was important to him. She was grateful for her dear husband.

As soon as Paul and Lyric were alone in the shed Lyric asked a question that had been on her mind for some time. She was sensitive to the way her grandma was telling the story and didn't want to appear as though she was running ahead of her, but she was almost thirteen and curiosity was getting to her.

"Grandpa I love the story Grandma's telling me and I understand I should be patient with the next part but there's something I'm dying to know and I don't think I'll be able to wait until she gets to it."

Paul laughed remembering when he was thirteen and needed to know everything right now!

"Oh, Honey that's dangerous ground you're asking me to walk on," he said, shaking his head with amused concern.

"I tell you what. You ask me the question and I'll be honest as to whether I can answer or not, how's that?"

"Ok, I guess that's fair," Lyric replied and took a breath.

" Mum already told me Grandma married an American Navy man, who was Aunt Apryl's dad, but what happened after that, "cause Grandma keeps hinting about something awful coming?"

Paul stopped what he was doing and turned to face the innocence of youth.

"Sweetheart, if there's any one question about your grandma's life I couldn't take responsibility in answering it would be that one!"

"Oh!" Lyric replied.

"Enough to say, honey, that what happened after they came over here is one of the greatest reasons why your grandma needs to tell the story. And I can't say another word so be patient and let's get on with this, OK?" And he gave her a squeeze.

Greg and Erin were outside having a cup o' tea sharing a quiet time with each other and Shy decided to retire to her room to mull things over.

She walked over to her window bench and retrieved a bunch of papers from underneath piles of bits and bobs and sat down at her window and began to read.

"I know Dad but I just wanted to be here with you and the family as soon as I could," Kieran explained to her father why she'd come down to Edinburgh sooner than they'd expected.

All those years she had felt unloved by him. All those years she felt nothing but an idiot in his eyes and who knows what could have been different if he'd at least told her the words: "I love you."

But she'd promised herself on the journey down that she wasn't going back to past hurts and as she opened her bag and unpacked some things she'd need for the night, she looked around the familiar room. Kieran breathed in the smells of her childhood still able to feel her mother's presence in the rooms in which she had grown up.

After unpacking she decided to go down stairs to put the kettle on. She walked past her mum's room and stopped for a moment. She couldn't go in.

Sensing her mum was one thing, but to see her clothes and personal things where she last left them was another. It was too soon to be able to face that.

The funeral was on Monday and Kieran had nothing suitable to wear apart from a little black skirt she'd brought with her, so later that day she went to a thrift store she knew of, fairly close by, that sold good quality clothes she could afford.

She found a pretty peach colored blouse, feeling her mum wouldn't want her dressed in all black and then she caught the bus home.

The family was content just to "be" for the rest of that day and when eight o'clock' came Kieran decided to call it a night.

She slumped into bed but couldn't get comfortable on the lumpy aged mattress. As she tossed and turned she sighed "I miss you so much Mum," and her heart felt heavy with the dull ache of grief.

In the dark of her room that night she tried to drift off to sleep and when she eventually did, she had dreams of a darker kind, filled with guilt and regret of not having lived the life her mum had wished for her.

The weekend was strained with everyone trying hard to just get through time and avoid public sharing of their own private grief.

It felt surreal. It felt like playing a part in some weird out-of-that-dimension play, and Kieran wasn't sure whether it was better that way or not. They all just got through until Monday morning.

Chapter 34
Unrelenting Cruelty

"I'm going in the shower, Dad. Please try and eat something!"

Kieran had made some tea and toast and laid it under the mirror in the kitchen where he always shaved.

"Aye, I'll try a wee bit, Kieran."

There was no point in nagging him.

As Kieran was putting the finishing touches to her makeup thinking about the irony of what she was doing, she heard the front door bell.

She ran downstairs knowing her dad probably wouldn't have heard it and there stood a vision of blonde loveliness.

Her sister was striking and even on that day she looked beautiful.

Growing up Kieran always felt the dowdy one compared to Jo's strawberry blonde hair and deep blue eyes, but there was never envy, just pride that she was her big sister.

Jo was an inch shorter than Kieran and curvaceous, with an all year round tan. She dressed in bright colors, more like Scandinavian style and she prided herself on being different from the average Scot.

Kieran, on the other hand, had a style of her own and with her chestnut hair and bright green eyes, definitely took after the Welsh coloring. She had a more elegant way of dressing but every now and then the rebel would pop out. In all Kieran was just an old fashioned kind of girl.

The rest of the morning flew by and before she knew they were standing in the tiny chapel awaiting the service to begin.

Her mum was being cremated which seemed such a shame to Kieran somehow, but she had no say in the matter. Everything had already been taken care of.

She kept glancing at her dad making sure he was OK, then wondered what she could have done if he hadn't been.

They filed into the tiny sanctuary and lined up in the first row. The atmosphere was somber yet surreal and Kieran stood still and waited. She didn't cry. It seemed as though the man performing the service was talking about someone else. Everything felt drab and impersonal and Kieran thought of the irony that a complete stranger should be talking about her mum and she got mad.

But then she had no voice. She wasn't included in the funeral preparation or even wondered whether she had a right to be. All she did know was it wasn't right for a total stranger to be talking about her mum.

The service ended and her Mum's casket disappeared through a red velvet curtain trimmed with heavy gold brocade and in that instant Kieran felt her loss. "Goodbye Mum."

At that moment in time Kieran felt completely alone, as though the people that stood around her were strangers also. She felt like an orphan left in the hands of people she didn't know.

The next part was what she was dreading the most.

The coming together of friends and family and Kieran knew if she could hold on until the mourners had partaken of some refreshments, she'd be fine.

It shouldn't take too long, she thought to herself as they pulled up outside the building her family had chosen.

"What is this place, Jo?"

Jo told her it was The Miners Club and explained that it was very reasonable in price and close to the crematorium.

It was a large hall which seemed to emphasize how small the group was that had come back to share time with the family.

Kieran felt sure the day would end soon and after an hour or so of some distant family members sharing their condolences with the family the guests began to taper away until finally the last one left. Kieran breathed a sigh of relief.

As the wait staff began to clear the tables her immediate family began to head towards another room.

"What's happening now Jo? Aren't we going home?"

Jo replied in a lowered voice. "Dad doesn't want to go straight home, Kieran, so we thought we could sit in the club for a while."

"What!" Kieran couldn't believe her ears.

They were going to spend the rest of the day they had buried their mum in a men's club. Complete with dart board and drunken miners!

That day was a painful example of what she'd believed all through her life. She didn't belong in this family. The only one she felt remotely related to had now gone.

Why couldn't they understand that, spending that day in a bar would have been disrespectful to Mum? Why was she apparently the only one to feel that way? Was it her? Was it always Kieran's fault for daring to question?

She felt sickened but sat quietly.

Hours passed and Kieran sipped her pineapple juice trying hard to remain inconspicuous within the group around her. She held on to every ounce of will to hold back tears and then she thought of her dad. He must be dreading to go back to that house. He must be dreading to face life without his mate.

Kieran's heart dissolved to mush and she went over to speak with him.

"How are ye' doin' Dad?" She asked as she sat down beside him, daring to pat his knee with compassion. But when he turned, Kieran saw something in his watery blue eyes that made her wish she hadn't spoken.

"I'm doin' fine, but you! You're just nothing but a bloody idiot! Nothing but an idiot with what you've done with your life!"

If he had stabbed her in the heart it wouldn't have hurt more!

"You caused your mother so much grief over the years; you were the one that made her sick with worry!"

Kieran couldn't believe what was happening and she stood up to run.

Run away from these strangers who'd given her so much grief through the years. Run from the torment of their words. Run from her father's lack of love.

As though that wasn't enough to contend with, before she left, her sister-in-law, who was the worse for what she'd consumed, chimed up with another precious little gem.

"Not drinking, Kieran? You're just a boring little bitch!"

It was like playing the part of victim in a black comedy of errors!

She couldn't quite grasp when it had turned from grieving for her mother into an all out assault on Kieran. But it had, and in her defense she ran.

She refused to waste a moment of the pain of losing her mum on retaliating against their vile accusations. Her mum would have been disgusted with all of them!

But unfortunately it didn't get any better. Jo followed her to the bathroom but couldn't quite understand what had taken place. Strange, thought Kieran in between trying to catch her breath and making sense of this outrage.

As she tried to explain to Jo what they'd said Kieran couldn't quite grip why Jo was defending them.

"Everyone's just overwrought with grief, Kieran."

"I'm going home to pack, Jo. I just want to leave quietly, so I'll call a taxi and leave. You can all stay here." Kieran managed to squeeze the words out in between sobs.

But then more hell broke out!

"Don't be silly, Kieran, just wait until Dad's ready to leave."

Kieran tried to find a phone when they started to blame her for causing a commotion. Now she was being blamed for over dramatizing, apparently like she always had. She was the bad guy yet again, the scapegoat that everyone gets to lob missiles at and blame for everything that happens in the world.

On the way home in the taxi her brother-in-law landed the final blow and Kieran snapped.

"You were the one that killed your mother," He spewed.

The earth as Kieran knew it stopped turning at that moment and all of a sudden everything fell into place. Jo shouted at her husband to stop it but it was too little, far too late! He has said the unspeakable.

"Oh! So I'm the only one that caused my mum worry am I?" Kieran was almost foaming at the mouth with righteous rage. "I guess it couldn't have been that you got my sister pregnant when she was only sixteen or that my brother sent his kids over from S. Africa because their marriage was a mess!" She took a breath. "Or perhaps it wasn't because my dad came home every Thursday night, drunk as a skunk, sometimes bleeding from fighting with Tom, Dick and Harry and breaking his promises time and time again. "No it couldn't possibly have been any of that that caused my mum pain and worry, it was all little old me wasn't it!"

The taxi arrived at the end of the street and Kieran opened the door and jumped out, her heart breaking and pounding at the same time.

As she waited for them to catch up, realizing she couldn't open the door they both started in on her again and Kieran had had enough. She turned slowly to her sister and took a deep breath.

"Jo, if you know what's good for you, you'd better shut up right now! You won't want to know how many beans I could spill if I was forced to!"

Suddenly everything went quiet and all of a sudden they had nothing to say.

"What do you mean, Kieran?" Jo dared to ask.

"You really don't want to know do you?" Kieran asked crushed her sister had joined in the attack.

And they both backed down, Jo's husband with a quizzical expression.

Kerry, Jo's daughter opened the door and saw the ravaged look on everyone's face, but Kieran didn't wait to explain.

She ran upstairs and began to throw clothes into her suitcase determined not to spend one more moment in this house that was no longer home. As she sat on the case to push down the overspill of clothes, a knock came to the door but she didn't answer.

"Kieran it's me, Dad, can I please come in?"

As much as he'd hurt her all through her life and especially that day she couldn't ignore his request. She opened the door and they sat down on the bed.

He asked her what was going on!

Are you kidding? You have to ask me, it wasn't obvious to anyone but her? She thought to herself, suffocating under the absurdity of the day, but she kept that hidden.

She didn't mention what he'd said at the club. There was no use. She shared how Jo and Frank had attacked her in the taxi and she had had enough and was going home.

All he could do was make excuses for everyone's behavior and there seemed little regret. The brief conversation ended with him actually saying the words "I'm sorry and I love you," but it was too late.

She appreciated the effort and said she loved him too, but it was still too late.

Far too little! Far too late!

She just felt sorry for him. Sad for his loss and the lonely life that spread out before him, but she couldn't relent and knew that this was the time to create boundaries.

"Dad I'm sorry but I can't stay here after all that's been said, so I'm going home."

Kieran sneaked downstairs to call a taxi and went back up to wait, praying that no one else would come up to talk her into staying. She wasn't pouting or causing drama but rather just tired of the charade. She was sick of feeling like an oddball. She was sick of not having a place in a home where she could release her emotions without being branded as some kind of trouble maker or freak.

They could grieve their mum's passing in their own way, and if it made it easier for them to blame her then so be it.

The taxi came and she left silently without another word to anyone and as it made its way through the darkened streets of Edinburgh the driver asked if she was OK. He noticed she looked upset.

"I'm fine, thank you," she replied politely. "I came down for my mother's funeral today," she added and he said he was sorry for her loss and continued driving without interrupting her thoughts further.

When they arrived at the station he helped her to the ticket office with her luggage and when she tried to give him a tip, he refused saying it was his pleasure.

There are still some nice people in the world, Kieran thought to herself as she made her way to the platform. She boarded the train and found a little corner to snuggle into and she settled down for the journey that lay ahead.

Kieran felt grief far deeper than words could ever explain. On that train journey home she grieved the death of her mum, and the only family she'd ever known was gone now too.

The darkened image of her own reflection in the window haunted her as the taunting words came back to kill her softly just one more time. They replayed over and over again in her troubled mind forcing tears to spill over once again.

Was it me? She questioned, racked with the guilt of those cruel accusations.

Was I responsible for killing my mum?

The lies were spinning their web of deceit throughout the passageways of her mind, taking her to the brink of insanity with the pain they had caused.

But then she became outraged at the injustice. Suddenly knowing the truth, as though a breath of reassurance billowed past her like a soft breeze from heaven, Kieran relaxed and took a deep breath in.

"Thank you," she whispered to her mum's memory. She knew her mum would have hated what they'd done that day, and she suddenly felt sorry for them. Gradually the gentle rocking of the train helped her to fall into a peaceful sleep.

When the train finally arrived in Montrose she called a taxi and after two hours of travel, Kieran was glad to be home in her sanctuary and away from all the recrimination of the last few days. She refused to allow those cruel words to haunt and destroy her so she kept focused on the whispers of truth she'd heard on the train.

The following day she called Danny and he brought Megan back home. She'd missed her 'wee lamb' and the two of them spent that day and night relaxing, talking about everything Megan had done over the weekend with her dad and brother. It was so good to be back home where she was loved and appreciated.

As she tucked her wee lamb into bed and kissed her goodnight, the phone rang and she went to answer it praying it wouldn't be a member of her family. She wasn't ready for that conversation and wouldn't be for a very long time.

"Hello" she said quietly.

"Hey, Kieran its Martin; where have you been I've been calling all week and..." Kieran interrupted him before he went any further. He sounded extremely agitated.

"Martin, just wait a moment, will you," she told him with a firmness he'd seldom heard before. "My mother died and I went down to the funeral," was all she said in reply and there was silence for a moment. He apologized and Kieran listened but wondered if he ever truly meant what he said.

For a split second she'd been given a glimpse into the true man and for that instant she felt a warning resonate deep in her heart. He's not to be trusted.

It was obvious he didn't like the brush off, but this time she meant it and would not back down. She said a quiet goodbye and hung up the phone.

She was emotionally exhausted from all that had taken place in the last month and the last thing she needed in her life was more trauma. She just needed time to herself. Kieran took the rest of the week off to spend time with Megan. After the long rest she felt her spirits lift.

For the month that followed she began to grow stronger and made the decision to reclaim her life. She found a lawyer who charged a reasonable rate she could pay a little towards every week and within a few months she was divorced.

To have that burden finally lifted was a relief, but bittersweet. She grieved the death of a marriage and family unit she had hoped in the beginning would last forever, but now it was time to move on and so she celebrated new beginnings.

There was a knock at the door that made Shy jump and she glanced at the clock on her dresser. Two hours had passed and it was almost time for dinner!

She got up and placed what she was reading back in the window bench.

"Come in," she said, and Lyric walked in.

"Grandma, we're done working in the shed and Grandpa asked about dinner."

"Oh darlin', I got carried away reading and I didn't realize the time."

"Well let's go down stairs and have a look in Big Bertha, shall we."

Big Bertha was the nick name they'd given the fridge. Paul had bought it after a long search for the right one and it was delivered when Shy was out. She arrived home and looked at it aghast!

Big Bertha stuck out at least nine inches from the counter space that had been designated for a, normal size fridge and Shy was in complete shock when she saw it. She'd never had a fridge that big before and was tempted to send it back.

However, after a couple of days and the blessing of a name, they grew accustomed to the monster fridge and named her Big Bertha.

Shy and Lyric were met with a behind sticking out of the fridge when they entered the kitchen and Shy slapped it playfully.

"Hey! That hurt!" Paul replied rubbing his touch with slight exaggeration.

Lyric laughed at the playfulness of the two grownups she adored and shook her head, "You guys are funny."

Shy got leftovers out and within half an hour five delicious platefuls of steaming hot goodness were making their way to the table Lyric had set.

"I'm amazed at how you manage to throw a terrific meal together in such a short time, Grandma!" Lyric remarked with a mouth full of food.

"Lyric!" Erin was just about to chastise her but she interrupted.

"I know, I know I'm sorry, but it's so good!"

They chatted and enjoyed their last meal together, for a while at least, and when they finished Lyric and Erin cleared away the dishes.

"I don't think Grandma will be able to finish the story, Mum," Lyric said sharing her disappointment with Erin as they filled the dishwasher.

"Well honey there's plenty time to catch up when we come back for Christmas."

But Lyric looked crushed.

"I can't go that long without finding out, it'll just kill me!" And Erin laughed at her daughter's exaggerated declaration.

Noticing how hurt Lyric looked she stopped what she was doing and apologized.

"Oh I'm sorry, sweetheart, I didn't mean to make fun." Erin wrapped an arm around Lyric's shoulder. "I realize how much you love Grandma's storytelling but…"

Lyric interrupted her. "Mum, this is different! It's not just any story, you know. It's Grandma's story!"

Erin was well aware what her mum had shared with Lyric and she was touched her daughter was taking it so to heart.

"You're a good girl." Was all she could say and kissed her baby on the forehead.

"Maybe we can change our schedule a bit. Let me talk to Dad. OK?"

Before Lyric could get too carried away Erin calmed her. "But don't get excited until we talk it over. I'm not promising anything."

"OK, Mum, I understand."

Erin left Lyric to finish the dishes and went to find Greg.

He was found quickly chatting in the family room with Shy and Paul and when Erin walked in they immediately knew something was up.

"What's up, honey?" And Erin sat down on the arm of his chair.

"Well, Lyric's a bit upset that Mum won't be able to finish the story before we leave and I wondered if we could stay one more day."

Greg looked a little concerned.

"We can't stay for a full day. Remember I have that meeting in the city at 4:00 with the new clients." He paused in mid thought.

"But we could stay at least until lunch time tomorrow, if that's OK with everyone else?"

Erin and Greg looked towards Shy.

"You could all live here if it was up to me, but what about Lyric's school?" Shy asked hoping she hadn't started something she couldn't finish literally.

"She doesn't start back until Tuesday. They've been installing a new heating system at the school and needed an extra day to get it all done."

"Well that sounds good to me," Shy remarked then added.

"And even if I don't get it completely finished, all real life stories are a work in progress and I have a wee surprise for our Lyric anyway."

Erin knew what she was talking about, or at least she thought she did, and smiled at her mum who winked back.

They shared the news with Lyric, and she was elated to say the least and after playing a few board games both Shy and Lyric went upstairs to continue the story for a while before bedtime.

Lyric climbed into bed and puffed up her pillows behind her.

"Now, Grandma, we left off where Kieran's mum, Great Grandma May that would be, died after a massive stroke and Kieran was waiting on news of the funeral. Then she gave her life to Jesus after watching The Christian show on television, but she wasn't completely sure what she'd done. Is that about right?"

Shy sat on Lyrics bed with her hands folded upwards on her lap in a gentile fashion that had always amused Lyric. She nodded in agreement.

"That's right honey."

And as though the shock of her mum's death wasn't enough, what lay ahead, as she prepared to go back down to Edinburgh, was to change her life in a way she could never imagine.

Lyric listened intently.

"Since we don't have too much longer darlin', once again I'm going to condense it a bit, OK?"

Lyric nodded thankful she was getting to stay a little while longer.

Kieran journeyed down to Edinburgh on the train once again, emotionally drained with all that had taken place of late. She was heartbroken and was already missing her mum.

When she arrived at her childhood home she immediately sensed the emptiness.

"In the attempt to cut a long part of the story short sweetheart, all I can say now is that the funeral was terribly hard to get through. Her family said mean things to Kieran that upset her even more and as soon as the funeral reception was over she left to go back home."

"What did they say Grandma?" Shy looked out the window beside Lyric's bed and stared into the black canopied silhouette outside. Her eyes brimmed with salty tears from memories she cared not to remember and she turned back to Lyric and took her hands in hers.

"Darlin' I truly hoped I'd be able to get through the whole story with you over Thanksgiving and I'm grateful to your mum and dad for giving us a wee bit more time, but I can't go on." She squeezed Lyric's hands.

"I can't go through it any more honey and I'm sorry for leaving you hanging but I'm not really." Shy took a long breath in and as she breathed out the stress of a lifetime seemed to dissipate. "Because, I have a gift for you."

"A gift?" Lyric asked now a little confused but intrigued nonetheless.

"Hold on a moment." Shy whispered.

She left the room for a few minutes and came back with a large bundle of papers stapled together. She sat down on the bed and stroked the cover that had two somewhat familiar pictures on the front.

"What's that, Grandma?" Lyric asked, her heart now pounding with excitement.

"This, my love; is a story of a lifetime. It's a story of Redemption and of Amazing Grace." Lyric was speechless.

"It's the story that tells the life of a wee lass named Kieran." Lyric sat up straight unable to suppress her surprise and opened her mouth wide, with eyes popping.

"It's my story, sweetheart, therefore its part of your story!"

"Oh Grandma! Is it a book? You've written a book! How absolutely cool is that!"

"Well, it's in the hands of the publisher as we speak." Shy confirmed.

And Lyric forgot she was almost thirteen for a moment and bounced up and down where she sat, clapping her hands together like a little girl of three.

As usual the child brought the emotion of the moment back to where it belonged; in the real life of today. Never to live in our tomorrows unless Jesus goes back there with us to heal the pain and sorrow that's in everyone's lives. To breath in His tender mercy of every day with a joy that surpasses all understanding!

It seemed that Lyric had a zillion questions to ask but Shy took back the manuscript and promised she would have it tomorrow, just before they left.

"You'll never get to sleep lassie and I'm not goin' tae' be blamed by your mum and dad for keepin' ye' up all night.

"Awe Grandma," was her reaction but Lyric now had a twinkle in her eye that uncovered her excitement.

Shy left her room and she heard Lyric say quietly before she slipped beneath the sheets. "My Grandma's an author. How cool is that!"

"Goodnight sweetheart."

"Goodnight Grandma."

Shy slipped into their bedroom where Paul was already asleep.

Good I don't need to explain anything until the morning. She thought to herself as she changed into her night gown and slipped under the quilt.

"Thank you for giving me permission to share our story, Papa!" Shy prayed to her best friend who knew it all and more, much more.

She drifted into the most restful sleep she'd had for a very long time and felt it was almost done. The legacy of a lifetime she was destined to share was almost complete. Or would it ever be? Perhaps not.

Chapter 35
Letters of Love

Shy had set the alarm for 5:00 a.m. assuming no one else would be up that early. Erin, Greg and Lyric would be leaving after breakfast even though they didn't realize it yet.

As much as she loved when they were home and hated to think of the months that lay ahead before seeing them again, Shy knew Greg would be more relaxed with his meeting if he had plenty time to spare.

She was at peace with the way things had turned out and felt exhilarated when thinking of the incredible mother and daughter experience that lay ahead for Erin and Lyric.

It might be arduous but there will definitely be the worthy prize of complete healing at the end with Papa's blue ribbon of blessings tied in a huge bow.

Shy knew the Holy Spirit would be there in the midst of question and answers encouraging in His ways of comfort, ensuring both girls of that safe place.

It feels so good to hand them both over into your loving care Papa. I thought I already had but I guess you keep teaching us lessons each day we walk closer. Shy's senses were ablaze with the spirit that morning. She sat down at her writing desk and took three sheets of the delicate blue writing paper Paul had bought her for her birthday and placed them side by side on the desk with precision, ready for her Papa to tell her what to write.

She was preparing the way for the girls to share the rest of the legacy. The words to both of them needed to be exactly what God wanted.

To My Darling Lyric

You have no idea what a privilege it has been to share this journey of a lifetime with you my sweet girl. I had hoped to complete the story over the course of the week, but when God has a different plan we just have to be obedient. Throughout the many, many years I have known Our Papa personally I have listened intently to His voice and this Thanksgiving was no different.

By the end of this week He told me to give you "Broken to Beautiful" and then the reason behind this change of timing became so apparent it made me wish I'd thought of it myself! He needs you to read this yourself sweetheart but to be within close council of your mom. I will of course still be here if you need to ask questions she might not have the complete answers to, so please call if you need me.

However, I honestly feel that the Lord has had deep purpose for the sharing of the story this way and many blessings of deep healing are sealed in the promise of His plan. You see darlin'; your mom has kept an awful lot of things to herself over the years with the sole purpose of protecting me. Sometimes from others who intended harm but much of the time from my own self condemnation.

She has done it out of love but Our Lord wants her finally set free from that burden and His timing is always perfect. I feel He will use the purity and intensity of a mother's love for her daughter to heal her through answering the questions you will so wisely ask. My prayer for you is that The Holy Spirit will be there in the midst of you both and will allow you to see all through Heavens eyes.

I must prepare you though, sweet girl, that the rest of the story will not be easy to read. There will be many life lessons to learn in the process but this time is most definitely for you and your mom to share.

Please be open to what God is whispering to you in the quiet places. my pet. Remember; that's where I first heard His voice, as I sat on the doorstep of my home so many years ago. You can only imagine how I felt all those years later when I found out it was He who had been whispering tiny fragments of love.

It was He who warmed my heart when the world outside seemed determined to cause a deep freeze. It was He who saved me from myself.

I love you, precious wee lass and Our Papa loves you even more so read on, warrior princess, and make sure to hold your mom when she needs to be held. Papa wants to clear out the cobwebs in the rooms of her memory she has so vehemently kept locked tight and I know with Blessed Assurance, He will be gentle with the healing that will take place.

Be Blessed sweet girl and know you are loved and are in my prayers.

Grandma Shy.

To My Wee Lamb
There are many ways I could begin this letter but the most important is to stress how much I love you and how proud I am to be your mum. We've taken quite a few journeys together Erin and not all of them pleasurable, but to take them with you made them all so much easier to bear.

You are indeed the delight of my heart, sweet daughter, and Papa is so proud of you. This new leg of the journey is for you and your daughter to share as you explore my labor of love together and like I said to Lyric if you need me, just call. There will be nothing too simple to ask or too difficult to share so please be brave, wee lamb, and let Jesus carry you through.

Be aware of the Spirit as He leads you through places you may have thought you had already laid aside, but in truth were locked up somewhere in the recesses of your heart in a valiant effort to save me from more pain. You have protected me long enough, little angel, and need to be free at last from the weight of such a tiresome burden.

Listen to your baby's heart, Erin, for she is wise indeed and has taught me a thing or two. Be honest and sure that she can handle whatever you have to say. Papa and I have given you permission to say anything you need to that will unlock the door to your freedom, so forge on and breathe in the new day that awaits.

For the times you may have thought I was unaware of your fears, I humble myself before my God and my daughter and ask forgiveness. I was aware of more than you could imagine, sweet girl. Perhaps, in the years that stretched out ahead of us, I neglected to speak the words you most likely needed to hear, in an effort to put the past to rest.

But; in reading the last part of the story with Lyric, I pray you will finally come to understand how aware I was during those years of extreme adversity. With Our Papa's help in filling in the missing pieces to the puzzle, I was allowed a deeper glimpse into your pain.

I need to share that with you so you can have your voice! And there lies the key to unlock the door where freedom waits. We have walked within 'the shadow' of death many times, dear heart, and survived to tell the story of our trials and in doing so we claim victory in Christ Jesus!

But until we shed the remnants of the past, giving every last thread over to God, we are unable to claim the full blessings of what he has in store, and I truly feel this is your time, wee lamb.

What lies ahead will take your breath away! Be courageous, sweet Erin, and know how necessary this part of the journey is so that you can soar and fly high. I love you but Papa loves you more so trust Him to take your hand.

Be Blessed, little Mama, and know my heart and my prayers are with you.

Mum Bum

To My Sweet Apryl

Hi, my sweet horse-loving girl! I hope you're well and enjoyed Thanksgiving. You blessed your old mama with a wonderful surprise, just turning up like that, and it truly was a time to give thanks, for me especially.

There is something quite amazing I need to share with you, Apryl, that may also involve your input at some time. Perhaps now or perhaps a little later on but I wanted to make you aware anyway. Intrigued daughter of mine who loves mysteries? Well read on.

There was only one person in our close family who wasn't aware I had written a book about our life journey and that's Lyric. You know how much she loves her grandma sharing stories from back home, but she was getting to that age where I thought she needed to know our legacy as an immigrant family so to speak.

I decided I would tell her the story just as I wrote it in the book a few years ago, knowing that one day I would share it with all my grandchildren, therefore passing on the legacy of a lifetime.

As the Lord would have it I wasn't able to complete the story over the Thanksgiving week, so He had me tell Lyric about "Broken to Beautiful."

I will give her the book to take home so that she can share the ending with her mom, knowing that there may be a tremendous opportunity for a complete healing to take place. We both know how many hurts of the past Erin has kept to herself and has done for years, so I feel Papa definitely has a plan in store.

This may affect you because Lyric loves to talk with you about a multitude of things she doesn't necessarily share with her mom or me.

I know you don't remember much about our life together before we set out on our own, sweetheart. However, you did experience all that involves being the child of a single parent, trying to be mum and dad and hold down three jobs.

Sometimes it was extremely hard on all three of us in different ways and Lyric might want to ask you questions on how it affected your life growing up.

Be truthful, Apryl. Papa and I give you our permission to share your heart.

There may be healing in that for you too, sweetie pie, even though you think you couldn't possibly be happier working the job of your dreams and heart's desire. But stuff gets locked away in our efforts to just get on with life, and because we give everything over to God, we think we become instantly healed from the past. But sometimes it takes time so please just be open darlin'. Lyric has a right to know and we have a duty to share and heal completely.

We've always been able to talk about difficult subjects and you have been more than willing to voice your opinions, at times a little too loud maybe. Ha! Ha!

Seriously though, sweet girl, you have the gift of sharing and reaching out to those who are hurting. You are a blessing, sweet Apryl.

I love you and I'm so proud of you. Papa looks down and smiles when He sees you at work, loving animals and children and He loves your heart.

Keep up the good work Munchkin! Oops! Sorry that slipped out! It's been a long time since I called you that, huh?

Be blessed, as I know you will be, and forever know how much you are loved and missed ever day. Be assured how happy and proud you make me and your Papa and take care of yourself too.

Luv Ya! Mom

Shy laid down her pen and stretched her fingers. She felt relieved to have the letters finished before the family got up and sliding them each into matching soft blue envelopes she sealed each one and took them downstairs.

She'd done all she could and knew God would be pleased. They were all in His loving care anyway, but that morning Shy gave them over willingly and completely.

The family got up soon after, being subjected to tantalizing aromas as they winded their way upstairs to every bedroom on the second floor.

Little Kylie had been set free from Lyric's room where she'd spent the night and was now wagging her tail eagerly to be let outside.

"Come on then, sweetie, we'll get you out before the rain starts. It looks threatening out there," Shy said to her furry confident as though she understood every word.

She checked the biscuits before letting Kylie back in; Shy got them out the oven and sat them on the stove top, adding to the delicious smells and sights of her kitchen.

Erin walked in, her big green eyes peeking out from under her usual morning hair do.

"Mornin,' Mum," she said, amidst a yawn that sparked off one from Shy.

"You either didn't get much sleep or you had too much," Shy remarked with a smile, always amused at Erin in the morning.

"I had an awesome sleep, thank you!"

Shy made a fresh pot of coffee and turned to her daughter who was leaning against the counter top picking at a warm biscuit.

"Sweetheart, I'm giving "Broken to Beautiful" to Lyric to take home so that you and Greg can get the early start you both wanted."

Erin stopped mid bite.

"But I thought that was being reserved until you'd finished the story."

"Well God has a way of changing the plans we make for ourselves doesn't He?"

Before Erin could reply she went on.

"He told me just last night that Lyric needed to read the last part herself but with you close by. You need to take over where I left off." And she turned around to face her wee lamb.

Erin was quiet but Shy could feel the thoughts racing around in her mind.

"You have to be able to talk to her about it all pet. You have to be able to use that voice you've kept silent all through the years."

Shy understood her daughter completely and knew that what she was being confronted with was probably the last thing she expected.

"But what if I break down? What if I can't talk about the stuff she asks me about Mum? You said that you would talk about it all with her."

Shy was concerned she'd opened up a hornets' nest but believed with conviction that this was what the Lord wanted.

Pouring out two mugs of coffee and handing one to Erin, she replied, "The mere fact that you're almost hyperventilating even thinking of it proves you need to do this, and you know what?" Shy stopped, looked down at her feet and as she inhaled she cupped her daughter's face in her hands and looked into her eyes. "You need to trust your beautiful, wise daughter who is turning into a young woman and you need to be honest and strong."

Tears welled up in Erin's eyes as she nodded in agreement. "I know Mum, you're right. I thought I'd put it to rest after all these years, but the very fact I still get upset must mean I haven't dealt with it like I should have. But you know what, I'm tired! In fact, I'm sick and tired of it still hurting and I'm going to take charge right now."

A declaration made by the strong daughter Shy knew Erin to be.

"That's ma' girl!" And Shy gave her a high five before hugging her tight just as Lyric walked in.

"What's all this mushy stuff about?"

"Well; good mornin' to you too, young lady!" Shy replied to her question as she grabbed hold of her grandbaby and hugged her just as tight.

"Good morning, Grandma, good morning Mum," Lyric stifled voice squeezed out as she struggled to breathe, nearly squashed by her grandma's hug.

"Go set the table for breakfast, honey bunch, if you don't mind."

"Sure!" was Lyric's reply as she busied herself around the kitchen.

The men came down to join them, and Shy shared what she had to tell them all.

"So ye' see it truly works out better for everyone doesn't it?"

All faces turned to look at one another not in the least bit surprised at her idea. Once again Shy had taken charge and created an answer to a little girl's dilemma that would suit everybody's interest perfectly.

"Sounds perfect," Greg replied with a mouthful of biscuit. Looking over at Erin with a sudden pang of concern he asked, "Is that OK with you honey?"

She squeezed his hand under the table and smiled. "It's fine."

"You know what I was thinking," Paul suddenly chimed in.

"What sweetie? What were you thinking?" and everyone laughed at Shy's easy way with her husband.

"Yeah, yeah, I know she humors me most of the time, but anyway, I was thinking we might drive up to the city and take in a few shows before it gets really busy for the Christmas rush."

Shy smiled and glanced over at her honey bunch but Lyric was first one out with a reply, "Oh yes! That sounds great Grandpa."

The rest of the meal was overtaken with discussion on which show to see and when they would go. Suddenly there was tremendous excitement in the air.

As Shy and Paul cleared up the breakfast things allowing the rest to finish packing, Shy gave her guy a big sloppy kiss, "You always know how to bring back the joy don't you?"

"It had never left, honey. But I sense there are hard things to be faced, so bringing a little sunshine into the midst of all that is a very good thing."

The young'uns eventually came downstairs struggling with bags. Paul helped them pack up the car, and within half an hour they were on the road back to the city.

Lyric stroked the book Shy had given her and took out the two letters she'd slipped inside.

"Before you start reading the book, sweetie, I would like you to read the letter I wrote you. Then you can either start at the beginning or where we left off in the story. Enjoy, my sweet girl, and remember to call," Shy had whispered in Lyric's ear before the car pulled away. "And don't forget to give the other letter to your mum."

Lyric opened her letter quietly in the back of the car and read. A few moments later with watery eyes and a swelling up in her heart of gratitude towards the grandma she loved, Lyric laid her head against the seat and slept.

When they arrived in New York the weather had already taken a turn for the worse, and as dark thunderclouds gathered in the overcast sky, Lyric was happy she had something incredible to keep her busy for the rest of that day and the next. Tuesday, and back to school, would come only too quickly so she was eager to get started. She threw her bags onto her bedroom floor and jumped onto the bed.

A sudden rumble of thunder gave her that familiar scared but excited feeling in her tummy and seconds later a crack of lightening made her jump. She loved reading, but during a thunderstorm was even more exhilarating for her.

She opened the book at the place where Shy had stopped the tale. Lyric was unable to wait any longer to find out what happened next, and she lay back against her pillows and read…

Chapter 36
A Shredded Heart

Kieran had been divorced for a few weeks but hadn't felt an urgency to spread the news.

It was disconcerting to her that she didn't seem overly eager to reach Martin either. She put it down to the culmination of traumatic events she'd gone through in the last six months. In fact in the last two years!

She was emotionally exhausted and didn't have the strength to make quick decisions with her life. She was also well aware that the base was scheduled to close within the next year or so, and departments were already beginning to wind down.

Kieran still pondered the thought of moving to Edinburgh feeling that the small town of Brechin held no promise for her future or her children's, but something deep inside made her feel the move would have to be farther afield.

But America sounded so final. She was terrified at the prospect of leaving her family and homeland, but then did she even have a family? In her heart the answer was a definite NO!

Her sister had called a couple of months after the funeral and they talked over what had happened. The trauma of that day was glossed over slightly because Kieran couldn't bear to keep grudges. She forgave everyone willingly, hoping lessons had been learned by all in the process.

News of her divorce must have spread around base via Danny because by the end of the week she received a call from Martin.

"I just heard Kieran! That means I can come and see you; I'm off restriction."

It was strange but Kieran's reaction to the news surprised her.

"Oh." she said. trying to sound enthusiastic. But her tone gave her true feelings away and Martin sensed it immediately.

"Well don't sound too happy!" He remarked sarcastically.

"Of course I'm happy, Martin, but I'm still recovering from my Mum's death. You can't expect me to bounce around the room," she replied, trying to convince herself as well as him.

He didn't sound as though he believed her and as usual made it all about him. Unable to tolerate his whining attitude Kieran made an excuse to hang up. She was completely confused.

Martin was too, but more than that he was mad and within a few hours he was at the flat.

As soon as Kieran saw him she melted. She didn't understand the magnetic charm he had over her but it was undeniable. All the doubts she seemed to have disappeared as soon as he kissed her and her resolve to be careful in making decisions for her life too quickly all but dissolved.

Within the months that followed Kieran fell into a torrid relationship with the man that would eventually steal her heart. Amid a rollercoaster of break up and make up she dared to believe she couldn't live without him. Even the passion of the many fights they had over the ensuing months became a drug to her senses that made her feel alive in a distorted way. She became swept up on a tidal wave of adrenalin rush!

When he was on restriction, she had regained her senses. The common ones that kept her grounded. But when he came back into her life, she lost all comprehension of normality.

She ignored the look in Megan's eyes when her wee lamb witnessed the arguments, becoming the proverbial ostrich and denying the existence of red flags. She became a junky addicted to a poisoned kind of love where kisses turn to punches and one's soul becomes lost in a passionate embrace.

The decision that would ultimately have to be made loomed in the not too distant future, and Kieran felt the need to broach the subject with her children. To leave their homeland and family behind was not going to be a willing choice by any of them, but it would have to be made if Kieran and Martin were going to follow through with their plan to marry.

Megan broke down and sobbed when Kieran gave her the news of their possible immigration to America. She didn't want to leave Scotland or her family. Ultimately she felt she had no choice but to trust her mum's decision, even if it meant doubting her sanity.

Perhaps that's what was at the root of all the chaos in Kieran's life. Was she continually depressed and looking for something to fill the lifelong void in her heart? Almost like being on a quest for the Holy Grail of happiness!

To an eleven year old, who loved her mum dearly, no matter what, to put her own fears at bay just to be with her mum was the only thing to do.

To Kieran, the choice was beyond painful, it was almost too hard to make. The undeniable pull on her heart to leave her country was too great for her to ignore, and she just knew that to stay would be the death of something. Something she wasn't completely clear of, but a nagging doubt deep down in her senses told her it wasn't being married to Martin.

Tommy became indifferent when Kieran spoke of going to America and eventually made it clear that he had no intention of going with her.

"What do you think it's going to be like over there, married to a black man? Do you think life's going to be easy?"

Kieran was shocked into a reality that hadn't often crossed her mind. In her heart, love was color blind!

"Tommy I understand your concerns, but I love Martin and I think we may have a chance of a better life over there," Kieran tried to convince him.

"I was devastated when you decided to leave and live with your father but it'll break my heart if you don't come with us Tommy," she cried, and she tried and she tried yet again to convince him but her son would have none of it.

Kieran realized what she was up against, so she tried to think of an alternative.

"If you decide to stay, there are the Mac Air flights. Military families use them all the time, and we'll be able to fly back and forth at least a couple of times a year."

Her heart was breaking but it was too late to turn back. The momentum of change had overtaken any other doubts, and although she desperately wanted Tommy to come with them, she also wanted what was best for him. If that meant staying in Scotland with his father and extended family, then she'd have to work at getting over her broken heart.

What was her alternative now anyway? To stay in this tiny town with no prospects and risk marrying a man much like her first husband? To move to Edinburgh and live beside a family that made her feel responsible for her mother's death? Or to step into a future she was beginning to feel destined to be a part of?

No matter how much she struggled with the heartbreaking decision Kieran just couldn't deny the tremendous temptation to leave Scotland. She had been searching for a truth that no one in her life had ever spoken of so far. But now Kieran felt she had found a clue to what her heart had been longing for all through her life. A truth she had been made aware of by a woman with the heart of an angel, on a television show she'd never seen before.

Martin invited her to a church on base one Sunday, and if Kieran had any doubt that America might hold the answer to that life long search, the service that day dispelled it. She became swallowed up by the lively praise and worship service.

Sharing life testimonies with Scottish families who had already married American servicemen gave her confidence that the choice she was making would be for the best.

The weeks passed and her mind spun in turmoil. Eventually, after visiting the church for a few Sundays in a row, Kieran decided to talk with the Pastor.

"Kieran, I understand that it's a big decision to make, but I don't think you need to have doubts about Martin. I've known him a while and I'm sure he's a good man who loves God."

A few weeks later Martins new orders came through. He was going home to America and was being transferred to the largest base in the country, Norfolk, Virginia.

"You almost sound as though it wouldn't matter to you whatever I decided Martin," Kieran told him the next time he came over.

They were talking about the future and Kieran felt Martin now had a blasé attitude towards her concern whether to stay or go with him.

"You know what they say happens when you assume Kieran," was his only reply, completely void of any compassion for her predicament.

When Kieran's divorce became final, Danny had stressed his concern that Martin had been using her all along and that as soon as his orders came through, he'd drop her like a hot potato.

At the time Kieran became defensive, positive Danny was speaking from bitterness, but for an instant his words rang loud and clear in her mind. Anger rose up in side and she struggled to stop panic from over taking. Had she been conned yet again? What a fool she'd feel if it were true.

The voice of doom screamed at her, engulfing her in irrational thought.

He loves me! Of course he loves me! She thought, fighting against the voice of logic and wisdom. Calm yourself Kieran. Take your time and think hard before making a hasty decision. But the pain of possible rejection was already beginning to take over and she became determined to make it stop.

By bedtime that night she was exhausted and curled up in the dark and prayed: God please help me make the right decision. I feel pulled to leaving Brechin. I know that I'm meant to be somewhere else, but America is so far away and I don't want to leave Thomas. I don't want to break Megan's heart. Help me please! I don't think I could survive the pain of rejection once again!

She cried herself to sleep.

The next day she called Martin and told him she would go to America.

He was leaving within a week and had already packed most of his things. The plan was that she would follow in three months, when they would then marry.

She still felt the nagging doubt that Martin didn't really want to go through with it but she couldn't give it credence. She couldn't admit that everyone had been right.

She couldn't believe she was the idiot they all believed her to be. She had to prove them all wrong.

For the next three months Kieran saved and packed and sold things that were too big to take with them and more important of all, she talked to her children to make sure they understood what was happening.

It gradually seemed to become easier for Megan or perhaps Kieran was fooling herself. Megan just wanted to be with her mum no matter what, and at that time her best friend's mother was remarrying and moving to Australia. That alone may have made it a little easier for Megan to accept.

Thomas was a different story. He refused to listen when Kieran tried to talk to him and acted as though it would never happen. He pretended it wasn't true because the truth was too painful for him to bear. The day before they were about to leave Tommy came to see her.

He stood before his mum and asked if he could come too, and Kieran felt her world slip from under her.

"Tommy you've ignored me for months." Kieran almost writhed with the pain and self loathing of a mother leaving her child behind. "I don't have the money to buy another ticket now, and you have nothing packed even if I did. We're leaving tomorrow!" she screamed hardly able to handle the heartbreak.

"Tommy, I've been trying for three months to get you to come with us and you've refused. Why have you changed your mind now?"

He looked down at the floor and shuffled his feet. "I guess I just couldn't believe it would actually happen."

"Look, Tommy," she said, looking into his eyes to make sure he understood what she was about to say. "I've bought return tickets, so we can come back home within two weeks if we decide we don't like it over there. But if we decide to stay, we can either save up and send for you or get back home on a regular basis with the military air flights. It won't be nearly as bad as it seems at the moment," she assured him praying it would all turn out.

"OK Mum, but I'll miss both you and Megan an awful lot," he said, struggling with the excruciating misery of a child rejected.

She hugged him for the last time, for a while at least, aching with the decision she'd made. Believing that destiny was pulling at her to be courageous she took a deep breath and remained strong. Nothing she'd gone through in her life that far could compare with the harrowing heartache of that day. But Kieran believed it wouldn't be long before she saw him again.

She stood at the window and watched as Tommy walked down the brae with his shoulders slumped and his head held low. Kieran would have that picture embossed in her memory for the rest of her life.

He would hate her, if he didn't already, and she'd deserve it.

Kieran truly didn't know what she was doing. She'd never felt more sickened with her own actions. For all the years she had stuck up for her baby boy, now it was she who was causing him more anguish than anyone else ever had. She hated herself for what she was doing but it was too late to turn back. How could she ever be forgiven for leaving him? How could she ever forgive herself?

The next one to face was her Dad and after saying goodbye to everyone in Brechin, Kieran and Megan made their way down to Edinburgh to say their last farewells to the rest of their family. Her father was his usual quiet self when they arrived and didn't say much about her decision to leave, but she did sense his concern. They hadn't spoken much after her mum's death but at least they had all come to terms with what had happened. They were leaving the following day, and before they left, her dad pushed some money into the palm of her hand.

"I don't need it Dad," Kieran tried to convince him, but he insisted.

"Just in case love," he replied, and a torrent of regret flooded every ounce of her. She hugged him, unable to think of anything to say but promising to call as soon as they arrived in America.

Little did she know that would be the last time she saw her dad again.

Drew was driving them to the airport which was an hour away and Jo had decided to come and see them off. When they pulled up outside the entrance to the airport her brother turned to Kieran and said, "I don't have time to park so I'll just drop you off here."

She felt sorrow quicken her heart. She was grateful to him for taking the time to drive her to the airport, but both she and her daughter were leaving for what could be a lifetime. It seemed he was happy to just drop them off, like a drive by departure.

But then perhaps he couldn't trust his emotions, or perhaps his anger with what Kieran was doing now with her life. Perhaps he didn't want to risk saying something he'd regret. Kieran would never know the answer but it all felt so very final and woefully heartbreaking.

This was it! She was taking the journey of a lifetime into the unknown. Into a future where only God knew what stretched out before them and Kieran was scared.

Megan seemed excited about flying but obviously sad about leaving everything and everyone she knew behind. As they found their seats in the enormous plane Kieran turned to her baby and squeezing her hand gently, she whispered, "We'll be OK."

Kieran laid her head back and inhaled. As she exhaled a deep sigh forced yet another prayer. A prayer that the promise she made to her wee lamb, who trusted her mum with her very life, would be kept.

The door of Lyric's room opened and her mum popped her head in.

"Just checking on you, sweetie. Are you OK?"

Lyric sat upright with a strange expression on her face.

"There's a letter for you from Grandma on my dresser. She asked me to give it to you but I was dying to get started on the book, sorry!"

Erin walked over and picking up the letter she said, "I'll read it later."

She sat down on the bed and rubbed Lyric's knee. "Is everything OK? You looked a wee bit sad or something when I walked in."

Lyric looked down and explained to her mum what part she'd just been reading.

"I really felt your pain, Mum. I'm so sorry you were put through that."

Erin smiled sadly, a glimmer of the eleven year old still evident in her beautiful green eyes.

"It didn't feel good, darling, leaving everything I'd ever known behind. And I can remember feeling that I hated Martin. Although that feels bad to say now, back then it was how I felt. I was really scared!"

Erin gazed out the bedroom window as though actually seeing ghosts from her past. "I just sensed he was lying and pretending to be someone he wasn't, and to be honest, I thought my mum had gone crazy. I wondered constantly why she couldn't see what I did."

She looked down at her hands folded tight around each other realizing she was extremely tense and so she consciously relaxed.

"We don't have to talk about it if you don't want to, Mum," Her little angel remarked, continuing the legacy of protecting one's mom.

"Well, darling, Grandma helped me to understand that perhaps this is exactly what I need to do. You see I thought that over the years I'd laid all my hurt to rest, but as soon as it comes up I still get terribly sad. If I were to be totally honest, I was probably more than a little mad, also, at my mum back then for making the decision that changed our lives."

It was hard to relive pain. It was hard to go back to places she had tried for years to erase from her mind. At the same time, it felt like a relief to actually say the words, as though a purging was taking place. Erin suddenly felt peace wash over her and she smiled and laid a hand on Lyric's.

"But then sweetie, I think of you and your dad and the wonderful life we have, and I feel a rush of gratitude towards her for being courageous enough to take that step into the unknown. And I think I now understand how painful it was for her at that time too."

Lyric just let her mom talk.

"I knew, even as an eleven year old, that we probably wouldn't have had a great life if we'd stayed in Scotland, but when I get terribly homesick I wonder sometimes what it would have been like to stay."

She sighed deeply.

"It all gets a little confusing when you're torn between two worlds. But then we can go back and visit now at least can't we? For years and years even that wasn't possible."

"Can we really go to Scotland, Mum?" Lyric asked, suddenly elated at the prospect.

Erin paused wondering what she'd started. "I think we should talk it over with the family, because it's way overdue."

In the midst of reliving years of trials and terrible pain, God was giving them the gift of hope. Something exciting to look forward to!

Erin had been really homesick lately. It came in waves with her. Sometimes she was completely happy and had no wish to leave the home she had now. But then she'd be hit with what felt like a tidal wave of dreadful longing to go back and visit the land of her birth and, of course, her father, brother, and extended family.

"Well sweetie I really need to get on with laundry for the rest of the week. Will you be OK reading?" and before Lyric could answer Erin went on. "I'm concerned it might be too much to handle on your own."

Lyric smiled. "Mum, I'm a big girl now. I can handle it, trust me."

Erin got up to leave a little reluctantly, but she had to get some work done.

"We'll have lunch in a couple of hours, so there'll be time for us to talk some more."

"OK , Mom," Lyric replied and added just before her mom closed the door, "And don't worry!"

Lyric loved her mom and thought of her as a hero. She had not only survived more than many, but she'd also kept such a peaceful sense of herself and the world around her. Now she was being given an even deeper glimpse into her fears during those years, and she felt privileged that her Grandma would entrust her with such a labor of love.

Lyric fluffed her pillows and continued with the story as; her mum glanced at the beautiful handwritten, soft blue envelope on the table.

Erin packed the washer full of whites, and sat down at the kitchen table to read her mum's letter and at the same time on the outskirts of an unassuming little town called Yardley a mother, a grandmother sat in her wildflower garden wrapped in a blanket of perfect peace.

As Erin unfolded the delicate blue paper that was every bit her mum, she thought of where Lyric was in the story and hoped she'd be OK.

She took a deep breath and read on…

To My Wee Lamb

There are many ways I could begin this letter but the most important is to stress how much I love you and how proud I am to be your mum.

We've taken quite a few journeys together, Erin, and not all of them pleasurable, but to take them with you made them all so much easier to bear. You are indeed the delight of my heart, sweet daughter, and Papa is so proud of you'.

As Shy's message unfolded a familiar lump formed in her wee lamb's throat.

This new leg of the journey is for you and your daughter to share as you explore my labor of love, and like I said to Lyric, if you need me, just call. There will be nothing too simple to ask or too difficult to share, so please be brave, wee lamb, and let Jesus carry you through.

Be aware of the Spirit as He leads you through places you may have thought you had already laid aside, but in truth were locked up somewhere in the recesses of your heart in a valiant effort to save me from more pain.

You have protected me long enough, little angel, and need to be free at last from the weight of such a tiresome burden. Listen to your baby's heart Erin for she is wise indeed and has taught me a thing or two. Be honest and sure that she can handle whatever you have to say. Papa and I have given you permission to say anything you need to that will unlock the door to your freedom, so forge on and breathe in the new day that awaits!

Her mum, her warrior queen, her cheer leader, and confident, and a valiant advocate for God's truth, gently guided her through life's many, many trials.

She was still there for her, paving the way for a complete healing.

For the times you may have thought I was unaware of your fears, I humble myself before my God and my daughter, and ask forgiveness. I was aware of more than you could imagine, sweet girl.

Perhaps, in the years that stretched out ahead of us, I neglected to speak the words you most likely needed to hear in an effort to put the past to rest.

But in reading the last part of the story with Lyric, I pray you will finally come to understand how aware I was during those years of extreme adversity. With Our Papa's help in filling in the missing pieces to the puzzle I was allowed a deeper glimpse into your pain. I need to share that with you so you can have your voice! And there lies the key to unlock the door where freedom waits.

We have walked within the shadow of death many times, dear heart, and survived to tell the story of our trials, and in doing so we claim victory in Christ Jesus!

But until we shed the remnants of the past, giving every last thread over to God, we are unable to claim the full blessings of what he has in store, and I truly feel this is your time, wee lamb. What lies ahead will take your breath away!

Be courageous sweet, Erin, and know how necessary this part of the journey is so that you can soar and fly high.

I love you but Papa loves you more so trust Him to take your hand.

Be Blessed little Mama and know my heart and my prayers are with you.

Mum Bum

Erin blinked back tears and folding the letter, she gently placed it back in the soft blue envelope. She cleared her throat and put the kettle on for that soul warming cup o' tea.

Lyric had lost her place when her mom came in to talk and she flipped over the pages to find the right spot….

"This is your Captain speaking!"

The voice over the intercom brought hushed anticipation into the plane where people had been watching a movie or were waking up from naps.

"We are approaching Norfolk International Airport at 12,000 feet and you will be able to see the city on your right as I bank the plane for approach."

"Mum, look, look out there isn't it beautiful!" Megan squealed with excitement as Kieran leaned over and took in the sight below. It looked like a fairy tale land with thousands of tiny gems sparkling in the midnight sky.

They had been traveling for fifteen hours including a one hour wait over in two different airports and they were exhausted. The plane landed and the two Scottish lasses embarked. They were a little apprehensive at what lay ahead and held each other's hand tightly.

As they walked down the long walkway leading to where friends and family waited Megan suddenly caught sight of Martin, and shouted "There he is!"

She let go of her mum's hand and ran the rest of the way throwing herself into his arms with a bear hug that took him by surprise. Martin hugged her back but without much passion, Kieran noticed, and a twang of something very real shot through her like an electric charge.

He looked up to see Kieran walking towards them with tears in her eyes. But the tears weren't for him. They were for her wee lamb. Kieran knew Megan was making a tremendous effort to show she was excited to see him and her mum's heart broke with a mixture of pride and desperate sadness.

The pride was self explanatory but the sadness was due to a sudden awareness of how her child was fighting against terribly contradicting odds. She hadn't wanted to leave her home and family and could have acted out like most pre-teens, but wee Megan was made of stronger stuff. She was born full of Scottish true grit and determination and as young as she was Megan seemed determined to make the best of the decision her mum had made.

She was a real trooper!

Kieran hugged him, "Hi, I've missed you so much," she said the words but something felt odd.

"I've missed you too," Martin replied and as they stepped back from the embrace he asked, "Is that new?"

He was referring to the cardigan she'd bought for the trip.

"Well, yes actually, I got it for the trip over."

He didn't say she looked nice and Kieran felt the question was more of a complaint for spending money.

"You look as though you've put on a little weight, Kieran."

She went quiet and tried to ignore the thump of her heart.

"Actually I haven't Martin, it must be the cardigan," Kieran answered the unnecessary remark with as much disdain as it deserved.

They picked up the bags from baggage and as she tried to still her mind from racing, the airport doors opened and her breath was suddenly stifled with suffocating heat she'd never felt before.

"Oh my gosh! What's that?" And Martin actually laughed at her expression.

"It's June, that's what it is!"

The drive home wasn't what she'd hoped for, but was it what she expected? And if so; why was she even here?

The city seemed so different from what they'd left behind. It was midnight so they couldn't see much apart from tree-lined streets and city lights and a rush of excitement suddenly coursed through her tired body.

Within ten minutes they arrived at the apartment Martin had rented.

"Wow! This is nice Martin," she complimented him on his choice trying hard to lay down supportive groundwork as soon as possible.

He'd had to get everything set in place for them coming over all by himself, and when they entered the apartment she was pleasantly surprised at the choices he'd made.

"Gosh! Martin this sofa set is beautiful! You've been working so hard!"

Megan was shown her room which was tiny but sufficient. The double bedroom was quite small, too, but the bed looked comfy and stylish and Kieran thanked him once again for working so hard for them.

She suddenly felt embarrassed that they'd be sleeping together before getting married, but then Martin had stayed over at the weekends sometimes in Scotland. It wasn't a way of life she felt happy sharing with her daughter, especially given what she'd witnessed before, but she knew they'd be getting married soon.

They were completely worn out and decided to call it a night.

Kieran kissed Megan goodnight and thanked her for what she'd done in the airport.

"That's OK Mum. I'm really trying to like him!"

"I know you are darlin', I know. Perhaps one day it won't be so hard."

Kieran was exhausted but as soon as she fell into his arms any fears she may have had were momentarily dispelled. She'd missed him terribly at times in between the uncertainty, but the allure was just as strong and she melted with his touch.

She'd never felt like that before. She'd never felt like she was drowning in a whirl pool of passion, but with Martin she did. He made her feel like the most exotic, sensual and desirable woman ever to have lived. She fell under a spell and almost feared for her sanity as she became bemused in an unfamiliar world of seduction.

Finally she fell into a deep sleep cradled in his arms. She loved him.

By the light of a new day, the America Kieran and Megan saw as they flew in at midnight suddenly became an entelechy of gaudy strip joints within close proximity to elementary schools and churches. Fast food establishments were prominent on every block, their neon flashing sign beckoning the natives to over indulge.

Rows and rows of car dealerships advertising the best deals were evident wherever she looked, as was the abundance of shopping malls.

The fast paced life style everyone seemed to enjoy, driving their convertibles and enormous SUV's, was scary for Megan and Kieran, even though they were accustomed to Edinburgh. Kieran's home town was an international city as big as Paris or Rome.

The melting pot of nationalities all busy going somewhere intrigued the two Scots as they wandered around their new environment. Looking into the faces of people going by as they tried to still their longing for home became a game of sorts as the girls discovered what made this great nation tick. But for many, many months home felt a very long way away.

As the girls discovered farther afield, the contrast of quietly serene, wooded parks and waterways with trail rides and miles of golden beaches helped them appreciate that perhaps they could get used to this brave new world!

Counteracting her memory of that first passionate night, within the first two weeks of arriving in America Kieran sensed warning signs!

She remembered the promise she'd made to Thomas. "If we don't like it within the first couple of weeks, we can come back."

Their whole life had been sent over to America so what did she have to go back to? There was no home left in Edinburgh and the thought of living with her father's silent condemnation sent shivers through Kieran!

There was nothing left in Brechin apart from her son, but then she no longer had a home so what could she offer him?

Their return date came and went and with it any chance of turning from the life she'd chosen.

The comparable essence of their new life within the confines of their tiny home and the oppressive heat outside became painfully apparent. But at least they could escape the heat.

There was no running from the atmosphere they were beginning to encounter when Martin came home.

Megan wasn't happy and Kieran had no option but to face the look of disillusionment in her baby's eyes each day. She questioned her Mum's logic in this life changing decision she'd made, but kept her true feeling hidden under a blanket of love and understanding.

To say they were now pressured into walking on eggshells in the apartment they struggled to call home was a gross understatement. They survived each day and that was about it!

Megan made some friends in the neighborhood so when she wasn't compelled to stay in her room because of the house rules, her wee lamb at the very least had some freedom outside.

Martin laid down those rules not long after they were married. In fact he gave the edict during his lunch break amidst a hurricane warning. If that wasn't a sign from God!

Kieran tried to make life as normal as possible for Megan, but when living with a ticking timebomb, it's impossible to hold on to normalcy.

He seemed to find great pleasure in making life as difficult as possible and they began to argue constantly.

Every time he sensed Kieran had had enough he would soften things up and become sweet, making her feel it was all worth it in the end, but at what price? It quickly became the early stages of control.

When he was at work during the day, she and Megan explored their new surroundings in an effort to convince themselves that life wasn't so bad.

Kieran's work permit was still in the beginning process so there was no point in looking for work yet. Finding a job would be her only chance of holding on to some kind of freedom.

It seemed Kieran had made yet another impossible bed, perhaps from within a moment of slight insanity. But somehow she believed she wouldn't be sleeping in it for the rest of their lives.

They had little to do during the long hot summer months but sit by the apartment pool, hoping to blend in with the normal families.

Both she and Megan gradually fell into an agreed alliance of how best to navigate this new, but hostile, life and a great part of the summer became a time of learning how to measure his moods swings.

In fighting to keep her head above water, Kieran didn't realize they were being dragged into an unfamiliar pattern; a pattern that was completely alien to them; a pattern that involved the vile nature of the cycle of abuse.

The life of neglect she'd suffered at the hands of Danny was nothing compared to what she'd stepped into with Martin. At least then it was only she who had truly suffered.

During that first summer in America Kieran and Megan would learn to depend on each other in a way they hadn't needed to before. Megan began to witness terrible fights that were usually brought on by Kieran's attempts at shielding her daughter from continual persecution.

He became a control freak and demanded that his rules of; how a home should be run, be carried out to the letter. Megan was forced to wash the dishes every night in a particular way and if she didn't comply with that chore with attention to minute detail, he would force her to start all over again.

She would have to wash the floor in the kitchen every night and if Kieran attempted to intervene a fight would ensue. She would inevitably land up black and blue.

Before long they began to feel like caged animals, living with their prison guard filling the dual role of tormentor. Then; just as quickly, he would switch back to the caregiver she'd fallen in love with. He'd romance her into believing he couldn't live without her.

He played on her gentle spirit and compassionate heart and convinced her it would get better. He played on controlling her mind. The cycle of abuse. It's named such because the situation continually circles from one scene to another, never staying in any one state for any particular span of time.

It begins with a few weeks of relatively normal family life. They would share outings as a family and watch movies together and barbeque. They'd even sometimes laugh and have fun.

Martin was a willing provider and helped around the house. He would go shopping with Kieran and Megan for school clothes, which Megan always hated, but at least he made an attempt.

For a couple of weeks life felt somewhat normal or average or whatever the term is given to a relatively healthy lifestyle; when one is caught up in this travesty, normal. is never in their vocabulary.

Then Kieran and Megan would sense a change, One day he would come home from work and as soon as he opened the door they knew that day had arrived.

They'd entered into the second stage. The atmosphere in the apartment could literally be, cut with the proverbial knife. He wouldn't talk much. He'd whisper seething complaints under his breath; his huge expressive eyes glared at them from under a frown of disapproval.

It was hard to suppress the anxiety this period of time caused in Megan and Kieran. They would try to act normal, within the restrictions of that household. But Kieran knew he sensed their angst, like a predator ready to pounce on its fear-filled victim

That fear caused nervousness, which in turn caused clumsiness. During this second stage poor Megan would inevitably drop something or spill something on the table, ultimately lighting a fuse in his crazed mind and with it Kieran's protective instinct took over. She'd try to suppress her outrage but usually failed miserably. Incontestable rumblings of anxiety and dread felt thick in the air and the count down began.

The days that followed would be the worse to live through. A tentative existence and nothing more for the two girls. Martin would come home from work, the oppressive silence heavy in the air, and refuse to eat the dinner Kieran had prepared.

Instead he'd iron a shirt!

'But that's quite normal' do I hear you say?

It wasn't the way he did it; slowly and purposely, taking his time to be absolutely precise in his preparation. Every tiny act he performed had a diabolic and twisted reason behind it. Every breath he took and every glance he gave was a ploy to cause angst.

He didn't talk, he just kept on ironing and Kieran would try to ignore the sound of the steam as he ironed and ironed; the tension building with every flattened crease! Sssss! Ssssss!

It doesn't typically take half an hour to iron one darn shirt but the pressure had to build in his sick mind.

No explanation but lots of slow preparation. He would shower and use his best cologne and it was all a perfectly staged undertaking to drive Kieran crazy!

It was a passive aggressive attempt at control. And as much as she hated to admit, it usually worked!

Kieran would slide into the 'no man's land' of not knowing what to do or say.

If she asked what he was doing or if she didn't it would inevitably provoke a fight. She always landed up for the worse!

During those first few days Kieran and Megan would try hard to stay clear and pretend it wasn't happening again!

Tick, tick, tick, went the time bomb, marking the days before it exploded!

The Third stage would arrive sometimes late, sometimes early but unfortunately always dead on time:

The girls would, once again, see it in his eyes as soon as he opened the door and their heart beat would quicken.

His eyes turned blood shot red with controlled rage and the girls knew that at any moment he would blow!

Attempting to stay out of his way in a tiny two bedroom apartment was unachievable!

The silent stage over, Martin would find fault with the tiniest of things to provoke the fight.

Sometimes a look from Kieran would initiate an accusation.

"Who's that?" He asked once when he caught sight of her staring through the sliding French doors into oblivion. She sat rigid with fear.

"Who are you talking about?" Kieran replied in all innocence.

"You were staring at the guy that walked past! Who is he Kieran?"

There was no right answer! There was no turning back from this point of no return and so she learned to take a deep breath and brace herself for the inevitable.

He grabbed her by the shirt or the throat, all depending on how enraged she'd made him. More often than not Megan would get in between them throwing punches at him to deflect his attack on her mum. But Kieran would push her away. "Get into your room Megan!"

Sometimes her wee lamb would obey the command but others she would stay and risk being hurt herself!

There was no hard and fast rule amid such chaos. There was only; what do we do to survive!

Megan's choice was; do I stay and protect mum, or do I run to my room and listen to her cries for help! There was no choice!

Kieran always suffered bruising somewhere on her body.

But even with that he grew wily. He didn't want the evidence to show, so he began to concentrate the fierce blows around the head area.

It left ringing in her ears for days. But no one could see the bruises on her scalp or feel the lumps on her head!

She would hurt for weeks and began to suffer terrible headaches, but Kieran was too ashamed to admit their tragic life to anyone.

At times she'd try and fight back but he always got the better of her and when it was over his tears would flow!

Within minutes he'd be on his knees begging forgiveness, his huge brown eyes blood shot now with remorse.

As her head pounded and her face beat red hot with the physical exertion of the attack she'd give in to his pleas and forgive him, time and time and time again.

Thus bringing them to the Fourth or 'Honeymoon stage':

Where 'normal' life would reign for a short season and he would act within the parameters of remorse which seemed genuine at the time.

Back to movie nights and shopping with the family so all the world could see what a happy family they were

Eventually the summer passed and Megan went to school. She met friends who did have ordinary lives and she pretended that hers was too. Well at least for a while. As she learned to trust she shared her dark secret with a few.

She guessed it helped a little to release her pent up agony and frustration.

Megan was loved by everyone at school, friends and teachers alike and through it all she kept up good grades.

Her Mom was broken but proud that her baby was trying to keep her life together and she prayed for the day they could break free from their tormentor.

Kieran needed to find a job and as soon as her work permit came through she applied for a position on the base in the cosmetic department. She got hired on the spot.

August came and went and Kieran was due to begin her job on the 15th of September and the cycle from hell continued.

Megan at least had school and friends to distract her a little from life at home but Kieran never minimized the trauma of their hidden life and the effect it was having on her wee lamb.

She was aware of her daughters' pain and fear at all times but all she could do was try and form a plan; knowing that it might take time.

They hunkered down and endeavored to make the best of their lot, attempting to keep as safe as possible.

A week before she began her new job Kieran began to feel unwell.

She'd been planning to make a trip to the doctor to secretly go back on the pill, but life or sheer survival got in the way and by September 3rd she found out she was pregnant!

Suffering from a multitude of mixed emotions Kieran made her way home.

'Perhaps the news of becoming a daddy might calm him down!" She hoped as she stared out the bus window.

"Perhaps he might realize what he's been doing?' Kieran thought with the prayer that this little miracle might make a drastic change in their life.

Although they'd never seen the inside of a church since arriving, Kieran yearned for that empty promise to be kept just like all the others; yearned to see evidence of the man who had led her to the little church on base.

She had never given up on the God she was searching for. She never got mad and blamed Him for leaving them, but she did feel ashamed.

She felt she was letting Him down just like she had her natural father and could no longer lift her face towards Him.

She hung her head in shame but became more aggressive with her prayers!

Kieran believed with all her strength that one day, either Martin would change, or they would have their freedom.

Unfortunately, nothing changed soon!

Chapter 37
Illusion Shattered

He had no compassion for her pregnant state and the cycle continued. Just before Kieran left for work one day a fight ensued once again.

One of Martin's particularly twisted habits was to goad Kieran into calling him the 'N' word.

"Go on Kieran you know you want to say it! You know that's what you're thinking!"

He would repeat the taunt over and over again, push, push and push until she was pushed over the edge! She gave him his reward!

Thwack! Another slap across the face but this time something in Kieran snapped!

She was around five months into her pregnancy and she couldn't bear the thought of bringing a child into this living hell!

Her clenched fists bore down on her already swollen belly and she screamed out to God to save them from this torment.

"God Please Help!" "I don't want this baby to be born into the nightmare!"

And Martin stopped his rage!

Her plea had obviously unnerved him and Kieran took that pause to do something to save them all.

She grabbed the phone and dialed 911.

Sobbing into the phone she explained what was happening and within minutes two officers were at the door.

They saw the welt on her face! They saw she was pregnant but decided it wasn't enough to arrest Martin. He was let off with a warning!

Kieran went to work as usual just to get away from him, but something had changed that day. Martin sensed she was gaining strength and he didn't like it.

From that moment on Kieran realized she had little alliance within the police department.

There was something in the officer's eyes that told her she was a fool. Told her she was getting what she deserved. Told her they weren't going to risk their safety for a stupid woman playing games with her life.

Kieran worked and Megan went to school and they suffered in silence.

But she was becoming drained with the weariness of this existence and after one more fight and one more attack she had enough!

It was the middle of December and everyone else was preparing for Christmas.

The store was busy and Kieran struggled through each day with Megan just trying to survive.

Kieran felt powerless after her last experience with the police. The last thing she needed was to see that look in their eyes that screamed out; 'it was your choice honey, live with it or get out!'

The day after the fight she picked up the phone book and called The Norfolk Shelter for families suffering from abuse. She couldn't keep her shame to herself any longer.

Throwing enough clothes in a bag for Megan and herself Kieran waited for her wee lamb to get home from school.

They packed as much of their lives as possible into a taxi cab and ran to safety.

The two Scots lasses spent their first Christmas in America in a tattered old house in a secret location of Norfolk, sharing the birth of Christ with ten other broken families.

The councilors were compassionate and gave them a private room, but many others had to share.

The rooms were dark and unfriendly but safe. The faces of some of the other women were gaunt and worn out as the common denominator of abuse bonded the roommates instantly.

There were rules of the house they all had to stick by and for a month Kieran and Megan shared the sanctuary and abided by the rules.

Megan went to school by bus and didn't breathe a word of their plight to anyone.

Kieran did the same.

If she worked the late shift Megan sat in the shelter alone terrified for her mother's safety. Kieran had to take two buses to work and had a long walk to the shelter from the bus stop. It was situated in a, not so great neighborhood and Megan counted the minutes each night until her Mum came home.

Kieran had enough money to buy Megan a little watch with a plain brown leather strap from the drug store across the street. She felt humbled and defeated!

What had she become?

What had she done to her child?

She had almost hit rock bottom but a little life inside her moved, telling her mum to hold on!

'Hold on for my sake Mummy!'

The women in the shelter were supportive and tried to encourage Kieran to begin a life free from their abuser.

The words were good to hear but reality was too hard to face especially now! She was five months pregnant.

A week after Christmas they went back.

Kieran knew she couldn't cope with Megan, a new baby and no job.

As much as she hated the choice of going back, the alternative looked even grimmer. She couldn't take Megan into 'special' housing set aside for homeless families.

At the very least back at the apartment they had some kind of comfort and Megan had her friends in the neighborhood.

And perhaps this was enough of a wakeup call for Martin to change.

Kieran prayed her decision to return wouldn't be fatal.

Unfortunately, within the next six weeks the violence not only continued but escalated until one tragic night!

"A-a-g-h! Oh No God P-l-e-a-s-e stop him!" an unknown yet familiar woman screamed as her pleas for help filled the darkened apartment.

Thrown down onto the hardwood floor the woman gasped for breath nearly suffocating under the tremendous weight of the man straddled across her.

Her swollen belly pressed down hard against the cold wood. "The b-a-b-y, you're hurting the baby!" she cried with exhaustion but the pounding of his clenched fists on her head was relentless and it seemed all she could do was give in to the protective instinct of a mother shielding her young and curl up into a tight ball to wait for his anger to subside……

(The nightmare hadn't just been a bad dream!)

Megan tried to help but this time Kieran forced her to her room.

The child curled up helplessly on her bed in the fetal position, her hands clamped over her ears to muffle her mum's screams for help!

After it was over Kieran could hear Megan crying hysterically from behind her bedroom door but she could only lie still on the cold hard floor.

His blows were particularly lethal that night! And she couldn't move.

Minutes passed and he came out of the stupor of fury that had engulfed him once again and he helped her to her feet.

Everything hurt!

Her head was pounding and her face felt swollen where she'd suffered most of the assault. But something else was causing her worry.

During the attack she had felt a terrible strain on her swollen belly. As the cold hard wood pressed up against the substantial mass of 190lbs that bore down on top Kieran suffered an odd impression of intense pulling deep inside her belly. She laid her trembling hands across the swollen mound to reassure her little one that mummy atleast was OK. She felt her baby move and relief washed over her.

Ignoring his usual pleas for forgiveness Kieran struggled to her feet and went to check on Megan.

They held each other and wept and Kieran promised herself silently that they would break free!

A few weeks later Kieran went to her 28th week OBGYN appointment and immediately sensed something was wrong.

The nurse practitioner listened for the heart beat and a frown appeared across her face. Kieran said nothing but watched as the nurse measured her stomach.

"Is there something wrong?" she asked finally unable to stifle her concern.

"Well Kieran I don't know yet but I think we should get you to the hospital."

"What!" She gasped and tried to sit up.

"But I can't go into hospital. I can't leave Megan at home alone!" and then she suddenly fell quiet. Had she said too much?

"But can't your husband look after her?" The nurse asked a little perturbed by Kieran's reaction.

Kieran looked down at her swollen belly and caressed her baby to reassure her everything would be ok!"Try as she may to stop the tears from flowing they spilled over and ran down her flushed face.

"She just doesn't like when I'm not there." And the desperate look of anguish was more than evident in Kieran's eyes.

"Well let's just get you to see the doctor in Portsmouth and we'll take it from there ok?"

Kieran was forced to stay in hospital on complete bed rest. The diagnosis was grave and the doctors didn't hold out much hope for the baby.

The amniotic sac had ruptured and they were concerned the baby's internal organs hadn't developed. The doctors were curious as to the cause.

Kieran had been experiencing intense bouts of sweating, especially at work, as she stood on her feet all day.

"Have your other pregnancy's been normal Kieran?" The doctor asked, sensing this woman was a little too quiet.

"Yes," was her only response.

She couldn't eat or sleep worrying about Megan, but her wee lamb assured her with every visit that she was doing fine.

Martin was being on his best behavior. He was probably concerned Kieran would 'spill the beans' of his diabolical behavior to the doctors, but she kept quiet. Knowing full well she held his future in the balance, Kieran was thankful he was doing his best for Megan.

Kieran was 32 weeks when she went into labor.

The 'c' section was a must given her age and Martin had been called. He came to the hospital with Megan and after they prepped her for surgery she assured them both she'd be fine.

The doctor thought there was something strange about the couple and couldn't keep his concern in any longer.

"Are you guys ok?" "You don't seem to talk much to one another."

Martin was at Kieran's head and she felt intense tugging on her lower region. Suddenly there was a loud, healthy cry!

"Thank you God! Our baby must be healthy. The doctors were wrong!" Her heart skipped a beat with joy!

The nurses took their little girl away to be weighed but didn't bring her back to Kieran.

Instead they took her to a side ward and she waited in anticipation.

After what seemed like an eternity Martin came into the room and held Kieran's hand. He looked different somehow, almost nervous but Kieran was too anxious to see their little girl to care.

Then the doctor came in to give her the news and suddenly she knew why Martin looked strange.

"No, no, no!" she screamed, the sordid truth of their pathetic life crushing her like a brick wall.

Kieran lay crying for hours and stared at the ceiling.

She didn't want to hear Martin talk. She didn't want to hear anymore 'I'm sorry's!'

She didn't want to go on forgiving the monster within this man she'd married!

She hated him and felt a wave of disgust rise up inside like putrid bile from hell!

Megan was heartbroken!

But at least she had her mum back.

After the painful job of buying a dress for Joy Linnet's funeral they drove down to Mississippi. Joy's remains were being flown down by the military.

That was the biggest mistake Kieran could have made.

It was only a week after Joy's death. Kieran was struggling with appalling pain and they drove 15 hours to Jackson.

Martin insisted Joy be buried down there with his family.

His family was compassionate up to a point.

The day after the funeral Kieran was in the back garden, sitting on a garden swing crying from her grief. Her breasts were hard as rocks and excruciatingly painful and she grieved for her baby girl.

Martin's mother asked him why Kieran was still crying and he came out and told her to pull herself together.

Kieran couldn't believe their lack of compassion and an argument broke out!

Within half an hour they were loaded into the car and back on the road, vile, depraved rap songs screaming at them from the radio.

Would the torment never end!

Kieran pleaded with him to turn it down but he was determined to make her suffer.

His reason; she had insulted his mother by staying outside to cry!

"Please turn it off Martin!" she begged distressed with what her wee lamb was being subjected to. "Please I beg you!"

He gloated and punished her for whatever his crazed mind convinced him.

Fifteen hours of torture! Fifteen hours of living hell amidst her grief and excruciating pain.

Lyric folded the book after keeping the place with a book mark and went to find her mom.

She was feeling overwhelmed and couldn't go on without talking with her.

Lyric stood at the kitchen door silently for a moment, watching her mom busily going about her work.

She'd had an incline over the years that they'd endured hardships when first arriving in the States but hadn't a clue as to how bad it was.

How can someone survive such grief and be willing to share the story?

She now had a different kind of admiration for the women she already loved and thought of as queens in their own little kingdoms.

"Mom, can we talk?" Lyric asked and Erin almost dropped the dish she was holding!

"Oh you scared me honey!"

Regaining her composure Erin said, "Sure come and sit down." "Grandma's chicken pot pie ok for lunch?"

Lyric smiled. "You bet!"

Erin cut two pieces and placed them on plates. She'd already set the table in anticipation of the arrival of a very hungry book reading girl and they sat down to enjoy a special treat.

"I didn't know Grandma gave you pie to bring home." Lyric stated her mouth full.

"You know what she's like. I think she's worried we'll all starve before our next visit!" And they both laughed at the remark.

"What did you want to talk about sweetie?"

Lyric paused for a moment unable to put all she had to say into question form.

"I guess I just wanted to say I had no idea you'd gone through that much trauma Mom!"

She pushed her pie around on the plate; her appetite suppressed for a moment and lowered her eyes.

"Well Lyric!" Erin replied placing her fork down. Leaning forward on her elbows she folded her hands under her chin.

"We didn't ever wear our lives on out shirt sleeves for the entire world to see. We were kind of ashamed that we weren't a normal family and it was bad enough going through it without talking about it all the time." Erin shrugged her shoulders. "I guess we just got used to keeping quiet."

She lowered her hands and sat back in her chair.

"When you survive that kind of thing you spend most of your life trying to forget about it!"

Lyric listened and her mom went on.

"Our life is safe and God centered and I guess I just got used to being happy, which is a really good feeling!"

Lyric smiled.

"I live every day in perpetual awareness of how blessed we are to have such a great life!"

Then she added.

"It's hard to read Mom but I want to get through it myself." "I don't want to keep taking you back there."

Erin grabbed her daughter's hand.

"Sweetheart; if you need to talk, you talk or ask questions or whatever!"

"Both Grandma and I are here for you and you know what?" Erin paused and without waiting for a reply she went on. "I'm truly beginning to realize I wasn't completely healed! But for some reason I now feel freed from something that must have been a remnant of our tragic past."

"Perhaps whatever that something was; was self imposed, but I feel free of it nonetheless!"

She sat back in her chair and gazed into the distance as though seeing her life afresh and from….. Well perhaps from heavens eyes.

"I have a greater understanding of grandma and all that she was really going through when I was questioning her silently."

Looking back at Lyric she said simply. "I realized she was human and made some terrible mistakes but never stopped loving me, Thomas or Apryl through the whole process. She never stopped fighting for us!"

There was a silent pause broken by Lyric.

"Oh Grandma's never stopped being a fighter all right, poor Grandpa!" and the girls laughed, picked up where they left off and finished their pie.

Lyric didn't read anymore that night and instead just relaxed with her mom and dad.

Greg's meeting went well and he picked up a movie on the way home.

Lyric made a huge bowl of popcorn and they snuggled in and enjoyed the movie.

Back in Yardley a happy older couple snuggled in to watch a movie also with Kylie in between and a smaller bowl of popcorn.

Thanksgiving had been a real treat this year and now they were looking forward to that special visit just before Christmas.

"I hope the girls will be ok." Shy wondered out loud.

"They'll be fine honey. The old apple doesn't fall too far from the tree you know."

Paul confirmed a truth of which Shy was more than aware and she cuddled into his arm and let out a long deep sigh.

Before Lyric went to bed that night she remembered a question she did want to ask her mom, but felt it hadn't been the right time. She sensed somehow it might take a while to answer so she wisely waited for that perfect moment.

That question being;

How did her mom cope with going back to him after the trip to the shelter?

When Lyric awoke she heard the sound of torrential rain against her bedroom window and smiled.

Perfect day for reading' she thought as she hopped out of bed.

She'd had a long lie in with the darkened morning sky and after breakfast she was eager to continue with the story.

"Is there anything you want to do today; apart from reading that is?" Erin asked smiling as she looked over at her little book worm.

Erin had taken an extra day off from her voice over work with a local agency and was thankful she had a flexible schedule.

She had created little character voices over the years, probably as a way of escaping the living nightmare of their life. As God would have it He made good out of evil and Erin had developed a lucrative career from her natural gift.

"Mum the weather's already dictated that today is definitely a 'stay at home' day, so I'll be fine just reading." Lyric announced.

"Hmm, thought as much!" Erin answered.

"You won't mind then if I run to the grocery store. We're out of milk, bread and a few other things I'll remember when I'm there."

She pulled her raincoat from the closet and buttoned it up.

"Could you get some of those nut cluster things I love? You know the 'healthy ones'!

Erin smiled. "Ok I'll get the 'healthy' nut cluster things."

"Don't answer the door! And only answer the phone if I ring twice first and then hang up!"

Lyric rolled her eyes with exasperation!

"Mum! We go through this every time you step out for a minute!" "I'm not three, I'm thirteen and quite capable of looking after myself and remembering the rules ok?"

Erin ignored her munchkin's attitude and replied."Yeah, I know honey but it's a mommy thing, so indulge me please?"

She closed the door and said a silent mom prayer. "Lord I know I pray this every day, but look after our daughter please!"

To Erin, one could never be too careful when it came to keeping our children safe. She walked down the steps and into the downpour.

Lyric curled up on the window seat in the family room and opened "Broken to Beautiful."

Duncan curled up at her feet rubbing his head against her and purring loudly. He truly didn't mind Mrs. Siedman but he preferred being with his family and especially his best pal Lyric.

Lyric found her place and settled in.

It took Kieran a while to eventually heal both physically and emotionally from Joy's death and Martin sensed she was gaining strength.

Her job had folded for the summer anyway, as they refurbished the NEX and she knew within a month she could go back to work.

Kieran had worked out that to make it on her own she would have to buy a car and get a second job.

For the first time since coming over here she believed it was possible!

Of course she'd need to take small steps so as not to alert the monster within, but this time she had her ducks in a row.

Within the first week of getting back to work she convinced Martin it would be wiser if she bought a little run around car and he wasn't opposed.

She applied for a credit card with a limit of $200 which paid for the down payment on a tiny Geo Metro and Martin actually co-signed the loan.

She guessed he was struggling with the idea of Kieran having more freedom, but then decided her idea would give him more freedom also.

Kieran tried to be as sweet as possible to cover up her true intentions and both she and Megan felt they were drawing up a strategy.

Chapter 38
The Way Out of Hell

After a year of surviving the cycle of abuse in their home, Kieran and Megan had gained enough sense of their reality to be able to navigate each situation as it arose. However, Martin also sensed the ground they were both gaining and was well aware of the unspoken alliance they had developed.

The four stages were still running their inexorable course. Their abuser unwilling or unable to stem the tide. It was just as painful to endure but Kieran now had three things she didn't have a year prior: a job and a car and hope.

He would play his games of control and it continued to feel intolerable. But now at least they had that quintessential blessing of hope. The tormentor tormented and the schemes he developed to punish became more tragic as time wore on.

Like:

Making threats if they ate food from the fridge,

Taking the television plug and phone cord with him when he went out.

When Kieran was at work Megan couldn't eat or come out of her room.

There was nothing about their life that was normal. It was simply an existence. They were treading the water of time until they could grab the opportunity for freedom and that time was coming soon!

Unfortunately Martin knew that too!

About six weeks after Joy's funeral yet another Stage Three was to stop Kieran in her tracks!

During this particularly savage attack he broke a bone in Kieran's hand and a neighbor called the police. A lone police officer stood in the doorway and didn't take one step inside.

"We received a call from a neighbor about a disturbance. Is everything OK?"

"Is everything OK? IS EVERYTHING OK!!!? Are you kidding me? Are you blind?"

Kieran sat on the sofa adjacent to the door, with matted hair and a swollen tear stained face. She was clutching a broken hand and couldn't believe the black comedy farce she seemed to have the starring role in.

Once again her hopes plunged like a sinking ship. She would never ask the police for help again.

Throughout the years that followed they suffered and struggled to break free, enduring many more bouts of violent rage.

Mother and daughter escaped their abusive life for a second time!

Although Kieran ran she felt defeated, the reason why? It was the day after another baby had been conceived.

After a very deliberate attack the night before, Kieran knew immediately she was pregnant again.

The counselors in the shelter were devastated for her but Kieran had no intention of carrying out the alternative of which they spoke. She was vehemently opposed to abortion and refused to even consider it.

A few days later they returned.

Lyric's heart began to beat faster and she paused for a moment to wipe tears from her eyes.

This was so hard to read but she was determined to carry on.

Suddenly, she felt the beating heart of that family, her family, and to give up reading would be to turn her back on them. She had to read on!

This time Martin left her alone during the full nine months, leading Kieran to believe he was capable of leading a conventional life free from the torment of his rage. Evidently the violence was a choice, and not a demonic rage he fought within himself. He had blown his cover!

Literally up to the day of Apryl's birth he behaved somewhat normal and almost likeable, but as soon as the bouncing, 9lb 1oz, baby girl was brought home, his demeanor changed.

Martin refused to allow Megan to touch her baby sister and the only release they had was when he went to work.

His ship was pulling out to sea in 3 months for a 12-week practice and the girls celebrated silently. Soon after, the ship would be deployed for six whole months and both Kieran and Megan longed for that day to come. Deployment day came and they found it hard to suppress their relief. He left, they relaxed and enjoyed baby Apryl, and she thrived. All three celebrated 12 weeks of bliss.

But the time flew by, and then Kieran got news of when the ship was pulling back in to port.

When she saw Martin walk towards her she caught a glimpse of a familiar expression, and her heart skipped a few beats with panic. Panic and dread, two words they knew so well.

His temperament was subdued and the usual strained atmosphere returned.

The girls strived to keep light spirits and the day after he got back Kieran and Megan asked if he wanted to watch a movie. His answer was barely audible but Megan had to return one anyway so she began to get Apryl ready to go.had to take movies back to the store, and she got Apryl ready as usual.

Martin had been given a day off work and he told Kieran to leave the baby with him.

Her instincts screamed at her to stay.

"Just go, Kieran. She'll be fine with me," he demanded, but she was terrified to leave.

The day before Martin had tried to pick Apryl up, but she'd screamed for her mama, and Kieran noticed rage in his eyes. Apryl's reaction was not unusual. She was only six months and didn't know him.

But he didn't understand. To him it was rejection. He couldn't even try to comprehend the mind of an infant. It was always about him.

He saw the indecision and glared at her, "Kieran go!"

She had to make a quick choice. If she stayed a fight would break out. If she left Apryl would cry and God knows what he would do.

The store was literally five minutes away. Perhaps if she ran she could get back quickly enough to prevent anything from happening. Perhaps she was overly concerned. Apryl was his flesh and blood. Surely he wouldn't hurt her!

Her life depended on split second decisions!

Megan wanted to go with her mum so they left together hearing Apryl scream in the distance. They ran like the wind. Got to the store and threw the movies down the shoot and ran back! They were gone no more than ten minutes and when she opened the door they were met with silence.

Martin was watching TV.

"Where's Apryl?" Kieran asked.

"She's in her crib," he replied without taking his eyes off the screen, and Kieran sensed something was wrong.

As she stepped quietly into the room she saw her baby girl lying on her back not uttering a sound. That was unusual for Apryl. If she was awake she needed to be held or played with.

Kieran glanced over at her baby who smiled and kicked her chubby legs. She picked her up and held her then something told her to check her body. Nausea was stirring in her stomach as she carefully laid Apryl down and undid her clothing.

As she took off her diaper Kieran noticed a long red welt across her tummy and her heart pounded.

That wasn't there this morning, she thought and she picked her baby girl up and held her tight. Apryl wasn't giving Kieran any indication that anything was wrong with her physically but she still felt the need to speak to Martin.

He denied knowing anything about the welt, of course.

The mark ran directly underneath the waistband of her diaper so even if Kieran did alert the authorities she thought they would think her crazy.

Just another over protective Mom!

Apryl seemed fine but her instincts told Kieran he'd done something.

She never left her alone with him again during that month. And then she knew he'd be gone for six whole months.

For the four weeks prior to the six month deployment Martin tormented Kieran in a new, particularly sadistic way. He suddenly shunned her. He wouldn't touch her and even began to sleep on the sofa. He made her feel rejected.

Some may think Kieran should have celebrated this particular form of torture but it was actually a familiar source of pain for her; just like she'd felt most of her life growing up. Martin seemed to be playing on the rejection she'd felt from her father. It had become glaringly apparent to Kieran that she had married another selfish man-child, who gave her very little in the way of companionship or cherished love.

His silent moods grew even more sinister and the atmosphere in the apartment more strained than ever, but in a different way. She didn't realize at the time but he was obviously infuriated at the Navy for getting in the way of his plan of control.

For a whole six months Kieran, Megan, and Apryl would have the opportunity to relax and actually be the happy family Kieran longed for, and Martin couldn't stand it! He was insensed that none of them appeared heartbroken at him leaving. So he had devised another method of control.

Kieran dropped him off at the dock on the day he left and the silent treatment continued. As much as she fought against how this was making her feel she couldn't deny how much it hurt. He was a master at the art of control.

She heard nothing from him for over a month, then she received a letter. Kieran stood in the kitchen reading and her heart quickened!

All the emotions of the last two years of their abuse-filled life rose up to the surface. Every terrifying rush of fear, every soul-destroying blow, and every putrid word heard swamped her senses!

The words she read were pure poison! But she stood transfixed unable to put the letter down. Vile rage gushed from the pages and Kieran felt sick to her stomach. What had she done to deserve this? But worse still; how could he make her feel this way thousands of miles apart?

She thought she'd gained strength. She thought there was nothing more he could do to hurt her. She was on the thresh hold of breaking free and from thousands of miles away he had baited her yet again.

Kieran sank down onto the kitchen floor and cried. Why was she determined to self destruct? Why was she willing to put herself and her children in danger?

She wrote back and tried to be strong with her choice of words but he must have sensed her weakened state. His letter had done the trick! From then on Kieran wrote him a letter of pure love and encouragement every day for five months. She had been spurned from the man who was meant to show love.

She had to climb that mountain! She had to gain his favor back!

And as the remnants of her strength and conviction to break free swirled and disappeared like dishwater from a sink, the enemy had a field day with her!

Within a few days another letter lay in the mail box and she opened it and read.

"Please, please forgive me Kieran! I was insane with grief over leaving you and the girls. I didn't know what I was saying! I love you desperately! I can't live without you Kieran!"

This was the love she'd yearned for! This was the passion she had longed for!

And he'd done it again!

Kieran wrote to him every day for the rest of the cruise. She made up packages of all his favorite things and she wrote and poured out her soul in the love letters.

Both she and Megan enjoyed Apryl and wallowed in a five month hiatus of perfect family life, but secretly Kieran admitted to missing him. She longed to read the poetic words of love he returned in reply and he seduced her once again from a distance.

Then he came back.

More quickly than she could have imagined, they were plunged into the familiar pattern and every time it happened she was snapped out of her illusion.

What had she been thinking? Life with him will only ever be more of the same over and over again. The next time a fight broke out Kieran gained the strength to call the police.

They believed her this time because children were involved. Trips to court ensued and as disillusioned as Kieran had become with herself, and Megan had become with her mother, they spent the next three years gaining back the momentum towards final freedom!

Yet another trip to the shelter became necessary as the attacks became more frequent and finally the police were called for the last time!

Martin was arrested because this time his victim was his baby girl!

Kieran had found a new apartment for herself and her two girls. She had gained the courage to tell Martin face to face and it sounded as though he'd finally come to terms with the fact.

However, when they moved out Kieran's compassionate heart overruled common sense and she gave in yet again!

He had no place to go and she told him he could sleep on the sofa in her new apartment until he found somewhere else to live. She wanted a divorce!

In less than a week after the move, he called her one night when she was working her second job at a grocery store.

Kieran had cooked dinner and left Megan in charge of Apryl.

At nine fifteen she received a call at the store where she worked until midnight.

"Kieran; I'm sorry! It's always been my fault. All the years we've been together I've been to blame and I know that now. I need help Kieran."

There was something eerie in the way he spoke and Kieran's senses were alerted.

"What's wrong, Martin? Are the girls OK? Is Apryl OK?" She felt a wave of panic wash over her as he tried to convince her not to worry.

"They're fine Kieran. I just had to tell you. I know now. It's all my fault."

She hung up the phone and grabbing her car keys from her purse, she yelled at her boss, "I have an emergency at home. I need to go!" And she flew out the store, got into her car and was home in ten minutes.

Kieran entered the apartment and Martin was lying on the sofa watching television.

Apart from the TV there was an ominous silence in the place and she asked, "Where's Apryl?"

"She's in the bedroom," he replied without taking his eyes off the show.

Kieran's instincts were screaming! There was something wrong with her baby!

She opened the door quietly and walked over to her crib, the beating of her heart loud enough to be heard. Looking down at her angel she knew.

Apryl was lying with eyes wide open, staring up at the ceiling obviously traumatized. There were two large brown marks one on each of her cheeks that looked like friction burns.

Kieran tried to be calm and when Apryl saw her mommy she smiled and kicked the covers off her legs. She stretched out her chubby arms and mommy bent down and picked her baby girl up.

Calm overcame Kieran and she walked into the living room and said, "It will look a lot better for you if you call the police and give yourself up."

Martin didn't say a word. He got up, went over to the phone and called 911.

Two uniformed officers and a detective arrived within ten minutes of the call and told both of them to sit down.

Kieran was holding Apryl on her lap and as she explained all she knew. She turned her baby's face towards them, showing them what she'd found when she came home.

Disgust was evident in their eyes and after the detective was certain Kieran had nothing to do with her child's injury he took them into the kitchen to take photographs of her wounds.

They led Martin away in handcuffs and Kieran didn't see him again until the court date two days later.

By that time the courts had quite a file on the family, and the judge had had enough!

He convicted Martin on five counts, including four previous assaults on Kieran and Megan, and sentenced him to five years in jail.

"Oh my gosh!" Megan exclaimed shocked at the severe sentence.

Even her daughter had become somewhat brainwashed, Kieran thought to herself as her husband was led away.

Martin served only five months of the five year sentence.

When he got out he lived for a while in The Mission, a homeless shelter for men in downtown Norfolk and when Kieran found out where he was her soft heart couldn't stand it. After all the pain and suffering he'd caused them all she still couldn't stand to see him in a place like that.

She'd kept his clothes and took them to the shelter. When she was there, he saw her getting ready to leave and stopped her in the hallway.

She was beguiled by more sweet talk, but this time it reached into her soul. He shared with Kieran that he'd given his life over to God in the jail, and had spent the whole five months on the floor set aside for those of faith.

"We had Bible study every day, Kieran, and I really feel my life has turned around."

Of course he looked humble! He was living in a shelter with hand-me-down clothes; who wouldn't?

Did Kieran now see what her heart had longed for?

She had prayed for years that he would change and be freed from his demons. He had played his last hand. He had gambled that the God card would work and who knows, perhaps at the time even he believed what he was saying.

It had worked on Kieran and that was the main thing. He'd suckered her once again.

However, at least this time Kieran was wise enough to grill him for a few months before giving in completely.

He got a job at a local bakery and she watched from a distance as he buckled under and worked. They spoke often and eventually he shared that his time in the shelter was almost up. He had been in the roach-infested place for two months and as nervous as she was to trust him again Kieran knew she couldn't walk away from the marriage after he'd shared his conviction from God.

"Mum, he can't be trusted. We've been safe for months! Please don't believe his lies again!" Megan begged her mother.

"He may have changed, Megan. God can work miracles!"

When Martin was in jail they found a church and had attended the Sunday service as often as they could. Kieran felt herself drawing closer to God.

Not once in the last few months had Martin given her cause for concern. And Kieran knew she couldn't stand by and do nothing when he became homeless.

By the end of the month she allowed him back into the apartment.

"You can stay until you find somewhere else to live, Martin," she stressed making sure he understood this time.

"Megan looks after Apryl when I'm at work, so please don't interfere with our routine. I put Apryl to bed before I leave for work, so she shouldn't waken anyway. And please don't bother Megan."

It was an indirect warning but Kieran was now laying down her house rules!

Her state of mind confused loyalty with keeping herself and her children safe and she was also confusing what God wanted for the family.

She honestly believed she couldn't walk away for good unless the final last chance was given.

The final last chance was given only two weeks later!

Martin left the bakery and found a job working construction. He promised he was trying to find a place to live. Each day she questioned Megan to make sure he wasn't doing anything behind her back.

"He's been OK, Mum, but I just want him gone for good!"

"He's not stupid enough to go against his word this time, sweetie. I'm going to give him one more week to find somewhere to live then he can find a friend to stay with if he hasn't found a place by then."

Kieran had begun working overnight at the airport in the parking facilities. Although the graveyard shift went against her natural body clock the pay was twice what she'd been earning at the grocery store.

She left just before 10:00 p.m. after having worked her part time day job, some days until 5:00 p.m. Although she was exhausted with the unnatural schedule she was happier being able to put Apryl to bed before she left.

Kieran realized it had also taken quite a burden off Megan's shoulders.

She'd normally be home by 6:15 a.m. and make the girls breakfast.

She'd get Apryl dressed and then take her to her day job, as nanny for a doctor.

Kieran would clean their house and get Mandy, the doctors' daughter, ready for school. After dropping her off at her private school downtown she'd then take Apryl to daycare, so she could then get some sleep.

By that time it was around 9:30 and she'd have her second wind.

Sleeping during the day in an apartment complex didn't come naturally and most days she went without.

She'd then pick Apryl and Megan up around 2:00 p.m. and either pick up Mandy and wait for her father to come home or just go straight home and start on dinner.

It was a horrendous schedule but it provided for her girls so she didn't complain.

When Kieran came home that particular morning she went to waken Apryl.

Martin had already left for work.

Her little girl sat straight up in bed, a look of horror on her face and she asked frantically, "Where's Daddy, where's he gone?"

Kieran was taken aback. "What do you mean, munchkin? He's at work."

Apryl began to scream, her arms flailing wildly.

Kieran grabbed her child and rocked her back and forth thinking she'd had a terrible nightmare, but then Apryl pushed her away.

"Daddy, Daddy is bad, Mommy. Daddy is bad!" And fear suddenly gripped Kieran's heart.

As she tried to calm her down she asked Apryl to explain and between heart rendering sobs she eventually got the story out.

Apryl pointed to her forehead and pulling back the hair from her face Kieran saw the lump!

She couldn't believe her eyes and tears streamed down as she ran to the kitchen and got some ice.

"The bastard! The bastard! I'll kill him this time! So help me God I'll kill him!"

Kieran placed a cloth filled with ice over the enormous lump on her baby's head. Apryl tried to explain she had woken up crying for Mommy and then her daddy came in and got really mad! He punched her with his fist on her head!

"I'm sorry, darlin'. I'm so sorry, Apryl; it's all Mummy's fault. I'm so sorry darlin'."

Kieran rocked her back and forth and cursed her stupid gullible nature. She'd believed Martin when he said he'd given his life to God in jail.

She'd never take him back but she was thankful he'd finally woken up to the truth. He needed God to deliver him from the rage inside him. But she shouldn't have trusted him. She shouldn't have put her children at risk and she hated herself all over again!

She was exhausted with life. Run down with the chaotic schedule she kept, but nothing was an excuse for stupidity!

She had to call the doctor to let her know she wouldn't be at work.

And then she made another call.

Kieran called Martin at work pretending it was a family emergency and screamed at him down the phone!

Every diabolical word she could think off came out of her mouth. Years of pent up frustration of giving her life over to a crazed control freak spewed forth, as the dam built from six years of hope crumbled.

The fury she had for her own inadequate behavior over the years raged on as she cursed words that had never been in her vocabulary.

And finally, completely drained she listened to his pathetic excuse.

All he had to say was, "You can't do a darn thing. Kieran! By law; you can't throw me out, and you can't risk calling the police. The court will take the girls away from you!"

Kieran hung up the phone.

She was a fool. In fact she was more than that! She was nothing, absolutely nothing but a bloody idiot and she deserved that title!

She could have been responsible for........!!!!!! She couldn't even bear to think what. But now, that day, it had ended!

Kieran checked on Apryl and caught her sliding out of bed. She ran to her mommy and cried and cried.

"It's OK darlin'. It's going to be OK. I'll never let that happen ever again, OK munchkin?"

Apryl nodded her head and Kieran asked her to hold the cloth over the bump.

It already looked better.

She picked up the phone and called 'the woman's shelter'.

She told them that Martin had hit Apryl this time but she didn't mention the events of the last eight months.

He was right. They would have taken the children from her.

Chapter 39
How to explain the madness?

Lyric snapped the book shut unable to go on, her heart quickening! She was surprised at how much she'd been able to read. It was hard! It was terribly disturbing! But now she needed answers. She looked out of the rain spattered window and tried to still her mind. It was racing with questions and she had a strange unsettled stirring in her heart. What was she feeling towards the woman she'd known all her life?

The woman she admired and respected and loved so very much. She had understood and had compassion and empathy towards Grandma Shy throughout the whole story so far, but now she was disappointed and enraged!

How could she have put her mom in that kind of danger over and over again? How could she have risked the life of her own baby over and over again?

Lyric needed to know and she needed to know right now!

Her mom was still out shopping so she had time to call Grandma before she got back. But then, just as she picked up the phone Lyric suddenly remembered the woman she was calling; her beloved Grandma Shy.

She remembered the many times Grandma had shared wonderful stories and had given her such wise advice.

She remembered how much her own Mom loved her so.

She remembered how much everyone loved her and suddenly she remembered one more thing!

She'd written a book about the truth! She had been completely honest about everything she'd done wrong and all the bad decisions she'd made. She never needed to be that truthful. She could have been content to lock the memories in a closet, like so many people do with their family skeletons!

She did it to reach out to others! She did it to help stop the madness!

Who am I to be mad at my Grandma for making mistakes? Lyric let out a long, deep sigh and dialed. The phone rang a few times and Paul picked it up.

"Hi, Grandpa, it's Lyric."

"Oh hello sweetheart, how're you doing?"

"I'm fine Grandpa how are you?"

Paul explained he'd been working in the garage and asked if she wanted to speak to Shy.

"Well yes actually that's why I called. Not that I didn't want to talk to you of course!" She added.

"Oh I know, my love, let me call Grandma and say hi to your mum and dad will you?"

Lyric told him she would and waited for Shy.

She heard Grandma pick up the phone and suddenly became nervous. Fighting back tears she said a soft, "Hello."

"Hello munchkin! Oh what's wrong with ye' darlin'!" Shy asked suddenly aware Lyric was crying.

In between trying to catch her breath Lyric explained.

"Well I was reading a lot of the story yesterday and today, and Mom and I talked a bit, but then when she was out shopping I kept reading and felt as though I was getting really mad at you! And I didn't like it, so I called!"

"Awe, ma' pet! Maybe I shouldn't have given you the book. Maybe I should have waited," Shy replied, and then she stopped. "But ye' know honey bunch. She paused for a moment, "God has us do things His way, for His purpose and I'm not going tae' argue with Him."

Lyric laughed and a huge burden lifted off her young shoulders. That's my grandma! She thought.

"I'm guessing you might be talking about when we were living with Apryl's dad?"

"Uh Huh, that's the part."

"Well. ma' love. it'll take a long time to explain all that. Are ye' willin'?" Shy asked.

"Yes Grandma I am. I won't sleep tonight if you don't tell me."

"Well you get comfy OK?"

Lyric sat down on the window seat and stared out at the rain soaked streets.

"I'm ready, Grandma."

"Well I'm just going' to jump right in at the deep end, I guess," Shy began, a little apprehensive of what to say, but her Papa made the way clear.

"Martin had romanced me. He had convinced me he couldn't live without me, playing on my compassionate heart. He lied his way through life like it was second nature to him. Which of course it was, but back then I believed his lies to be truth.

"I desperately wanted this new family to work. I desperately believed he was just as much a victim of his own pain, therefore I stayed. I not only stayed, but I went back time and time again. And that's what upset you sweetie!"

Lyric grabbed a cushion and hugged it tight.

"There were very few people in my life back then that cared enough about me and the girls to tell me the truth. To tell me how dangerous it was in either taking him back or going back after a stay at the house. To tell me how to get out and stay out! The councilors at the shelter tried but their advice obviously wasn't what I needed.

"I was a loner by nature. I didn't need groups of friends to affirm who I was. But that part of my personality fell right into my abuser's game plan."

"What do you mean by that, Grandma?" Lyric asked.

"Abusers take a long time to lure their prey into a place of trust, sweetheart. It doesn't just happen over night!

"He found out as much information about me as he could during the first few months, allowing me talk, allowing my broken heart to share. I had been romanced by this guy for two years prior to coming to America, Lyric."

Shy took a breath as she remembered the decent into hell!

"Although by that time he had given me some reasons to be concerned, I had fallen under his spell and by then it was almost too late. I was more confused about who I was at that point in my life, than any other, given the events that led up to the relationship. And that's exactly what his aim had been: to destabilize me, to confuse me so much that I felt he knew and understood me better than anyone else.

"He began to control everything I thought and everything I did. He began to control my life."

Lyric was quiet on the other end of the phone as she tried to put herself in her grandma's shoes. But it was hard! No, more than that it was impossible!

She'd had a wonderful life full of support and guidance and unconditional love from her parents and grandparents, how could she even begin to understand?

But then she'd been reading the story. She knew Kieran from childhood!

Lyric listened in that quiet place and God suddenly allowed her to see the bigger picture of Kieran's life.

"Grandma, it didn't just start with Martin did it?" And without waiting for an answer she went on. "It began way back there when Kieran was a little girl!"

Tears of grace spilled over as Shy now listened to her grandbaby. She felt the pounding of her heart as a child revealed the tragic truth!

She saw the correlation between her childhood and her life as a grown up.

Words spoken at home, from those who are meant to love and cherish, set a child up for a life full of brokenness and years of fighting against a lie.

In Kieran/Shy's case, it had led to abuse! Shy pulled herself together.

"That's exactly what "Broken to Beautiful" is all about, precious girl. That's exactly what God revealed to me as he walked with me back through years of pain. I've never used my pain to excuse wrong decisions, Lyric. I've never blamed anyone else for putting myself and my children at risk.

"But when God revealed the truth the enemy has kept buried under the rubble of my life, it became my duty to share the lessons, to share the legacy of a lifetime searching for Papa. To share the redemption we can only receive from the blood of Jesus Christ."

Lyric jumped when she heard the front door open.

"It's just me, sweetie pie, I got your nutty things!" Erin shouted through to her little book worm, she assumed was snuggled in all comfy cozy.

The door of Lyric's bedroom opened to reveal a rain soaked mom and immediately she sensed something was up.

"Are you OK, Lyric?"

Lyric nodded and smiled.

"Grandma, Mom's just come back so I'll hang up now."

"Sweetheart, did I answer your questions. Did I explain enough?"

Lyric smiled and replied. "You did fine, Grandma, honestly I see it more clearly now, you know; the whole picture. But there is one more question."

Erin closed the door sensing they needed their time.

And Shy waited.

"Why do you call God "Papa," Grandma?"

Shy smiled and her heart soared

"I call Him Papa, sweetheart, because He's not just the God of the Universe to me anymore. He's the God that saw every step I took and every trip that made me fall. He's the God who whispered into my heart even when I didn't know Him, with tender words full of unconditional love. He was the Father I'd always longed for. That's my Papa and I know He loves me! And that's why I call Him Papa, sweet girl, because I feel Him in my heart."

Shy was so grateful He had revealed Himself to Lyric through questions. Words never seemed adequate enough to explain a life of trauma. She realized Lyric didn't want to say too much in front of her mum. Not to hide, but rather to save unnecessary pain. She was just as much a trooper as Erin!

"God Bless you sweet girl. I'll talk to you later."

"Bye, Grandma, I love you."

"I love you too ma' darlin'." And Shy hung up and just sat.

Lyric closed the book and went through to see her mom.

"Was that Grandma?" Erin asked stating the obvious but Lyric knew her mom by now. She knew she didn't like to be invasive and strived to give Lyric her space.

"Yeah! But I called her actually."

Erin turned round to face her. "Was the story getting too much?"

Erin knew it was time to be open about it all. She knew her mum's passionate belief in a family being open and honest, even about painful matters.

As soon as they finally broke free from their life of torment and her mum's mind began to clear and grow stronger, she vehemently stood against anything hidden. Even to the point of pushing Erin to talk and be more open about difficult to talk about issues. In was in her wee lamb's nature to keep things to herself. Shy knew that was a bait of Satan and was determined to tackle him head on in every battle. She was a warrior, in Erin's and Lyric's eyes.

"It was and I found myself getting really angry at Grandma, so I called her."

"That was the right thing to do, sweetie. You wouldn't have been able to let it go otherwise."

Erin knew her daughter really well and sometimes too well according to Lyric!

"Yep! And I wouldn't have slept either."

"Are you almost done?" Erin asked hoping there wasn't too much more. Hoping she'd finish well before Christmas.

"I am, and the conversation I had with Grandma was awesome!"

"She really clears things up doesn't she?"

"Grandma has such a simple way of getting at the truth that sometimes I wonder why everyone else makes stuff so complicated!"

Erin laughed.

"I know! And then she always rounds it up with; To Him the Glory!"

"That endeared me to her even more because I know she really means it!" Erin stated.

Lyric nodded in agreement and got sidetracked by the bags. One of them held her nutty treat.

"Hey, young lady it's almost lunch time!"

"Awe just a few, please!"

The girls spent the rest of the day relaxing and enjoying each other's company. Lyric decided to take a break from the story and just pottered around doing nothing in particular.

In an ivy covered cottage on the outskirts of Yardley, two people in love just enjoyed the rest of their day too. As Shy and Paul sat down to dinner that night they talked about the phone call.

"She's another amazing product of a happy God-centered home, sweetheart!" Shy remarked having shared most of the conversation she'd had with Lyric.

"Oh she's something else, honey, that's for sure!" And they ate and talked and later on took a long walk down their quiet country lane.

Chapter 40
Finding her way Home

Shy rose the following morning to embrace the beautiful day. The sun was shining and a gentle breeze rustled golden leaves as they clung on to the trees in all their glory.

She let Kylie outside and made a pot of coffee for her usual quiet time with the Lord. But this morning, before she began, she felt drawn to another piece of writing.

She had several copies of the manuscript, having gone through many rewrites and thought she had another completed version upstairs in her window seat.

This morning she felt compelled to refresh her thoughts of the journey; to renew her gratitude to God for guiding her home to Him. She went back upstairs to fetch the other copy and the delicious aroma of fresh brewed coffee beckoned to her to come back down! She found it, all thumb marked and dog eared and clutching it in her hand she slipped quietly downstairs.

Shy loved being alone for the first few hours in the morning. Understanding her heart's desire for that quiet time Paul had willingly sacrificed himself for another two hours in bed.

Shy poured her coffee and buttered a toasted muffin. She got situated in her favorite armchair, in her favorite room.

It was glorious outside but she knew she would be distracted by nature and the beauty of her surroundings. She knew she wouldn't get a word read. Sipping her coffee and resigning herself to being obedient, Shy took a bite of her muffin and began to read.

A final bid for freedom and something inside Kieran had changed once and for all. Martin had crossed the invisible line in the sand and he'd mocked the will of the Father.

Kieran had trusted him for the last time because of his declaration of faith and this time he'd not only fallen from grace, but he'd violated that trust.

He'd played on her search for the simple truth of faith, years before in Scotland when he'd invited her to the Baptist Church on base. He knew then, that would lure her in and he bargained on it again.

This time he was wrong!

She would never, ever, trust him again. Kieran knew there was a race against time. He didn't have a ride back from his job but she was nervous he would concoct some dramatic lie to leave early and hitch a ride back.

She couldn't afford to linger so began to literally throw clothes and personal items into as many garbage bags as she could find.

Kieran walked up and down the stairs umpteen times becoming worn out with the feat of packing up their life, but adrenalin kept her going. She threw food into plastic bags and toiletries into shopping bags and then Apryl joined in with her toys.

"Can I bring my favorite things Mommy?" A little angel asked, a little scared but a little excited. It felt like an adventure!

There was urgency in the way Kieran was acting that conveyed to her baby girl that this time it was for good!

"Munchkin, you can bring whatever can fit in the car, OK?"

All her toys, Kieran thought to herself as she marched up and down the stairs loading the car to full capacity. And she fought back tears as they blinded her vision.

Got to keep strong! Her mother's heart reminded her.

Megan's room was another mountain to climb. Kieran threw in necessities first, then personal items to keep her wee lambs soul from crushing, went next.

But what Kieran didn't realize was if Megan had seen her mum at that moment, she'd be happy to leave with only the clothes on her back!

There was a definite, finality to the madness, in her actions that day.

An "I've had enough with this garbage in our lives" attitude that would have made anyone that knew her cheer her on!

"Go Kieran, Go Kieran, you can do it! It's your birthday! It's Freedom Day!"

She made room for one more item as she emptied Megan's room and carefully packed things tightly around the car seat.

The car was now a Plymouth Neon she had upgraded to a few months prior. At that moment she was thankful for the blessing of much more room.

"Ok now, munchkin." Kieran looked down at the huge brown eyes staring up at her. "We have everything apart from you, Megan, and..." She took a long pause for effect hoping to bring a little sunshine into the drama of the day.

"The television!" She concluded.

Apryl's face was priceless! "We can take our TV?" She asked her eyes big like saucers.

"Yep! We sure can, angel face, now come on let's go!"

Kieran drove to the house absolutely exhausted. It was midday already and she'd had no sleep since the day before but she kept going. Freedom was worth it, at all cost!

Some of the workers at the shelter helped unload yet another family's life, wondering whether this would be the last time. They were so used to victims returning to their abuser time and time again. In fact sometimes it took up to seven times before they eventually gained the strength to stay away for good.

Unfortunately, all too often they would see women go back for the last time. They wouldn't get out of their situation alive! Kieran had no time to ponder such a tragic truth. This time was the last for her and the girls.

At 2:30 p.m. Kieran sat outside the school and watched the expression on Megan's face as she saw her mom and Apryl.

"What's going on?" She asked, perhaps a little fearful, perhaps a little hopeful.

"We've left, Megan. We've left for good! And this time there's no going back, I swear to you with my life."

Megan cried and Kieran cried and Apryl hugged them around their legs, being strong for her family. Then she joined in. They walked towards the car and Kieran told her daughter what had happened.

She wasn't surprised of course and neither should Kieran have been.

But for some women it takes a final something. Something like the final straw! Or even an over play of the enemies hand for them to say: enough!

Enough of the control, enough of the misery in their lives, enough of the madness! They drove back to the house and Megan knew her mum was serious when she saw the TV. Suddenly it all seemed funny! Terribly tragic, but funny. Kieran asked her what was so amusing.

"I kind of believed you this time Mum, because I saw something different in your eyes and the way you held yourself, but......" Megan paused trying to suppress the laughter but failed miserably. In between hilarious, rib cage breaking roars, she explained that she believed her completely when she saw the TV!

They laughed and laughed and then the laughter turned to tears and back to laughter and by the time they got it all out they were spent.

Years and years of pent up pain and fear and frustration to end all frustration, was dispelled through laughter.

How good is Our God!

The month was crazy busy, trying to work and find a new apartment. Kieran was thankful for an awesome tax refund that year, and they were able to shop for some things for the new apartment they eventually found.

This was real! It was really happening! And gradually Megan believed there was no going back.

They'd fought for years for their freedom and it tasted so very sweet when it finally arrived.

Chapter 41
Closer and Closer

Kieran was aware the airport job had to come to an end. She was getting less sleep than ever before, living in a house full of ten other families so, she applied for the Norfolk Police Department. Her rationale then was; to use her experience as a kennel person/dog handler with The Ministry of Defense Police in Scotland, to get just one job that would provide for her girls.

But, apart from it causing panic in the heart of her children, Megan especially, Kieran didn't realize what she was up against in a man's world!

She passed the written test and was the only woman to do so, in that group. The next step was agility and physical fitness. The day came and as soon as she saw the look on the examiners face her heart sank!

But the group of guys she was with quickly became her personal cheerleaders.

She lined up for the first phase: a hundred yard dash in 17 seconds. Kieran's heart pounded. She had never been a good runner at school but she was determined to beat that clock!

The ground was uneven grass filled with little potholes and half way down the track Kieran felt a muscle in her thigh pull. She didn't stop!

The African American Sergeant pressed his stop watch. "18 seconds you're out!"

He declared with hard to conceal relish written all over his face.

"Awe come on Searg!" The guys yelled back, fully aware of what was going on. "Give her a break! She was only one second short."

The 'gracious' sergeant gave Kieran another chance and as she limped up to the start she gritted her teeth with tenacious intent!

"Go!" And Kieran ran like the wind, excruciating pain in her thigh causing her to wince, but she wouldn't give up!"

"18 seconds again, you're out!"

The men knew the truth of that day. They knew she had been singled out and labeled by the good old boys network.

As Kieran limped away from the field she held her head high and shouted good luck to her cheerleaders!

Another week of the grueling schedule passed, until the morning Kieran fell asleep at the wheel of her car! She was driving Mandy to the private school she attended, and Apryl was in the back, in her car seat.

Kieran blacked out at the wheel and came around with the girls, high pitched squeal; "Where are we going?"

She'd turned right instead of going straight and had fallen asleep for only a few seconds, but it was enough to have put them in extreme danger. She called in sick that night and had a good night's sleep to recover from a whole year of exhaustion.

The following night she handed in her notice. Kieran didn't have a job but somehow knew in her heart God would provide. Her faith was still in the early stages of discovery but she sensed He was taking care of them..

When she got home from work that day she bought a paper.

In the centre of the "jobs wanted" section there was a full page ad for a big department store in downtown Norfolk: "Associates needed $10 per hour, no experienced needed, will train."

It wasn't police pay, but at least it was as much as the airport.

She prayed the doctor would allow Megan to help out with Mandy so she could keep that income also. Resolutely she applied.

Kieran was hired on the spot for the Lancome counter in cosmetics. It scared her more to be a beauty consultant/ makeup artist, than a police dog handler! Go figure!

The enemy was still trying to attack, convincing her she was and never would be good enough! But God had a purpose. He'd had His hand on little Kieran all through her life, broken hearted with her pain but conscious of the lioness within her heart.

She'd valiantly fought the enemy for years even though she was ignorant of whom her adversary was. But now she was growing more aware each day. It was around that time God led her little family to a church where they would begin to grow in their faith. His plan for Kieran and her girls was being put into action.

They attended the church as often as they could and for the years that followed lived the rollercoaster life of a single parent family enduring the challenges together. Megan had to transfer to another high school she hated and would never grow accustomed to, Apryl was going through an extended terrible-two's season and Kieran was just as tired, but she was getting sleep.

They bathed in their freedom and celebrated every day, through every trial. Her walk towards the God she'd been searching for grew closer.

Deep within the channels of her heart Kieran was freshly aware of a love relationship with her Father in Heaven growing ever deeper and with it, her resolve to find the simple truth. One day as they sat in church as it began to fill for the morning service she heard a voice directly behind her, "Kieran!" the voice said in a deep resonant tone.

She turned around and no one was there. "Did you call me? Are you two playing around?" The two girls looked at Kieran and then each other. "No!" they replied in unison wondering now whether their mum might have lost it completely!

"Kieran," the voice said once again but deeper and crystal clear. Suddenly Kieran knew!

Suddenly she knew God had called her name!

She didn't know what to do with it! But she sensed to be still and wait! Kieran didn't panic; she didn't question or tell anyone. She just hunkered down and waited.

Just before Megan's 18th birthday Kieran was finally able to file for her green card, the legal document an immigrant needs to live and work in the US. The whole process takes years and cost money. A lot of money and that in itself is another story; a story to be told at a later date!

Kieran worked long hours, the doctor allowed Megan to help and they gradually became an extended family. They went to church, and Kieran read the word and drew closer and closer to God her Father.

After working for three and a half years with Lancome, Kieran found out about a position available as a makeup artist for the very Ministry she'd prayed with all those years prior.

The American show with the angel! The show that led her to give her life to Jesus 12 years previously in Brechin, Scotland, as she had cried out to the God of the Universe for help!

Shy stopped and gazed out the window into her wildflower garden. A flutter of something colorful caught her eye and she stepped closer. On the window-sill outside a butterfly with delicate wings of blues and yellow lay almost motionless, as though clinging to the last breath of life. A fragile memory from a distant past suddenly tugged on Shy's heart and tears welled up in her tired eyes as she remembered her doorstep. As she dried the salty flow her gaze deepened and the delicate creature fluttered its wings, its beauty magnified by an unexpected ray of sunshine and as though the Creators breathe had suddenly touched its tiny body it flew. She smiled and watched as it flitted from flower to flower celebrating its tenacity for life; holding on to hope with fervor that it could fly once more. She sat down and laid her head against the soft cushion on her favorite chair and reflected.

What a journey! What an amazing search and longing to find the simple truth! A truth she had felt deep in her heart as a child that dared to question.

Looking back through her life Shy, or Kieran as we've come to know her, had discovered living proof that God had never left her. He had been patiently waiting on her every step of the way and without realizing it she too had clung on to hope.

Thousands of miles away in what seemed another lifetime in the little town of Brechin, she had given her life to the Lord when she didn't know the real meaning of what she was doing. Who would have thought that that declaration of faith and trust would eventually lead her to work for the very ministry she'd prayed with all those years ago!

That wasn't just coincidence! Only God knew!

She now looked forward to spending the rest of her life in perfect peace, within a family who knows God intimately; who shares the truth and dares to keep it simple!

All those years later!

From the cruel words spoken within an otherwise loving home that crushed her spirit! The terrible fall into sin! The trauma of divorce and a broken family! All those thousands of miles traveled across an ocean of hope as a destiny unknown tugged on her heart.

Years of abuse from either a victim trapped in bondage of his own, or a willing servant of evil!

The list could go on and on..............

But now, in her life story so far, Kieran's Papa was calling her home!

He was patiently leading her down the path towards a complete healing!

But that's another part of the story perhaps for another time. And so the legacy of a lifetime will be passed on, from generation to generation; passed on with love so that no one is left behind......

This is a simple story of Redemption; a story of hope for broken hearts......The story of "Broken to Beautiful."

To Him the Glory!

The End

Or Perhaps just the beginning...............?

Epilogue

How very far I have come
Reflections on a Life by Sheila Summers

How many long years have passed full of adversity and trials of immeasurable proportion, alone in a strange country knowing no one and nothing but the rage of a man devoured by anger, evidence of a deep brokenness of his own.

If you have read my story you will already know that I am not an author of eloquent words full of deep wisdom and underlying messages that would be the topic of conversation amidst the patrons of the 'writers guild book club meetings', but rather I believe myself to be a conveyer of the simple truth as directed by My Heavenly Father and lover of my soul.

I sat in church one Sunday morning about two years ago with my two girls, early for a change, waiting quietly for the sanctuary to fill and the service to begin.

"***Sheila***!" a deep voice called, just behind me to my right and as I turned to see who was calling my name I realized there was no one within sight. I turned back and asked my daughters if they had spoken or heard my name being called.

"We didn't hear a thing Mom" they both replied minus the usual look of mischief I was used to witnessing when they were up to something.

"Hmm! Must have been my imagination" I thought to myself but as the last word of wondering fluttered through my mind I heard it again;

"Sheila" with a deep clarity like no other voice I'd known before and I snapped my head around much quicker than before, my heart now pounding knowing without a doubt I hadn't imagined it twice. But then I felt warmth engulf me like suddenly being wrapped in a familiar, cozy blanket from many years before and another lifetime away, as though I was being cradled in His tender love reassuring me that whatever He was calling me to was not to be feared.

I knew it was the voice of my God!

It would eventually take me another year before I felt Him say this time:

> *"Sheila I want you to write your story and I will not forsake you in the dark places, but rather, in the telling of your testimony, I will heal you of wounds of which you were completely unaware. Be strong and fear not."*

Calm came over me and I began to write.

For all those who knew my fear of computers and my complete inability to type with more than one finger at a time, taking a few moments to pause in between to search for each letter, the shock of witnessing my new found gift was just as real to them as it was to me!

I can remember calling Patrick, another of God's blessings, to ask him if I could read what I'd written so far and he graciously complied, in his innocence, to be the listener of no more than a few paragraphs at the most. Well, almost a complete first chapter later he replied in total disbelief "I can't believe you've written that much already!"!

"Me neither!" was my reply but throughout the writing of my story as I sat in disbelief watching my fingers fly over the keys and during many times when revisiting those dark places which had held so many painful memories, I have felt more like a scribe rather than a self-directed writer, and I have indeed been healed in places I was completely ignorant of ever having been wounded.

How Great is Our God!

That HE should bother with little me, whom I thought to be nothing more than an insignificant member of society, with little to offer anyone other than my children!

Yet, HE spoke in a clear voice and commanded me to write and so I was obedient and wrote.

He took me on a journey of discovery to help me understand the who's and why's of my life and I now write this epilogue with a crystal like clarity of seeing that journey through Heaven's Eyes and with Our Father heart.

The Church of Scotland; with its dark ancient exterior and cold unwelcoming interior was, to most children of elementary school age, a foreboding place where strict rules of conduct were implemented and the loving heart of God was only fleetingly referenced to by the Minister, who would stand high above the congregation behind the ornately, carved pulpit retaining an obvious distance from the very people he was trying to reach. As he would look down and read from the bible with a strained sing-songy voice that was surely designed to separate himself even more from us mere mortals, I was nonetheless touched by Gods hand and therefore, giving the Minister the benefit of the doubt, probably received some lesson of sorts from his sermons.

I longed to find out more about God but was raised within a home and culture that spoke more about religion rather than faith.

The difference between Catholics and Protestants was made prevalent during my childhood because of the 'troubles' between Northern and Southern Ireland and was spoken about most nights on the news. We'd witness the atrocities being carried out by both sides on a regular basis watching in horror as yet another car bomb was set off in some busy thoroughfare of a city gearing for Christmas with many innocent victims paying the price for the ignorance and futile beliefs of extremists, confusing me even more as to the difference between believing in a loving God and religion itself.

My home life was relatively normal, I could only guess and we lived with the generally accepted knowledge that we were loved by our parents because words of endearment were seldom spoken, but they fed and clothed us and worked hard to provide a safe shelter for us and taught us morals and values, yet I wondered constantly of a greater love.

I felt terribly lonely most of the time growing up as the youngest of four and seemed aware of an unspoken 'something' in our home that never was revealed to the 'baby' of the family. Whether this was all my imagination or not, and I'm more than sure I will never find the answer to that unspoken 'something', but never the less whatever 'it' was, helped make me feel like an outsider in my own home.

In our home there were never conversations at the dinner table or even enquires into how our day had been, yet we were there and lived our lives together with a quiet acceptance of; this is what life was.

When telling of how I had cringed at the word 'idiot' when I was just a little girl, as it had been spat at me quietly from an otherwise good man, my father, I suffered terribly from guilt; feeling I was committing an unforgivable betraying of father and daughter trust.

Even as I wrote honestly of how the Lord had revealed that word as the root of a deep pain I had carried all through my life, I still felt the need to compare all the good things my father gave and did for me, as though torn between a bonded loyalty towards him and understanding the grave effects that one little word had on me.

No matter how many times I danced standing on my daddy's feet or how many wonderful scones and cakes I had devoured as soon as they emerged from the oven hot and delicious, that tiny little word came crashing down like a brick wall to crush my spirits.

My face would flush and tears would try and well up but my resilience would force them back. Heart beating loud enough to hear as it broke a little more each time that cruel word was spoken, I would then lower my head hoping my long chestnut hair would hide my shame.

The mountain I saw before me that measured the distance I had to climb to gain his favor back from being 'nothing but an idiot' was too high for such a little girl who only wanted to hear the words *'I love you and I'm proud of you, Sheila'.*

In the years that lay ahead, the unspoken 'something' would become a familiar visitor to the atmosphere with in my home, as I grew to witness an invisible battle of sorts being played out between my parents, with my future being used as the weapon of choice between the two.

Coming together in agreement with each other would have been the right and proper thing to do in this situation of career choice, however, as long as we were just meant to accept that my parents loved one another it would also be more than apparent that the conflict between them seemed to have a life of its own and obviously had to survive. So the battle lived on and I chose dance and with it an ongoing sense of guilt the expense of this choice had incurred on their otherwise working class livelihood.

But no one understood my internal struggle.

I had no other choice but to carry on; giving up would have meant letting down the only person in my life who actually saw something in me to be proud of, even though her dream was a little more than unrealistic; it was impossible!

Although I persevered I instinctively knew I wouldn't be able to make it as a professional dancer but yet I carried on. I was living my mothers' dream of becoming someone for her to be proud of but yet struggling with a continual nagging assurance burned into my very soul that I was an imposter, truly then I must be 'nothing but a idiot'.

Harsh words spoken from someone who was meant to love and encourage and words that may have possibly changed a life of promise to one of bad choices leading finally to abuse.

I came to accept however, that my parents did their best for all of us and I love them and appreciate them in a deeper more profound way than ever before.

They helped make wonderful memories for us of Christmas and summer holidays and taught us manners and life values and were there for us as much as they could have been, but without having an understanding of a personal relationship with Jesus Christ they denied us the greatest gift any parent can give a child.

My father was a quiet man with an inability to communicate love and tenderness to his youngest child and perhaps to the others also. I now know however with blessed assurance that his weakness in that area was not my fault and I was therefore able to give up the guilt of feeling like the daughter who was portrayed as never being pleased with her life, making one foolish mistake after another and move on to loving myself unconditionally. I no longer feel guilty of admitting that I needed and deserved that from him but never received it.

Now I can look at those fragmented years of my childhood with a new found compassion for a father and mother I loved deeply and still to this day appreciate for all they did give to me, but I'm left to feel terribly sad for the lives they continued to live void of the greatest gift of all, Jesus Christ.

They are no longer with us in body but I pray that in spirit they will be able to understand once and for all the little girl who loved to dance and sit ever so still on the doorstep of their home wrapped in a blanket like a little orphan waiting to go home.

On this journey I have learned of Gods unconditional love and tender mercy as I had never fully understood before. True to his promise, He was with me all the way, tenderly revealing to me how deep rooted those hurts truly were and how well I'd managed to cover them up for so many years in my search for The Truth. He unraveled the lie I had been led to believe most of my life and so I was finally able to forgive myself for all that I'd felt responsible for throughout those years, thus releasing me from the sentence of guilt, sometimes dealt out from family, but mostly of my own volition.

My Heavenly Father helped me to understand that guilt and shame are baits of Satan that will keep us in bondage for eternity unless we allow Him to set us free.

I lived my life throughout childhood carrying with me a terrible burden of guilt, never understanding why but feeling I was responsible for all the wrongs within my world and to be called an 'idiot' only served to enforce the lie. As an adult I made a poor choice of life partner who, apart from blessing me with two beautiful children, became the perpetrator of neglect which led me to spiral downwards into a pit of despair creating loneliness like I'd never experienced before.

The neglect my children and I suffered then led me into the arms of a do good predator and so once again I chose to keep my sanity but lost my dignity by having an affair which ultimately led to divorce and a second marriage.

This new choice however, was to lead my daughter and I away from the protection of our family and homeland to America, the land of opportunity and freedom.

How ironic to think; that this hope for a brighter future only served to lead us into danger beyond my ability to comprehend.

I survived the death of my first child in this new marriage from Hell as predator turned into abuser and the distant echo of cruel words turned a hearts desire to be cherished into the poisoned kind of love where passionate embrace turns into a fight for one's life.

Grieving over the loss of a baby girl whilst trying to protect my eldest daughter and suffering a terrible longing for my son who chose to stay behind in Scotland, I then fell pregnant again and nine months later gave birth to another precious baby girl.

The road ahead became a battle ground where broken bones and bruises led to one court case after another culminating in my husband's eventual arrest and sentence to five years in jail. He only served five months.

Six years from having arrived in America, after going through the trials of a lifetime including four visits to a battered woman's shelter, my two daughters and I finally escaped for the last time and began our long searched for journey into freedom.

Having the courage to take that final step allowed God to show me the path He had laid out for me even though I'd deviated from it many, many times.

He taught me how to revisit situations from my life that had haunted me for years by looking at them from a different advantage point, like viewing the slow motion replay footage from a football game, analyzing each thought in each situation with Him by my side waiting to catch me if I fell, reassuring me with a great sense of peace. In turn this discovery gave me a deeper insight into the why's of what I had been feeling during those life events that had caused so much pain.

However, writing my story was much harder than I thought and it would be remiss of me to candy coat the certainty of renewed pain I suffered through taking this journey with Him, but it was all completely necessary.

He had to help me see the deep connection between those cruel, little words spoken and the lie I had been led to believe.

Finally He helped me to understand that we are not only all sinners in need of a savior with no exceptions, but we are also equally precious in His sight.

In accepting this truth I was then able to look back at my father and the two men in my life who'd been responsible for inflicting so much turmoil, in a different light, seeing them for the first time through Gods eyes and forgiving them all with unconditional love, still to keep my physical distance intact to remain safe.

This life journey from the ancient city of Edinburgh, to the stark beauty of the Scottish Highlands and then eventually to America has been long, arduous and extremely painful, but eventually I arrived at this destination full of blessings of unimagined proportion.

The journey I took with Our Father became the ultimate quest for the truth and I would do it all over again if necessary because, I have finally been set free!

But it doesn't have to end there with me.

If this story strikes a familiar chord with you or anyone you know then the agony can stop now!

God is waiting for His children to turn to Him and you are one of His children. He wants to bring you home to His embrace, freeing you from the shackles of abuse and condemnation.

I urge you brother and sister alike; to listen to this simple story of redemption and understand the message. We all have to become more aware of how the enemy weaves his lies and deception throughout our lives and come to realize the reality of the battle that is being waged on a daily basis; the battle for our souls and well being of the unity of family.

The enemy despises anything that resembles family unity and is lying in wait to destroy.

Each word of insult to our children will serve only to break down their confidence and eventually set them up for a lifetime of failure.

Each time we show them anything less than a united front within the structure of the home we will be laying the groundwork for their marriages to come.

The message comes back to the simple truth;

To Love one another as you love yourself.

However, if you have not been taught how to love yourself and have been forced to believe in a lie throughout your life then turn to Our Father and he will show you the child you have always been in His eyes. And then the healing will begin.

The look of utter astonishment on Katia's face when I told her I could give her a first-hand account of what it was like to be a victim of abuse, as she prepared for her weekly show with the Christian television ministry we both work for, was incredulous to say the least.

"What are you talking about Sheila, how could you possibly know?" was all she could say in answer to my declaration.

As I began to explain, condensing my story as much as possible, I took a step outside the reality of it all and as I heard myself talk I realized how distant that life had become and how truly renewed I am into being the woman God made me to be. Yet in so many ways I am still the little girl who sat on the doorstep so many years before listening quietly for His voice whispering into my heart.

This brought me to understand that from birth we are all innocent and pure and are cherished by Our Father, but if we never hear the message of the simple truth and grow up unaware of God's love, we become even more susceptible to the lies of the enemy and can then fall victim to the traps he sets.

My utter joy resounds as I celebrate the great wisdom He has imparted to one who once thought herself to be insignificant in the grand scheme of life and I now stand tall and declare with a loud voice that;

I am a cherished daughter of the King!

Acknowledgement

How do you tell the story of a lifetime and who do you bring along for the ride? Answer: Who so ever loves you enough to take the arduous journey with you!

To God my Father, my Papa, my deliverer; who loves me unconditionally and that means no matter what! Who saved me from myself, all the while whispering softly into my heart. Who is using my pain, my sin, my redemption to reach others in need: Thank you Papa.

To My dear sweet husband; love of my life, incredible man of God and omnipresent giant for justice, protector of me from myself and an extraordinarily consistent source of encouragement and strength for me and my children. The man my Papa prepared to love me like no other, breathing life into my broken heart, returning to me the years the locusts had stolen: Thank you, my love.

To my Girls; who have supported me throughout our life together including the three long years of writing, at all times sensing when I needed my space, or just asking me if I needed anything when the going got tough: Thank you, sweet daughters.

To my Son; who forgave me, and has turned his 'broken into beautiful' by being the best father any child could wish for. I applaud you sweet son and tender heart: Thank you from Mum Bum.

To my parents; for giving me life, for doing the best you could do with a child full of questions, for loving me in the quiet places when you were mad enough to spit, for providing a home safe from the outside world even though there was pain within: Thank you Mum and Dad.

To my sister and brothers; who were a part of my childhood even though we were like passing ships in the night, who probably tried to understand me but certainly had their work cut out: Thank you siblings.

To My Co-workers; who allowed me to bounce ideas off them now and then and whose encouragement helped validate my efforts when I was drained: Thank you, dear sisters in Christ.

To Dearest Trish; editor extraordinaire, one of the busiest women I've had the pleasure to meet and loving wife of David: Thank you for sharing the journey with such compassion.

To a wonderful publishing company; who dared to take a chance!

To all those whose paths I've crossed and have encouraged me in my humble mission to reach out to those who are still broken: Thank you.

My prayer is that in the presentation of this life long journey and testimony, I have done and will continue to do justice to this work which God has placed on my heart to reach out to those who remain broken.

If you are ready to break free from your brokenness, visit me at my website

www.mybrokentobeautiful.com.

About the Author: Sheila Summers

Sheila Summers is a woman of quiet grace that knows the road from broken at home to beautiful in the Lord. She grew up in a working class home in Edinburgh Scotland where dance and a desire to be a wife and mother turned to desolation and despair. Today Sheila lives in the Hampton Roads area of Virginia with her daughters and husband.

Her mission and calling is to reach out to those still trapped in what she has come to know as the *Poison Kind of Love*, when hugs and kisses turn to an endless cycle of verbal and physical abuse. But Sheila is living proof that there is a way out and a source of rescue that can bring about healing, forgiveness and redemption

And in all of it, Sheila Summers is quick to say:

"To HIM Be the Glory!"

BUY A SHARE OF THE FUTURE IN YOUR COMMUNITY

These certificates make great holiday, graduation and birthday gifts that can be personalized with the recipient's name. The cost of one S.H.A.R.E. or one square foot is $54.17. The personalized certificate is suitable for framing and will state the number of shares purchased and the amount of each share, as well as the recipient's name. The home that you participate in "building" will last for many years and will continue to grow in value.

Here is a sample SHARE certificate:

YES, I WOULD LIKE TO HELP!

I support the work that Habitat for Humanity does and I want to be part of the excitement! As a donor, I will receive periodic updates on your construction activities but, more importantly, I know my gift will help a family in our community realize the dream of homeownership. ***I would like to SHARE in your efforts against substandard housing in my community!*** *(Please print below)*

PLEASE SEND ME __________ SHARES at $54.17 EACH = $ $__________

In Honor Of: ______________________________

Occasion: *(Circle One)* *HOLIDAY* *BIRTHDAY* *ANNIVERSARY*

OTHER: ______________________________

Address of Recipient: ______________________________

Gift From: ______________ ***Donor Address:*** ______________________________

Donor Email: ______________________________

I AM ENCLOSING A CHECK FOR $ $__________ PAYABLE TO HABITAT FOR HUMANITY <u>OR</u> PLEASE CHARGE MY VISA OR MASTERCARD *(CIRCLE ONE)*

Card Number ______________________________ Expiration Date: __________

Name as it appears on Credit Card ______________ Charge Amount $ __________

Signature ______________________________

Billing Address ______________________________

Telephone # Day ______________________ Eve ______________________

PLEASE NOTE: Your contribution is tax-deductible to the fullest extent allowed by law.

Habitat for Humanity • P.O. Box 1443 • Newport News, VA 23601 • 757-596-5553

www.HelpHabitatforHumanity.org

LaVergne, TN USA
04 March 2010
174986LV00003B/5/P

9 781600 376887